The Serious Business of Growing Up

A Study of Children's Lives Outside School

Elliott A. Medrich, Judith Roizen, Victor Rubin, and
Stuart Buckley

UNIVERSITY OF CALIFORNIA PRESS

Berkeley · Los Angeles · London

University of California Press
Berkeley and Los Angeles, California

University of California Press, Ltd.
London, England

Copyright © 1982 by The Regents of the Univerisity of California

First Paperback Printing 1983
ISBN 0-520-05071-1

Library of Congress Cataloging in Publication Data

Medrich, Elliott A.
    The serious business of growing up.

    Includes index.
    1. Children—California—Oakland—Time manage-
ment—Case studies. 2. Time managment surveys—
California—Oakland. I. Roizen, Judith. II. Rubin,
Victor. III. Buckley, Stuart.
HQ792.U5M42   305.2'3'0979466   81-7630
                                        AACR2

Printed in the United States of America

1 2 3 4 5 6 7 8 9

Soon as three o'clock rolls around,
You finally lay your burden down.
Close up your books,
Get out of your seat,
Down the hall and into the street. . . .

Chuck Berry,
"School Days"

Preface to the Paperback Edition

In the two years since completion of the hardcover edition of *The Serious Business of Growing Up*, many of the issues and trends described in this volume have received considerable public attention. Not only families and schools, but most of our social institutions are facing new challenges as they attempt to meet children's needs. Many of these challenges result from changes in the activities and resources available to children in their hours outside school.

Elementary school enrollments are once again on the upswing, and there is even faster growth in the proportion of school-age children from families in which both parents work or in which a single parent is employed. Not surprisingly, the so-called "latch-key child" has become symbolic of the extraordinary changes taking place today in family structure and the economics of family life. Images of youngsters left on their own before and after school and even into the evening are common fare for the media. There is growing concern about this among school authorities and other professionals who work with children, as well as among parents. Where do the children go and what do they do? Are they happy and safe? Are they missing some important part of growing up?

In this volume we recognized the latch-key phenomenon, and the documentation of these children's circumstances we hope will contribute in some small way to a more effective social response.

The response which we make to the demographic and economic shift that is changing the nature of children's out of school lives will be partly expressed through the cultural, educational, and recreational activities which we provide. In the years since our fieldwork was completed, the fiscal status of these kinds of programs has markedly deteriorated, especially in agencies supported by local tax revenues in low and moderate communities. In California, for instance, budget austerity imposed by Proposition 13 resulted in proportionally larger program reductions in libraries, parks, recreation, school sports and extracurricular activities than in other functions of local government. In our research over the past two years we have observed similar changes in the many other states with tax and spending limitations or depressed economies. As a consequence of these lower budget allocations, a wide range of publicly provided children's programs have raised or introduced fees to cover their costs, or have turned to private fee-charging agencies to replace lost programs. As we note in this volume, however, such actions are fraught with potential inequities if access to out-of-school services becomes limited to families with substantial economic means. Easy accessibility to children of all backgrounds should remain a central social priority as services are reorganized in response to budgetary stress.

Our inquiry into children's time use also led us to profile in detail the things that pre-adolescents actually do outside school. Some of the findings reflected the historical continuity of children's interests and behavior patterns. On the other hand, other findings captured ephemeral trends and fads. Kung Fu classes and citizens' band radios, for example, were the rage several years ago, but cause hardly a ripple of excitement now. Were we to conduct a similar survey today we would no doubt find video games and personal computers in a prominent place among children's activities. However new and novel these high technology pastimes may be, they call forth in parents many of the same concerns that they have always had about their children's use of time: How can we see that children use their "free time" to become prepared for the workplace of the future? How do we strike the balance between children's freedom and responsibilities, between their growing powers of choice and family household rules?

Sometimes the social reactions to these new phenomena reflect our desire for a "quick fix," even if that leaves the fundamental issues unresolved. Thus numerous communities have legislated restrictions on young people's access to video arcades, even as they reduce the budgets for the presumably more constructive recreational alternatives. And while there is a boom in classes and summer camps for young people to learn about and enjoy computers, many school districts face serious long term shortages of money and qualified teachers for teaching even basic mathematics and sciences. We need to narrow the gap between what we expect from young people and the resources we provide to help them reach these expectations.

So many important experiences of growing up take place in the hours outside school that we cannot afford to leave them unexamined. We hope that this research stimulates others to delve more deeply into these aspects of childhood, and to use what is learned to create effective, humane and equitable social policies.

Elliott Medrich
Victor Rubin
May 1983

Contents

Foreword

Robert Coles

When I worked with Southern children going through the severe stresses of school desegregation during the early 1960s I kept wondering how so many boys and girls under the most strenuous of pressures (including, often enough, mob violence) managed to do so well. I asked their teachers again and again for an explanation, only to find them puzzled as well. I turned, of course, to the parents of the children, but most often found a similar sense of perplexity. Once in a while, though, there was a helpfully forthcoming child—and a surprising kind of elucidation: "I don't know what else we can do, but keep going to school, and keep hoping the white people will settle down, and stop being so upset about us. I saw one woman shouting 'nigger, nigger,' and it's my own aunt who's worked right in that woman's house, and now she worries that I be so bad for her kids' school! After school, I'm glad to be away from noisy white folks, hollering at us. I'm glad to be playing on our street, and going to my cousin's, and we go to the stores and get candy, then we look in the windows of other stores, and we meet people, and we go to the playground. When I get home for supper, I'm feeling great! I've forgotten all the trouble I went through, just to enter that schoolhouse, and then leave it!"

A ten-year-old boy, sick and tired of the senseless racial hatred he nevertheless had to contend with, yet able to explain the manner of his daily recuperation. I have never forgotten

that account, a lesson of sorts to an observer who had a fairly
narrow way of regarding the lives of children: their family life,
their education, their mental life—meaning their dreams, worries, fears, hopes. That young black was reminding me (tact-
fully, as always, but pointedly, too) that there were hours of
the day I'd lost sight of, and important events I hadn't taken
the trouble to consider. Over the years I've tried to make up for
my blind spot by taking notice of what children do "after
school," or "before supper," or "after supper," and so on. The
result has been, commonly, surprise and wonder at the continuing enterprise, the originality of mind, the shrewdness, ingenu-
ity, and sheer exuberance of the young, as they take advantage
of minutes and hours and as they poke around, take stock of
things, and make all sorts of headway with respect to a particular hobby, or activity, or form of pleasure.

This book brought back to my wife and me a good number
of those children, and brought back, as well, lots of memories
connected with the so-called afterschool life we happened to
watch. The authors have an obvious love for children, an abid-
ing interest in their lives, and a willingness to learn from them,
as opposed to using them as pawns in yet another ambitious
social science scheme. The result is a series of lively instructive
essays on a theme of central importance, indeed—the manner in
which young people give shape to certain hours of the day. The
result, too, is a thoughtful, reflective kind of writing, a response
of sorts on the part of observers anxious to accommodate with
words and ideas the spaciousness of any given child's life. It
would have been all too easy for these talented social scientists
to have run some willing boys and girls through one or another
"schedule" of tests, then come up with some of those sweeping
generalizations we have learned in this century to swallow so
easily and gratefully. Instead, the writing in the pages that
follow is wonderfully novelistic—that is, full of details, qualifi-
cations, amplifications and, not least, ambiguities—even (God
forbid!) a few moments of suspended judgment, of ironic
amusement.

Especially interesting, and telling, are the comments on television. It would have been easy for a new group of investigators
to play that issue to the hilt: decry, once again, the stupidities

and banalities of television, so much a part of the life of America's children. But these authors are too honest and too discerning to walk that road. They prefer to remind us that the issue is not what children in general do with their spare time, so to speak, but how their various activities emerge from the particularity of their lives: each boy and girl a member of a certain family, at residence in a given neighborhood of one rather than another region, nation, and so on. What seems a waste of time to some of us, may for some others be the best of all possible alternatives. Of course, no one who has read our best novelists would be surprised at such an outcome of a study; but we are getting places, one dares hope, in the social sciences, and particularly, in the field of child development, when the kind of intelligent, suggestive, tactful work that this book offers connects so impressively with the line of argument of, say, George Eliot in *Middlemarch*: "Our passions do not live in locked chambers, but, dressed in their small wardrobe of notions, bring their provisions to a common table and mess together, feeding out of the common store according to their appetite."

Preface

Shaping and improving the quality of everyday experience, wrote John Dewey, is the purpose of education. "Save as the efforts of the educator connect with some activity which the child is carrying on of his own initiative independent of the educator, education becomes reduced to a pressure from without. It may, indeed, give certain external results, but cannot truly be called educative."[1]

Education is a constant reorganizing or restructuring of experience. It has all the time an immediate end . . . direct transformation of the quality of experience. . . . Education . . . adds to the meaning of experience, and [increases] ability to direct the course of subsequent experience.[2]

"Becoming educated" for Dewey meant more than scholastic achievement, more than mastery of specific skills and kinds of knowledge. Becoming educated meant integrating the lessons of the classroom with the full range of lessons learned out of school.

This is a study of how children use their time out of school, in Dewey's terms, one side of the education equation. It focuses on eleven- and twelve-year-olds growing up in different circumstances in Oakland, California, the sixth largest city in the state. Based on a survey of these children and their parents, it is an exploratory effort with three objectives: (1) to describe systematically the kinds of things children do when they are not in school, (2) to examine the range of opportunities and constraints that shape children's time use and their attitudes toward time use outside school, and (3) to develop a perspective on nonschool time use, its purposes and meanings for children, for their parents, and for our culture generally.

Our work stands in contrast to many studies of children's daily lives. Often children play a passive role or no formal role at all in the research process. Those interested in children's out-of-school activities or their time use typically conduct observational studies, or they survey parents or other adults—teachers, recreation leaders, or youth workers—who may know something about these matters. This is done even though children certainly know more about many aspects of their out-of-school days than anyone else possibly could. Recognizing this to be the case, we concentrated our data collection on the children themselves. We felt that nothing else would yield a child's perspective on out-of-school life. While parents were surveyed on related issues, principally they provided the background against which we examined the children's responses.

As an interdisciplinary team of social scientists—sociologists, psychologists, and urban planners—we believe that much of our contribution lies in the quality of the data we have to present and the uses others will be able to make of it. In this sense, we view our work as exploratory in terms of our approach to each type of time use and tentative in terms of our conclusions.

Although we view our field survey as important and useful in its own right, we were not able to do all that we had hoped. First, despite generous support from several sources, budgetary constraints made it necessary to limit our study to children living in a single geographic area. Optimally, we would have sampled children throughout the San Francisco Bay Area, and our research would have been more representative of the general urban population of America. Second, rather than surveying only preadolescents, we would have sampled children of several age groups, making it possible thereby to describe time use at different stages of life. Neither geographic nor age group constraints, however, diminish the importance of the issues or the mode of exploration, as we shall argue in the first chapter. Third, in our effort to summarize in this volume as much data as we could (in part for the convenience of researchers), we found it necessary to compromise one of our secondary objectives. Our data are rich in intimate, anecdotal reports. A number of open-ended questions that we asked our young respondents invited detailed analyses in their own right. But for this summary volume, we invariably fell back on a largely quantitative, statistical presentation. The result is less personal than we had intended it to be. We have written, however, other books, monographs, and papers addressing aspects of the data which do retain much of that anecdotal material.[3]

This volume, along with several others, culminates a five-year research effort by the Children's Time Study. The project was begun in 1973 under the leadership of principal investigator Charles S. Benson, Professor of Education, University of California, Berkeley. Benson had been researching the problem of inequality in the allocation of funds to schools and school districts and its impact on children's educational attainment. His ongoing interest in equity issues led him to ask whether nonschool services suffered from inequalities that might similarly affect a young person's chances in life. In 1974 Benson was joined by Elliott Medrich, and together they undertook a preliminary investigation of service inequality across a range of nonschool, publicly provided programs for children. They concluded that equity issues aside, these programs played a relatively minor role in the daily lives of most young people; a major study of them would contribute only minimally to understanding the relationship of out-of-school life to matters of equal opportunity. With this in mind, Benson and Medrich broadened the scope of the project, proposing an exploratory study of children's time use outside school as a way of defining differences in children's daily experiences which might influence their future prospects generally. They were joined by Victor Rubin, who helped develop a research plan and a field survey strategy. Judith Roizen, then at the University's Survey Research Center (SRC), was recruited to assist in the drafting of instruments. After the field survey was completed, she became part of the project staff and participated in the data analysis. Mary Milos took on many of the tasks of managing the fieldwork and helped organize the data for analysis. A year after the survey was conducted, Stuart Buckley was invited to take on some of the research responsibilities. Ultimately, chapters of this volume were written by various individuals, then revised collectively. We all share responsibility, therefore, for the presentation that follows.

We four coauthors owe thanks to a host of supporters for their assistance, their time, and their faith in our abilities. At the top of the list is Charles Benson, who in his inimitable style helped us take an idea that was his and make it into a research problem of our own.

The three directors of the Childhood and Government Project—Robert Mnookin, John C. Coons, and William G. Riggan—lent financial and intellectual support. This study would not have been possible had they not taken an interest in the inquiry and provided a provocative and stimulating work environment.

Our research was funded by three institutions: the Ford Foundation, the U.S. National Institute of Education, and the Carnegie Corporation of New York. In particular we wish to thank James Kelly and Terry Saario at Ford for their assistance and personal commitment to this study. They enthusiastically encouraged us from the inception of the project and certainly inspired us to move into these heretofore underexplored research issues. Once the data were collected, Denis Doyle (now at the Brookings Institution), David Mandel, and Lauren Weisberg at the National Institute of Education provided several major grants that helped us complete our analysis. They challenged us to move beyond the narrow scope of our academic inquiry and to utilize our data to address problems of interest to educational professionals and practitioners as well. Frederic Mosher, through the Carnegie Corporation's grant to the Childhood and Government Project, provided partial funding for the Oakland field survey. His support was crucial to our project, for the success of the study depended in large part on data collection of high quality.

Many other people helped us along the way. At the Survey Research Center, University of California, Berkeley, special thanks to William L. Nicholls II (now at the U.S. Bureau of the Census). Bill coordinated the field survey, spent endless hours working with us and our team before, during, and after the data were gathered. Thanks also to Charlotte Coleman, Sheila Leary, Heidi Nebel, Karen Olson, Claire Risley, and Barbara Wolfinger, all at Survey Research Center, who shared significant responsibility for aspects of the fieldwork. Merrill Shanks and Jack Citrin, former directors of the SRC, were ready and available to us when, inevitably, practical problems of scheduling and coordination arose. These people, and others at the center, helped to make our field effort an extraordinary success, and for this we are forever grateful.

We are also indebted to the many officials at the Oakland Unified School District who helped us organize our research, particularly Robert W. Blackburn (then acting superintendent of schools) and Alden W. Badal (then associate superintendent of schools). Of course, a special note of thanks to those who made this study possible, our respondents, the 764 children and their parents who participated in the Time Study field survey.

The staff of the Children's Time Study—each and every individual associated with us—contributed to the work appearing in this volume. Lena Johnson served as our intrepid programmer with assistance from Greg Boudreaux. Research associate Mary Berg critiqued our early drafts, and assistants Celia Politeo, Anthony Rodrigues, and Carolyn Weil did many of the important tasks that facilitated our work in the field and our subsequent analysis. Shan Hernandez labored over the manuscript and skillfully managed its final production.

Finally we wish to thank those at the University of California Press who so capably assisted us prior to publication of this volume. We are indebted to Stan Holwitz, Assistant Director, for his special interest in our research, to Shirley Warren, Senior Editor, who shepherded our volume through the production process, and to Mitch Tuchman, who edited our manuscript and surely improved our presentation.

It has been a challenging time for us, and we hope that this volume will inspire others to undertake related ventures that may lead to an increasingly sophisticated, child-centered view of daily life and childhood.

PART I
Research Strategy and Setting

one
LIFE OUT OF SCHOOL

Five days each week, thirty-six weeks each year, most children six to eighteen attend school. This important, shared experience of childhood is central to everyday life. No other child-training institution is as highly valued by adults. Opinion surveys show consistently over several generations that Americans view "a good education" as crucial to ensuring a better life for the young.[1]

The notion that each child begins life with equal chances to learn and to succeed regardless of social origin has been a cornerstone of American ideology. Over the past few decades, however, we have come to understand the difficulty of achieving social equality through education. Not only do children come to school with significantly different intellectual capabilities but also with very different family and social situations. Their backgrounds, which affect their values, attitudes, and experiences, further diminish the likelihood that all will attain the same scholastic success. There has been a growing recognition that in terms of their futures, what happens to children outside school is as important, at least, as what happens to them in school.

This book is about children's lives outside school—the hours away from the classroom. The role of out-of-school life as an influence on the prospects of the young has received some attention, albeit indirectly. Many studies of school achievement, for instance, have concluded that to understand why children perform differently in school one must look beyond academics to family backgrounds and the home lives of students. This was one of the motivations for our research.

In one important study of school achievement, Christopher Jencks writes that "variations in what children learn in school depend largely on variations in what they bring to school." More specifically, with regard to why the schools cannot make adults "more equal," Jencks argues, "Children seem to be far more influenced by what happens at home than by what happens in school. They may also be more influenced by what happens on the streets and by what they see on television."[2]

This follows James S. Coleman's major study of educational opportunity, which found home life to be a critical factor influencing achievement: "The sources of inequality of educational opportunity appear to lie first in the home itself and the cultural influences immediately surrounding the home; then they lie in the school's ineffectiveness to free achievement from the impact of the home and in the school's cultural homogeneity which perpetuates the social influences of the home and its environs."[3]

Coleman argues that since schooling is fundamentally a common experience, especially when viewed against the disparate nature of family life, the school's contribution to the child's educational achievement and social development is a matter of the relative intensity of influences. "If the school's influences are not only alike but very strong relative to the divergent influences [of home and neighborhood], then two groups [of children] will move together. If school influences are very weak, then the two groups will move apart . . . complete equality of opportunity can be reached only if all the divergent out-of-school influences vanish."[4] It is apparent that these out-of-school influences represent an important problem for those concerned with equalizing educational outcomes and improving children's opportunities generally.

While it might not be clear just how life outside school influences schooling and academic achievement, it is recognized as a powerful determinant. But just how important? How powerful? Attributing a "significant" variation in school performance to this poorly defined set of circumstances and experiences is unsatisfactory. One is left with the impression that home life has a black-box effect on schooling—and not only on schooling, which, after all, is just one of many broad cultural contexts shaping children's perspectives of and their preparation for adult roles.[5]

Sara Lawrence Lightfoot effectively describes the complex relationships among school, home, and other realities of a child's world.

The social system and life of the school are shaped by the sociopolitical and economic structure of the community of which it is part. Great disparities exist in the education and schooling offered to children from various communities that are reflective of differences in race, ethnicity, and social class. These glaring disparities not only represent economic inequities but also differences in political realities, cultural idioms, and ethnic histories. These powerful structural and societal forces surround schools and deeply touch the lives of teachers and children. The encompassing force of the external world offers either promise and hope or despair and denial to young children and teachers. So as one studies life within classrooms, one must always be cognizant of the prevailing power of the external realities—the world of streets, families, churches, playgrounds, garbage dumps, and movie houses into which these children will run when they leave the constricting (or safe and secure) boundaries of school each day.[6]

These contexts are the settings for the out-of-school activities that are the focus of this study. One of our objectives is to demonstrate that educational researchers' general awareness of these realities can be extended into a systematic exploration: a prying open of the black box.

A related theoretical basis for this approach is found in Urie Bronfenbrenner's application of an ecological model to the study of human development.[7] In that formulation, a child's development is seen as a function of complex interactions among systems and settings in which behaviors take place, those that are immediate and experiential and those that are more distant, impersonal, and even structural in nature. Bronfenbrenner writes: "The ecology of human development involves the scientific study of the progressive, mutual accommodation between an active, growing human being and the changing properties of the immediate settings in which the developing person lives, as this process is affected by relations between these settings, and by the larger contexts in which these settings are embedded."[8]

The children in our study, like most young people in America, share a general day-to-day structure of time use, defined in part by their relationships to school, paid employment, and domestic work. School is nearly universal, of course; access to the labor market is extremely limited; and involvement in the domestic economy is minimal compared with past generations. Many historians have described family life in eras when children made significant contributions to the household economy through chores, work alongside parents, or income earned outside the home. In those situations the structure of a child's day was not so different from an adult's, nor were age groups as extensively segregated as they are today. The advent of compulsory schooling and laws restricting child labor were only the most prominent factors in the long-term transformation of child rearing that accompanied industrialization. Some scholars contend that adolescence was "invented" early in this century to account for the increased number of years during which young people were considered unproductive and in need of supervision and training.[9] The after-school hours are a similar kind of invention. This block of time has become distinct, ironically, through its ambiguity. It is a negotiable zone that is not wholly education, work, or free play.

Today the management of out-of-school life presents some uncomfortable problems for parents. For many working mothers, single parents, and other busy adults, organizing a child's after-school day can be a continuing preoccupation. Consider the growing demand for both child care (for preschool children) and supervised after-school recreation services (for older children). There is certainly no consensus regarding how these needs ought to be met. Some parents look to the public sector, and others to employers. Still others feel that any sort of organized intervention would represent a gross abuse of authority, overstepping the boundary between what is the public's concern and what is not. In fact, questions of boundaries between family and state are tested frequently in relation to children's out-of-school lives.

Within the family, too, out-of-school life is often a source of tension. One reason is that while many aspects of a child's day fall squarely under the control of adults, out-of-school time is less clearly adult-dominated. What children do and what parents want them to do can provoke considerable stress. While not inherently irreconcilable, parent and child perspectives on television viewing, doing chores or homework, or playing in the street often cause disagreements, anxieties, and frustration. Furthermore, psychologists, educators, and child development experts have put many parents in a guilt-inducing bind. Parents have been persuaded that what children do when they are not in school is important in terms of future prospects, but they may not have the time, energy, or resources to ensure their children a rich set of out-of-school opportunities.

These concerns suggest that out-of-school life is more than leisure. Characterizing the out-of-school day as "free time" is both a misunderstanding of child-rearing conditions and an underestimation of the circumstances that affect children's use of time. The substance of out-of-school life is the product of many opportunities and constraints linked to family, peer groups, neighborhood, and community environments. Since these environments differ greatly for the children in our study, so does their use of time—although the factors affecting their activity patterns are not as straightforward as one might anticipate.

Social scientists are searching for regularities in behavior. This, after all, is the essence of their science. But much of this volume describes complexities in daily life, child-rearing practice, and family management, such that clear, expected regularities in time-use behavior among social groups are hard to identify. In fact, all kinds of circumstances and idiosyncratic situations underlie whatever superficial commonalities of time use are in evidence. Unfortunately many analyses of this kind of data do not probe beyond the association of time use with a few background variables. A goal of our analysis is to show how numerous aspects of family life and social background create divergent uses of time even among children whose activity patterns, at first, may seem quite similar.

We will also argue for a somewhat less judgmental view of what is good and what is bad in terms of time use. There are often mitigating factors that necessitate suspending judgment. For example, it is often said that television is "bad" for children. Maybe it is not a good idea to watch a great deal: at the very least, most agree, it is bad for one's eyes and creative instincts. But consider a family living in an unsafe neighborhood. The mother may demand that her young children come right home after school and stay inside (for their own safety). Television may be the best alternative in that not so uncommon situation. It could still be argued that the child should read a book instead. But suppose he or she cannot read very well. Is television still a "bad" use of time?

Time use by children is often the product of so many constraints that we must carefully consider our own biases and perspectives before making judgments. In describing differences in time-use behavior, we are trying to gain some appreciation for the complexity and difficulty of day-to-day life, which may make choices that run counter to conventional wisdom seem very rational indeed.

EQUALITY OF OPPORTUNITY

Since researchers view family background and out-of-school life as sources of in-school achievement disparities, several related questions suggest themselves. In a world in which children grow up under very different conditions, is life outside school similarly characterized by unequal opportunities? What might such differences mean in terms of children's ultimate life chances? To what degree are the things children do, like to do, or are allowed to do when they are not in school matters of choice or reflections of social-structural constraints?

Subsidiary questions concern children's access to and use of facilities and services provided by local government. Over the past two decades important judicial decisions, complemented by a substantial literature in the social sciences, have identified a range of public services, from parks and libraries to street lights and sewers, which have been allocated unequally among neighborhoods in cities of all sizes nationwide. By design or by historical happenstance some residents are denied equal access to services to which they are entitled.[10] These neighborhood-level inequalities may be especially important to children since they spend most of their out-of-school time relatively close to home. A park or playground or library that is far away may be effectively impossible for a child to utilize. To that degree, their time-use "opportunity set" is constrained. The study of out-of-school time can provide some basic data on the effects of access to municipal services on children's behavior and their social and intellectual development.

FAMILY, HOME LIFE, AND TIME USE

Changes in work roles and family structure have become a significant topic of debate and concern. The growing number of single-parent families and mothers in the paid labor force has spurred speculation about "the new family." Relatively recent data indicate that fully 52.3 percent of married women with children ages six through seventeen were in the labor force, along with 41.9 percent of married women with children between the ages of three and five.[11] These proportions are rising. Since a majority of families now have a working mother, it is important to understand how daily life is organized when mothers are less available to their children. By studying out-of-school time we can assess some of the consequences of this trend: how children whose parents work manage their out-of-school lives, what a child's day looks like when no adult is home after school, and whether in two-parent families fathers are substantially involved with their children's activities outside school.

Out-of-school life must be examined also in light of the changing functions of the American family. Kenneth Keniston writes:

Over the last centuries, families have not only been reduced in size but changed in function as well; expectations of what families do for their children have also been reduced. Mothers are no longer automatically expected to spend the whole day with their four year olds: fathers are no longer expected to train them in skills for a job. No one imagines that parents will try to manage a child's raging fever without help or teach a ten year old set theory in mathematics. As the forms of life have changed, institutions with a great deal of technical expertise have grown up to take over these functions, while parents have gone out to jobs that are less and less comprehensible to their young children. Conversely, children need training and experience to prepare them for a world already strikingly different from that of a generation earlier when their parents were growing up. As a result, families today have drastically changed in their functions and powers, especially in their power to raise children unaided.[12]

These kinds of changes do not leave families without a *raison d'être*. To the contrary, attention tends now to be focused on the psychological burden and nurturing aspects of family life. Keniston continues:

Some needs and tasks appear even more concentrated in families than in the past. Among these is fulfilling the emotional needs of parents and children. With work life highly impersonal, ties with neighbors tenuous, and truly intimate out-of-family friendships rare, husbands and wives tend to put all their emotional hopes for fulfillment into their family life. Expectations of sharing, sexual compatibility, and temperamental harmony in marriage have risen as other family functions have diminished.[13]

Although issues of changing family demography and family functions have received considerable attention, researchers are only now beginning parallel empirical analyses of what these mean in day-to-day family life. There is surprisingly little written about the things that parents and children actually do together, this at a time when many traditional aspects of the relationship have been lost or compromised. This study redresses that gap. We believe that children's out-of-school behavior is an effective framework within which to examine child rearing and relations within the family, and the substance of contemporary, day-to-day family life.

SOCIALIZATION : TIME-USE ORIENTATION AND SEX ROLES

Parents, peers, television, and any number of institutions inculcate attitudes toward time use. These attitudes constitute pivotal determinants of out-of-school behavior and can have clear policy implications. For instance, it is possible to analyze the degree to which children do educational activities outside school. This may be a time-use orientation that we wish to encourage, and from our survey we can learn the circumstances under which it commonly occurs. In this sense, use of time is an expression of larger socialization forces that create predispositions to certain behaviors.

Time use as a socialization issue also involves questions of sex differences in out-of-school activity patterns. At a time of heightened sensitivity to the ways in which children learn behaviors "appropriate" to their gender, the organization of many out-of-school activities, once taken for granted, is being reexamined. Movement away from thoroughly sex-linked activity patterns accompanies changing values, attitudes, and child-rearing practices. Our survey provides a current and detailed description of boys' and girls' (and parents') attitudes toward activities that have been associated, traditionally, with sex role socialization. If reducing sex-stereotyped behavior represents an important social objective, it might be necessary to teach boys and girls to recognize a broader range of time-use alternatives, just as efforts have been made to redefine their understanding of career possibilities.

THE DOMAINS OF OUT-OF-SCHOOL LIFE

Identification of the five domains of time use, the analytical focuses of this book, required a certain amount of preliminary research. Prior to designing the survey instruments, we conducted a series of informal discussions with Bay Area sixth-graders in school classrooms. Our objective was to have children of the age group we would be studying describe for us in a general way their activities and interests outside school. These sessions were followed by fairly structured, exploratory interviews with children, mostly in their own homes, on different aspects of out-of-school life. We were searching for some generic categories, ways of describing types of out-of-school activities that would be meaningful to children coming from a wide range of backgrounds. These discussions and interviews, together with a review of related literature,[14] yielded five categories of activities:

1. Children's activities "on their own" (alone or with friends) without significant adult supervision or involvement

2. Children's activities with their parents

3. Children's in-home and out-of-home chores, jobs, and responsibilities

4. Organized activities, including participation in recreational and cultural programs supervised by adults (other than the children's parents)

5. Television viewing.

For the most part, activities that fall into these categories structure a child's weekday afternoons and evenings. The categories are not mutually exclusive but they represent different dimensions of daily life.

In all, we are concerned with approximately a seven-hour period, roughly from three o'clock in the afternoon until bedtime, around ten or ten-thirty in the evening. Daily time commitments among four of the domains, on average, are:

Television—three to four hours

Time on own (exclusive of television)—two to three hours

Parent-child time—less than one and a half hours (including some television time)

Chores, related responsibilities, or jobs outside the home—less than one hour.[15]

The fifth domain, organized activities, absorbs out-of-school time on the order of four to five hours a week. For the most part, these activities take away from children's time on their own, but the amount of time is relatively small and the activities tend to take place only once or twice a week.

There is a fundamental distinction that divides the five domains. Three—television, chores, and organized activities—represent specific kinds of activities. The other two—on their own and parents and children together—encompass a much broader range of experiences. We view them as types of time use within which to analyze some, but not all, activities that could be included in a thoroughly comprehensive analysis. Distinctions among the domains and the activities comprising them will be sharpened at the beginning of each chapter in part two.

The effect of time use in one domain on time use in other domains is not necessarily straightforward. Spending a large amount of time on some activities may diminish the amount of time spent on other activities, or it may not. Watching television does not automatically mean that fewer chores get done. The effects may be complex and idiosyncratic, and very difficult to identify systematically. Even so, at several points in the study, we tested various conceptions of displacement in an effort to describe linkages among the domains.

Our analysis differs in an important way from most quantitative "time-budget" research. In contrast to that approach we examine each time-use domain largely without regard to allocation of minutes and hours, since focusing on precise time commitments would not only be difficult but invariably would mask many differences in activity patterns. (The estimates of time allocation noted above are merely suggestive; they were drawn directly from data available in our study, derived from calculations based on the total number of out-of-school hours in the average day, or based on data collected by others.) Chapter two explains the reasons for our use of a variety of time-use measures, each appropriate to a specific domain and research objective.

It should also be understood that these domains, no matter how many hours they occupy each day, describe children's "public lives" only. For many reasons we have chosen not to probe private behavior, such as sexuality and drug use. In this sense we do not claim to have a complete portrait of daily life. Rather we have deliberately selected a set of activities and behaviors that illustrate aspects of children's behavior, opportunities, and experiences in daily life.

PLAN OF THE BOOK

In this chapter we have placed children's time use outside school into a research and policy context. The following two chapters probe the "problem" of time and time use and describe our methodological approach, the study setting, and the nature of the respondent population.

Part two, chapters four through eight, analyze the five time-use domains. Each begins with a detailed description of one of the domains and the distribution of children's time use among its activities. The determinants of time use are then explored, taking particular note of the factors that account for variation in behavior within the domain.

Chapter nine places our analyses into perspective, linking them with larger social and political concerns.

two

THE STUDY OF TIME AND TIME USE

Time, like money, is a scarce resource that can be spent in different ways. Time, unlike money, is allotted equally: everyone shares the same amount—a minute is a minute—and no one can add to it or regain it once spent. "We cannot build up a stock of time," writes Staffan Linder, "as we can . . . a stock of capital."[1] Time use reflects priorities and predilections, opportunities and constraints.

The existence of a temporal dimension to all human experience, despite persistent interest in the subject, has not led to the development of a distinct, rigorous social science of time. On the one hand, time-centered studies, in theory, "offer alternative quantitative criteria that would extend the narrow definition of benefit and cost to include the social or human dimension."[2] On the other, time studies contain an inherent bias of their own, which might be called "chronorationalism," the assumption of rationality in the allocation of time.[3] This familiar assumption is often expressed in metaphorically quasi-economic terms: time is a "fixed sum resource," allocated among a range of competing possibilities.

Quasi-economic models are hardly sufficient for explaining actual behavior. A complex mix of individual, familial, and social-structural factors shapes and constrains our use of time, so it is unclear to what extent an activity represents a conscious choice from among a perceived set of alternatives. F. Stuart Chapin writes that, with regard to time use, an individual's activities are "the result of . . . incentives and constraints serving to mediate choice . . . with some activities directly traceable to positive choices, and some attributable to negative choices in the sense that constraints overshadow opportunities for choice." He goes on to say that the "propensity to engage in an activity is determined by a set of energizing factors (motivations and thoughtways predisposing action) and a set of constraining factors (roles and personal characteristics preconditioning action)."[4]

Many researchers do not analyze these constraining factors systematically, however, preferring to work with simpler models of individual choice. Not surprisingly, a large number of time-use studies focus on parts of the day when people are thought to be exercising the greatest amount of choice. But even during these periods, such as when adults are not at work, their time-use options may be limited in important, if less apparent ways.

The distinction between work activities and other activities defines most of the primary categories of time use found in the literature. Sebastian deGrazia provides a traditional formulation, writing that each twenty-four-hour day consists of four kinds of time: work time; work-related time, such as commuting; subsistence time, such as sleeping, eating, and shopping; and free time (a residual category somewhat ambiguous in nature).[5] The presumption is that this leftover block of time is discretionary, at least more so than other types of time. A slightly different model is proposed in a study of time use in the USSR that identifies five categories: work time, nonwork time connected with production, housework, free time, and leisure and personal maintenance (eating, sleeping). "Free time is considered part of the general fund left after calculating the time needed to meet imperative obligations."[6] Others have arrived at rather similar descriptive typologies.[7]

Most time studies assume some degree of chronorationalism while at least acknowledging the existence of some decision-making constraints. Most also delineate roughly comparable categories of time. But in other respects, time-use research has developed along distinct disciplinary lines that have little in common. In order to understand how different approaches to the problem of time use have influenced our study, it is necessary to examine some of the methodologies employed throughout this diverse literature.

METHODS OF MEASURING TIME AND TIME USE

Time use must be understood in terms of what is being measured and what the measure is supposed to indicate. Time-research methodologies do not focus on a single dependent variable. In some studies the issue is "how much": people are differentiated in terms of the amount of time they commit to particular activities; the variable is described in terms of minutes or hours. In other studies the issue is "what": people are differentiated by the nature of their activities; the variable is the activity itself, often studied without regard to the amount of time spent doing it.

Time Budgets and Activity Systems Analysis

Most studies of time take the form of time budgets and activity systems analyses. The time budget consists of

itemized and measured accounts of how people spend their time within the bounds of a working day, a weekend, a seven-day week or any other relevant period. . . . This conventional name (time budget) has some metaphoric justification, since very many studies of this kind are concerned primarily with the proportions in which the twenty-four hours of the day are allocated. . . . This type of investigation is indeed somewhat similar to the procedure by which the allocation of funds for different purposes in financial budgets is analyzed. . . . The fund of time which is being allocated to various activities . . . serves simply as a frame of reference for setting out the temporal proportions of people's engagement in the gamut of their daily activities.[8]

Time budgets, typically kept in diary form, inventory and categorize time use, emphasizing the duration of activities as the basis for comparing behaviors among subpopulations.

"Time geography" and activity systems analysis are related, yet somewhat distinct approaches that introduce a spatial dimension into the temporal pattern. Time use is explored with reference to what is done, how much time is involved, and where each activity takes place. Time geography, pioneered by the Swedish geographer Torsten Hagerstrand and his associates, highlights the social nature of time use by building complex models to describe the interactions among individual activity patterns. Activity systems analysis, which developed out of Chapin's research, focuses more on the propensities of the individual and the opportunities available as he or she makes time-use decisions. Hagerstrand's and Chapin's theories of behavioral constraints on time use are now commonly included in conceptual models.[9]

From the standpoints of research objectives and field methods, George Lundberg's classic investigation of leisure time in Westchester County, New York,[10] and Pitirim Sorokin and Clarence Berger's national time-use survey[11] were historical precursors of contemporary time-budget studies. More recent works utilizing national and international samples provide examples of other styles of academic and policy-related time-budget research.[12]

Some of the earliest time-budget research explored changes in behavior resulting from governmental policy initiatives and interventions, and life-style transformations. Time budgets, for instance, confirmed the success of the labor movement in its efforts to reduce the length of the working day.[13] Time budgets have also documented the changing allocation of time across three primary activity categories: work, sleep, and leisure. The many studies that have examined these basic relationships need not be reviewed here, but taken as a group they clearly reflect important social trends and changes in the nature of daily life.[14]

In the USSR time-budget studies have been used to examine how particular economic policies affect industrial efficiency. Perhaps the most comprehensive time studies, which provide an important historical record, are those undertaken in Hungary as part of the decennial census, specifically designed to measure changes in living patterns and life styles from one decade to the next.

Some other specific applications of the time-budget methodology include Kathryn Walker and Margaret Woods's study of the household routines of working women,[15] and analyses of daily commuting patterns by urban planners.[16]

Single-activity Time-use Studies

Time budgets and activity systems analyses paint comprehensive portraits of the day or parts of the day. By contrast, studies of single activities or groups of similar activities are more selectively focused. Some place no emphasis on the amount of the time commitment at all, for the issue is whether the activity is done rather than how much time is devoted to it.

Television viewing, of interest to researchers because it occupies so much time and is thought to affect the time devoted to other activities, is particularly amenable to study as a single activity.[17] Researchers have assessed its place in a child's day, for instance, explored the conditions under which they watch, and examined television's relationship to competing opportunities.

The single-activity approach has also been a traditional way of researching children's participation in organized recreational activities. In the early 1950s the University of Michigan conducted a study for the Boy Scouts of America, describing differences between boys who were involved in organized programs like the scouts and those who were not.[18] In this and similar studies, the propensity to participate, not time allocation per se, was the central issue. Even so, as with some television research, analysis of this one kind of activity was used to understand the nature of children's time-use choices in a broader way.

A third kind of study utilizing the single-activity approach is represented by surveys of children's outdoor recreational interests and by studies of children's use of services and facilities provided by municipal agencies. Reports such as those of the Outdoor Recreation Resources Review Commission[19] and the British Travel Association[20] have explored children's preference for organized (as opposed to unstructured) outdoor recreational activities, and differences in participation rates among many kinds of sports activities. Related single-activity studies of children's use of public parks, recreation centers, and other services have examined the conditions under which children choose or are able to use these facilities.[21]

There is, then, marked contrast among studies of single activities. Some involve detailed exploration of one type of time use, intending to understand its particular import. Others focus on one type of activity for the purpose of describing and inferring generic time-use "orientations." Unlike time budgets, these studies employ a deliberate selection of activities for examination, a strategy that we adopted as we defined the five time-use domains of out-of-school life.

Activity Enumerations

Like studies of single activities, the enumeration shifts away from preoccupation with duration as the principal measure of time use. The objective of the enumeration is not to account for time spent engaged in different activities, but to profile the kinds of things that are done. Much of the research on the subject of children's use of time takes the form of enumerations. In fact, to the extent that there is a historical record of how children's time use has changed over the past several decades, activity enumerations provide some of the best source material.

Typically an activity enumeration resembles a checklist. An activity is mentioned and the respondent reports whether he or she takes part. Other questions are asked sometimes in an effort to understand the significance of activities in which the respondent participates: "Is it a favorite activity?" "How often do you do it?"

Activity enumerations are often narrow in scope, poorly suited to holistic explorations of time-use behavior. John Robinson and Philip Converse write that "information of this kind is limited to certain forms of relatively salient, unusual and temporally 'chunked' activities."[22] In some cases there is no way of evaluating the relative importance of the enumerated activities to the respondents or grounds on which to distinguish everyday from extraordinary activities.

But a carefully constructed enumeration instrument can provide a sketch of experiences in some sort of rough, time-bounded framework. These data can be used for purposes of describing activity patterns across social groups. Time-use enumerations thus are often employed to illustrate complex, class-linked norms and behavior patterns.[23]

By examining leisure-time activity enumerations, one can say a good deal about children's time-use patterns generally.[24] Studies suggest that among preadolescents (the population of special interest to us in this volume) there is a preference for informal and unstructured activities; greater interest in doing things with friends than with parents; evidence that schools are a central feature of the child's social, if not intellectual life; an insatiable desire to do things that cost money; clear differences between children who do a lot of one type of activity, such as sports, and those who do not; and, generally, preferences for activities that maximize freedom. Interpreted this way, activity enumerations represent indirect explorations of time use (indirect in the sense that they do not involve recording time allocations in the traditional fashion).

CHILDREN'S TIME USE

The Conceptual Dilemma

The Western world has developed a rough ideology of time. This ideology, with both religious and metaphysical roots, emphasizes the need to be industrious, purposeful, and productive during our short lives. Time, like everything else, must be utilized economically, hence chronorationalism. Hans Meyerhoff writes that time is "charged with significance for man because human life is lived under [its] shadow."[25] Time is something of a tyrant, a cruel reminder of the transitory nature of life. "It unfolds in one direction only, as a constant challenge or as a source of frustration, moving toward an open future of novelty and creation or toward a closed future of oblivion and deaths."[26] We may not be awestruck by time's finite nature, nor need the idea of scarcity be shared by all for it to be the dominant world view.

Most adults live in some sort of time-bound framework. The responsibilities of daily life encourage the development of regular, relatively discrete patterns of work, sleep, and nonwork activities. Because of responsibilities at home and away from home adults are more likely than children to treat time as a scarce resource. Children are less able to fit their activities into adult-defined categories. The tempo of their lives is different from that of adults, so it is not surprising that their sense of time differs as well. Children are infrequently the subjects of time research, in part because such studies are predicated on an adult perspective of time: time does not "mean" the same thing in a child's world. Psychologists like Piaget[27] and Fraisse[28] have argued that most children do not even understand the idea of time until adolescence. Hence, calculating how much time children spend doing different things may be quite difficult and not an especially useful way to judge what particular activities mean to them. This is a problem given the classic time-research methodology wherein the amount of time spent doing something is taken to be a measure of its importance.

There is other evidence indicating that children are generally less aware of the temporal dimension of daily life. Television researchers have found that children systematically underestimate their viewing time.[29] Others note that it is difficult for children to account for the amounts of time actually devoted to various activities, whether habitual or unusual. This suggests that attempting to measure precisely how intervals of time are spent may conflict with the logic of childhood. Children may not allocate time in ways that represent trade-offs or that necessarily provide evidence of the value or importance attached to particular activities.

Several other aspects of childhood also present conceptual dilemmas for researchers and must be taken into account in any study of children's time use. First, by virtue of their youth children share certain interests, preferences, and skills in common. Hence, we would expect to find that their uses of time are quite alike in some respects. Second, all children are dependent: they live under the care of adults, are generally fed, clothed, and sheltered by them, and have few, if any, material resources of their own. As a result, adults influence, if not control, their time use.

Let us consider the implications of these two phenomena. Children learn and play many of the same games. In general they can establish rapport with one another by drawing from this fund of shared experiences. Philippe Aries has examined some of the history of this social commonality.[30] Psychologists have traced the cognitive and developmental import of children's play behavior, which demonstrates a high degree of similarity at each age level regardless of social background, reflecting the fact that there are many things that children are not yet able to do because they lack the skills, exposure, or opportunity. These limitations serve to reinforce shared behaviors. At a given age children like to do and are able to do many of the same things. That is, children tend toward similar patterns of time use although they do not all have the same opportunities to develop particular interests or skills. By contrast, as they get older, fundamental sorting mechanisms like income, education, and occupation will begin to lead to distinct patterns of time-use behavior that are not as evident in youth.

Because of their dependence children also share similar experiences. Adults, in the role of parent, generally establish dos and don'ts, cans and can'ts. When, for instance, they tell children to come home immediately after school and stay in the house, when they believe that girls should be raised more strictly than boys, time use is affected, confirming that children's time use is inherently less free than adults'. While an adult's time is constrained by class and role expectations, children use time within a particular constellation of parental child-rearing imperatives.

Methodological Problems

While not restricted to time studies of the young, several methodological problems should be mentioned because they did establish critical limits on the structure and substance of our inquiry.

We know intuitively how complex time-use patterns actually are. We might for example, watch television, do housework, talk on the telephone, and baby-sit all at the same time. Time research is not well equipped to account for the complex transactions of daily life. Converse and Robinson put the problem this way:

. . . time in itself is meaningless. It must be subdivided and the resulting slices paired up with bounded, categorizable activities in order for time budget work to proceed. And however dissectable time may be as a working currency the infinite facets and blurred boundaries of human activities are not . . . the reliable sorting of behaviors into meaningful equivalence classes remains an Achilles heel of the whole procedure . . . (but) double entries are not welcome as they spoil the neatness of the 24-hour totals. . . .

Quite apart from ambiguities surrounding the psychological or functional meaning of a behavior for the actor, few categories of overt activities are not rimmed with marginal instances. Some of these are of such rare incidence that they would have negligible effect on an aggregate of time budgets. But this is often not the case, particularly with coarse coding schemes, and it is futile to draw elegant quantitative comparisons of time allocations between studies that have sorted the same activities into different bins.[31]

Researchers have no solution for these kinds of problems. Most acknowledge them as technical concerns and press forward. Coding schemes simplify, reducing the count of simultaneous activities to primary and secondary ones without regard to functional or psychological priority. Data collection procedures, particularly the use of diaries, discourage serious consideration of the meaning of activities for the respondents themselves. "Eating" can be "maintenance" and/or "leisure" or even "work" (for a food critic). "Reading" can be "work" or "leisure" or both. A person's day may be characterized by the researcher in a way that is hardly meaningful to the individual.

In a study of drug users, for instance, Herbert Blumer showed that many teenagers carry a normal load of activities yet perceive all but a fraction of their time use to be unimportant.[32] Following Blumer, we can construct two hypothetical, yet equally plausible summaries of the same youth's day:

School	6.0 hours
Socializing at park after school	1.5 hours
Eating	0.5 hours
Relaxing, watching television, talking on the telephone	5.0 hours

or

John said that getting high with his friends was the only important activity of the day. It would have been so whether it had taken place at the park, at a friend's house or while watching television at home after dinner.

The difference is not simply a function of reporting format (quantitative versus prose) but reflects a problem common in time studies, calling attention to the difficulty of interpreting time-use data.

It is easy to see, then, how the after-school day may appear to be tightly organized when portrayed by an adult as a time budget but amorphous when described by a child. Children, after all, are less sensitive to the clock, and less able than adults to describe what they do with their time in terms of hours and minutes allocated to different activities. Our own field experiments indicated that child respondents had difficulty attaching a measure of time even to activities that they had done in the very recent past. Therefore, attempting to focus on the specific amounts of time devoted to particular activities may not be an appropriate or realistic way to elicit from children information about daily life. Deriving a measure of time use that was not solely a report of hours and minutes devoted to different activities was one of the fundamental design problems that we had to confront.

The Linkage of Time Use and Social Class

Although studies of time have been conducted for many purposes, perhaps the most important applications are those that explore the relationships between time use and social class. Time use, it has been argued, is the product of powerful social forces that create different opportunities, predispositions, and activity choices among particular populations. Although this point is asserted frequently, there have been surprisingly few empirical studies of the origins of time-use values and orientations. Some relevant documentation can be gleaned from literature outside the time-research tradition. While these studies do not necessarily measure time use rigorously, they do attempt to relate life circumstances to adult and child perceptions of time and, in turn, to children's time-use behavior.

Circumstances and their impact on children's time use must be viewed in two stages, first involving parents' perspectives on time and its disposition, and second, the emergence of children's values regarding time. At the most general level, circumstances shape an adult's sense of what is possible, thereby influencing his or her attitude toward time as well as toward children's use of time. If opportunities seem limitless, this is conveyed to the child. If opportunities seem limited, it is hard for a parent to act as if such constraints did not exist. Either way the perceived values of time and time use are affected.

As Lillian Rubin writes:

For the child—especially a boy—born into a professional middle-class home, the sky's the limit, his dreams are relatively unfettered by constraints. In his earliest conscious moments he becomes aware of his future and of plans being made for it—plans that are not just wishful fantasies but plans that are backed by the resouces to make them come true. All around him as he grows, he sees men who do important work at prestigious jobs. At home, at school, in the neighborhood, he is encouraged to test the limits of his ability to reach for the stars.

For most working-class boys the experience is just the reverse. Born into a family where survival is problematic, he sees only the frantic scramble to meet today's needs, to pay tomorrow's rent. Beyond that, it's hard for parents to see . . . such boys face a "series of mounting disadvantages"—that is, poverty, lack of education and occupational guidance, no role models in prestige occupations, no personal contacts to help push careers along—all come together to create a plan for the future and form a vicious circle from which few ever escape. It is in this process that the class structure is preserved—as if in ice—from generation to generation.[33]

Arlene Skolnick sums up the differences:

. . . working class and poor people are often described as passive, lacking in the ability to delay gratification and fatalistic—believing that luck rather than hard work leads to success. Rather than reflecting deeply rooted inadequacies of personality, however, these differences—to the extent that they exist at all—may reflect realistic assessments of the opportunity structure and the amount of control lower income people actually have over their lives.[34]

Messages passing from parent to child about time and time use are in part a function of whether parents believe that they can manipulate the child's environment advantageously. It is reasonable to plan and prepare for the future if success seems likely. In this sense the likelihood of success becomes a factor influencing how time is valued. Accordingly, many parents who do not feel that they can assure their children's future prospects place proportionately greater faith in institutions such as schools, which they feel are more able to affect their children's development and chances in life.

Jules Henry argues that for people who are politically impotent, economically disadvantaged, and have little hope that the quality of their lives will improve, the time-bound, regularized world of the middle class makes little sense. Henry found that in the housing projects he studied, the lives of many poor blacks were relatively unstructured, and that in their world "a scheduled event may occur at any moment over a wide spread of hours or perhaps not at all. They believe, however, that in the highly organized world of whites it occurs when scheduled."[35] This suggests that depending on one's circumstances, time may or may not be viewed as a scarce resource, requiring careful allocation.

The issue of the time horizons of poor people has become fraught with ideological overstatements and misunderstanding of ethnic values. We have sought to avoid these pitfalls by surveying our respondents' perceptions and uses of time directly and explicitly, rather than inferring their time horizons from general or indirect observations, as has often been done. We do not claim pure, scientific objectivity, of course, but our conclusions may have a more solid foundation than those of many who have sought explanations for poverty in the "present orientation" of the poor.

The ways in which social class is linked to time use, thereby reflecting different perspectives on time, is the focus of many investigations. With regard to studies of this sort focused on children, Margherita McDonald and her coauthors provided the classic formulation, hypothesizing that "children from different social class backgrounds engage in leisure activities which are quantitatively and qualitatively different."[36] The University of Michigan Boy Scout study[37] and later Bernard Goldstein[38] found that children from upper-status homes were exposed to a wider range of out-of-school activities. M. Ward Cramer reported that children from upper-income families participated in a much larger number of organized activities and groups than other children did.[39] Celia Stendler, in a study of elementary school children, concluded that children from lower-class backgrounds tended to have more freedom and spend more time in unsupervised play. Middle-class children were more likely to have their free-time activities supervised by their parents. Stendler also argued that as early as the completion of grammar school, children's leisure-time interests and activities were conditioned by class and status considerations.[40] August Hollingshead came to much the same conclusion, finding that children from lower-class homes overwhelmingly preferred informal to structured and unorganized to organized activities when compared with their middle-class age mates.[41]

A word of caution is necessary. These studies define class in different ways; some in terms of income; others in terms of fathers' occupations; still others in terms of multivariate measures of social status. These inconsistencies make it difficult to know exactly how, or whether, different background variables are affecting particular aspects of time use in different ways.

While most research reports strong relationships between class and time use, this is not always the case. According to some researchers, and consistent with points we have made earlier, time-use patterns look more alike when children are younger, although there may be subtle, and important, differences in content and structure. It is not until well into adolescence, during high school and even later, when both age and the social sifting devices of adults—money and education, for instance—begin to pull children in very different directions, such that leisure-time activity patterns diverge notably by class. Similar observations had been made as far back as the Lynds's 1920s study of Middletown.[42]

Goldstein found similar activity patterns among young children of all social backgrounds.[43] R. Clyde White argued that activity patterns remain similar among children, diverging when they get older, as they "settle into the ways of the class to which they belong."[44]

This is not to suggest that other factors might not intervene, influencing children's attitudes toward time as well as their behavior, preferences, and opportunity sets. Bronfenbrenner, for instance, found that middle-class children were expected to take care of themselves at an earlier age and to accept more responsibility around the home. Furthermore, he noted that participation in tasks and activities that are regularized and scheduled influences the way a child's sense of time develops.

Hence, coming from a home of higher social status seems to convey a more adultlike consciousness of time (and, perhaps, its "economic value").[45]

Other things, including gender, also affect a child's understanding of time and activity choices. We found that girls in our survey were bound by rules less likely to be imposed on boys. These often centered around time: how late the child could play outside, watch television, stay up, and so on. Further, some girls regularly cooked meals and baby-sat their siblings, activities that necessarily require more clock consciousness.[46]

Other research, such as Barbara Heyns's study of summer school,[47] further supports the notion that sex is an important determinant of time-use behavior. Along the same lines, utilizing an older age group, Coleman's study of adolescents revealed: "The general pattern of these leisure pursuits, showing considerably more activity among the boys, is indicative of a situation that seems to be quite general in the adolescent community: boys have far more to *do* than girls . . . our society seems to provide a much fuller set of activities to engage the interests of boys."[48] Interest in time-gender and time-gender-class linkages increased among researchers in the last decade. Various findings suggest that many activities display sex-related differences that thoroughly overwhelm social-class differences.

Most of the studies mentioned here do not explore the impact of different aspects of individual background on time use. Few define what they mean by social class, and it is often hard to tell when similar dimensions of background are being compared. In chapter three we contrast our "life-circumstances perspective" with these traditional, often ambiguous, social-class formulations.

SURVEY AND INSTRUMENT DESIGN

In designing this study we drew on all three time research strategies: budgets, single-activity analyses, and enumerations. From the outset, we were committed to a child-centered study, with young people themselves as the primary respondents. Recognizing that children are less conscious of time than adults are, it did not seem appropriate to attempt a traditional time budget. Considering the myriad methodological and conceptual difficulties, focusing on the amount of time children spend doing different activities made little sense, for we knew that they are not reliable reporters of duration. An alternative approach preserving both the child-centered perspective and the emphasis on what children do with their time was to develop a modified enumeration model. Thus, within a time-bound framework, we were able to examine in detail the five time-use domains. The enumeration alleviated many classification problems, for we could examine specific kinds of activities with considerable precision.

Several points affecting the design of our questionnaires must be made. We began this study cognizant of the fact that many field surveys of preadolescent children had been suspect in the past because the data were thought to be unreliable. Often the real problem seems to have been that those who designed surveys expected too much from youngsters, asking them questions they may have been unable to answer. Then, when the responses were found to be unstable over time—when children changed their minds about their answers—it was argued that they were indeed unreliable social survey subjects.

Pauline Vaillancourt addressed this issue experimentally. On several occasions she administered identical surveys, asking children questions concerning self and family, politics, and political attitudes, then examining responses to see if and how they had changed. She found declining stability as questions moved from immutable characteristics ("Are you a boy or a girl?") to facts ("Who is president of the United States?") to opinions ("Do you agree or disagree . . ?"). She concluded that (1) the more personal the subject matter, the more stable the response, and (2) attitude and opinion questions meant relatively little to children and were, therefore, susceptible to high degrees of instability.[49]

Others have discovered that children often do not know basic family demographics: parents' education, parents' occupations, family income, and the like.[50]

Most younger children cannot answer these kinds of questions, so it is probably not reasonable to ask them.

We took account of these problems in designing our field

survey by focusing on aspects of daily life that are, we believe, salient to children. Hence, we feel that their responses are more likely to be accurate and stable. To confirm this hypothesis, three months after data collection was completed the children in our sample were contacted again, mostly by telephone, and asked a subset of questions from the field survey. Analysis of this data shows that across all socioeconomic and ethnic groups responses remained remarkably stable.[51] This check suggested to us that instruments well attuned to the child's world, which build on children's competencies and knowledge, can be extremely accurate and analytically useful.

With regard to the fieldwork format, we conducted pretest experiments utilizing self-administered time-use diaries, closed-ended questionnaires administered in school classrooms, mail questionnaires, telephone interviews, and personal interviews. Upon evaluation, we concluded that a personal interview, rather than any kind of self-administered protocol, would enable us to meet our basic research objectives and at the same time ameliorate many special difficulties associated with surveying young people.

First, personal interviews would minimize the problem of reading and comprehension skills. It would not be necessary to write questions to the lowest common denominator. As we have shown in other papers, the setting from which the sample was drawn included children who were virtually nonreaders as well as children reading at or above the high school level.[52] An interview would improve the chances that all respondents would understand the meaning of each question, and with careful preparation, interviewers could significantly enhance the quality of responses and level of detail that could be elicited from respondents.

Second, a personal interview could cover much more ground in a fixed amount of time than any kind of questionnaire could. Interviews hold children's attention better than any other format and permit the addition of many questions and areas of inquiry that otherwise would need to be excluded.

Third, the interview avoids the aura of a test. Though a few children were uncomfortable and reluctant to speak with us, most of the children in our sample were impressed and excited that someone would come to speak with them individually in an adult fashion. They seemed happy to be involved and interested in providing careful answers to what they perceived to be serious questions.

Fourth, from a pragmatic standpoint, we found that it was less difficult to get permission to interview children in their homes than it was to administer any kind of instrument at school or any other location. Parents were most likely to allow their children to participate in the study if they had some idea of what it was about, who was asking the questions, and why.

Fifth, interviewing children at home allowed us to involve parents in the study. Together, children and parents would provide a richer and far more comprehensive picture of children's out-of-school life than either could alone. With two data sources it became possible to focus the children's interview on their activities—what they did, what they liked to do, and where they spent their time outside school—and at the same time have their mothers answer questions designed to explore child-rearing practices, socialization priorities, and attitudes toward different aspects of out-of-school life. Moreover, not only could we avoid asking children questions they were less likely to be able to answer accurately but also we did not require parents to presume omniscience and full awareness of their children's every move.

Questions for children did not require that they report time allocations in hours or minutes. When it was necessary to determine approximate levels of commitment, a time frame was selected which fit the logic of the domain. If an activity tended to be done frequently, the child would be asked about participation in the last week. If it tended to be done infrequently, a much longer frame of reference was used. In our field experiments this appeared to make sense to our young respondents. On some activities that we wished to explore in detail, we asked parents specific questions about the amount of time their children spent doing them. In these instances, however, we limited ourselves to types of activites that parents might know about, such as television-viewing time.

The instruments, then, reflected a set of field research techniques carefully organized around a larger theoretical perspective, certain analytical constraints, and preliminary data-gathering experience. With this as background, chapter three describes the study setting and the survey population as well as problems associated with analyzing time-use data in terms of the social class and life circumstances of respondents and their families.

three
THE SETTING AND THE SAMPLE

For children the neighborhood is more than a geographical setting. It is a social universe. Since children are only minimally mobile, the things they do from day to day are, in part, shaped by the nature of the physical environment in which they live. [1] Streets, parks, schools, and other public amenities influence children's activity patterns in a number of ways. Similarly, the neighborhood as social environment also has a powerful impact on children's time use. We live among people like ourselves: children spend most of their time with friends from families not unlike their own, thereby reinforcing shared socialization priorities and practices. The interplay between physical space and social space represents a crucial dimension of the time-use dynamic. [2]

Traditional time research is almost singlemindedly concerned with the complexity of activity choices. Issues of the environmental context are largely ignored. By contrast, in this study, the diversity of the setting itself is viewed as a highly significant background factor. Our sample of 764 sixth-grade students came from twenty different Oakland neighborhoods, heterogeneous in ways that demand description in their own right—just as we must carefully disaggregate the social characteristics, the life circumstances, of our sample. Hence, we pay special attention to the features of the survey neighborhoods as well as to the nature of the study sample, as both affect the analyses that follow.

CHILDREN IN FIVE NEIGHBORHOODS

Oakland, California, is often viewed as San Francisco's poor sister city across the bay. While it does indeed share many problems typical of American inner cities, it is also a community with strong local traditions and unique accomplishments. For instance, its container seaport is the second largest in the nation. Its major league sports teams brought more championships to the city in the last decade than did teams in any other city in the country. Its culture and politics have fostered distinctive, widely recognized music, architecture, and social movements.

Within this city of worldly reputation rests a city of neighborhoods. These are of special concern to us here for the neighborhoods are the vantage point from which we shall explore the daily lives of children and families. The neighborhood map reflects more than a century of ethnic succession, of building booms, urban decay and renewal, and now of "gentrification."

Our respondent population lived in a great variety of neighborhoods characteristic of those found in most every large city. We begin our introduction to the study setting by describing five Oakland neighborhoods (of the twenty sampled) which we visited in the summer months after the field survey was conducted. The descriptions are based on the reports of children living in each area, so they provide something of a child's perspective. The rigors of poverty and the advantages of wealth can be measured by statistics, but there are also more subtle qualities in the physical and social environments experienced by children, as these accounts remind us.[3]

Mountainside

You do not see children when you drive the hilly streets of Mountainside. There are no sidewalks. Many houses are set back from the road, their windows turned to catch a view of San Francisco Bay. There is something rural about Mountainside, a feeling of isolation, a sense that residents want to be left alone, and these hills provide them with privacy.

The shops, gas stations, and library are clustered in "the village" at the base of the hill. Here, adjacent to the school, is a landscaped park and recreation center where year-round programs attract children and adults alike.

It is not easy for children to get around in this neighborhood. Many of the hills are too steep for bicycles and skateboards. Children have to walk most places or be driven. There is little public transportation available. Consequently children tend to spend much of their free time close to home. They play baseball and soccer in diamonds they have painted on the streets. They build tree houses and rope swings and share them with children who live nearby.

The only public building in the residential area itself is the fire station, a focal point near where children gather for spontaneous games of softball. If their families are members, children have access to the tennis clubs, the swimming and cabana club, and the riding stables, but they usually have to ride up to them with their parents because there is no other way to get there. The Mountainside Recreation Center at the bottom of the hill, run by the city's Parks and Recreation Department, is something like those clubs. It has fine facilities and offers a variety of things for children to do—tennis, art, and dancing classes—for which they seem grateful. Many are avid participants probably because there is so little public play space in the hills. As a result the center is one of the most successful in the city.

For the children of Mountainside it can be as much as three or four miles to school. Many takes buses or are driven by their parents. The children report that their best friends are those with whom they have things in common. One girl whose closest friend lived next door was asked if proximity was the reason for their relationship. "No," she replied, "I choose to be with others who are active like me."

Except for the firemen at the station, the children interact with few adults other than their parents, and that does not seem to bother them. They were bored even by the prospect of doing things with their parents, or their siblings, although they often had no choice but to be in their company because they have so few opportunities to do things and go places on their own.

Rosewood

Each house in the Rosewood area is surrounded by its own lush shrubbery. Few have fences. They merge yard upon yard into one lavish slope of greenery. The sidewalks mark the only boundaries. These are rambling and generous, and the children ride their bicycles along them and play softball in the connecting streets.

The neighborhood, in classic fashion, is centered on the school. Anyone in the area can get there in less than seven minutes. The children have developed many alternate routes over the years. There are the stone steps that climb the hill. There is an easy route down which they can ramble when tired. An occasional detour takes them through a friend's backyard or over a fence to avoid a dog or crabby neighbor.

The area's only public space is a city block that houses the elementary school and its playground. The children say they walk up here often in summer "to see who's around," although till late afternoon it is often too hot to play there. When it cools off they sometimes check out sports equipment at the playground but leave before the older kids "take over." Then they congregate in rugged places, odd lots abandoned and mostly inaccessible to adults. These plots all have names inherited from children bygone; the origins of the names are now unknown. "Astro" at the top of a hill is embraced by a sweeping view of the bay. Two alleys converge there, creating an ideal place for games of tag and chase. "Pioneers Trail" on the rise of another hill is suitably rutted for biking and sliding.

The neighborhood works well for children. Since there are many young families on every block, Rosewood is dense with children. Finding friends poses no problem. One has the sense, however, that children select their close friends with care. The heterogeneous character of the neighborhood appears to some extent to shape friendship patterns. The majority of Rosewood children are white (61 percent), but a large proportion are black (31 percent). From the things children said it seemed that as they got older they chose to associate less with children who were "different." It is not possible to determine the degree to which friendships based on racial matching are motivated by the children's inclinations or their parents'. Nevertheless a kind of sorting seemed to dominate social relationships among the children of this diverse, middle-class neighborhood.

Bancroft

There are no sidewalks or street lamps in the Bancroft district. The roads are narrow and patched with asphalt. Pickup trucks and old cars line the unpaved shoulders. Most of the houses cannot be seen from the street. They are small and hidden behind huge oaks, apple trees, and vegetable gardens. Grass grows in fringes near the low fences that separate yards. Where children play, growth has been trampled to stubble.

In this neighborhood families were less agreeable to having their children interviewed. Parents were sometimes suspicious and on several occasions hostile. In Bancroft both parents are likely to work, and children are frequently left on their own when not at school. Parents expect their children to remain close to home and want to know where they are at all times.

Because they are required to stay near home, the children know more about their own yards and those immediately adjacent than do children from other neighborhoods. They know the fenced-in areas well: the sagging trees and ladders, the mounds of dirt, the discarded boards and boxes. This is their turf.

Their time is often spent in the company of brothers and sisters. Children are close to their siblings and appear to prefer their stable companionship to the host of neighborhood friends common in other areas. Sixth-graders in the Bancroft area ordinarily leave their block only to go to school, run an errand, or keep an appointment. Their reticence can be attributed in part to the heavy flow of traffic through the area. The school and park both front on a heavily traveled thoroughfare adjacent to a freeway exit. Furthermore, these facilities are unattractive and uninviting: the schoolyard is often unavailable for play; the park is dangerous because of its proximity to the freeway. As in the case of all children we talked to, Bancroft's sixth-graders are clearly intimidated by the older people who frequent these facilities.

The director of city parks and recreation programs for the area agreed that parents there are more protective than in other parts of the city. She said that when children go to the park, parents will often wait there while they play and then escort them home. As a result, it is difficult to get children to participate in planned activities at the recreation center.

Glenn

Glenn begins abruptly beyond the block of trucking companies and shipping warehouses that crowd the freeway exit. Where the billboards and storefronts stop, flowers, sparsely planted, spring up along the sidewalks. The houses look like fortresses. Most are brashly painted in colors that accentuate their imposing characters. In other parts of the neighborhood the houses are smaller, blander, hidden among each other. In this area apartments are more common. Neighbors sit on bannisters. There are many more people on the streets and more children hanging around than in other areas.

Although buses and large trucks run through continually, there are no stop signs, even on the most heavily traveled streets and alleys. Shops and churches are located mostly in one area. The triangular stores on the corners create a sociable atmosphere. On one block there are three churches—Solo Cristo Salvo, Ebenezer Church of God in Christ, and the New Jerusalem—each with the same kind of Portuguese stained glass. Even in broad daylight they are locked.

At the top of the hill stands the junior high school. Most of Glenn's sixth-graders will be enrolled there somewhat reluctantly. It has a forbidding appearance. There is no grass anywhere in sight. The gates are locked and the windows boarded up during the summer. Vandalism rates are very high. One child said she was afraid to go there because "the kids are rough."

At the bottom of the hill the gate is open at the parochial school. A concrete and redwood church stands beside it. The playground adjacent to it looked well used—but only by older children.

Glenn Park, near the elementary school, is an oasis in the midst of the neighborhood. The park is a long hill of grass that slopes into the street below. The recreation center at the top and the tennis courts appear popular. Even late on a workday morning many parents are there with children. Old people are there, too, some picnicking.

The houses of Glenn are very orderly and packed with small luxuries: a padded bar in one corner, an aquarium, a color television in the kitchen. The children frequently had televisions of their own or stereos.

Play space is a problem, especially since many children, boys and girls alike, enjoy team sports. Often they play in vacant lots and side streets, some strewn with old tires, paper, and glass.

Children in the Glenn neighborhood are rarely alone during the day. They go into each other's houses and around the neighborhood in loosely knit groups. They are always on the move. Even when they are simply killing time with friends they are usually "going around." One boy said, "Sometimes we just walk to the pier on Seventh Street. It's six or seven miles. We might go into a store and sit for a while."

Glenn is a neighborhood with strong ethnic ties. Sixty-four percent of the families are black, 27 percent Hispanic, just 3 percent white. Friendships seem to be formed along ethnic lines, and tightly knit adolescent gangs are common. When children talked about friends, they did not mention ethnicity unless it was different from their own. One girl, describing the neighborhood, carefully enumerated the racial characteristics of each of the families in her housing complex. She mentioned only those of similar ethnic background when asked who among these she considered to be her friends.

Eastside

The streets of the Eastside neighborhood are stark. Debris collects at the curb. Fences claim the yards that soften rows of small faded houses. There are no trees except in the better-tended gardens. Weeds push through the asphalt of streets and schoolyard. Yet despite its physical appearance, the neighborhood is vibrant with street life.

Many Eastside families migrated here in the 1950s and retain ties with the South. They talk about relatives or recent vacations in Kentucky, Alabama, or Louisiana.

The children of the Eastside neighborhood, like the children of Glenn, spend their time in groups. On a summer day, even before adults have left for work, many children have congregated on the street. First thing in the morning and again at lunchtime some take advantage of free meals at the community center. More than half of the neighborhood children are eligible for these meals. The children take their trays outside to observe and talk to other children coming from all over the neighborhood to eat.

Eastside children thrive on the company of their peers. The children on a block call most everyone a friend. Best friendships seem to be related more to proximity than to the compatibility of interests characteristic in Mountainside. Eastside sixth-graders number older people, including their parents, their friends' parents, and shopkeepers, as friends. In contrast with neighborhoods in the hills, there seemed to be few loners among Eastside children. The idea of spending time alone did not even seem to present itself as a viable social option. Perhaps the high density of families with younger children would make it hard for a child to be a loner anyway.

Within a certain radius of their homes the children were familiar with innumerable places that held an attraction for them. Corner stores seemed especially fascinating. Children wandered in and out, calling owners by name and making inexpensive purchases. One boy, during a lag in the activities of the morning, darted into a corner drugstore and emerged with packs of gum that he shared with everyone around.

The schoolyard can be reached in five minutes from anywhere in the area. The children's rambling takes them by it several times during the day. If there are no older children around, they stop and talk or play basketball. Since there are other schools and open playgrounds nearby, they can congregate elsewhere if necessary.

The Community School, run by the Black Panthers, provides play space and special activities for neighborhood children. Martial arts classes are sponsored throughout the summer. Many children have taken these classes and are skilled in self-defense.

Eastside children are especially interested in team sports. There are certain spots for playing baseball and kickball, which are very popular. These are dead-end streets or vacant lots. The place where the scoutmaster lived was mentioned several times when the children talked about where they met to hang around. Age seems to matter less in this area. Skills count. Hence it is not uncommon to find a broad age range of children getting together to play ball. Many adults join in the evening games.

The children talked a little about the condition of their neighborhood. They appreciated the fruit trees accessible to them and pointed out the lemons and plums. Two boys mentioned that littering was a problem. As they walked along, they tossed their gum wrappers behind them. One did not care if anyone saw him, but the other waited until he thought no one was watching.

THE STUDY SETTING

Oakland is a "minority majority" central city. Demographic changes have occurred rapidly over the last two decades (tables 3-1 and 3-2) with the proportion of minorities of all races increasing from 26 percent in 1960 to 54 percent in 1977. Furthermore, if the number of traditional family households continues to decline, in another decade fewer than half the households will be what the Census calls "family units."

These changes reflect national trends: fewer children per family, increasing segregation of senior citizens in the inner city, exodus of middle-class families with school-age children to the suburbs, and related phenomena. The other core cities of the San Francisco Bay Area experienced the same kinds of changes, including net loss of population, although the metropolitan area as a whole continued to grow.* In all these cities, correlates of declining population have included smaller average household size and lower school enrollments.

In Oakland the white and nonwhite populations are very different in terms of age structure as well as economic status. The black population is younger and more family-based than the white (table 3-3). The white population is increasingly composed of the elderly, of households of unrelated young

---

*Bay Area cities that lost population after 1960 include San Francisco, Berkeley, and Richmond, as well as Oakland. San Jose continued to grow, largely because of its annexation policies.

TABLE 3-1. Ethnicity and Total Population of Oakland

	1960		1970		1977	
Ethnicity[a]	Number	Percent	Number	Percent	Number	Percent
Black	83,618	22.8	124,710	34.5	148,811	44.7
White	270,523	73.6	213,512	59.1	153,694	46.1
Other minorities[b]	13,407	3.6	23,339	6.4	30,550	9.2
Total	367,548	100.0	361,561	100.0	333,055	100.0

SOURCES: U.S., Bureau of the Census, *Census of Population and Housing: 1960 Census Tracts, Final Report PHC (1)-137 San Francisco-Oakland, Calif. SMSA* (Washington, D.C.: Government Printing Office, 1962); *Census of Population and Housing: 1970 . . . PHC (1)-189 . . .* (1972); and "Special Census of Oakland, California: April 26, 1977," *Current Population Reports, Series P-28, No. 1563* (January 1979).

[a]In addition, enumeration of Hispanics showed: 1960: white and Spanish surname, 22, 729 (6.5 percent of city population); 1970: all individuals with Spanish surname or language, 35, 372 (9.7 percent of city population); 1977: not available.

[b]Category consists of five groups (1970 populations in parentheses): Chinese (11,335), Japanese (2,405), Filipino (3,633), Native American (2,890), and other races (3,076).

TABLE 3-2. Household Composition: Oakland

	1960		1970		1977	
	Number	Percent	Number	Percent	Number	Percent
Family households	96,269	71.9	89,233	64.3	79,753	57.2
(Husband-wife)	(79,946)	(59.7)	(69,998)	(50.4)	(53,419)	(38.3)
(Other with female or male head)	(16,323)	(12.2)	(19,235)	(13.9)	(26,334)	(18.9)
Households of single or unrelated individuals	37,574	28.1	49,598	35.7	59,762	42.8
Total households	133,843	100.0	138,831	100.0	139,515	100.0
Persons per household	2.69		2.53		2.33	
Median age: male	34.7		29.7		28.3	
female	36.5		33.5		29.7	

SOURCES: U.S., Bureau of the Census, *PHC (1)-137*; *PHC (1)-189*; and *Series P-28, No. 1563*.

TABLE 3-3. Ethnicity and Household Composition: Oakland, 1977

	Total population		Black		White		Other	
	Number	Percent	Number	Percent	Number	Percent	Number	Percent
Family households	79,753	57.2	36,142	63.4	36,872	50.7	6,739	67.7
(Husband-wife)	(53,419)	(38.3)	(19,008)	(33.4)	(28,885)	(39.7)	(5,526)	(55.6)
(Other with female or male head)	(26,334)	(18.9)	(17,134)	(30.0)	(7,987)	(11.0)	(1,213)	(12.1)
Households of single or unrelated individuals	59,762	42.8	20,688	36.4	35,865	49.3	3,209	32.3
Total households	139,515	100.0	56,830	100.0	72,737	100.0	9,948	100.0
Persons per household	2.33		2.59		2.03		3.00	
Median age:								
male	28.3		21.5		33.1		26.2	
female	29.7		24.1		38.3		26.6	

SOURCE: U.S., Bureau of the Census, *Series P-28, No. 1563.*

adults, and of families with few or no children. The median age of whites is more than twelve years older than blacks, and the average household size is significantly smaller.

The demographic profile of the public school system (from which our sample was drawn) is considerably different from that of the city as a whole. With regard to the ethnic characteristics of the schools, there has been an important transformation in recent years. To begin with, data from 1970 and 1975 indicate that there was a dramatic withdrawal of white students from the public schools during that period. The 1970 census shows that there were 26,709 children under age five living in Oakland and that 33 percent were white. The elementary schools' enrollment five and one-half years later, when that cohort constituted the majority, was only 19 percent white: almost half the white preschoolers in Oakland had moved or were otherwise not enrolled in the system.

By this token many questions of school desegregation have become moot. The white minority is concentrated in a few schools. In thirty-five of Oakland's fifty-eight elementary schools three-quarters of the students are of a single race, and in another twenty a majority are.

As the city's population has declined so has public school enrollment, the latter at a more precipitous rate. The city lost 7 percent of its 1970 population by 1977; the public schools lost 13 percent of their 1970 enrollment by 1976. Further declines are projected.

The school population is also poorer than the city population as a whole. In 1970, 38 percent of the children attending the public schools were from families receiving public assistance in the form of Aid to Families with Dependent Children (AFDC) (a proportion that has remained almost constant since then), while only 12.2 percent of all Oakland's families and 16.6 percent of all residents were below the census' poverty level at that time.

Exact comparison of the economic status of the school and city populations is not possible because of the lack of equivalent data. Nonetheless, in some respects such a comparison would be tautological. That is, the presence of children is correlated with younger heads of households, larger households, lower-than-average incomes, and other factors that spell lower socioeconomic status. In almost all major American cities, even those with very wealthy populations, the families of school-children tend to be relatively less well off than the general population. When, as in Oakland, the public school population is further reflective of larger demographic and residential housing patterns that segregate poor and nonwhite families, then the comparison will show even greater differences.

Though aggregate statistics indicate that the Oakland public schools' population is relatively disadvantaged, there are wide disparities within the district, from school to school and, in some instances, within schools. The proportion of children from AFDC families attending each elementary school, for example, ranged from a low of 0.9 percent to a high of 99.1 percent in 1975. Median incomes for elementary school attendance areas, using 1970 census data, varied from $4,715 to $20,476, with a citywide median of $9,626.

Oakland is divided in two: the hills and the flatlands. These labels symbolize the extremes of wealth and poverty, respectively. Hill families are predominantly white and well off. Flatland families are predominantly minorities with low incomes. Both white and minority families of moderate income live at the base of the hills—in between the extremes. Black and Hispanic families are more likely to live in low-income neighborhoods even if their personal income is not low. This is due to discrimination in the housing market and, to a much lesser extent, to choice on the part of those who stay. As the black population of Oakland has grown, however, members of its upper social and economic strata have sought homes in more desirable neighborhoods. Consequently certain areas in the hills, adjacent to less prosperous black areas, have become predominantly black. There are one or two thoroughly integrated upper-middle-income areas (including one in our sample).

There is not much of a white working class, other than people in or near retirement, left in the city. Increasingly, whites living in lower-status flatland areas are young singles, childless couples, or retired persons rather than families with children.

The city's elementary school attendance districts average around 6,000 residents and encompass areas of about one-half mile square. Major pedestrian barriers such as freeways, railroad tracks, or boulevards form their boundaries. Within these areas, most children walk, or could walk, to school relatively safely in eight minutes or less. There is no intradistrict busing plan, so virtually all elementary-school age children attend school near their homes. For many people, especially children, the name and extent of their perceived neighborhood coincides with the school attendance area.

Neighborhoods embody important forms of collective social responsibility for the welfare of children. Neighborhood life retains great significance for children as a context for socialization. When it comes to publicly provided facilities and programs, we discovered that "who you are," which pretty well defines "where you live," is a fair proxy for "what you get" (table 3-4).

Generally, upper-status neighborhoods enjoy better children's services, particularly parks and recreation facilities. One study of per capita expenditures in Oakland documented variation among neighborhoods of between $90 and $487 per capita.[4] On this basis, higher-income neighborhoods (which also tend to have significantly lower population densities) seem to fare much better than lower-income areas, although the correlation between per capita spending and neighborhood socioeconomic status is not an absolute measure of quality or access. Two neighborhoods of similar low socioeconomic status in our study sample had significantly different parks and recreation spending and service levels (table 3-5). The area that was better served had been developed at an earlier time and had a lower density of children. Yet even that neighborhood was below the citywide average on some indicators, consistent with the overall correlation of service quality and socioeconomic status.

Parents' subjective perceptions of service quality, as crucial as actual differences in quality, are quite clearly related to ethnicity and socioeconomic status, and not in surprising ways (table 3-6).

Although in the aggregate Oakland's children performed far below average on state standardized scholastic achievement tests, parents generally rated the schools very favorably. Forty-two percent told us they were very satisfied with their children's schools, far more than felt that way about other services.

TABLE 3-4. Availability of Neighborhood Services[a]

	Mean score
Ethnicity	
Black	72
White	121
Asian	125
Hispanic	73
Family income	
Less than $5,000	70
$5,000-$9,999	80
$10,000-$14,999	79
$15,000-$19,999	88
$20,000 or more	109
Mother's education	
Less than high school diploma	68
High school graduate	80
Some college	88
College graduate and above	117
All respondents	84

[a]The scale incorporated contextual data on availability of libraries, parks, recreation facilities, and school-based afternoon programs in the twenty sample neighborhoods. The higher the score, the better the service for that group of respondents (minimum = 30.0; maximum = 240.0).

TABLE 3-5. Parks and Recreation Facilities for Two Areas in Oakland of Similar Low Socioeconomic Status

	Citywide average	Neighborhood	
		A	B
Number of recreational facilities in district[a]	14.75	10	20
Per capita investment in parks and recreation	$206	$108	$172
Additional park acreage needed to achieve minimum standard (2.5 acres per 100 population)	12.9	57.4	31.2

SOURCE: City of Oakland, Department of Planning, *Open Space, Conservation and Recreation Element* (1976).

[a]All figures refer to data for the junior high school area in which the sample elementary school is located. Facilities include: softball diamonds, baseball diamonds, tot lots, tennis courts, outdoor pools, recreation center buildings, and gymnasiums.

TABLE 3-6. Neighborhood Services Judged by Parents to be "Better than Average"[a]

	Mean score
Ethnicity	
Black	5
White	15
Asian	11
Hispanic	6
Family income	
Less than $5,000	6
$5,000-$9,999	6
$10,000-$14,999	6
$15,000-$19,999	9
$20,000 or more	13
Master sampling strata[b]	
Low status	5
Middle status	8
High status	17
All respondents	7

[a]An index based on the number of services that respondents characterized as "better than average" in their neighborhood compared with the rest of the city. Services included schools, police, recreation programs for children, libraries, parks, and buses.

[b]Sampling strata are defined in the following section of this chapter.

Another 41 percent were somewhat satisfied, leaving less than one-fifth of all parents to say they were dissatisfied. (By way of contrast, neighborhood recreation programs, parks, and public safety were rated unsatisfactory by roughly half the parents.) Of all public agencies, the schools were viewed as the most accessible: 45 percent of all parents thought they had a good chance of getting school principals to act on a complaint, while only 7 percent considered their chances poor.

Much of the relatively favorable rating of the schools is the result of their greater familiarity to parents. In opinion research, familiarity usually breeds not contempt but appreciation, all other things being equal. Perhaps too the enormous importance attached to schooling makes parents more reluctant to admit dissatisfaction, for the options, short of moving, are few. As expected, there were higher than average satisfaction levels in higher-income neighborhoods where schools were considered the best in the city, and, among the parents of children who were doing well in their studies.

Virtually every mother in our twenty sample neighborhoods had visited the school, talked with teachers, and learned something about what goes on there. By contrast, recreational and cultural services were well known to only a small number of mothers, occasionally visited by more, and largely unknown to most. Their sixth-graders are at an age when they are less well served than either younger or older children. They are "in between" children's and adults' book collections at the library; and they are too small to use the playgrounds when the older ones want the space (often they are unceremoniously forced aside). Add these problems to the general malaise of cultural and recreational services endangered by their worst budget crises since the Great Depression, and one can begin to understand why they received relatively unfavorable ratings. Five times as many parents thought that their neighborhood recreation programs were below average as thought they were better than average, and for parks and libraries the ratios were not much better. When parents and children were asked to suggest what could be done to improve the neighborhood, most of their suggestions involved providing new parks and recreational facilities.

While no parents were completely happy with the services provided to their children, there was a great deal of variation in their relative satisfaction. An aggregate index of perceptions held by parents of all backgrounds regarding six services demonstrates widespread belief that families living in well-to-do, predominantly white neighborhoods receive better services. Thus both objective and subjective indicators of the level and quality of children's neighborhood services show definite variation across the city. These differences have important consequences for children and their out-of-school time use (see particularly chapters four and seven).

A PORTRAIT OF 764 FAMILIES

Our survey sample was designed to capture the full range of circumstances characteristic of families with children in the sixth grade attending the Oakland public schools. To obtain this representative cross section of the community it was necessary to interview children and parents from twenty Oakland neighborhoods (see Appendix B).

The data we used to define such a sample population turned out to be highly correlated with the characteristics of the families that were actually chosen (table 3-7). When the twenty school neighborhoods were ranked by overall socioeconomic status, the characteristics of the individual families living there fell into predictable patterns: families from schools of highest social status (Master Stratum I) scored higher on a composite "relative advantage index." These families were the smallest, the parents the oldest in the sample. The higher-status areas contained most of the white and Asian families, while areas of lowest social status (Master Stratum III) were virtually all black and Hispanic. On all of these variables—ethnicity, life cycle, and economic status—the schools of intermediate status (Master Stratum II) were the most heterogeneous.

Survey respondents were predominantly minority, mostly low- and middle-income, and principally educated at the high school level or above (table 3-8), but there are significant differences within our sample (table 3-9). These differences affect family life, child-rearing practices, and the nature of children's experiences out of school. We describe extensively the socioeconomic circumstances faced by Oakland's larger ethnic groups, as these are undeniably important to our analysis. At times in our analyses, ethnic differences in time-use patterns are not readily explicable by controlling for other variables. Our explanations are modest in these situations, for anything more would require ethnographic studies of the specific content of child-rearing practices and time-use behaviors among diverse cultures.* Indeed, given the importance of ethnicity in our time-use analyses, we hope that such studies will be undertaken in the future.

Household composition is another dimension on which the sample can be divided. The majority of children (57.6 percent)

---

*Furthermore, in ethnographic terms ethnic identities would themselves require more specificity than our general categories such as Asian, Hispanic, and white.

TABLE 3-7. Distribution of Selected Characteristics among Sample Families, Unweighted and Aggregated by School Area (percentages)

	Black	White	Asian	Hispanic or other	Mean score on relative advantage index[a]
High status					
(Master Stratum I)					
School 1	21.1	50.0	26.3	2.6	3.0
2	5.4	86.5	8.1	0.0	3.0
3	17.1	74.3	8.6	0.0	2.9
4	17.5	60.0	17.5	5.0	2.6
5	35.7	45.2	16.7	2.4	2.8
6	6.5	67.7	12.9	12.9	1.7
Middle status					
(Master Stratum II)					
School 7	16.7	11.1	61.1	11.2	1.9
8	40.5	37.8	21.6	0.0	1.6
9	83.7	14.0	0.0	2.3	2.6
10	73.0	16.2	0.0	10.8	1.9
11	94.9	2.6	0.0	2.6	2.4
12	61.4	4.5	9.1	25.0	1.1
Low status					
(Master Stratum III)					
School 13	76.1	6.5	4.3	13.0	1.3
14	70.3	8.1	0.0	21.6	1.0
15	85.4	4.9	0.0	9.8	1.6
16	100.0	0.0	0.0	0.0	1.0
17	91.9	2.7	0.0	5.4	1.2
18	100.0	0.0	0.0	0.0	1.2
19	87.5	5.0	0.0	7.5	1.2
20	100.0	0.0	0.0	0.0	0.9
Total sample	59.8	24.2	9.2	6.8	1.8

[a]This index consisted of a measure of family income, mother's education, family structure, and other related terms: the higher the mean score, the higher the advantage.

had two parents living at home. Most families (87.7 percent) consisted only of parents and children, with no extended family or unrelated individuals in residence. Most families had three or fewer children living at home (2.6 children were the mean). Eleven percent of the sixth-graders had no siblings.

Black children were most likely both to have only one parent at home and to have an extended family. Their mothers were, on the average, somewhat younger than those of white children,

TABLE 3-8. Study Sample Characteristics (vertical percentages)

		Unweighted (N)
Ethnicity		
Black	59.8	(457)
White	24.2	(185)
Asian	9.2	(70)
Hispanic and other	6.8	(52)
Family income		
Less than $5,000	17.4	(133)
$5,000-$9,999	20.9	(160)
$10,000-$14,999	16.0	(122)
$15,000-$19,999	14.4	(110)
$20,000 or more	24.2	(185)
Not available	7.1	(54)
Mother's education		
Less than high school diploma	22.8	(174)
High school graduate	27.9	(213)
Some college	31.4	(240)
College graduate and above	16.1	(123)
Not available	1.8	(14)

TABLE 3-9. Ethnicity, Income, and Education[a] (vertical percentages)

	Black	White	Asian	Hispanic
Family income				
Less than $5,000	27.9	9.1	5.0	39.0
$5,000-$9,999	31.0	13.8	15.4	15.4
$10,000-$14,999	15.9	15.5	26.0	27.9
$15,000-$19,999	11.9	20.2	11.3	15.8
$20,000 or more	13.3	41.4	42.3	1.9
Weighted (N)	(485)	(128)	(45)	(34)
Mother's education				
Less than high school diploma	28.5	13.3	23.2	64.8
High school graduate	32.6	21.4	38.3	13.2
Some college	32.0	33.7	18.9	16.6
College graduate and above	6.9	31.6	19.6	5.4
Weighted (N)	(517)	(134)	(47)	(36)

[a]Does not include respondents of "other" ethnic groups or cases where data on income or education were not available.

yet the average number of children per household was somewhat higher. Both Hispanic and Asian families were more likely than blacks or whites to have two parents in the home. These distributions generally conform to national survey and census data (table 3-10).

The ethnic distribution of sample families along a measure of per capita income (table 3-11) is not very different from the distributions of total family income (see table 3-9). The per capita measure, however, is a somewhat more accurate representation of material resources available to each child. Whites and Asians are better off than blacks and Hispanics. This differential is diminished but still quite evident when marital status is taken into account (table 3-12).

The traditional nuclear family (father as breadwinner, mother as full-time housewife) represents only a fifth of the sample. The female-headed welfare family (a single, unemployed mother and her children) accounts for only 14 percent. The majority of sampled families fit neither category (and those who do match these nominal descriptions are diverse in other ways).

There are some newer images of family life, however, which in recent years have become a part of American popular consciousness. Our respondents, surveyed in 1976, were a harbinger of contemporary patterns. Two related aspects of the home environment—family structure and mother's labor force status—showed extraordinary diversity. Both can be expected to influence children's time use for they are significantly linked to parents' time availability (see chapter five). With regard to the former, there are fewer "adult hours" in a single-parent family. And with regard to mother's employment, although families with single working mothers or two working parents may be "time pressed," one might expect that these families could substitute material resources (income) for time resources. Perhaps if the sample were more homogeneous and there was a single type of one-parent family or a "typical" family with the mother working, we could test such a hypothesis directly. Maternal employment, however, means different things in different ethnic groups, economic classes, and family structures.

Although there are nearly equal numbers of men and women in the labor force, the households with the greatest income are

TABLE 3-10. Ethnicity and Number of Parents in Household (vertical percentages)

Parents at home	Black	White	Asian	Hispanic	Other	All families[a]
One	51.8	23.7	7.3	37.3	9.5	42.4
Two	48.2	76.3	92.7	62.7	90.5	57.6
Weighted (N)	(512)	(133)	(48)	(37)	(12)	(742)

[a]Data not available in 22 cases.

TABLE 3-11. Ethnicity and Annual Income per Family Member (1975)[a] (horizontal percentages)

Ethnicity	Income per family member					Weighted (N)
	Less than $100	$100-174	$175-299	$300-499	$500 or more	
Black	23.5	23.6	20.1	20.6	12.2	(471)
White	5.7	9.0	16.0	32.6	36.0	(127)
Asian	0.0	9.8	35.1	22.3	32.9	(45)
Hispanic	37.3	21.5	25.4	11.8	3.9	(34)
Other	17.4	28.6	11.7	29.7	12.6	(11)

[a]Data not available in 76 cases.

TABLE 3-12. Ethnicity, Family Structure, and Income (vertical percentages)

Family income	Black		White		All families[a]	
	One Parent	Two Parents	One Parent	Two Parents	One Parent	Two Parents
Less than $5,000	41.8	10.8	26.7	4.1	41.9	8.4
$5,000-$9,999	39.0	22.9	30.0	8.2	36.8	18.6
$10,000-$14,999	10.8	21.1	23.3	13.3	12.5	20.2
$15,000-$19,999	5.6	19.7	10.0	23.5	5.7	19.9
$20,000 or more	2.8	25.6	10.0	51.0	3.0	32.9
Weighted (N)	(249)	(223)	(30)	(98)	(296)	(392)

[a]Data not available in 76 cases.

predominantly those with a male earner. Virtually all of the employed men in the sample held full-time jobs, with some employed well over forty hours per week. A slimmer majority of working women, 70 percent, were also employed full time (in female-headed families that proportion was higher). Thus it was not the part-time nature of some mothers' work that caused the income inequality between male- and female-headed households. In fact, part-time work was, in our sample, largely the province of relatively well-to-do, white, married women. Black women were more likely to work full time if they worked at all.

Whites are more likely than blacks to have two-parent families, two-earner families, and high-income families. Yet the proportion of families with two full-time earners is higher for blacks than whites,* despite the fact that less than half the black households in our sample had two parents living in the home. The total income of one- and two-earner families differed by ethnicity (tables 3-13 and 3-14). Here it is clear that the income returns for each ethnic group are very different: blacks on average made less. In other words, each group does not have the same income/time substitution factor. A black mother working full time is nowhere near as likely as a white mother working full time to pull the family into a relatively high-income bracket. Similarly, if a white mother in a two-parent family is not working, it is still very likely that the family has a high income, four times as likely as it is in the case of black families (table 3-15).

CONCLUSION

In stressing the limitations of any single-variable summary of social status, and by emphasizing the different meaning that the same measure might have for different groups, we are consistent with contemporary notions of social stratification.[5] Definitions of class and status involve several hierarchies of variables, and researchers can no longer substitute measures of economic, social, and cultural resources for one another as if they mean the same thing (perhaps they never really could). Similarly, indices that summarize all dimensions of social class and family status may miss essential underlying differences among groups. This, then, is the theoretical problem. It is one with which we must contend, since one of the primary objectives of this volume is to

---

*It is highest of all for Asians, where more than 93 percent of all families had two parents in the home.

TABLE 3-13. Ethnicity and Labor Force Status of Parents (vertical percentages)

Earners per family	Black	White	Asian	All families[a]
Two full-time	19.8	15.1	34.1	19.3
One full-time, one part-time	6.8	20.0	24.7	10.2
One full-time only	34.2	46.5	32.8	37.4
One part-time only	6.7	6.1	1.4	6.7
No earners[b]	29.7	9.1	5.7	23.8
Not available	2.8	3.2	1.3	2.6
Weighted (N)	(515)	(133)	(47)	(746)

[a]Data not available in 18 cases.
[b]Unemployed or not in labor force.

TABLE 3-14. Families with Incomes above $15,000 per Year (percentages of families within each earner category)

Earners per family	Black	White	Asian	All families
Two full-time	72.0	90.0	53.0	72.7
One full-time, one part-time	36.3	81.5	63.6	56.8
One full-time only	20.1	61.0	50.0	41.4
One part-time only	10.3	16.7	–	11.6
No earners[a]	–	–	–	–

[a]Unemployed or not in labor force.

elaborate the linkages among measures of social class and family status and children's time use.

Beyond the theoretical dilemma there is an empirical reality that must be recognized. We have seen that life-circumstance variables are distributed differently across our respondent families, particularly when they are stratified by ethnicity. Since we are principally concerned with the consequences of these circumstances for time use, rather than with the imagery of status and class, we are obliged to analyze and report time-use behavior in terms of a wide variety of background characteristics, rather than a few summary measures.

Our sample reflects the convergence of these theoretical and empirical issues. We have seen how easily simple equality of income and education, which appear to place people at similar

TABLE 3-15. Ethnicity, Mother's Employment, and Family Income (vertical percentages)

	Black				White			
	Mother's labor force status				Mother's labor force status			
Family income	Works full time	Works part time	Single parent (mother not in labor force)	Two parents (mother not in labor force)	Works full time	Works part time	Single parent (mother not in labor force)	Two parents (mother not in labor force)
Less than $5,000	11.7	41.2	58.0	8.1	3.8	5.5	68.6	6.1
$5,000-$9,999	32.7	22.5	32.9	33.9	16.5	7.6	22.7	12.9
$10,000-$14,999	16.9	14.9	4.0	32.5	14.5	16.7	8.7	15.4
$15,000-$19,999	14.8	17.1	2.5	14.8	13.9	31.5	–	23.0
$20,000 or more	23.8	4.3	2.6	10.7	51.2	38.6	–	42.5
Weighted (N)	(203)	(64)	(112)	(84)	(37)	(32)	(8)	(47)

resource levels, may not really do so at all. Probing more deeply, it becomes clear that the resources available to families in our sample vary in many other ways that are unique to each subpopulation. By exploring how families are positioned on different dimensions of circumstance—ethnicity, income, education, family structure, and mother's labor force status—we can portray in greater detail the variety of situations under which children are being raised today.

PART II
Five Time Domains

Introduction

The following five chapters, exploring the domains of out-of-school time use, were written in parallel fashion. Each begins with a brief conceptual statement, an effort to define some of the important social concerns associated with the domain. The activities that comprise the domain are then identified, followed by an analysis of the factors underlying patterns of activity.

We begin each domain analysis with a common set of independent variables, those discussed in detail in chapter three plus a few others, such as gender, which were mentioned only in passing. The common set is then pared down as we focus on a smaller number of variables that have descriptive power for particular domains.

The subjects of these chapters clearly have multidisciplinary appeal. This is advantageous, yet potentially problematic. On the one hand, we have provided a summary of time use in each domain. On the other hand, the analyses may not meet all of the requirements of specialists in some fields who might feel that the work should be structured around one set of themes or variables.

To maintain the level of generalization that we felt appropriate, we chose a heavily descriptive mode of presentation. This reflects several considerations. To begin with, since systematic studies of children's out-of-school lives are so rare, we determined that tabular analyses would be well suited to the interests of researchers and practitioners concerned with youth, of parents, and of other readers eager to learn more about each of the time-use domains. Second, as we argued in chapter two, we could not collect strict time budgets from our preadolescent sample. As a result, given the form of our survey we did not have available the interval variables necessary for certain types of statistical analysis. Similarly, some multivariate analyses would have required compromising the detail and richness of the data—the essence of our presentation—without significantly enhancing our understanding of the determinants and structure of children's time use. However, in other papers, monographs, and books that are products of the Children's Time Study research program, we have utilized a variety of quantitative and qualitative methodologies, each selected to meet particular analytical requirements within the limits of data capabilities.

Two technical notes are in order. First, the tables in each chapter report weighted results: our findings are generalized for the whole preadolescent age group in the Oakland public schools, not just the sample. The specifics of the weighting scheme are described in Appendix B. Second, the size of the sample did not make it possible to include all respondents in every phase of each domain analysis. Sample size constrains researchers regardless of the mode of analysis they select, and ours is no different in that respect. For that reason, many tables report responses for the entire sample (labeled "all children" or "all families"), while detailed description is often limited to our largest respondent categories: black and white children.

four

CHILDREN ON THEIR OWN

Our society segregates children from adults to an unusual degree, prescribing distinctive life styles for them and establishing a panoply of specialized institutions to serve them in relative isolation.[1] In spite of this, or perhaps because of it, we worry that preadolescent children spend too much time on their own, either alone or in the company of their peers.

Many feel that children this age should be within safe distance, if not under the actual supervision of adults most of the time. They should move each day from one sphere of adult influence, the school, to another, the home, as rapidly as possible. When this ideal goes unrealized, as it often does, a "problem" is readily inferred, either in parenting or in the social provision of child care.

Most parents are aware of these normative expectations. Nearly three-quarters of the children in our sample reported that they went straight home from school whether an adult was there to greet them or not. Fully 87 percent said that after school a parent or some other adult "wanted to know where they were most of the time."

Researchers support this perspective as well. Many argue that when children are on their own important developmental opportunities are foregone and antisocial behavior is inadvertently encouraged. Bronfenbrenner, for example, describes what he refers to as "the vacuum left by the withdrawal of parents and adults from the lives of children."[2] This vacuum, he argues, is "filled with an undesired—and possibly *undesirable*—substitute of an age segregated peer group."

Although issues of age segregation and parental contact may be important, they tend to understate the value to children of free time and to overstate just how free that free time is. Concern over the isolation of children from adults should be balanced by appreciation of the many ways in which a child's private moments are constrained and shaped by the adult world. Childhood, though it possesses a distinctive language and culture, is after all a stage of life thoroughly dominated by the process of growing up and preparing for adult roles.

Children's activities on their own often reflect and anticipate adultlike norms and social processes. In the apparent spontaneity of child's play there is compelling evidence of how deeply social controls extend and how fragile and limited natural freedom is. Nevertheless, the image of children on their own has symbolic appeal. Consider Mark Twain's portrait of Huck Finn and Jim floating down the Mississippi River (evoking far more than the images of midnineteenth-century America intended by the author)[3] and William Golding's *Lord of the Flies* (presenting a disturbing morality tale in which a group of shipwrecked children rule their island paradise by terror).[4] Scientific literature recognizes similar tensions. An example is Piaget's discussion of the schoolyard game of marbles. His portrayal of the schoolyard as a microcosm of the social world is particularly valuable for the way in which it reveals the blend of creative potential and submission to rules that characterize childhood.[5]

In our analysis we try, accordingly, to balance our presentation, emphasizing neither how free nor how controlled is the time children spend on their own. Instead we treat that time as relatively unstructured (in contrast to the time they spend with adults and in more organized settings) but revealing in its own way the informal means of socialization to adulthood.

THE ACTIVITIES OF CHILDREN ON THEIR OWN

We asked children two questions: "What do you like to do when you are alone?" and "What do you like to do when you are with your friends?"[6] Individually children did not volunteer many responses to these open-ended questions, even after probing by the interviewers. Collectively, however, the range of responses was enormous: we coded ninety-nine categories in all (even though participation was concentrated in a much smaller number).[7]

Perhaps the most striking feature of this domain is the difference between solitary and group activity patterns.[8] Children overwhelmingly said they liked to do more physically active things when they were with their friends. Only when they were alone were they likely to pursue sedentary pastimes.

To compare among children, tables 4-1 and 4-2 present data in terms of the frequency with which different groups of children gave specific responses to the questions about their activities alone and with friends.

The largest categories of response were team sports (for activities with friends) and television, reading, and homework (for solitary activities). Since space considerations prevent us from analyzing all the activities children mentioned, we have selected team sports and reading for detailed examination.*

Team sports, played by most children when they are on their own, are physically active, group activities taking place for the most part out of doors. Reading, by contrast, exemplifies a solitary, indoor, and in a conventional sense, more intellectual use of time.

Sex and ethnic differences pervade the domain. Team sports accounted for 45 percent of boys' responses but only 26 percent of girls' responses. They made up over 40 percent of black children's responses but only 22 percent of white children's responses (table 4-2). Reading, while accounting for roughly comparable shares of the total responses of all groups of children, displayed a contrasting tendency (table 4-1).[9] Girls (48 percent) and boys (37 percent), black children (39 percent) and children from other ethnic groups (46 percent) said they read for fun when they were alone.[10] (Additional survey data on the

---

*In chapters such as this which involve a large number of activities, one or more have been singled out for intensive analysis. We argue that the patterns and determinants of time use exhibited by these exemplary activities characterize the entire domain. This approach represents a manageable way of moving from simple description of activity patterns to explanation, since it is not possible to undertake detailed analyses for every activity mentioned in the domain overviews.

TABLE 4-1. "What Do You Like To Do When You Are Alone?" (percentages who do each activity)*

Activity	Boys	Girls	Black	White	Asian	Other	All children
Collecting	3	1	1	2	5	0	2
Pets	8	7	6	14	6	6	8
Making/fixing/ playing with models	13	0	6	9	4	4	6
Art	8	12	9	15	14	8	10
Crafts[a]	1	7	3	7	1	5	4
Play instrument/sing	4	4	3	7	6	3	4
Listen to radio/music	12	21	12	24	19	34	16
Television viewing	36	32	33	28	55	38	34
Read/write	37	48	39	46	68	54	43
Homework	6	9	7	10	10	6	7
Bicycling/ skateboarding	14	9	11	16	7	11	11
Basketball	8	3	7	4	1	1	6
Catch, ball, Frisbee	6	3	4	4	3	6	4
All other sports	15	11	12	17	6	11	13
Going places	4	2	4	2	4	0	3
Playing games (general)[b]	11	9	10	12	13	5	10
Role-playing games[c]	2	7	6	5	1	0	5
Board games	5	8	7	10	7	1	7
Phone	2	4	4	0	0	1	3
Domestic tasks/ cooking/shopping	5	10	9	7	5	6	8
Resting	14	11	13	10	18	7	12
Other	4	3	3	7	1	0	3
Weighted (N)	(370)	(394)	(530)	(134)	(49)	(51)	(704)

*We coded the first three responses to this question. On this and the following table we reduced the number of categories by combining those that were related and contained less than 1 percent of the total responses. A few activities of special interest were retained as separate categories regardless of frequency mentioned.

[a]Chiefly pottery, needlework, woodwork
[b]Children's games, e.g., hopscotch
[c]E.g., "house," "war"

TABLE 4-2. "What Do You Like To Do When You Are With Your Friends?" (percentages who do each activity)*

Activity	Boys	Girls	Black	White	Asian	Other	All children
Hobbies[a]	12	8	8	17	12	3	10
Listening to radio/music	0	5	2	6	1	5	3
Television viewing	3	4	2	7	7	2	3
Reading/writing/homework	3	6	4	2	3	12	4
Baseball	51	30	45	29	22	26	40
Basketball	44	8	29	16	19	20	26
Football	32	4	19	12	12	12	17
Kickball	14	31	27	11	10	20	22
Soccer	4	1	1	4	7	7	2
Softball	1	3	2	3	3	0	2
Volleyball	0	8	5	1	1	12	4
Gymnastics	2	4	2	6	4	0	3
Skating (all types)	1	10	6	7	4	5	6
Swimming	5	7	5	13	3	3	6
Tennis	1	3	2	3	5	4	2
Bicycling	28	31	29	38	22	17	29
Skateboarding	15	4	7	13	15	12	9
Dance	0	3	2	2	0	0	2
Tetherball	0	7	4	3	4	3	4
Catch	5	4	3	7	10	11	5
Other sports, physical activities[b]	20	15	17	17	20	16	17
Going places - free	7	12	11	4	14	11	10
Going places - fee	5	8	7	6	4	4	6
Going places - unspecified	5	8	6	8	4	12	7
Playing - general	27	37	32	37	24	37	32
Role-playing games	3	7	4	10	7	5	5
Board games	10	14	10	17	28	5	12
Socializing	16	25	19	28	24	21	21
Shopping	3	8	5	7	4	4	5

TABLE 4-2. (*Continued*).

Activity	Boys	Girls	Black	White	Asian	Other	All children
Other	1	4	2	5	3	5	3
Weighted (N)	(370)	(394)	(530)	(134)	(49)	(51)	(764)

*We coded the first five responses to this question.
[a]Collecting, pets, models, arts and crafts, playing instruments.
[b]Chiefly bowling, Ping-Pong, fishing, hiking.

frequency with which the children read for fun was consistent with this pattern, so in much of the following analysis we also use these more detailed data.)

To the extent that any of the activities represented in tables 4-1 and 4-2 was collective, took place out of doors, and was active, boys were more likely to participate than girls. This is not to say that girls had no interest in physical activities. Quite clearly they did. Physical activities remained girls' most favored activities when they were with friends, and most of the activities they engaged in were at least as strenuous as those of boys. But their overall participation rate was somewhat lower. Furthermore, the physical activities they most commonly engaged in were either individual or two-person activities or indoor activities, such as dancing.

Most other activities in the domain fell into approximately the same pattern. Girls were less likely to play outdoors and with large groups of friends and more likely to play in and around the house. They reported doing domestic chores twice as often as boys on their own and outdoor activities like bicycling and skateboarding somewhat less. Even in terms of hobbies, the responses suggested sex-linked clusters of activities. Making and fixing things were reported exclusively by boys, while girls reported expressive hobbies, such as painting, drawing, and other arts and crafts. The differences in the actual content of these activities may be small, yet the children in our sample seem to have done one type or the other with little overlap.

With few exceptions, children's activities on their own did not vary directly with their families' material resources. This is probably because few of the activities children did on their own involved expensive equipment or large monetary outlays. When the latter were required, it was much more likely that parents were also involved in some way. It is, thus, all the more interesting that ethnic differences in this domain (given the association between ethnicity and wealth) were as pronounced as sex differences.

Consider the ethnic differences associated with reading and related activities. Black children reported reading less frequently on their own than did other children. They were also less likely to do traditional hobbies and more likely to say that television viewing was a major activity when alone (table 4-1). The importance of reading when alone or of engaging in hobbies is not entirely clear, although it may reflect a certain set of values and predispositions. It is possible that children who did not engage in such activities had ample functional equivalents. Particularly in the case of hobbies, those thought to be educational in the traditional sense may, in fact, be expressions of different cultural values rather than active ingredients in the acquisition of vital skills.

Interpreting the origins and significance of these sorts of ethnic and sex differences can be problematic and value laden. Children's activities are neither undertaken as the result of pure individual choice nor are they completely determined by parental socialization practice or larger, social-structural conditions. To understand these activity patterns—particularly to the extent that we wish to know whether they represent unequal opportunities—we must consider other factors that influence children's time-use decisions. Here we shall focus on peer relations and qualities of the physical environment, which have an especially important impact on this activity domain.

CHILDREN'S FRIENDSHIPS

Adults are often ambivalent about children's relationships with their peers, their attitudes varying with social context and the age of the child. Peer relations are universally regarded as crucial to psychological and social development, especially among relatively young children.[11] At the same time, many parents and professionals worry that children, especially adolescents, might "get in with the wrong crowd." This, it is assumed, might undermine adult-approved values and attitudes and lead to socially unacceptable behavior.

Sociologist Talcott Parsons analyzes the school class, describing the positive functions of the peer group: detaching the child from the family, instilling more universalistic norms, and encouraging broader allegiances and dependencies. Yet, the peer group may also propel the child unavoidably into what he calls "adult-disapproved" activities.[12]

James Coleman makes a much stronger statement about the conflict between the values and behavior patterns of high school peer groups and the objectives of modern education. Even so, in much of his work, Coleman proposes harnessing peer groups toward achievement-oriented objectives;[13] and, in his major study on educational opportunity, he argues for exposing underachieving school children to the presumably salubrious benefits of daily contact with privileged, high-achieving peers.[14]

Finally ghetto ethnographers, such as Lee Rainwater,[15] whose research deals with adolescents, or Carol Stack[16] and Eliot Liebow,[17] who focus primarily on adults, exhibit this ambivalence toward many aspects of peer culture with particular clarity. They see peer groups among the poor and minorities they have studied as important support systems in a world of minimal opportunity. They are keenly aware, conversely, of how peer groups reinforce patterns of behavior that may preclude material success or integration into mainstream culture.

To view the peer group only as problematic can lead to an unnecessarily negative portrayal of its role and import in the lives of the young. For example, a study of sixth-grade schoolchildren by John Condry and Michael Siman theorizes, after Bronfenbrenner, that children's peer group affiliations are in large measure the product of adults' withdrawal from their lives. Condry and Siman find that "peer-oriented" children are more likely than "adult-oriented" children to admit antisocial activities and negative feelings about themselves. Their explanation of this difference is that those children who do not have prominent adult figures in their lives take out their negative impulses on themselves and on society.[18]

These findings may be unimpeachable in their context, but they come uncomfortably close to the traditional adult characterizations of compliant children as good and more questioning, rambunctious children as bad. Nothing in Condry and Siman's research indicates, for example, that adult-oriented children are not merely conventional and their peer-oriented counterparts healthily self-critical. And most important, these findings suggest a polarization: they do not admit to the possibility that children's peer affiliations may be positive and complementary to, rather than exclusive of, good relations with adults.

The Condry-Siman research is by no means an extreme: it reflects a surprisingly common orientation to children's friendship patterns and peer relations, which our data lead us to question. We try to keep the issue of children's peer groups in perspective, recognizing tensions between the peer group and the demands of the broader society but appreciating its positive developmental functions as well. We are cautious in our interpretations because, to the extent that we found "problems" associated with peer groups, both the nature of the problems and the degree to which they were exhibited among children from different backgrounds followed a more complex pattern than we would have expected had we focused strictly on the articulation between youthful peer groups and adult society.

Almost 90 percent of the children in our sample said that they usually played with children other than their siblings after school and on weekends. Even those who said they usually played alone were able to give the names of frequent playmates or to mention activities involving other children when asked what they liked to do on their own. Friends are thus a virtually universal part of the lives of children this age. Solitary children are concentrated heavily only in the smaller ethnic groups set apart within the city by language or relatively extreme cultural differences. While 8 percent of the black children and 13 percent of the white reported no playmates, the proportion rose to 35 percent for Asians and 19 percent for other minorities.

The median number of close friends listed by the children was three, with more children reporting a greater than a smaller number (mean 3.4). In effect, there was no sex variation,[19] but variation by ethnicity was striking: black children consistently

reported more friends than either whites or those of other
ethnic backgrounds (table 4-3).

We knew that the number of friends varied with the potential
availability of children in the neighborhood, and that black
children lived in areas densely populated by children: 42 percent lived in high-density neighborhoods compared with 10
percent of white children. Still we had some basis for conclud-
ing that black children are raised in an environment that assigns
more importance to friendships than are white children because
when we controlled for population density, large ethnic differences remained.

The significance of friends to children of different ethnicities
did not follow the patterns that we would have predicted,
however. First, the differences pertained principally to girls:

TABLE 4-3. Number of Friends and Child Population Density[a] (horizontal
          percentages)

Child population density	Number of Friends			Weighted (N)
	1-2	3	4-5	
Low				
Black	25	29	46	(53)
White	40	27	31	(41)
Asian	*	*	*	(7)
Other	*	*	*	(3)
Total	33	29	39	(104)
Medium				
Black	29	19	52	(214)
White	35	26	41	(66)
Asian	23	40	37	(22)
Other	24	21	55	(16)
Total	30	22	48	(314)
High				
Black	16	23	61	(222)
White	24	38	39	(11)
Asian	*	*	*	(1)
Other	18	44	38	(22)
Total	17	26	58	(256)

* = small *n*s

[a]The density factor is derived from 1970 census tract data. For a given neighborhood: low density = less than 2 children (age 5 to 19) per acre; medium density
= 2-5 children per acre; high density = more than 5 children per acre.

75 percent of black girls said they would like to have more friends compared with 56 percent of white girls. Boys, both black and white, expressed the same sentiment in about 60 percent of the cases.

Similarly we found a relation between family size and the actual and desired sizes of peer groups. The larger the family, the more likely the child was to report having fewer friends and wanting more. Where siblings substituted de facto for friends, the substitution was less than satisfactory: 87 percent of children with five or more siblings compared with 54 percent of only children wanted more friends.

This is particularly interesting because in the sample as a whole the desire for friends was entirely unrelated to the actual number reported. We also considered whether such "family effects" might underlie some of the sex differences in children's desire for friends. Tied to the home because of limited mobility and greater domestic responsibilities, girls might have experienced a sense of reduced opportunities for making friends and socializing. This was not the case however: being part of a larger family also created a desire among boys for more peer group support.

Friendship patterns affect the nature of the activities children pursue when on their own. We found, for instance, that among blacks and whites the more friends a girl had, the more likely she was to play team sports. Among boys, those with at least two friends were more likely to play team sports, but beyond that the number of friends did not seem to matter (table 4-4).

The sex composition of the peer group was also important. Very few children claimed any members of the opposite sex among the friends they named, though many more girls (18 percent) than boys (9 percent) did. And those girls who numbered boys among their friends were far more likely to say that they played team sports when on their own than did others (table 4-5).

These data suggest, first, that differentiation in activities is quite firmly entrenched by this age in terms of sports participation, even in the informal settings we are describing; and second, that patterns are only partly attributable to the actual size of the peer group (girls after all reported as many friends as

TABLE 4-4. Children Playing Team Sports on Their Own and Number of Friends (percentages).

Ethnicity and sex	Number of friends				
	1	2	3	4	5
Black					
Boys	47	90	70	88	86
Girls	55	41	58	68	75
White					
Boys	48	67	61	37	70
Girls	10	39	34	35	70
All Boys	49	81	69	80	84
All Girls	33	41	50	62	74

TABLE 4-5. Girls Playing Team Sports on Their Own (percentages)

Ethnicity	Reporting no friends of opposite sex		Reporting friends of opposite sex	
		Weighted (N)		Weighted (N)
Black	59	(201)	78	(42)
White	36	(49)	57	(12)
Asian	17	(10)	25	(3)
Other	49	(20)	68	(4)
Total	53	(279)	71	(61)

boys did). There are also indications that sex segregation among friends influences activity patterns and that, with regard to certain kinds of outdoor group games, girls' time use may be much more strongly affected by sex segregation than boys'.

The peer group did not affect the ethnic differential in team sports participation very much: black involvement in team sports still outweighed white involvement (table 4-4) for both boys and girls, a finding that may well reflect the role sports play in the opportunity structure of the black community.[20]

While we hypothesized that team sport participation would be positively related to friendship patterns, we suspected, in contrast, that more gregarious children might read less frequently than more solitary children. We thought further that this tendency would be more pronounced among the disadvantaged, especially blacks, for whom the peer group is so significant. Finally, we thought that boys, since they do more outdoor activities than girls, would show these effects more clearly. In fact, we found none of these things (table 4-6). Tendencies were in the opposite direction.

Reading seemed to increase slightly where we had expected it to decrease, that is, among children with larger numbers of friends. The data are suggestive rather than conclusive, yet, we feel, important. The aggregate patterns display an interesting relationship between ethnicity and sex. There was very little relation between number of friends and reading for white children. White girls even showed the pattern we had originally anticipated: an exchange between friends and reading. Among black boys there was a strong positive relationship between

TABLE 4-6. Reading and Friends (horizontal percentages)

	Boys only				
	Number of days per week read for fun				
Number of friends	5-7	3-4	1-2	Less than 1	Weighted (N)
1	11	33	30	26	(27)
2	12	26	37	25	(57)
3	19	15	32	30	(79)
4	20	17	31	30	(77)
5	21	26	38	16	(106)
All boys[a]	18	23	35	24	(367)

	Black boys and girls only				
	Number of days per week read for fun				
Number of friends	5-7	3-4	1-2	Less than 1	Weighted (N)
1	12	26	28	34	(29)
2	13	24	38	25	(79)
3	21	14	38	27	(108)
4	18	21	33	28	(95)
5	21	29	36	13	(172)
All black children[a]	19	23	36	21	(523)

[a]Includes those reporting zero or more than five friends.

friends and reading; for black girls the association was more muted, chiefly taking the form of differences in the proportions of children who read very infrequently.

For some children, then, the peer group seems to have exerted very little influence upon reading as an activity chosen when on their own, while for others its impact appears to have been positive.[21] For the latter, this could be related to attitudes toward the school environment: among those who had difficulty in school, the peer group may well have had an ameliorative effect on their interest in intellectual pursuits such as reading. (In the section "How Children View Their Time," below, we explore the psychological correlates of reading in a way that supports this kind of speculation.)

None of this means that peer groups did not foster some of the problems suggested in many studies. Our findings indicate, however, that peer groups may have broadened the range of activities children generally engaged in on their own and, in certain instances, encouraged less sex-linked and sex-stereotyped behavior. These friendships- and peer group-related time-use patterns may be specific to the age group we studied. Nonetheless, these children were on the brink of adolescence and, given the literature, it would seem important to understand how, why, or under what circumstances the benign activity patterns associated with these peer groups might become problematic in future years. Further, given these findings, it seems equally important to explore the circumstances under which children's friendship patterns represent a positive rather than a negative force in their time-use activity patterns.

THE SPATIAL CONTEXT

The physical environment plays a crucial role in children's lives when they are on their own.[22] Many of their activities take place outside the home, so the quality and nature of this spatial context influences their time use. A study by Iona and Peter Opie notes, "Where children are is where they play. . . . Indeed, the street in front of their home is seemingly theirs, more theirs sometimes than the family living room; and of more significance to them very often than any amenity [provided by local government]."[23]

In point of fact, since children are minimally mobile, they have a particularly heavy investment in the physical environment close to home and spend little time away from it.[24]

The physical environment offers opportunities for children to play, but it constrains their activities as well. Problems of where to play, how to get there, and whom to play with are matters of intense concern for children and parents alike.[25] As the Opies suggest, children are infinitely flexible, making do with what is available: their activity patterns, in part, are a product of an environment that all too often is poorly suited to the tempo and style of childhood.[26] Writing about Paris, Bruno Frappat contends:

There is plenty of reason to doubt whether urban life ... is compatible with the rhythms of childhood. It's rare that a child can find a patch of grass to tumble on in a Paris park; the municipal lawns are literally for the birds, and the kids are confined to the gravel paths. . . . Still children have the sidewalks when they can manage to stake claim to some space . . . and on condition that they don't get in the way of passing housewives laden with the day's shopping. Chalking out a game of hopscotch has become a feat of daring, and in places a sacrilege whose telltale signs are immediately obliterated by vigilant grownups.[27]

Children often invent their own play spaces: everything from streets to vacant lots to open space is fair game. But their age, safety considerations (both personal and traffic safety), the terrain, and access to different kinds of facilities affect their mobility and autonomy when they are on their own.[28] Children have an irrepressible urge to carry their activities and social interactions out of their homes, both because they may not have all the space and privacy they want or need and because the adventurous nature of their games and explorations requires a more expansive and challenging setting.[29]

When asked where they and their friends usually played, the preadolescents in our sample most often mentioned their own homes and yards or those of friends. Public spaces were mentioned much less often and organized play areas hardly at all. Nevertheless, while predominantly home-based, children of this age have begun to widen their range (table 4-7). A majority mentioned playing in some public spaces. Boys were more likely to mention public than private spaces, and more of them played

TABLE 4-7. Where Children Usually Play When on Their Own (percentages)

Location	Boys	Girls	Black	White	Asian	Other	All children
Home or yard	53	74	64	65	69	49	64
Friend's home or yard	53	61	56	66	63	45	57
Schoolyard	36	29	37	21	29	22	33
Park	26	22	28	14	15	18	22
Street	12	16	12	16	25	18	14
Vacant lot	12	6	9	8	5	4	69
Recreation center	7	3	6	3	0	0	5

Play in Public and Private Spaces (percentages)

Children reporting they play in	Boys	Girls	Black	White	Asian	Other	All children
Public spaces[a]	75	56	70	51	59	54	65
Private spaces[b]	71	87	78	81	86	74	79
Both public and private spaces	45	42	48	32	46	28	44
Exclusively in public spaces	30	13	22	19	14	26	21
Exclusively in private spaces	25	44	30	49	41	46	35

[a]Parks, schoolyard, streets, vacant lots, recreation centers.
[b]Homes and yards.

exclusively in public spaces than exclusively around their homes and the homes of friends.

For girls the pattern was reversed: with the exception of the street as a place to play, they strongly favored private spaces. Thus they were less likely to play at schoolyards and recreation areas, as well as in more adventurous open spaces such as vacant lots. While concern about safety might seem a plausible explanation for this, we are unable to tie either parents' or children's fears about neighborhood safety to actual use of space. There were two reasons for this paradox. First, children who expressed safety concerns did so from experience. For example, more children who perceived the schoolyard as a place frequented by threatening teenagers, and so feared for their safety, had played there themselves. Concern about safety, in other words, while a preoccupation, did not seem to act as a deterrent. Second, a variety of factors other than safety affect choice of play areas.

Consider schoolyards, the most accessible public play areas and the ones most often used by our respondents (table 4-8). Our findings show both a relationship between frequency of schoolyard play and involvement in organized after-school activities taking place on the school grounds, and a relationship between schoolyard play and mobility (walking, bicycling, or being driven between home and school). It is clear from these data that both access and opportunity were more prominent

TABLE 4-8. Schoolyard Play (percentages)

	Less than 1 day per week	1 or 2 days per week	More often
Sex			
Boys	38	25	36
Girls	53	23	23
Ethnicity			
Black	38	27	35
White	63	18	19
Asian	73	19	8
Other	54	19	26
All children	46	24	30
Children who participate in no activities before or after school	55	23	23
Children who participate in at least one before- or after-school activity	34	27	40
Child walks or bikes home from school	42	26	32
Child is driven or takes bus home from school	67	14	18
Parent satisfied with neighborhood safety	45	27	28
Parent dissatisfied with neighborhood safety	47	21	33

antecedents of schoolyard use than safety, although they did not fully account for the sex and ethnic differences observed.

Black children were no more likely than others to play only in public spaces nor less likely to play in private spaces. They were more likely, however, to report playing in both kinds of spaces. The major difference between black and white children's patterns had to do with the proportion of each group that played in the houses and yards of their friends. While black children played as often as white children in their own homes and yards, they were much less likely to play in those of their friends. Black children playing together more often played outside and in public spaces.

This may have been related to the nature of domestic space. In the first place, purely physical considerations played an important role. About one-quarter of the black children sampled lived in apartment buildings (as opposed to single- or two-family homes) compared with less than 10 percent of white children, 2 percent of Asian children, and 20 percent of children of other minorities. Living in a multiple-unit dwelling was associated very clearly with greater use of public space.

Privacy or lack of privacy in the home also may have affected children's propensity to play in their own houses or yards or their friends' houses or yards (tables 4-9 and 4-10). Less privacy (not having a room of one's own or living in a multiple-unit dwelling) discouraged play in such settings among all income groups and all ethnic groups except whites. Even white children, if they lived in multiple-unit dwellings, were less likely to report playing in friends' homes.

It would be a mistake to overemphasize the extent to which children use public space to compensate for a lack of private space. We have already noted that girls are less likely to play in public spaces. Similarly, there are important intervening factors other than the size and nature of the dwelling unit that affect how children relate to the physical environment outside the home, in the neighborhood, and in the city beyond.

There was, for instance, a clear distinction between places children commonly went with their parents or other adults, such as restaurants and churches, and places they were likely to

TABLE 4-9. Children with Rooms of Their Own (percentages)

Ethnicity and income		Weighted (N)
Black		
High income	48	(65)
Medium income	31	(135)
Low income	25	(286)
White		
High income	64	(53)
Medium income	69	(45)
Low income	34	(29)
Asian (all)	36	(49)
Other	32	(51)
All children	35	(713)

TABLE 4-10. Play Location and Dwelling Unit

Children who play in friend's house or yard (percentages)				
	Black	White	Asian	Other
Child lives in				
Single-family or 2-family dwelling	60	68	69	47
Multiple-unit dwelling	42	48	35	41
Children who play in their own houses or yards (percentages)				
Child lives in				
Single-family or 2-family dwelling	67	65	73	59
Multiple-unit dwelling	54	66	51	43

visit on excursions alone or with friends, such as movies, parks, and libraries (table 4-11; see also chapter five). The latter were more likely to be visited by boys than by girls, by black children than by white.

Among children in our sample, boys were more mobile than girls, blacks more than children of other ethnic groups. This is even more evident when we look at children's activities while on

TABLE 4-11. Children on Their Own Visiting Nearby Places (percentages)

Place[a]	Boys	Girls	Black	White	Asian	Other	Percent of all children who go on their own	Children who go on their own as percent of all children who go
Movies	4	3	5	2	10	2	4	51
Park	6	4	5	3	3	4	53	64
Restaurant	2		1	1	7	1	1	2
Church	1	1	1	1	14	2	15	2
Library	3	3	3	3	4	2	35	6

[a]In descending order of percentage of children visiting each place, whether on their own or not.

Summary Index: Visits to Nearby Places on Their Own (percentages)

Number of places[a] child has visited on own in the sixth grade	Boys	Girls	Black	White	Asian	Other	All children
No places	17	24	14	34	41	29	32
One or two places	56	57	58	56	48	55	56
Three or more places	27	19	28	10	12	16	23

[a]Movies, park, restaurant, church, and library.

their own outside the neighborhood (table 4-12). We asked the children about visits to a large number of cultural and recreational facilities in the Bay Area. Children who went to these places generally went either with parents or on school field trips. Only a small proportion of visits were made by children on their own.

The data on children's mobility in the urban environment reflect patterns documented in the literature in recent years. Many studies of children and the city have focused on the lack of opportunities for ghetto children to move freely about the neighborhood and larger community. Their "mental maps," or perceptions of familiar territory, have been found to be more

TABLE 4-12. Cultural and Recreational Sites Outside the Neighborhood Visited by
Children on Their Own[a] (vertical percentages)

Number of places	Boys	Girls	Black	White	Asian	Other	All children
No places	39	50	37	56	62	71	45
One or two places	44	38	47	34	36	23	41
Three or more places	17	12	16	10	3	6	15

[a]List of 15 places, including urban and rural parks, lakes and beaches, zoos,
skating rinks, sports arenas, and museums.

restricted than those of other children.[30] Barry Wellman's
empirical study of "spatial cosmopolitanism" among urban
adolescents, however, shows that inner-city minority youth
exhibited greater cosmopolitanism both in attitudinal and
behavioral terms than did suburban children.[31] Wellman's findings are consistent with our own to the extent that children
living in inner-city neighborhoods were more likely to travel on
their own around the city than their counterparts in high-status
neighborhoods on the outskirts of Oakland. In a paper written
in conjunction with this study, Berg and Medrich report, for
example, that the physical features of hilly, less urban neighborhoods that delighted adults were far less ideal for children
because of the limited opportunities they offered for play and
the way they constrained children's access to other parts of
the city.[32]

Of course, many more of the higher-status children, who
tended to live in the outlying neighborhoods, came from
households with cars, so their reduced independent mobility
was somewhat offset by more frequent rides from parents. Use
of public transportation by children was negatively related to
income and was more common among blacks. Furthermore,
although most children, especially those from higher-income
families, had bicycles, it was only public transportation that was
associated with real mobility: the bicycle is not a viable means
of exploring the city beyond the confines of the neighborhood.

One additional point is worth noting. Those children who
tended to use public transportation when they were on their

TABLE 4-13. Children's Transportation and Mobility on Their Own (percentages)

	Have bicycle	Rides bus alone at least once a week
Sex		
Boys	73	40
Girls	68	29
All children	70	34
Ethnicity		
Black	67	42
White	84	19
Asian	71	11
Other	63	8
Black children		
High income	80	34
Medium income	72	36
Low income	61	47
White children		
High income	95	14
Medium income	81	12
Low income	63	44
Inside neighborhood		
Children who go no places	77	19
Children who go 1-2 places	68	34
Children who go 3 or more places	68	45
Outside neighborhood		
Children who go no places	70	23
Children who go 1-2 places	72	38
Children who go 3 or more places	64	56

own did not, however, use the Bay Area's rail rapid transit system, BART. Not a single child reported using the BART system while going places alone or with friends.

Highly mobile children tended to have more friends than less mobile children did, so it was not surprising to find that these more gregarious children also did more group activities, such as team sports. Mobility was particularly associated with higher rates of team sport participation among girls. Girls who ranged about their neighborhoods more freely were involved in sports activities on their own as often as less mobile boys (table 4-14). The factor of range, however, did not really affect the already high levels of sports involvement reported by black children.

TABLE 4-14. Children Who Play Team Sports When on Their Own (percentages)

	Boys	Girls	Black	White	Asian	Other	All children
Location of play							
Both public and private spaces	73	49	65	47	25	50	61
Public spaces only	76	80	84	52	71	62	78
Private spaces only	71	44	62	43	50	52	53
Number of places child has visited on own in the sixth grade[a]							
No places	67	46	71	37	34	48	55
One or two places	73	49	65	49	48	59	60
Three or more places	78	63	75	61	38	49	72

[a]Combined list of places inside and outside neighborhood. See tables 4-11 and 4-12.

Play location had a similar impact on team sports participation. Children, especially girls, who reported playing only in public spaces were more likely than others to undertake team sports. This is hardly surprising since these games usually require the playing fields or courts provided in public recreational areas.

HOW CHILDREN VIEW THEIR TIME

Most of our interview was devoted to activities, but to some extent we did explore subjective issues such as children's experience of time. We asked children how much time they felt they had to do things they liked to do; how often they felt bored; how constrained they felt by obligations to do things they would otherwise not want to do; whom they would like to spend more time with; and whether or not, on balance, they would rather have things be different from the way they currently were. We also constructed a rough index of self-esteem (table 4-15).

Few children said that they had too little time to themselves, though girls were somewhat more likely than boys to complain

TABLE 4-15. Children's Feelings and Perceptions of Their Time (percentages)

Children who	Boys	Girls	Black	White	Asian	Other	All children
have "not very much" or "hardly any" time to do the things they want to do	9	15	12	20	12	9	13
have to do lots of things they do not like to do	45	45	51	33	26	35	45
often feel bored and do not know what to do after school and on weekends	36	46	41	41	34	49	41
would like to spend more time doing things with their parents	80	82	82	75	74	86	81
wish they had more close friends	61	71	68	67	67	79	67
would be different from themselves if they could	43	47	50	38	30	33	45
score low on self-esteem index.[a]	29	29	32	22	19	30	29

[a]For a description of this index see table 4-17 footnote.

of a shortage. If this was the result of, say, greater domestic responsibilities, it was apparently something girls accepted since they were no more likely than boys to say that they had to do many things that they would rather not do.

That children said they had plenty of free time does not necessarily mean that they had many ways to fill it. In fact, many felt that they had little to do that was worthwhile or interesting, and a high percentage of children reported that they were often bored, at a loss for things to do, and that they wanted more friends. Perhaps, as Bronfenbrenner suggests, this dissatisfaction stems from the lack of adult contact and involvement in their lives, for almost all children said that they would like to spend more time with their parents.

The reports of boredom, however, support a different, less parent-centered interpretation. It was children who felt that they had less time to do things they wanted to do who were more likely to report boredom; similarly, it was those who wanted more contact with friends, not those who would have liked to have had more contact with parents, who reported high levels of boredom. Furthermore, variations in perceptions followed sex and ethnic lines: black children more often than whites said they had to do many things they did not wish to do; girls more often than boys said they were bored and wanted more friends.

Children's feelings about time were related to the things they actually did. Consider team sports and reading once again. Children who played team sports said they were bored less often than children who did not (table 4-16). Girls who played team sports, however, were still more likely than boys who played team sports to complain of boredom.

Reading presented a different pattern, one that was related to children's feelings of constraint and self-esteem (table 4-17). This was clearest when viewed by ethnic group. Black children, as noted earlier, were more likely to say that they felt their time use was constrained and to report low self-esteem. Black children who read regularly, however, were no more likely than their white counterparts to have low self-esteem.

TABLE 4-16. Boredom and Participation in Team Sports (percentage of children saying they are often bored after school and on weekends)

	Boys	Girls	All children
Child plays team sports alone[a] or with friends	33	42	37
Child does not play team sports alone or with friends	45	50	48
Total	36	46	41

[a]This may seem paradoxical, but children did mention team sports activities as things they did while alone—and no one who has seen a solitary child shooting a basketball for hours on end should doubt them.

TABLE 4-17. Reading on Own and Selected Perception Items

Number of days per week child reads for fun	Reading and self-esteem[a] (percentages of children who score low on self-esteem)				
	Black	White	Asian	Other	Total
Read 5-7 days per week	13	13	*	*	14
Read 3-4 days per week	36	29	*	*	33
Read 1-2 days per week	34	19	*	*	30
Less than once or never per week	42	27	*	*	41
Total	32	22	19	26	29
Weighted (N)	(169)	(29)	(10)	(15)	(202)

Number of days per week child reads for fun	Reading and time constraints (percentages of children who have to do things they do not like to do)				
	Black	White	Asian	Other	Total
Read 5-7 days per week	43	24	*	*	36
Read 3-4 days per week	45	27	*	*	39
Read 1-2 days per week	54	44	*	*	48
Less than once or never per week	58	42	*	*	57
Total	51	33	26	35	45
Weighted (N)	(271)	(44)	(13)	(18)	(345)

* = small ns

[a]The self-esteem measure consisted of a series of items from the interview schedule point scaled low to high. See Appendix A, child's interview, question 44 (items 4 and 5) and question 30 (items 9, 10, 14).

And regularity of reading for fun was associated with reduced perceptions of constraint, though less dramatically. This may indicate that success at conventional, adult-approved activities, such as reading, has significant psychological consequences for children's feelings about themselves and their time-use.[33]

These examples, while by no means conclusive, suggest that for children opportunities to do particular activities, to be with friends, and to be relatively free of obligations have a significant impact not only on their behavior but on the way they experience and feel about their time as well.

LINKS TO OTHER DOMAINS

We began this chapter by contrasting several images of childhood: childhood as a time of independence, freedom, and exploration; childhood as a period devoted to preparing (in rather controlled environments) for adult life; and childhood as a stage of development in which the most basic features of adult social interaction emerge. We confront the contrasting perspectives whenever we observe and describe children's behavior during their freest hours and when we assess adult attempts to direct children's interests and actions: the things children choose to do when on their own are not necessarily comparable with the choices they make when under adult supervision. Still, even on their own, children's activity patterns are not entirely free from the influence of the adult world.

That girls participate less than boys in organized sports has been viewed widely as an example of sex differences in socialization.[34] Specific programs, even legal action, have been aimed at increasing access to athletic opportunities for girls of all ages. With our data we can see if girls involved in adult-organized, structured sports activities also tend to do more of these things on their own.

Similarly, many feel that parental participation in children's educational development affects children's attitudes toward school, their out-of-school behavior, and in turn, their prospects for scholastic success.[35] As a result, a variety of programs has been designed by educators to encourage and enable parents to become more directly involved with children in activities at home which may enhance school achievement. With our data we can observe whether (and in what ways) engaging in such activities with parents is associated with the pursuit of similarly "proeducational" activities when children are on their own.

What then is the relationship between playing sports in an organized context and in the more informal setting when children play on their own? The data in table 4-18 may indicate a transferral of organized to informal behavior, or it may merely identify children already involved in sports on their own who also took advantage of organized opportunities. The majority of girls who played two or more organized team sports did not also play sports when they were on their own. The pattern among these girls may reflect the absence of opportunities in unorganized settings (a notion supported by evidence reported earlier in this chapter). Among boys and among children of all ethnic groups generally, participation in organized sports was quite clearly associated with greater involvement in informal team sports activities.

Girls' participation in unorganized team sports did not approach boys' rates of participation. This was true even for those girls who did take advantage of organized opportunities. This is not to say that organized programs did not ameliorate sex differences in sports participation somewhat. Rather, all children's behavior was affected by the level of organized services available to them (see chapter seven). At present it may be more meaningful to consider absolute changes in girls' participation rates, not changes relative to boys. Change may be manifest initially in organized settings and only later on in informal

TABLE 4-18. Contrast of Organized and Unorganized Team Sports Participation (percentages of children who play unorganized team sports)

Number of *organized* team sports child participates in	Boys	Girls	Black	White	Asian	Other	All children
0	66	49	63	40	33	54	55
1	77	60	73	56	50	50	71
2 or more	84	48	78	72	50	50	79

settings (where opportunities for girls still seem more constrained).

With reading there was a different pattern. We had expected that parental involvement in children's educational development outside school might encourage reading for fun. (We dealt with the general issue of parental involvement in out-of-school life and scholastic achievement in another monograph.)[36] Indeed, among all ethnic groups, except Asians, parents' helping children with schoolwork was directly associated with informal reading (table 4-19). There were some important ethnic differences however. For instance, although more black children than white said that they rarely read for fun, among black children whose parents helped them with their schoolwork the proportion who said they rarely read for fun was significantly reduced (to a level about equal to that of other groups). If we look at the proportion of children who did read regularly for fun, by contrast, parental encouragement, while still a factor, did not reduce the ethnic disparity. This suggests that parental influ-

TABLE 4-19. Reading for Fun and Parent Involvement in Schoolwork

(percentages of children who seldom or ever read for fun)				
	Black	White	Asian	Other	All children
Parent helps child with schoolwork	13	13	4	18	13
Parent does not help child with schoolwork	26	17	4	8	20
Total	21	15	4	10	17

(percentages of children who read regularly for fun)				
	Black	White	Asian	Other	All children
Parent helps child with schoolwork	24	35	15	23	26
Parent does not help child with schoolwork	15	29	37	10	19
Total	19	33	30	13	22

ences may have had a minimal threshold effect, but they did not by themselves intensely motivate children when they were on their own.

The intrusion of parents and the adult world on children's activities when on their own is complex, as we have seen from this brief analysis of team sports and reading. Yet it is important to keep these kinds of connections in mind. As we turn to the domains of time use that bring children into contact with parents and other adults, we must be cognizant of the fact that although many of these interactions are expected to affect children's behavior when on their own, things do not always happen in the way or to the degree intended. On balance we must be careful not to assume that children's time use on their own is either free of or thoroughly tied to larger socialization phenomena and familial child-rearing objectives.

CONCLUSION

In this chapter we have surveyed children's time on their own from a variety of perspectives. We described generally the activities that comprise the domain and the social and physical milieus in which they take place. We also examined children's attitudes toward their time and finally the extent to which participation in particular activities is related to adult encouragement and involvement.

We found that different variables account for or underlie activity patterns in the domain. Thus we attributed girls' lower participation in team sports, and active group pursuits generally, to several things: lesser access to friends and restrictions on spatial mobility in some cases, minimal opportunities and little exposure in others. Yet even girls who had more friends and were more mobile did not match the participation rates of boys in active pursuits like team sports. Perhaps most surprising, girls who did these activities (and, therefore, had time-use patterns more like boys') were still more likely than boys to complain of boredom and feeling at a loss for things to do while on their own. Similar findings characterized differences in children's time use for many of the activities in this domain.

Throughout the chapter we have described time use among particular groups of children. With respect to sex and ethnicity, we found fundamental differences in activity patterns, and apparently in interests, skills, and opportunity structures. But the differences were of degree rather than of kind, and in many respects (as we suggested in chapter two) of lesser degree in this domain than in those to be examined in subsequent chapters.

This is in some ways encouraging, for it means that children's time use while on their own is not thoroughly conditioned by class and family status. The picture we have presented suggests that children are impressionable and flexible, and that they desire and respond to a broad range of time-use opportunities and varied peer and community activity contexts when they are on their own.

five

CHILDREN AND PARENTS: TIME TOGETHER

Parents today are beset with time problems. Commuting adults, mothers of very young children, and mothers who work outside the home often have too little time. Mothers who cannot find employment or do not want to work and those whose children are grown may have too much. Fathers and mothers alike have to find time for their children, their jobs, their spouses, and their other interests. Some are caught in a no-win situation. Many take second jobs in order to provide luxuries—or even necessities; others may commute long distances in order to reside in what they consider good child-rearing environments and, in either instance, wind up feeling guilty about being away from the family so much of the time.

In his classic volume, published in 1956, one of William Whyte's organization men captured the double bind when he said, "I sort of look forward to the day my kids are grown up, then I won't have to have such a guilty conscience about neglecting them."[1] His children are now adults themselves, the contemporaries of parents in our sample. When compared, the families of the organization men of the 1950s and the families in our sample are hardly similar—and our sample is a fair reflection of emerging trends today. For one thing, in many of our sample families both parents were employed. For another thing, the structure of the nuclear units was very diverse: there were a large number of single parents raising children alone. Given these realities, which we suppose are affecting child-rearing practices and the nature of time children and parents spend together, we can infer that in the last two decades the number of "time-pressed families" has increased.

Over and above the changes in family structure and labor force demographics restricting time together, there may also be changes in the quality and substance of child-parent interactions. Bronfenbrenner finds a link between the two issues: "Children used to be brought up by their parents. . . . While the family still has the primary moral and legal responsibility for the character development of children, it often lacks the power or opportunity to do the job, primarily because parents and children no longer spend enough time together in those situations in which training is possible."[2] What was once thought to be a trend toward greater permissiveness in child-rearing norms, Bronfenbrenner argues, may reflect essentially decreasing contact between parents and children.

With these established and putative trends in mind, we turn to the time parents and children do spend together. We look at some particular activities they pursue and examine how much time parents have for their children and the "types" of time that characterize their interactions.

There are numerous points from which to view the ecology of family time. A linguist studying a two-year-old's verbal interactions with his or her mother sets the spotlight in a different place than the social psychologist looking at the small-group behavior of the family unit. The time frame may be the same, the group may be the same, but the problem and relevant dyadic-triadic relationships may differ. When the family is together, the parent is usually playing many roles simultaneously, and very often the children are involved not only with the parents but with each other as well. Much child-oriented time is the secondary activity of parents but the primary activity of children. For the parent, time together may be work, for the child, leisure.

Little is known about the things eleven- and twelve-year-olds typically do with their parents or about normal variation in family activities. With data from our survey we are able to describe the everyday activities of children and their parents together. We expect to see social-class and ethnic variations reflecting different constraints on time use and different child-rearing norms. As Walter Miller has argued with reference to the import of subcultural variation, "The pivotal meaning of social classes to the student of behavior is that they limit and pattern the learning environment; they structure the social maze in which the child learns his habits and meanings."[3] By extension, this suggests that not only the learning environment but most aspects of family life as well are fundamentally different for children growing up in different circumstances.

THE CHANGING CONTEXT OF FAMILY TIME

In earlier times families spent most of each day together. This has changed as the family has changed. In the Puritan household, for example, parents were charged with all aspects of the child's development from education—secular and religious—to preparation for a trade. These children, regarded largely as miniature adults, were also included in most common social intercourse along with their parents.[4] In this sense, most time was family time. The day was not segmented as it is now; family members spent most of their waking hours including leisure time in close proximity. The family was physically close because, in one way or another, everyone was involved in related productive activities and maintenance of the household. This is captured in Michael Young and Peter Willmot's description of nineteenth-century farm life.

The children learnt by doing what their parents showed them. At six or seven the son of a farming family was taken under the charge of his father, running errands, fetching tools, taking his father's meals out to the fields, and, as he grew older, he was taught the more difficult jobs of tending the animals, shearing the sheep, ploughing the fields, and getting in the harvest. Likewise, the mother prepared her daughter for the bearing of children, the cooking, the care of animals, the handicrafts and the work in the dairy.[5]

Changes in the economy and in primary and secondary schooling and the development of a variety of specialized child-serving institutions fundamentally altered the nature of family life. These changes have been accompanied by greater segregation of age cohorts and the separation of extended kin from the conjugal family. As many aspects of children's socialization and education have been transferred outside the family, the time spent together has decreased substantially and the functions that families perform have changed. Many parental responsibilities are now residual, consisting primarily of those aspects of child training and caretaking left undone by others. One consequence of these changes is the dramatic decrease in time spent on the physical care of children and the correlative increase in nonprimary activities and interactions. There is today considerable variation among families of different backgrounds in the substance of and the values underlying child-parent nonprimary time use.

Concentrating on historical changes in the roles and functions of families may mask other factors influencing family time-use choices. Thus in the same decades that Rose Kennedy raised her nine children in a setting she describes with some restraint as "more fortunate than most—having the domestic help and money that I required,"[6] conditions in the Boston slums were not unlike those documented earlier by Jacob Riis.

In three [flats] there were two [families] to each. In the other twelve each room had its own family living and sleeping there. They cooked, I suppose, at the one stove in the kitchen, which was the largest room. In one big bed we counted six persons, the parents and four children. Two of them lay crosswise at the foot of the bed, or there would not have been room. A curtain was hung before the bed in each of the two smaller rooms, leaving a passageway from the hall to the main room.[7]

Obviously family time cannot have a single meaning when some parents must struggle for a few minutes of solitude, while others "borrow" children back from the governess. Then as now child-parent time together is not just the product of physical proximity, for it reflects class-related and resource-related norms and values surrounding child-rearing practices and priorities. In this chapter we look broadly at the relationship between family circumstances (particularly poverty and maternal employment) and patterns of family time use.

POVERTY, LOWER-STATUS FAMILIES, AND TIME USE

Although a great deal has been written in the last fifteen years about poor and lower-status families (especially about poor minority families), little data has been generated to answer the question posed by Daniel Moynihan a decade ago: "In what ways are the poor different from others: and how did they come to be that way?"[8]

Surprisingly few empirical descriptions of day-to-day family life have been forthcoming in the years since the inception of the antipoverty programs of the Great Society. This is the case even though many social programs were intentionally designed to compensate for perceived deficiencies in the family lives of the poor. The critique of lower-status families and poor, minority families frequently has included descriptions of home life embedded in a "culture of poverty." Oscar Lewis describes it thus:

On the family level the major traits of the culture of poverty are the absence of childhood as a specially prolonged and protected stage in the life cycle. . . . Other traits include high incidence of maternal deprivation; lack of impulse control; strong present time orientation; with relatively little ability to defer gratification and to plan for the future.[9]

To the extent that these characteristics are exhibited, they would seem to affect directly the kinds of time children and parents spend together. It should be noted, however, that other studies of lower-class subcultures and family life emphasize certain strengths associated with adaptation and coping, qualities that may not be dysfunctional at all: the family " as the repository of a set of survival techniques for functioning in the world of the disinherited."[10]

Images of time use in poor families are implicit in many social programs. The schools project a prototypical view. Children from poor families are assumed to be "culturally disadvantaged," lacking, among other things, the kinds of parental interest, interaction, and guidance deemed essential to scholastic success. To correct such presumed deficiencies, programs such as Title I Compensatory Education of the Elementary and Secondary Education Act (ESEA) have taken on a variety of supplemental enrichment functions, functions that other families are thought to perform as a matter of course. The view of the family implied by the constellation of services aimed at bolstering academic achievement among disadvantaged children suggests that poor school performance in part reflects inappropriate norms and values concerning time and undesirable time-use choices.

We cannot measure the outcomes of family time in terms of children's educational success, ultimate life chances, or well-being. However, we can explore differences among families by looking at time use in relation to two different theories of the organization of family life. One theory argues that poor and lower-status families differ from others only in that, in the aggregate, they display certain characteristics disproportionately. The second theory argues that those of low status are the only group with these characteristics. To substantiate the former, we would expect to find many similarities in family time use among social groups, with some noticeable differences. To verify the latter, we would expect to find dramatic differences between lower-status families and all other families in the use of time. This exploration enables us to see if we can identify distinct family time-use patterns, practices, and values among social groups, differences that support one or another "deficit" model.

MATERNAL EMPLOYMENT AND FAMILY TIME USE

Probably no aspect of family life would be expected to have a more direct impact on the amount of time parents and children spend together than the labor force status of the mother. This does not speak, of course, to the nature of the interactions that take place, although the issues of quantity and quality of time together represent concerns not entirely distinct.

In recent years a good deal of attention has been devoted to the return of middle-class mothers to the labor force.[11] In the past mothers, especially mothers with young children, worked mostly out of economic necessity. While this has long been a fact of life among lower-income families, it has now become characteristic across the economic spectrum. The effect of this trend on child rearing remains relatively unexplored although there is a good deal of uneasy conjecture about its implications. In some circles it is viewed as evidence of the breakdown of family life or, at least, as potentially damaging developmentally and emotionally for children. But there is not a lot of evidence on this matter and what little exists is hardly definitive.[12] We can address some of the relevant issues with our survey data, exploring whether there are substantial differences in time use between families in which mothers work and families in which they do not. Independent of social-class variation, do children whose mothers work have different sorts of out-of-school experiences?[13]

Our survey sample is helpful in that the majority of mothers worked part or full time, and within each economic and ethnic group significant numbers of working and nonworking mothers were represented. Hence the possibility of some useful comparisons. While we cannot analyze the psychological and emotional consequences of maternal employment on children (although these are important concerns), we can examine nonprimary interactions,[14] an increasingly important aspect of family time for preadolescents. On these we have good data, and just as we can compare child-parent time use in families that are poor and in families that are not, so too we can compare child-parent time use in families in which mothers are employed and those in which they are not.

Previous research on family time has concentrated primarily on measuring either the total amount of time parents spend with children or measuring the time spent on specific activities.[15] Here we look at family time-use patterns more generally and from several perspectives. Since we are particularly interested in time-use variations associated with various aspects of life circumstances—income, education, ethnicity, family structure, and parents' labor force status—we shall proceed to a high level of data disaggregation.

PARENT AVAILABILITY

Estimating Parents' Time with Children

Empirical estimates of the time parents spend with their children vary considerably.[16] To an extent this variance is a function of the ways researchers define activities. "Primary" (direct) care is distinguished from "secondary" interactions;

physical care is usually distinguished from nonphysical care; and time in the presence of children, "contact time" as measured in some studies, includes all time whether or not a child-oriented activity is taking place.

Estimates of all of these types of time vary both cross-nationally and by important stratifying variables. Fathers in Eastern Europe spend considerably more time with children than do fathers in Western countries. Men from higher social classes in many countries spend more time with children than lower-class men do. Employed mothers, East and West, spend less time with their children than housewives do. And women from Eastern European countries use weekends to "make up" time with their children, while Western wives focus more attention on their spouses. John Robinson, author of *How Americans Use Time*, estimates that parents here spend about nineteen hours a week in contact with their children, a little more than half of that on primary and secondary care activities, the rest on activities with children simply present. Two-thirds of primary care is custodial—feeding, clothing, chauffeuring, and so forth—rather than interactional.[17] This suggests that a good deal of nonphysical care does not receive the full attention of parents but is an adjunct to other activities, something that may account for the fact that the great majority of children in our survey seemed to want more parent time.[18]

Perhaps the most careful and comprehensive estimates of parental time with children come from a study by Kathryn Walker and Margaret Woods. They estimate that nonphysical care of family members account for about half of all family activities. Here again definitions specific to their study make comparisons difficult:

Nonphysical care of family members included all activities related to their social and educational development. Activities classified as nonphysical included helping children with lessons, reading to children or other family members, chauffeuring children or adults for any purpose except physical care, and taking care of the family's pets.[19]

As they note, however,

It was recognized that the area of nonphysical care would be subject to varying interpretations; for example, playing with a baby or young child was likely to be looked upon by many as nonwork. In developing the category, it was decided that only the mother could classify the activity accurately and that there would be some variations in the classification. When the mother thought the particular activity engaged in was intended for the education or socialization of a child, it was classified as nonphysical care; when it was considered a purely pleasurable activity engaged in as a family social activity, it was classified under the general heading used for activities other than work.[20]

According to Walker and Woods, under one hour per day was spent on nonphysical care in two-parent households in which the youngest child was between six and eleven.[21] Estimates for working mothers (0.5 hours per day) were slightly lower than for nonworking mothers (0.7 hours per day). Fathers spent considerably less time on these activities, averaging about 0.3 hours per day. Activities shared by the whole family, such as visiting or going out together, were not included in these calculations.

While the provision of nonphysical care varies by age of the youngest child and employment status of the mother, according to Walker and Woods almost 90 percent of the parents of children aged six to eleven had given this kind of care to their children during each day studied. Among older children (those who are beyond elementary school) both the time devoted to nonphysical care as well as the frequency of activities together with parents declined.

Data of this kind neglect the fact that nonphysical care is considerably more intractable to measurement and more indeterminate in meaning to the child than physical care. The mood of the parent, the receptiveness of the child, the nature of competing demands for the parents' time all determine the quality of interaction. Parents can be helping with schoolwork, playing a game, or talking to a child and yet not really be available intellectually or emotionally. Several important facts, however, emerge from data of this type: (1) nonphysical care of children is most often secondary to something else the parent is doing; (2) the time parents spend with children can be contracted or expanded to accommodate demands on the parent such as those related to work; and (3) the older the child, the less time parents feel they need to devote either to physical or nonphysical care.

In order to estimate the variation in time parents could have available to children, as well as to look at the characteristics of those who are "time poor," in our survey we analyzed data on the amount of time parents spent away from children.[22] Work time emerged as the most significant constraint on family time. For example, a single parent working full time (at a paid job outside the home) was likely to be more time poor than a single nonworking parent; two parents working full time were likely to be more time poor than a two-parent family in which one or both adults worked less than full time.*

Work Patterns and Parent Availability at
Key Periods of the Day

The majority of mothers and fathers in our sample worked. The patterns of work varied by family type, family income, parents' education, and ethnicity. The traditional family configuration—father working and mother at home—was characteristic of fewer than a quarter of all sampled families. In slightly less than half of the families at least one parent was out of the labor force (table 5-1). In 24 percent of black families the nonworking parent was a single mother with a low income, while in white families the nonworking parent was most likely a mother in a middle- or upper-income, two-parent family. Having a mother at home occurs most frequently among economically advantaged whites and disadvantaged blacks. Hence, time poverty as defined by parents' labor force status was most likely to be a problem among lower- and middle-income families with two working parents and lower-income families with a working single parent.

---

*While analyzing our survey data, we attempted to develop a measure of time poverty that included: number and ages of children; labor force status of adults in the household; and estimates (taken from other studies) of the amount of time adults spent on housework, leisure, and personal maintenance. We found, however, that as a way of estimating time available to children, these complex indexes did not prove to be much better than the rough proxy of parents' labor force status.

TABLE 5-1. Parents' Labor Force Status (vertical percentages)

Family structure and parents' labor force status	Black	White	All families
One parent			
Working	27	15	23
Not working	24	6	18
Two parents			
Both working	28	36	30
One working	17	38	23
Neither working	4	3	4
Single father	1	2	1
Weighted (N)	(497)	(132)	(726)

TABLE 5-2. Family Earnings Structure (vertical percentages)

Earning structure	Black	White	All families
One earner			
Mother works full time	21	12	18
Mother works part time	6	4	6
Father works full time	13	34	19
Father works part time	1	2	1
Two earners			
One works full time, one works part time	7	20	10
Both work full time	20	15	19
No earners	30	9	24
All other patterns	3	3	3
Weighted (N)	(515)	(133)	(745)

In 19 percent of all families, both parents worked full time (table 5-2). In most of the families in which the mother was the only earner, she worked full time, and there were more of these families (24 percent of the sample) than there were families in which the father was the only earner (20 percent). The work pattern often thought to be the best compromise between child-rearing demands and economic needs—one part-time and one full-time earner—was relatively uncommon (10 percent). In 24 percent of the families, there were no earners at all.

TABLE 5-3. Work Schedules (vertical percentages)

Schedule	Black		White		All families	
	Mothers	Fathers	Mothers	Fathers	Mothers	Fathers
Normal work week (Monday through Friday)	61	58	49	62	58	60
Weekdays only, but less than 5 days	3	2	11	1	5	2
One weekend day and weekdays	14	16	18	18	16	18
Weekends and some weekdays	15	18	17	18	15	18
Weekends only	2	6	1	–	1	–
Not available	4	1	4	1	5	3
Weighted (N)	(280)	(211)	(74)	(95)	(415)	(375)

TABLE 5-4. Work Shifts (vertical percentages)

Shift	Black		White		All families	
	Mothers	Fathers	Mothers	Fathers	Mothers	Fathers
Generally days	71	48	56	66	67	56
Generally days (returns late)	2	2	2	3	2	3
Generally days (leaves early)	–	6	1	1	–	6
Swing shift (generally 4 P.M. to midnight)	8	9	4	3	7	7
Graveyard shift (generally midnight to 8 A.M.)	3	4	4	1	2	2
Irregular, full time	5	14	8	16	6	14
Irregular, part time	5	2	20	5	9	2
Works, but no other information	7	16	5	4	6	10
Weighted (N)	(289)	(211)	(74)	(95)	(415)	(375)

Most employed parents had a "normal" workday (daytime hours) and a normal workweek (five weekdays) (tables 5-3 and 5-4). In a fair proportion of cases, mothers (about 20 percent) and fathers (about 25 percent) worked six or even seven days a week. Work patterns of white mothers suggest more control over work hours than all fathers or black mothers had (table 5-4). Nearly a fifth of the employed white mothers worked part time and at irregular hours, an arrangement that could be organized to respond to children's needs if the employee had a say in setting her schedule.

We can pose the question of parent time another way: not in terms of amounts of time, but in terms of availability at particular times of day. Key periods of a child's day include breakfast, the after-school hours, dinner, and bedtime. Generally at least one parent was home at these times. Rarely was the mother out of the house for the morning meal, the evening meal, and at the child's bedtime. Work schedules seldom forced mothers to be absent regularly during breakfast or dinner hours (15 percent of cases). A large proportion of the fathers returned from work after 7:30 P.M., suggesting either a late dinner for families or a pattern of parents and children eating separately.

After-school hours present a serious management problem for working parents. This is a time when children are often tired, hungry, and in need of adult support and supervision. In 27 percent of the families studied, there was no adult home after school. This varied by family type and labor force status of the mother (tables 5-5 and 5-6). In only about 10 percent of two-parent families with one working adult were children at home alone after school compared with almost half of the children with single, working parents. Most families in which the mother worked part time appeared to have enough flexibility to arrange for an adult to be present after school. So although work patterns may have placed great stress on families and created difficult time demands, most families appeared to be organized in such a way that at least one adult, most often the mother, was available during key times of the child's day.

Norms and Rules Regarding Family Time

The norms and rules governing key periods in the child's day present a different window on the amount of time parents and

TABLE 5-5. Families with No Adult Home after School[a] (percentages)

Ethnicity	Family structure	
	One parent	Two parents
Black	30	26
White	43	20
Asian	*	26
Other	17	13
All families	30	23

[a]This table shows the proportion of families with no adult at home after school. By way of comparison, 39 percent of single parents were not home after school, and in 31 percent of two-parent families no parent was at home.

* = small n

TABLE 5-6. Families in Which Neither Father nor Mother Was Home after School (percentages)

Mother's labor force status	Black	White	All families	Weighted (N)
Works full time	65	70	66	(290)
Works part time	18	13	20	(120)
Not in labor force (single parent)	16	29	16	(133)
Not in labor force (two parents)	11	7	9	(183)

children spend together. Families can lengthen or shorten the time they spend together, for instance, by the setting of bedtimes. Children can be told to be in the house early or late in the evening, for dinner with the family or not. We found considerable variation in these norms and rules.

Dinner time for many families is an important time in the day, when parents and children can be together to sort out the day's events and plan for tomorrow. We examined rules and time schedules before dinner among our sample families. In 61 percent of families children were called in for dinner rather than having to be in at a specific time. This suggests both that children were near home most of the time and that most families did not establish rigid schedules. Fifteen percent of the children were allowed to come in when they wanted. This is related in part to the fact that not all families sat down to eat together and in part to differences in families' attitudes toward time. In the lowest-status black families between a fifth and a quarter of the children perceived the norm as permissive ("I come in when I want") compared with fewer than 10 percent of children from the highest-status black families. This pattern differed from that of white families. Very few children in white families, regardless of status, were allowed to come in when they wanted. Children from lower-status white families were more likely to have a definite time when they had to be in. Nearly half the white children with definite schedules had to be in before 6:00 P.M. compared with about 10 percent of the black children.

There was also significant variation in dining patterns. Fifty-seven percent of families (81 percent white, 47 percent black) ate together. Twenty percent (4 percent white, 28 percent black) ate separately (table 5-8). It was especially uncommon among white families, but not among black families, for each person to eat separately. Although there is little social-class variation in dining patterns among white families, black families show marked differences. In black families with a highly-educated mother the proportions eating together differed little from comparable whites (table 5-9). But in black families with less highly educated mothers, it was as common for each family member to eat separately as for all to eat together. These aspects of the structure of family life were not unrelated. In families that ate together, only 10 percent of the children could come in when they wanted; where they ate separately, 35 percent.

It might be expected that norms and dinner time schedules vary according to the time constraints on parents, especially mothers. But this did not prove so (ethnic differences remained more significant). Whether a mother was employed full time, part time, or not at all had little effect on when her children came in for dinner (table 5-7) and whether her family ate together (table 5-10). Fathers' work patterns also had little effect, except to make it slightly more likely that some family members ate separately.

Regular bedtimes were the general rule for 60 percent of all children although specific bedtimes varied (table 5-11). Children

TABLE 5-7. Time Children Come in before Dinner (horizontal percentages by group)

Mothers' labor force status	Black			White			All families		
	At a definite time	When called	At will	At a definite time	When called	At will	At a definite time	When called	At will
Works full time	21	60	18	42	50	6	23	59	17
Works part time	23	60	16	15	74	10	22	64	12
Not in labor force	21	58	20	32	58	9	23	60	16

TABLE 5-8. Family Dinner Patterns (vertical percentages)

Dining pattern	Black	White	All families
All eat together	47	81	57
Some eat together	25	15	23
Each eats separately	28	4	20
Weighted (N)	(530)	(134)	(764)

TABLE 5-9. Family Dinner Patterns (percentages)

	All eat together			Each eats separately		
Mothers' education	Black	White	Total	Black	White	Total
Less than high school diploma	35	82	45	35	*	34
High school graduate	47	91	56	28	*	36
Some college	54	76	61	24	*	31
College graduate and above	68	79	75	14	*	5

* = small ns

TABLE 5-10. Family Dinner Patterns (percentages)

	Black		White		All families	
Mothers' labor force status	All eat together	Each eats separately	All eat together	Each eats separately	All eat together	Each eats separately
Works full time	45	28	83	*	52	22
Works part time	45	29	89	*	63	17
Not in labor force	47	28	75	*	57	20

* = small ns

TABLE 5-11. Bedtime on School Nights (vertical percentages)

	Regular bedtime			No regular bedtime		
Time	Black	White	Total	Black	White	Total
Before 9:30 P.M.	40	59	46	14	35	15
9:30–before 10:00 P.M.	20	24	19	10	20	13
10:00–before 10:30 P.M.	30	14	26	27	17	27
10:30–before 11:00 P.M.	4	2	4	13	18	16
11:00 P.M. or later	7	1	5	35	9	29
Weighted (N)	(236)	(68)	(356)	(154)	(30)	(211)

with no regular bedtime stayed up later for the most part than the others. In either case black children tended to stay up considerably later than white children. Socioeconomic status effects on bedtime were not strong, nor did they explain ethnic variations. Although low-income parents did not have less time available than other parents for their children (as has been suggested in some descriptions of these families), there were variations in how the day was organized. In these families the child's day tended to be more loosely structured than in other families, and it is possible that these parents consequently spent less time in close interaction with their children than did parents in more structured households.[23]

CHILDREN AND PARENTS: ACTIVITIES TOGETHER

The great majority of parents make varied use of their time with their children, engaging in many different kinds of activities. Most children and most parents of all backgrounds reported going places and doing things together. Only a few children reported doing nothing at all with their parents.

We asked two questions designed to elicit perceptions of time spent together. When asked, "How often does your child go places with adults in the family?" most parents responded, "frequently." About 90 percent said they did so at least a few times each month (table 5-12). When asked, "How often do you do things with your parents on weekends?" children reported much less frequency (table 5-13).* Of the 20 percent of children who said that they hardly ever went places on weekends with their parents, slightly more were black than white, and more from single-parent than two-parent families. In part this is explained by income. The poorest children in the sample reported hardly ever going places with parents twice as frequently (25 percent) as the wealthiest (12 percent). Similarly, black parents of all backgrounds, single parents, and poor parents were less likely than others to respond "frequently" to the question (table 5-12).

---

*The question asked of parents was more general; it focused on "going places." In contrast, the question asked of children specified a time frame but included a wider range of activities.

TABLE 5-12. How Often Child Goes Places with Adults (vertical percentages)

| | Black | | | White | | | | | |
	One parent	Two parents	All blacks	One parent	Two parents	All whites	All families	Low income	High income
Few times each week	39	51	45	54	72	68	49	39	62
Few times each month	45	41	43	44	25	29	41	45	34
About once a month	10	7	9	2	2	2	7	12	3
Less often	6	1	3	0	1	1	3	4	1
Weighted (N)	(264)	(247)	(529)	(31)	(101)	(133)	(761)	(165)	(139)

TABLE 5-13. "How Often Do You Do Things With Your Parents on Weekends?" (vertical percentages)

	Black	White	All children
Every weekend	14	20	16
Most weekends	29	25	27
Some weekends	37	40	37
Hardly ever	20	15	20

Measures of family circumstances explain some of the variation in time use. None, however, is a singular, consistently strong predictor of types of time use or types of activities children and parents do together. This is so because, as noted in other chapters, measures of family circumstance admit of competing theories. For example, a difference in patterns of time use among single- and two-parent families reflects (1) material differences—more single-parent than two-parent families are poor; or (2) time pressure—mother's labor force status and/or family size may make less time available for each child; or (3) some complex interactions among these factors. Similarly, if we find that parents with a higher level of educational attainment pursue more activities representative of "high" culture in the community, an explanation may still be elusive. These parents may believe that spending time with children in this way contributes to school success and to educational achievement, or they may feel more comfortable in such places.[24] There may also be other shared beliefs about child-rearing practices associated with higher levels of educational attainment which interest parents in activities of this type.

We know that many of the questions we asked children about activities with their parents could be interpreted in more than one way.* A question such as "Do you ever play games together with your parents?" can mean anything from a daily chess game

---

*We rely here more on data from the children's interviews than from the parents' questionnaires for several reasons. First, the questions we asked children about activities they did with their parents were detailed. Second, children were less likely to give "socially approved" responses (a common problem in studies of parent-child interactions). Third, our descriptions of the other time-use domains also rely principally on children's reports.

to a five-minute game of tic-tac-toe once a month. But our interest was not in great specificity; the issue was one of perception and behavior. If children say that they play games with their parents, we assume that for these children parents' participation in their games meets their needs or, minimally, is satisfactory enough to evoke a positive reply.

As in chapter four, we examine a sample of activities rather than a comprehensive list. First, we look at activities families do at home, then at things they do outside the home, and third, at the types of things they do most often together to facilitate the child's involvement in other activities.

Activities at Home

Questions about activities at home with parents evoked a considerable variety of responses (table 5-14). Almost all children said that they had watched television with parents in the last week or two. Fewer than half (37 percent) said that they had worked together on hobbies or special projects during that period. It is interesting that children from families of different types (single- or two-parent families) with varying economic resources and varying time constraints (mother does or does not work full time) were equally likely to report having done most of the at-home activities with parents which we asked about. Asian parents were less likely to do these activities, except television watching, with their children. In general, minority children were less likely than white children to report doing hobbies with parents, although with respect to games and hobbies there was relatively little variation (table 5-15). Families play games together more frequently than they pursue

TABLE 5-14. Activities at Home with Parent(s) (percentages)

Activity	Black	White	Asian	Other	Low income	Single parent	Mother working full time	All children
Play games	73	65	47	53	69	69	72	69
Work on hobbies	36	54	26	24	30	34	40	37
Do homework	55	54	31	29	51	51	48	51
Watch television	86	85	92	90	86	87	83	86

TABLE 5-15. Games and Hobbies with Parent(s) (vertical percentages)

Activity	Black	White	Low income	Single parent	Working mother full time	All children
Hobbies						
At least once a week	13	12	8	10	12	12
Two or three times a month	10	15	7	10	10	10
About once a month	10	16	11	10	10	11
Less often	3	12	4	4	7	5
Never do	64	46	70	66	60	63
Weighted (N)	(529)	(134)	(165)	(316)	(290)	(763)
Games						
At least once a month	34	22	31	27	30	30
Two or three times a month	22	20	24	26	23	21
About once a month	8	10	8	7	11	8
Less often	8	13	5	8	7	10
Never do	27	35	31	31	28	32
Weighted (N)	(530)	(133)	(165)	(316)	(290)	(763)

hobbies, but families of different types do both with comparable frequency.

Among families in our survey homework was a rather important child-parent activity. In eighteen of the twenty schools in our sample principals said that homework was assigned in sixth-grade classes. In turn, the majority of children said that their parents helped them with their homework. Asian children were significantly less likely, however, than either blacks or whites to say parents helped them, yet their school achievement (in the aggregate) was the highest in the city. We have explored this issue in other work;[25] here it is sufficient to say that our data suggest that social stereotypes about school and family life may be in error: children of single parents, low-income parents, and black parents are as likely as others to report spending time working with their parents on school-related activities.

Television viewing is the most frequent child-parent activity, taking up the most time in a day or week. Nearly half the children in the study said that they watched television with parents every day (table 5-16), a proportion only slightly smaller than the number who reported that they usually ate dinner with their parents. Asian children, again, were less likely to report this every day (28 percent) compared with white children (46 percent) and with other minority children (about 46 percent). Differences in family viewing in relation to mother's education were dramatic, especially among whites. This is a function of different attitudes and values toward both television in particular and toward time use in general (see chapter eight).

Going Places

Providing exposure to the community is an important educational and social task that often falls to parents. It has been assumed that children differ in the extent to which their parents take them places, exposing them to community resources and activities. A number of social programs, in fact, have addressed the issue of who goes where with whom: "disadvantaged" children are assumed to be those less likely to come from families that do these things.

Children were asked several questions about going places in the community (table 5-17). The most general questions asked how often the child went to five different types of places; whether they usually went alone; and, if not alone, with whom. All of these activities were done by the majority of children, including going to the library (the least frequent of the activities surveyed). White children were less likely than blacks to report going to church. Blacks were less likely to go to restaurants.

TABLE 5-16. Children Who Watch Television with Parent(s) Every Day (percentages)

Mother's education	Black	White	All children
Less than high school diploma	53	77	53
High school graduate	48	70	49
Some college	47	42	46
College graduate and above	37	21	27

TABLE 5-17. How Often Children Go Places (horizontal percentages)

	Once a week	Few times a month	Once a month/ few times a year	Hardly ever/ never	Usually go with parents[a]
Restaurant					
Black	21	30	16	32	35
White	31	36	17	15	62
All children	24	30	17	28	41
Movies					
Black	28	37	18	17	17
White	9	30	50	11	26
All children	22	34	26	18	19
Park					
Black	44	24	16	16	10
White	31	24	24	21	20
All children	41	23	18	18	13
Church					
Black	47	18	9	26	39
White	37	7	9	47	33
All children	44	16	9	30	37
Library					
Black	15	23	13	48	3
White	11	28	28	33	15
All children	14	24	17	45	6

[a]These percentages are not related to columns 1-4.

Otherwise, ethnic differences on these items were insignificant: only restaurant and church going were typically family activities (where "family" included at least one parent), and most were done with someone in addition to parents (such as siblings). Movie going and playing in the park, fairly frequent activities for the children, were by and large not family activities. The differences between the proportion of black children reporting going to the park frequently (at least once a week) and the proportion going with parents was especially large. The same pattern held for library visits. Clearly, from this sampling of activities, it is reasonable to conclude that preadolescent children have much greater exposure to the community than is reflected only in the things they do with parents.

Using a different type of question to measure both exposure and child-parent interaction, we asked children about a wide range of specific places: whether they had ever gone, whether they had gone during the school year, and with whom they had gone most recently. Included were certain well-known local and regional parks, beaches, cultural facilities, and entertainment centers. On the list were free activities and those charging entrance fees, places representative of "high" and "popular" culture, and indoor and outdoor activities. (For a complete list of the activities see Appendix A.) Nearly two-thirds of the children had gone to at least one of these places with their parents in the last school year (table 5-18). Half of the low-income group had not; black children were half as likely as white children to have gone to any of the places with their parents. White children, generally, had not only been to at least one place with parents but 39 percent had visited three or more places with parents compared with 20 percent of the black children, 22 percent of the Asian children, and 15 percent of the other minorities.

A larger proportion of white children than children from any other ethnic group reported having gone to all types of places with parents, regardless of family structure or income (table 5-19). The ethnic difference in cultural activities is especially noteworthy. Three times as many white as black children reported doing one or more of these activities. For each item, except outdoor activities, children with a single parent and those from families with a low income were less likely to have done these things together.

Single-parent families, white and black, were less likely to have gone to high-fee places and indoor places (some of which

TABLE 5-18. Number of Places Gone with Parent(s)[a] (vertical percentages)

	Black	White	Asian	Other	Low income	Single parent	Working mother (full time)	All children
0	41	19	36	35	50	43	37	36
1 or 2	40	42	42	50	35	39	41	41
3 or more	20	39	22	15	16	18	23	23
Weighted (N)	(530)	(134)	(49)	(51)	(165)	(316)	(390)	(764)

[a]See Child's Interview Schedule, Question 58 (Appendix A).

TABLE 5-19. Places Gone with Parent(s) by Type[a] (percentages)

	Black	White	Asian	Other	Low income	Single parent	Working mother full time	All children
Cultural	10	35	16	3	8	11	12	14
High fee	31	44	22	27	25	26	37	33
Indoor	33	58	38	26	26	27	36	37
Outdoor	49	69	53	57	46	51	54	54

[a]Aggregation of items in Child's Interview Schedule, Question 58 (Appendix A). In this table and in those following, categories are not necessarily mutually exclusive.

also charged high fees), but the differences were not large (table 5-20). With respect to visiting these types of places, single-parent black families were not significantly different from two-parent families, white or black. White families and families with higher incomes were more likely to do a great number of activities overall, in part because they do more fee-charging activities.

The difference in the number of outdoor places children had gone was surprising. Significantly fewer black children went to these places with parents. This may be related to the fact that

TABLE 5-20. Places Gone with Parent(s)[a] (percentages)

	Black		White		All children	
	One parent	Two parents	One parent	Two parents	One parent	Two parents
Indoor						
0	75	59	48	39	73	55
2 or more	7	17	27	28	9	18
Outdoor						
0	52	48	23	34	49	43
2 or more	21	25	34	42	23	29
High fee						
0	76	61	59	54	75	62
2 or more	6	12	11	14	6	11
Cultural						
0	91	89	64	64	89	83
2 or more	2	1	15	14	3	4

[a]Same aggregation of items as table 5-19.

black children went to more places around and outside the neighborhood on their own; their mobility patterns were considerably more expansive than those of their white counterparts. We also expected low-income families to substitute activities at outdoor, no-fee places for activities at indoor, fee-charging places. To some extent this occurred as all types of families used cost-free outdoor facilities, while costly facilities were used principally by higher-income families.

With the exception of the lowest-income group, material resources had only a modest impact on the overall number of places children went with parents (based on an additive index of visits to specific places) (table 5-21). Income did, however, have a substantial effect on types of places visited (table 5-22). It influenced attendance at places that charged a fee ("high fee" and "indoor"), and it had a strong effect (among whites) on propensity to attend cultural activities. This is probably a function, however, of different interests among parents with different levels of education rather than simply a reflection of income (table 5-23). What persists at all levels of income and education are ethnic differences, even when comparing white and black families of higher levels of income and education.

Facilitation

Time spent by parents facilitating their children's involvement in out-of-school activities is quite different from time spent at home or going places. Parents and children spend much of this time together, often driving from one place to another. Other facilitation time is spent with the parent as an adult participant: room mother, den mother, coach, and so on. And,

TABLE 5-21. Child Went One or More Places (All Types) with Parent(s) (percentages)

Family income	Black	White	All children
Less than $5,000	49	76	51
$5,000–$9,999	63	70	65
$10,000–$14,999	57	90	63
$15,000–$19,999	70	80	74
$20,000 or more	62	85	73

TABLE 5-22. Child Went One or More Places with Parent(s) (percentages)

Family income	Cultural			High Fee			Indoor			Outdoor		
	Black	White	All children	Black	White	All children	Black	White	All children	Black	White	All children
Less than $5,000	8	13	8	26	46	26	27	34	26	44	76	46
$5,000–$9,999	10	15	10	27	37	29	30	39	32	55	67	57
$10,000–$14,999	10	50	15	40	33	33	38	63	38	44	80	53
$15,000–$19,999	10	38	18	38	41	39	39	57	47	58	70	59
$20,000 or more	16	40	25	46	55	47	46	70	55	47	70	59

TABLE 5-23. Children Scoring Zero on Additive Index of Cultural Activities with Parent(s)[a] (percentages)

Mother's education	Black	White	All children
Less than high school diploma	92	80	92
High school graduate	94	83	92
Some college	87	58	82
College graduate and above	81	53	69

[a]A score of zero means that a child attended none of the cultural activities surveyed (See Child's Interview Schedule, Question 58, Appendix A).

of course, parents spend time as the child's "agent," registering for groups and lessons, for example—time not necessarily spent together.

Although mothers driving station wagons loaded with Little Leaguers to the big game are a commonplace of television commercials, a popular caricature of middle-class family life, little data exist that indicates how typical this type of time together is for parents and children. Our survey included a variety of questions pertinent to facilitation. Here we examine three types that are most often done with the child present: driving, seeking and signing, and volunteering. (Seeking an organized activity may involve some initial parent *or* child time and perhaps some parent time alone.)

For many activities that parents and children do together a car either is a necessity or makes participation much easier, hence more likely. In nearly a third of our sample families (30 percent of black families, 7 percent of white families) parents had neither a car nor a driver's license. Controlling for both, however, black and white parents were about equally likely to report that they had driven their children places and with the same frequency. Forty-two percent of all parents said they drove children as often as a few times a week. A much larger proportion of white (32 percent) than black (4 percent) parents reported driving their children somewhere every day—and it was thought to be too often (white, 20 percent; black, 7 percent). White and Asian parents were considerably more likely than black parents to have driven children to and from lessons and groups and to have enrolled them personally. Several explanations are conceivable: differences in time available for such things, parents not available at key periods (afternoons) because of work, or differences in values regarding the activities themselves.

To look at some of the related social correlates, we created a four-point index of facilitation made up of items having to do with driving, seeking, and signing. Half of the single-parent families compared with just over a third of the two-parent families scored zero on the index (table 5-24). Almost twice as many blacks as whites scored zero, and only a third as many

TABLE 5-24. Facilitation Index Summary Score (horizontal percentages)

Ethnicity and other characteristics	Facilitation index score				Weighted (N)
	0	1	2	3 or 4	
Black	41	35	10	14	(530)
One parent	50	37	6	7	(265)
Two parents	35	33	13	19	(247)
Mother's labor force status					
Works full time	38	33	10	19	(218)
Works part time	36	37	16	11	(68)
Not in labor force, one parent	55	39	3	3	(118)
Not in labor force, two parents	51	32	9	8	(97)
White	21	29	14	35	(134)
One parent	23	37	16	24	(31)
Two parents	20	26	14	40	(101)
Mother's labor force status					
Works full time	25	30	14	32	(40)
Works part time	6	30	19	45	(32)
Not in labor force, one parent	*	*	*	*	(8)
Not in labor force, two parents	26	24	13	37	(49)
All families					
One parent	50	36	7	7	(316)
Two parents	36	28	13	23	(429)
Mother's labor force status					
Works full time	39	30	12	19	(290)
Works part time	30	33	14	23	(120)
Not in labor force, one parent	55	38	3	3	(134)
Not in labor force, two parents	43	28	10	19	(183)

* = small *n*s

scored three or more points on the four-point index. Among blacks, those parents with more time available did less facilitating for and with their children.

Mothers' labor force status, which might have been expected to affect levels of facilitation, had little impact. More nonworking than working mothers scored zero, and fewer scored three or more.

Income and education were very strong determinants of facilitation (table 5-25). The lowest-income respondents were twice as likely as the highest to score zero on the index. Only 8 percent of the high-income, white respondents scored zero compared with more than one-third of the high-income blacks. Half of the high-income and a third of the middle-income whites scored three or four compared with a much smaller proportion of blacks.

TABLE 5-25. Facilitation Index and Family Income[a] (percentages)

| | Facilitation index score | | | | | |
| | 0 | | | 3 or 4 | | |
Family income	Black	White	Total	Black	White	Total
Less than $5,000	57	48	58	4	16	4
$5,000–$9,999	46	50	47	7	10	9
$10,000–$14,999	36	24	33	18	37	20
$15,000–$19,999	37	20	31	19	30	25
$20,000 or more	35	8	23	22	51	36

Facilitation index and mother's education[a] (percentages)

| | Facilitation index score | | | | | |
| | 0 | | | 3 or 4 | | |
Mother's education	Black	White	Total	Black	White	Total
Less than high school diploma	67	62	67	2	8	4
High school graduate	45	24	42	7	27	12
Some college	32	22	29	19	34	23
College graduate and above	20	1	10	33	54	42

[a]Includes only those respondents with driver's licenses and cars.

Differences between the scores of the least- and most-educated mothers were even larger.

Parents were also asked about helping with the activities that their children were involved with in school and out of school. Substantial numbers of parents of all backgrounds volunteered, and the associations between income or education and volunteering were only slightly stronger for white than for black mothers. Working mothers were about as likely as nonworking mothers to engage in some form of volunteering (table 5-26). Single parents participated somewhat less often, possibly because of time pressures, but among those who did, black single parents were more likely to work in classrooms, while white single parents more often helped with organized activities outside school. Among two-parent families white mothers volunteered more frequently than black mothers.

The relationship between facilitation and life circumstances suggests that some activities may nearly always be beyond the reach of less-advantaged children. When we return to the issue of facilitation (chapter seven), our focus will be the relationship between these parental actions and children's actual activity patterns. Organized after-school programs vary greatly in the amount and kinds of parental facilitation they require.

INTERCORRELATIONS AMONG CHILD-PARENT ACTIVITY SETS

We have tried to show that families chose how they spent their time together from a relatively small, common set of activities. From one socioeconomic group to another we found little variation in the proportions of families spending time together at home, considerable variation with regard to facilitation.

We have offered little evidence for the "only difference" theory whereby low-status and low-income minority families are different from all others in their family time use. No single variable accounts for all or even most of the variation in how families spent time, nor were those who scored low on our various measures of parental availability to be found in any single group. Low-status families made up a significantly larger

TABLE 5-26. Parent Volunteering Time on Child's Activities (percentages)

Ethnicity and other characteristics	Room mother	Helps with organized activity	Weighted (N)
Black	38	31	(530)
One parent	37	29	(262)
Two parents	39	33	(246)
Mother's labor force status			
Works full time	27	35	(217)
Works part time	56	36	(67)
Not in labor force, one parent	46	26	(118)
Not in labor force, two parents	40	29	(97)
Low income (less than $5,000)	36	21	(135)
High income ($20,000 or more)	37	46	(65)
Low education (less than high school diploma)	29	15	(146)
High education (college graduate and above)	40	60	(36)
White	62	52	(134)
One parent	23	41	(31)
Two parents	75	57	(101)
Mother's labor force status			
Works full time	38	53	(40)
Works part time	80	60	(32)
Not in labor force, one parent	16	9	(8)
Not in labor force, two parents	83	54	(49)
Low income (less than $5,000)	32	17	(12)
High income ($20,000 or more)	75	55	(53)
Low education (less than high school diploma)	52	12	(18)
High education (college graduate and above)	74	65	(42)
All parents			
One parent	35	29	(312)
Two parents	48	38	(427)
Mother's labor force status			
Works full time	29	37	(288)
Works part time	61	41	(120)
Not in labor force, one parent	44	28	(134)
Not in labor force, two parents	51	34	(183)
Low income (less than $5,000)	35	20	(165)
High income ($20,000 or more)	55	49	(57)
Low education (less than high school diploma)	30	14	(206)
High education (college graduate and above)	60	62	(90)

proportion of families who spent little time, other than television time, together at home, however; and minority families, independent of their circumstances, were more likely to do few of the activities away from home reported here. (It is possible that a different set of activities might have yielded different results.)

To examine the intercorrelations among these different kinds of activities, a summary index of family activities was created by combining the data on at-home activities, going places, and facilitation. This represents twenty-two times that the child could report having done an activity with a parent (or having had an activity done for him or her). Mothers with little education were considerably more likely to score at the low end of this index (table 5-27). Controlling for both ethnicity and measures of status (table 5-28), we see that although higher-status blacks were less likely than low-status whites to score low on this index, they were considerably more likely to do so than were comparable whites. Nearly a quarter of the black families in which the mother had had some college education, for example, scored zero on at least two of the three activity sets. Similarly, middle- and high-income black families were considerably more likely than comparable whites to have low scores. It is especially noteworthy that these low scores do not appear to be a function of either family structure or available time. Both single- and two-parent black families had low scores more frequently than comparable white families. Even mothers, black or white, with larger amounts of available time (that is, those not

TABLE 5-27. Index[a] of Family Activities (vertical percentages)

Family activities index score	Black	White	All children	Mother's education	
				Less than high school diploma	College graduate and above
Low	11	3	9	14	5
Low-middle	28	12	25	39	4
High-middle	37	25	35	32	30
High	22	59	30	13	62

[a]Composite index construction from the three activity sets presented in this chapter (maximum score: 22 activity points).

TABLE 5-28. Index of Family Activities (percentages scoring low)

	Black	White
Mother's education		
Less than high school diploma	57	48
High school graduate	38	24
Some college	28	10
College graduate and above	16	1
Family income		
Less than $5,000	42	25
$5,000-$9,999	41	47
$10,000-$14,999	31	13
$15,000-$19,999	32	10
$20,000 or more	28	6
Family structure		
One parent	46	14
Two parents	32	16
Mother's labor force status		
Works full time	32	16
Works part time	24	9
Not in labor force, single parent	61	*
Not in labor force, two parents	39	21

* = small ns

working) did not appear to spend as much time doing family activities as those who were employed (table 5-28).

The perception by parents that many of these activities were best done, or were already done, by institutions such as schools may help explain differences in rates of participation. Trips to museums, parks, and other community facilities we asked about were often a regular part of school programs designed, among other things, to compensate for the perceived environmental disadvantage of poor children.* Children in schools that had these enrichment programs did, in fact, make more visits with their classes and fewer with their parents than their counterparts at schools without these programs.

How parents' attitudes and views of their responsibilities are affected by the school's involvement in these areas of children's lives is a relatively unexplored issue. Since Title I funds were

---

*The most important of these programs is ESEA Title I (1965). Of the sampled schools only those in Master Stratum III received these funds (see Appendix B).

allocated to low-income Oakland public schools (regardless of each attending child's individual circumstances) they reached children whose parents held a variety of outlooks on these "exposure" issues. Some parents may have taken for granted that the schools should facilitate children's exposure to these activities and would not have undertaken such trips themselves. Others simply may have allowed the school trip to substitute for an activity that they might otherwise have done with the child. Still others may have preferred that schools "stick to basics"; they may not have placed a high value on these experiences at all.

In other Children's Time Study reports we have attempted to explore more thoroughly the complex relationship between parents' priorities and school inputs.[26] Given the range of possible attitudes, interpreting variations in behavior is difficult. But, at the least, these data do suggest a wide variety of parenting styles that affected child-parent time together. There was a larger than expected group of children who did very few presumably educational, achievement-enhancing activities with parents. It is this group that we must study further if we are to understand the different ways in which child-parent time together contributes or might contribute to children's cognitive and intellectual development.

CONCLUSION

Family time can be described in a number of ways: by the simple availability of parents, by the rules that structure the family's day, by the kinds of activities that parents and children do together. Each way of defining time in this domain gives us a slightly different picture of family life and parenting and the effects of life circumstances on each. At the beginning of the chapter we asked some specific questions about child-parent time together in lower-status and poor minority families compared with higher-status and wealthier white families and in families in which mothers are employed compared with families in which they are not.

We found that the most time-poor families in our sample were those with two working parents or a single parent working full time. Independent of amount of time available, parents' labor force status, and traditional socioeconomic measures, most families managed to have an adult home during key periods in the child's day. Mothers who worked part time appeared to be in the best position to organize their work life to coincide with their children's schedules.

Families differed in terms of how the child's day was structured and whether or not time was provided for at-home activities. Black families were significantly less likely than white families to eat dinner together. Additionally, more black than white families and more low- than high-status families had what might be called permissive rules about after-school time schedules, dinner time, and bedtime.

We found more similarity in activities at home than activities away from home. Patterns in the latter reflected differences in family income and mother's education. Facilitation levels were surprisingly high in most groups; we did not find employed mothers doing less than unemployed mothers (except that they were less likely to be volunteers in children's activities).

On a composite measure of family activities (at-home, away-from-home, and facilitation) low-status families tended to score lower, and black families, independent of status, scored lower than whites. The availability of parent time (as measured by mothers' labor force status and number of parents in the home) did not have a strong effect on these scores.

The differences on measures of time use among families of different incomes, family structures, and ethnicities were not as pronounced as we expected. There was more variation in the type of activity choices than in their number. Of course, we do not know, from our largely behavioral data, how highly parents value these different types of activities with their children.

One last note: given the current debate about the consequences of maternal employment for children, it is particularly noteworthy that working mothers did not differ significantly from other mothers on these measures.

six
JOBS, CHORES, AND SPENDING PATTERNS

Virtually all the children in our sample had chores to do around the house at some time during the week, if not every day, and many with younger siblings looked after them frequently in their parents' absence. Few held paying jobs of any kind outside the home, and when asked to describe their activities "yesterday," even those children who had reported a lot of chores, outside jobs, or extensive baby-sitting usually failed to mention them. Instead they spoke of leisure activities, such as watching television, and routines, such as brushing their teeth; and they recounted going places to spend money rather than doing things to earn it.

The fact that nearly all children are expected to do chores but few regard them as significant is hardly surprising. Parents need their children to make some contribution to the household economy, but children usually prefer to do other things with their time and they do not feel that what they do to help out matters very much. Furthermore, chores are often a source of ongoing tension. The conflicts that surface around these activities—between children and parents and between parents themselves—encapsulate some complex questions about children's economic role in the family and in society at large and about parents' efforts and obligations to inculcate traditional work values.

In this chapter we assess children's domestic responsibilities and the role of these activities in socialization. We explore how work and work-related values figure in the experience of children of different backgrounds. We focus chiefly on the jobs children do when they are not in school, on their chores, and on their child-care responsibilities. In the context of this analysis it is necessary also to consider other elements of children's roles as economic actors, including their relationship to the money economy: where do they get their money, and what do they spend it on? Children are paid for some of the things they do but not for others. In this regard, we found it impossible to understand fully the meaning of activities they were not paid for without reference to their own and their parents' money management attitudes and practices.

CHILDHOOD AND WORK

Historical and Cross-Cultural Perspectives

Recent visitors to China have reported how elementary school children pack electric bulbs or perform other light industrial tasks in the classroom.[1] Such descriptions usually excite the same kind of uneasy attention aroused a generation ago by reports of the collective orientation of the Soviet schools. The dilemma is whether to categorize what is observed as tantamount to child labor and an indication of economic and pedagogical backwardness or as the kind of exemplary integration between work place and school many educators in this country advocate.

We confronted the obverse of this issue, for in our sample work and productive activity appeared to play, subjectively at least, a very marginal role in children's lives. The reasons for this are not simply ideological: even though American schools do not glorify work and production directly in the ways their Soviet and Chinese counterparts do, a strong work ethic still pervades most sectors of American society. Indeed, the Soviets and Chinese may go to such lengths to instill a work ethic in their schools precisely because such an ethic is less ingrained in the culture than it is in more highly industrialized societies.

The attenuated relationship between childhood and the world of work seems to be a shared characteristic of fully industrialized societies. The evolution of industrial, agricultural, and domestic production has increasingly restricted the extent and changed the character of children's work. Children in America today are often seen as exclusively future rather than present economic producers and their views of work and the work place are shaped largely by adult attitudes that focus on the paycheck more than on the quality or challenge of the work experience. It is not surprising therefore that children come to display a lack of interest in or awareness of the activities that will occupy the greater part of their adult lives. Yet this does not resolve our problem. The conflict remains between the impulse to protect children from the harsh realities of the work place and the labor market and the desire to provide them early with the skills to survive there once cast loose.

Most studies of the relationship between childhood and work essentially reflect these conflicting impulses: first, there is a perspective that takes for granted the value of anticipatory socialization of children into the routines and norms of work life;[2] and second, there is a critical position (pervading a good deal of the educational literature) which regards children's lives as already far too dominated by what Samuel Bowles and Herbert Gintis have called "the long shadow of work."[3]

Government bureaucrats and scholars concerned with problems of youth policy are apt to perceive only an unfortunate discontinuity between the insulated world of childhood and the central productive activities of the society. Some argue that it is this discontinuity that explains a wide range of youth adjustment problems. For example, the absence of a real economic role for young people is often associated with delinquency; if children had "meaningful" work opportunities, it is proposed, these problems would diminish.

The dangers of such approaches have been detailed often enough and do not need extensive treatment here. They range from failure to acknowledge the structural sources of unemployment and lack of skills on the one hand to the make-work character of many youth employment programs on the other.[4] Even the best programs are undermined ultimately by the facts that children are rarely regarded as bona fide workers in economies such as ours and that the kinds of work available are oftentimes peculiarly frustrating to a still-growing individual whose potentialities are relatively more open than those of many adults. Yet, many historical and cross-cultural descriptions of the relationship between childhood and work reinforce simplistic formulations of this sort. They conjure images of the complete integration of children into the work activities of society whether in the preindustrial past or the agrarian present. This picture is often coupled with the idea, most notably associated with Philippe Aries, that what lies behind the increasingly marginal economic status of children is a more fundamental change in conceptions of human development, a change involving the social rather than the biological definition of stages of life, such as childhood and adolescence. [5] Both of these assumptions—of the historical integration of children into the economy and of the "invention" of childhood—are potentially misleading and leave much unexplained. Serious scrutiny of the kinds of work children once performed in the United States, and still do perform in some parts of the world, shows that while they may have had more extensive and more demanding work responsibilities in, say, colonial America than they do today, in functional terms most young children's tasks were not so very different then: primarily light and sporadic chores performed in and around the home and its immediate environs.

Many of these tasks have become mechanized and industrialized, and as a result children no longer perform them. The process by which this occurred, however, offers clear evidence that it is mistaken to portray the dissociation between childhood and work as a smooth and secular trend.

The exclusion of children from the industrialized labor force took place over a long period and was accompanied by fierce conflicts. Between the rural child of the past, working alongside his or her elders, and today's child stands the child of the industrial revolution, sweating over looms or pulling coal trucks. It was not until the early twentieth century, after untold suffering, civil disorder, and depression of adult wage rates that child labor diminished and protective legislation was enacted in the United States.

The actual demise of child labor, moreover, did not come until new tasks were discovered for children. Child labor declined just as the need became apparent for a more skilled labor force with a particular set of work and authority-related values and attitudes. Children left the labor force to a chorus of opinion extolling the virtues of domesticity and of the institution that came to mediate between the home and the work place, the school. Exclusion from the world of work came with the arrival of a more refined, more prolonged preparation for it.[6] Even today, both at school and at home, there is plenty of evidence that children from a very early age are being prepared for the roles they will later perform as working adults. Norman Denzin, in an article entitled "The Work of Little Children," points out how children's activities and time use are often organized so that, like jobs, they are purposive, structured, and role oriented.[7] Similarly, Robert Dreeben and other critics of formal education argue that schools possess a powerful "hidden agenda" at least as important as the formal curriculum: their role is to inculcate the essential character traits of future workers and citizens.[8]

Finally, modern American children perform a wide range of tasks that would be recognized as work—and probably paid—if performed by adults. This includes not only a vast array of volunteer activities common among high school and college students but also sibling child care undertaken by preadolescents. Among children's traditional tasks, such child care has proven the most resistant to industrialization and professionalization. As a result, children's roles here may still expand as mothers' labor force participation increases.

It is inaccurate to describe modern American society then, as one in which children are entirely insulated from the world of work. The modern child, who must undergo a long and psychologically rigorous educational career to qualify for the simplest job, is every bit as tied to the economy of the day as that partly mythical child of the past or the agrarian present who shared wholeheartedly in the joys and fatigues of the adult world.

A better way of describing the present situation is that which is suggested by our data: while childhood and work may be connected in myriad ways, the linkages are no longer clear and subjectively experienced. Most theories of how children come to acquire work-related values assume too readily that such socialization works directly and unambiguously. According to these theories, values are imposed on the growing child which foster development into a responsible and obedient worker, even at the expense of creativity and individuality. Thus, Bowles and Gintis argue, the skills associated with academic achievement (as measured by school grades and test scores) are fundamentally traits such as docility and obedience which are functional for the jobs that most students will hold later on.

The reality we describe in this chapter does not directly contradict these theories, any more than it supports theories that children are thoroughly detached from the world of work. But it does suggest their inadequacy. We found it necessary to be less deterministic in assessing how work-related values are instilled and more aware of the complexity of the socialization process.

A variety of agents and institutions—parents, peers, schools, television, and a host of child-serving agencies—are all engaged to varying degrees in preparing the young for future work roles. We shall not try to address the particular contributions of each. Rather, given the nature of our data and given some of the things we have said in earlier chapters about the changing role of the family and the changing relationships of children and parents, we focus here on work and the development of work-related values within the nuclear family. We shall argue that parental socialization practices relating to work are linked to larger social structural considerations, part of a long evolving set of conditions that define the child's place in the work economy.

JOBS OUTSIDE THE HOME

The route to success is a newspaper route. Young people who manage routes just seem to be the kind destined for success.

They like doing their own thing. Earning their own money. Operating their own business. Building for the future.

As a result you will find (as surveys tell us) that young newspaper carriers stand out. They are self-reliant, responsible, and do better than most at school.

This is the text of an advertisement that appears regularly in the *San Francisco Chronicle/Examiner*. The advertisement for delivery boys and girls expresses a widely held belief in the value of hard work and in its individual rewards. We had thought that among children in our sample who worked this kind of work ethic would be particularly well developed. In fact, we found that very few children worked at all outside the home on a regular basis, and that there were few systematic differences between those who worked and those who did not. Neither was there much evidence that the parents of children who worked had value systems and beliefs different from the majority of parents whose children did not work. We were thus led to conclude that, for better or for worse, the newspaper advertisement is somewhat anachronistic and that an experience and set of values that may have been central to growing up in earlier generations is now limited to a very small minority.

Only about 15 percent of the preadolescents in our sample reported working outside the home on any regular basis. For two-thirds of them *regularly* meant once or twice a week. Less than one percent of all children held more than one job. With the exception of paper routes (17 percent of jobs), the jobs were virtually all tasks that would have been regarded as chores had they not been remunerated or had they been performed at home (the most common being yardwork and baby-sitting).

A handful of children did work with their parents, chiefly their fathers, at adult jobs, usually in family-owned stores or laundries, selling wares at flea markets, or helping with janitorial work. Only two children reported holding jobs independently that might just as likely have been performed by adults; these were a stock boy and a packer in a fortune cookie factory.

These findings reflect in part the age of children in our sample; studies of older teenagers show much higher rates of paid employment.[9] The findings also result from our choice of a more restrictive definition of what constitutes a job than that used in many studies. Mary Engel, Gerald Marsdon, and Sylvia W. Pollack, for example, asked children if they ever had worked for money and as a result arrived at much higher estimates of the number of "children who work" (70 to 80 percent).[10] Their measure is problematic for at least two reasons: first, if their definition was intended to portray the totality of children's work-related experiences, chores done in the home should have been included in their analysis whether or not they were remunerated; and second, if they were concerned only with the impact on children of work in the everyday sense of paid employment, occasional or nonrecurring events should have been distinguished from regular experiences. Regularity is an important characteristic of work, and its absence in children's work is highly significant.

This is not to deny that the line between actual jobs and chores is a fluid one, both in children's minds and in social reality. For this study we thought it essential to link children's jobs to regular, paid employment outside the home. For other research objectives a more expansive definition might be appropriate. The activities that we identify here as jobs were not necessarily distinct in content from those discussed in the section on chores that follows, but they were more organized economically. Analyzing them separately reveals a number of characteristics of the domain as a whole which would be less clear if they were combined.

Sex and family size were better predictors of which children worked than were ethnic and socioeconomic differences. Twenty percent of boys but only 11 percent of girls held jobs. Eighteen percent of only children, 17 percent of children with one or more siblings, 13 percent of those with three or four siblings, and only 11 percent of those from larger families worked outside the home. The decline was even more precipitous for children with larger numbers of younger brothers and sisters.

These patterns might suggest that the lighter the workload at home, the more likely the child was to work outside: girls generally and children from larger families tended to have more domestic chores. Nevertheless, children with jobs had roughly the same pattern of chores and responsibilities at home as other children. In the main, time spent on paid jobs must be viewed as a supplement to and not a substitution for time spent on other tasks. Only among children who did jobs more than a few times a week was there evidence of substitution: 9 percent of these children had no chore responsibilities compared with only about 1 percent of those who had no jobs or did jobs only once or twice weekly. There was somewhat more substitution in the case of child care, but it, too, was confined to children with the heaviest job commitments. One-half of the children with frequent job responsibilities did not care for other children as opposed to one-third of all others (including those with jobs once or twice a week).

Children's work was not in any significant way associated with their parents' world views and child-rearing philosophies. Paradoxically, the single relationship of any magnitude was that parents who ascribed greater importance to luck as a factor influencing their child's future prospects were more likely (19 percent as opposed to 12 percent) to have children with jobs. The only other attitudinal item linked systematically to children's employment was concern for safety. Working means greater exposure to the risks and dangers of city life, and only 8 percent of the children whose parents worried a lot about their safety had outside jobs, compared with 17 percent of other children.

To the children themselves jobs were clearly valued, at least as a means to income. Median weekly earnings were $4.00 as opposed to median allowances of $1.50. These earnings were roughly proportional to the number of days worked per week, and more of those who held jobs were otherwise without access to money from their parents. Finally, the children who held jobs were more likely than other children to save money or put it aside for necessities and less likely to spend it on things like candy and other treats (table 6-1).

But even working children spent most of their money on nonessentials, and this may help explain why they failed to mention their jobs when describing what they did after school on a typical day. Their jobs were viewed less as a way of spending time and more as a way of earning money to spend, as though the two were virtually unrelated.

Some employers seem to be keenly aware of contemporary preadolescent attitudes toward the world of work. In contrast to the advertisement in the *San Francisco Chronicle/Examiner*, the *Washington Post* recruits boys and girls this way:

THINK OF IT AS A STEREO, A NEW TEN SPEED, OR A WALLET FULL OF CASH. . . . Delivering the Washington Post is a job that'll fill

TABLE 6-1. Children's Jobs and Spending Patterns (percentages)

Employment Status	Save their money	Buy candy and nonessentials with their own money	Have things they must spend on	Must spend on bus fare	Must spend on lunch	Weighted (N)
No job	26	55	21	11	7	(647)
One job	31	48	23	10	10	(83)
Two jobs or more	31	39	34	24	15	(34)

your pockets but not your time because as a Post carrier you can make up to $100 or more every four weeks and still have your afternoons and evenings free.

HOUSEHOLD CHORES

Table 6-2 shows the list of chores about which we questioned both the children and their parents, together with the frequencies with which the children said they performed each one. The list includes almost all the activities children of this age could reasonably be expected to perform on their own. (Grocery shopping was excluded from this list of chores after pretesting, which indicated that it was rarely done by children alone.)

We constructed two measures of overall chore performance (table 6-3): the number of chores a child claimed to do at least once a week (that is, the range of chores) and the total number of times each week chores on the list were performed (that is, the time spent doing them). Most children performed three or four chores each day and slightly more than half of those listed every week.

The most frequently performed chores took relatively little time and were not central to the organization of the household. They required little creativity or initiative and were likely to become important or receive notice only when left undone. Thus children were more likely to empty the garbage than cook, more likely to make their own beds than anyone else's.

Refinements of this pattern were quite striking. For example, children were more likely to clear the table than to set it. This is not entirely explained by the frequent informality of family

TABLE 6-2. Children's Chores (percentages)

Chore	At least once a week according to:		Number of days per week[a] (according to child)							Mean number of days per week
	Parent	Child	1	2	3	4	5	6	7	
Make bed	88	90	5	6	4	2	2	2	66	5.4
Clean room	83	87	27	12	7	3	2	1	33	3.5
Clean house	63	79	27	12	7	4	3	1	21	2.8
Set table	32	39	6	6	6	3	3	1	16	1.6
Clear table	49	67	9	8	7	5	3	1	31	3.1
Do dishes	63	71	10	11	10	7	4	1	22	2.7
Work in yard	41	51	29	8	3	1	1	–	5	1.1
Empty garbage	63	70	17	13	8	5	2	1	22	2.6
Care for pets	37	45	4	6	4	3	1	1	28	2.3
Help cook	40	47	14	10	6	4	3	1	7	1.4

[a]These columns sum to column 2 only approximately since some children who claimed to perform a chore weekly did not say how frequently they did so over the course of the week.

TABLE 6-3. Chores Performed Weekly (horizontal percentages)

4 chores or fewer	5 - 7 chores	8 chores or more
15	52	34

Estimated time children spent on chores[a]
(horizontal percentages)

None	Low	Average	Above average	High
2	12	43	33	10

[a]Calculated from the numbers of chores listed above times the number of occasions on which it was performed each week. The scores are grouped as follows: low, 1-14; average, 15-28; above average, 29-42; high, 43-59.

meals since children were also more likely to clear the table than to do the dishes. (Credit the fear of breakage perhaps, although accidents are as likely en route from the table as in the sink.)

Given the types of chores children performed, it is hardly surprising to find that they viewed them as relatively unimportant. There are, no doubt, still some children whose lives are burdened with heavy domestic responsibilities, but so far as we could tell they were not numerous enough to be represented in our sample.[11]

While children's responsibilities may be unimportant in terms of time requirements and in their own reports, they may be crucial to parents. To the working mother, for example, having to pick up after a child at the end of a very long day may be the proverbial last straw. Thus, it is not surprising that the children of working mothers in our sample did have a somewhat greater range of chores and responsibilities and spent more time on them (table 6-4). No matter what the chore, they were somewhat more likely to have to do it than were children of nonworking mothers. In cooking and cleaning the differences were marked, although in most other cases they were not great.

Though the absence of a second parent might also be expected to affect the level of children's chore responsibilities, there was very little difference between one- and two-parent households (table 6-5). Indeed there was some indication that the presence of a father increased the chores a child did. This unanticipated finding testifies to the minimal contribution most men made to their household economies. But according to Walker and Woods, fathers in most cases still contribute more than all their children together, so it is not clear why at least

TABLE 6-4. Children's Chore Responsibilities (horizontal percentages)

Mother's labor force status	Number of weekly chores			Weighted N
	4 or less	5-7	8 or more	
Works full time	13	49	38	(290)
Works part time	13	45	42	(120)
Not in labor force	17	55	28	(328)

Mother's labor force status	Estimated time children spent on chores (weekly) (horizontal percentages)			
	Low	Average	Above average	Very high
Works full time	10	44	35	10
Works part time	14	35	39	12
Not in labor force	14	46	28	10

TABLE 6-5. Family Structure and Children's Chores (horizontal percentages)

Family structure	Number of weekly chores			Weighted (N)
	4 or less	5-7	8 or more	
One parent	14	56	31	(317)
Two parents	16	49	36	(447)

some responsibilities are not shifted onto children rather than mothers if the father is absent. It may be because the kinds of tasks—heavier and more mechanical—which men traditionally perform about the house are difficult to reallocate to children. Even so, we would expect that single mothers, saddled with additional tasks, would transfer some of their lighter responsibilities to children. Since this seems not to have been the case, and since children in two-parent families had slightly heavier responsibilities, it may be surmised that chores were not simply undertaken because the jobs needed doing. Chore assignments may well have expressed parents' values about how the household should be managed and how children ought to be brought up. Allowing this, we are in a much better position to understand children's chore performance, the content of their tasks, and variations in the level of activity.

In *For Her Own Good* (1978), Barbara Ehrenreich and Deirdre English argue that a substantial, and perhaps increasing, portion of household chores is concerned less with the production of goods and services and more with the reproduction of social relationships. They view the roughly constant amount of time housewives have spent on chores since labor-saving devices have become readily available as evidence of a "manufacture of housework." The home's loss of productive functions, they say, led to a "domestic void," which the elaboration of new and higher housekeeping standards attempted to fill.[12]

To the extent that housework is "manufactured," or subjectively created, in this way, children almost by definition are ill-suited to perform it. The psychological values realized by housework, for example, may require that it be performed by the housewife: it is not simply a necessary chore that could be done by any capable individual. In addition, socialization itself has become a more important, independent outcome of domestic life. Hence, children may be a proportionately greater drain on the homemaker's time now than in the past because socialization has become more of a separate obligation and less of a responsibility carried out in conjunction with other productive activities. In this sense, children are products, not producers, of domestic work.

That chores served important socializing functions is clear when we examine differences in the things that boys and girls were called upon to do and in the amount of responsibilities they had. Only chores culturally defined as masculine, such as taking out the garbage, were done by boys more often than by girls (table 6-6). Moreover, when the mother worked it was more likely to increase a daughter's than a son's chore responsibilities.[13]

The distribution of tasks among children in the family also illustrates the interplay of economic and socializing factors. Walker and Woods suggest that an only child contributes more time to housework than a child in a larger family. On average such a child works 1.2 hours per day; in families with seven to

TABLE 6-6. Chore Performance (mean number of days per week)

	Boys	Girls
Make bed	5.2	5.5
Clean room	3.3	3.7
Clean house	2.3	3.2
Set table	1.2	2.1
Clear table	2.6	3.6
Do dishes	2.1	3.3
Work in yard	1.4	0.8
Empty garbage	3.6	1.7
Care for pets	2.4	2.2
Help cook	0.8	2.0

Estimated time spent on chores (weekly)

(horizontal percentages)

	None	Low	Average	Above average	Very high	Weighted N
Boys	2	15	48	29	6	(370)
Girls	1	10	39	37	14	(394)

nine children, the total time expenditure of *all* teenaged children was only 3.4 hours per day.[14]

In our survey we found that some chore assignments—setting the table, doing the dishes, caring for pets—declined with family size, although others showed no systematic variation. This was also the case for our composite measures of chore performance. Conversely, some chores—cleaning the child's room, making the bed, and working in the yard—increased with family size, and the number of younger siblings present consistently increased the extent of obligations. The younger child was favored in all chores summarized in table 6-7; older children, especially the oldest, tended to do the bulk of the work. The amount of work done was less a function of how much there was to be done than of who was there to do it and of the expectations of parents who assigned the chores.

The interaction of gender and family position made the normative component even clearer: the presence of an older sister, for instance, lightened the load of a sixth-grade boy but not of a sixth-grade girl. Such differences were probably less the results of deliberate and conscious decisions on the part of parents than of unconscious and habitual patterns of socialization, at least as far as sex was concerned. Parents' reports of children's chores revealed that their perceptions of sex differences were less marked than those of the children themselves, yet there were some respects in which actual treatment of boys and girls may have differed (table 6-8).

Differences in chore performance across ethnic and educational lines were in many cases as large as differences by gender. Black children and those with less-educated mothers tended to do more cleaning and tidying, the chores that formed the bulk

TABLE 6-7. Family Position and Chore Performance (horizontal percentages)

Position in family	Number of weekly chores			Weighted (N)
	4 or less	5-7	8 or more	
Only child	20	42	38	(68)
Oldest child	12	49	39	(200)
Youngest child	17	57	26	(205)
Middle child	14	52	34	(291)

TABLE 6-8. Level of Child's Chores (parent's report, horizontal percentages)

	None	Low	Medium	High
Boys	1	36	43	20
Girls	1	30	43	27

How often child requires parental prompting to do chores

(horizontal percentages)

	Almost always	Few times per week	Few times per month	Hardly ever
Boys	35	42	10	13
Girls	28	43	10	19

of children's domestic work (table 6-9). Differences were much smaller with respect to less typical, more creative chores. But our summary index of chore performance showed little systematic variation by other indexes of social status and family background.

As a result, our findings cast doubt upon class-based theories of child rearing which posit that children of the middle class succeed in part because they have held significant responsibilities at home and thereby learned important lessons that build competence, self-esteem, need for achievement, and good work

TABLE 6-9. Ethnic and Educational Differences in Frequency of Chore Performance (mean number of days per week)

	Whites	Blacks	Asians	Others	Mother is college graduate	All Others
Make bed	4.1	5.8	4.8	4.7	4.9	5.4
Clean room	2.6	4.0	1.6	2.7	2.7	3.6
Clean house	1.7	3.2	1.4	3.1	2.1	2.8
Set table	2.8	1.1	3.1	2.9	2.3	1.6
Clear table	3.3	3.1	2.9	3.1	3.2	3.1
Do dishes	2.3	2.9	2.1	2.5	2.1	2.8
Work in yard	0.8	1.1	1.0	1.4	0.9	1.1
Empty garbage	2.0	3.0	1.2	2.2	1.8	2.7
Care for pets	3.9	1.9	1.9	2.3	3.3	2.1
Help cook	1.1	1.5	1.1	1.6	1.4	1.4

habits. Since our data fail to show important differences in chore performance along class lines exclusively, it is difficult to support such theories.

If anything, middle-class parents in our sample seem to be somewhat less intent on using chore responsibilities to inculcate discipline and traditional work values. Similarly, our data offer weak support for certain theories concerned with the socialization of middle-class children for achievement. Some critics of the educational establishment suggest that children from middle-class families are more likely to succeed in school and in adult life because their training at home prepares them especially well for the kinds of work discipline required by better paid and "more responsible" jobs. Contrarily, our data suggest that to the extent that doing chores was considered one way of developing values such as obedience and industriousness, these activities were more common among children from poor and less privileged families. It was in these groups that we found the firmest attachment to chores as a socializing mechanism.

In this sense, our findings are most consistent with those of researchers who have argued that, ironically, it is among lower-class families that one finds children receiving the heaviest doses of traditional, middle-class socialization. Rather than equating a middle-class upbringing with structure and responsibility at home and assuming its absence in lower-class households, a number of scholars have stressed instead the flexibility of the former and the rigid, or even authoritarian, quality of the latter. This perspective has a wide range of adherents, from the students of discipline patterns, like Melvin Kohn and his associates,[15] to the sociolinguists following Basil Bernstein [16] and to the historians of educational reform in the Progressive Era.[17]

Complementing this supposition, our data did indeed reveal differences among parents in terms of child-rearing practices related to chore assignments. When we asked parents at what age they thought their children would be ready to decide for themselves what chores to perform, black parents were more conservative (table 6-10). When we asked how chore responsibilities were actually decided, however, parents of all ethnic groups were split between a consensual and an authoritarian approach (table 6-11). We found no relationship between these decision-making rules and actual levels of performance (table 6-12). This shows that children's chore responsibilities were not arrived at in simple ways and that the frequency of chores was not solely a function of authoritarian child-rearing tendencies.

There are at least two reasons why we can only cautiously connect socialization models with our data on chores: first,

TABLE 6-10. Parents' Views on When Child Should Decide What Chores To Do (horizontal percentages)

	When decide			
Ethnicity	Decides already	7th or 8th grade	9th or 10th grade	11th grade or later
Black	17	16	22	45
White	25	21	25	27
Asian	40	17	15	28
Other	33	20	21	29

TABLE 6-11. Who Decides What Chores Child Will Do (percentages)

	Parent only	Parent and child together
Ethnicity	"Authoritarian"	"Consensual"
Black	50	47
White	48	48
Asian	53	38
Other	45	40

TABLE 6-12. Parents' Views of When Child Should Decide What Chores To Do and Estimated Time Spent on Chores (horizontal percentages)

When child should decide	Time child spent on chores				
	None	Low	Average	High	Very high
Decides now	3	7	45	31	15
7th or 8th grade	1	17	43	34	5
9th or 10th grade	1	16	45	29	9
11th grade or later	2	11	42	34	11

chores played a small role, at most, in the lives of the children; and second, as a result parents were uncertain as to the significance these activities ought to have had. Hence, children were asked or required to do chores for any number of reasons, of which none predominated. But if the link between chores and child-rearing orientations was muted (or different from what might be expected), this was not so in the case of values, attitudes, and uses of allowances and other "income" children received from parents.

CHILDREN'S INCOME AND SPENDING PATTERNS

Children's principal source of income was their parents. Even the majority of those children who worked also received allowances, in most cases larger than the allowances of children who did not have jobs. Parental practices on the matter of allowances varied enormously and in a fashion that seemed to reveal little about the material resources of the family and much about basic child-rearing values: it was not wealthier, but poorer parents who gave their children greater direct access to money.

White parents and those with higher incomes and higher levels of education (the latter not shown) had a much more controlling attitude toward money than others (tables 6-13 and 6-14). They were more likely not to give their children spending money at all, more likely to give it in the form of allowances rather than on demand, and more likely to give smaller amounts.

Consistent with these differences in parental behavior, the children themselves spent the money they received in markedly different ways.[18] Some children said there were necessities on which they had to spend their money. Some reported buying mostly candy and other nonessentials. Others claimed to save (table 6-15). It is noteworthy that black children reported more often both that there were things they had to buy and that they spent on impulse items. They were less likely to report saving.

Attempts to account for these ethnic patterns in terms of factors such as family income, parental employment, family structure, and family size were unsuccessful. Indeed the poorest children from one-parent families whose mothers worked

TABLE 6-13. Money from Parents (horizontal percentages)

Ethnicity and income	On demand	Allowance[a]	No spending money	Weighted (N)
Black				
High income	49	45	3	(65)
Medium income	53	44	2	(135)
Low income	58	39	1	(284)
White				
High income	23	60	15	(53)
Medium income	39	44	15	(46)
Low income	38	48	10	(29)
All Asian	22	53	22	(49)
All other	54	29	12	(50)
All children	49	43	6	(711)

[a]These categories were almost mutually exclusive. Only 1 percent of the sample reported receiving both an allowance and money on demand.

TABLE 6-14. Weekly Allowance (horizontal percentages)

Ethnicity	Less than $1.00	$1.00-1.99	$2.00-4.99	$5.00 or more	Mean allowance per week
Black	10	28	48	14	$2.33
White	30	44	24	2	1.00
Asian	47	37	15	0	1.00
Other	16	37	27	20	2.26

were less conspicuous for greater levels of spending on necessities than for greater outlays on nonessentials. It seemed clear that spending patterns were much more the product of basic attitudes toward money than of the simple availability of resources in the family.

This analysis should be qualified. First, we do not know the actual amount of money families spent on their children. It is possible that wealthier parents gave their children less money because they spent more on them, giving them things beyond the limits of their allowances. Poorer parents, who may have been unable to afford such things, may have allowed children

TABLE 6-15. Children's Use of Money Received from Parents (percentages of children allocating money to various uses)

	All children	Boys	Girls	Black	White	Asian	Other
Discretionary uses							
Saving	27	30	25	24	36	46	21
Buying candy and other nonessentials	54	51	56	59	43	27	49
Going places	19	24	15	22	15	8	11
Necessities							
All necessities	21	21	21	25	11	9	27
Bus fare	11	13	10	15	1	4	4
Lunch	8	7	8	8	3	4	19

greater discretion in making immediate, inexpensive purchases. But this, too, suggests differences in family attitudes toward money.

Second, we do not really know what the apparently more liberal attitudes of poorer parents meant. That poor parents indulge children more than wealthier parents is familiar folklore, and a number of ethnographers, most notably Liebow, [19] have argued that immediate gratification is the most rational response to the prospects of lifelong poverty and periodic unemployment. Thus while controlling access to money may make relatively good sense for parents whose children are being prepared for lives with secure jobs and regular incomes, it may be less logical if the income stream will be irregular and precarious. Contrary speculations are equally persuasive. Learning the value of money may be more important to those who do not have much, and poorer parents may give their children greater access to money so that they will understand its value at an early age.

While we are not prepared to make assertions confidently about the content of these value systems, we do think some modest conclusions can be drawn about the degrees to which families seem to emphasize the socialization potential of different kinds of behaviors. This seems particularly true if we contrast attitudes toward chores with attitudes toward money. Permissiveness in one area is coupled with control in another in a way not well accounted for by most of the literature. There is little consistency. For instance, parents in our sample who appeared to be trying to teach their children the value of money by regulating its availability did not necessarily try also to instill the value of hard work, at least insofar as children's chores were concerned. Those who made certain that their children contributed to the domestic economy, however, seemed less concerned with instilling financial responsibility through the regulation of allowances and access to money. In effect, more privileged parents seemed to have substituted money for work as the focus of their socializing efforts at home, while the less privileged no longer seemed to believe that they should teach their children that hard work is always accompanied by an opportunity to enjoy the material fruits of one's labor.

CHILD-CARE RESPONSIBILITIES

Jobs and chores appear to play minimal roles in the lives of children. One activity, however, is probably of increasing importance to families as mothers return to (or remain in) the paid labor force. Certainly, as long as institutional child care remains inadequate, preadolescents are likely to find themselves pressed occasionally into child-care service.

Child care by children is by no means a new phenomenon, although attitudes toward it in our culture are ambivalent, if not negative. Nevertheless, of all the activities described in this chapter, caretaking by children in our sample was perhaps the most important, both in terms of family needs and in terms of the impact of this kind of obligation and responsibility on the caretaker.

In her famous essay "The School in American Culture," Margaret Mead points out that in many societies the upbringing of young children is a responsibility that falls primarily to grandparents or to older children.[20] Many recent ethnographies bear this out.[21] Even in our own culture the ideal of exclusive parental socialization and child care is far from fully realized even though other caretakers are regarded by some as less legitimate.

Forty percent of the children in our sample reported baby-sitting as one of their responsibilities. This figure, however, is somewhat misleading. Most baby-sitting took place within the baby-sitter's family, so for all intents and purposes the 40 percent of the children in our sample who had no younger siblings lacked the opportunity for such responsibilities. It is true that some children baby-sit for other families, but this would have been quite unusual for youngsters of the age sampled. Only 3 percent of the sample said they baby-sat regularly outside their homes. Many of these twenty-six children (twenty-four of them girls) had no younger siblings. Those who did have younger siblings, however, and engaged in paid baby-sitting were, even so, more likely to baby-sit their own siblings than other children.

We confined our analysis of child-care responsibilities to the 477 children with younger brothers and sisters.* It is clear, first of all, that boys were just as likely as girls to do some baby-sitting (table 6-16). The picture changes, however, when we

---

*Tables 6-16 through 6-19 refer to this subsample.

TABLE 6-16. Baby-sitting Younger Siblings[a] (percentages)

	Ever	Almost daily	4 or 5 days per week	2 or 3 days per week	Once per week	Less often	Never
Sex							
Boys	65	8	5	15	15	22	35
Girls	67	13	8	17	17	13	33
Ethnicity							
Black	63	12	8	15	15	14	37
White	70	7	1	16	18	26	30
Asian	73	10	7	13	10	30	27
Other	78	8	8	23	18	20	20
Total	66	10	7	16	16	17	33

[a]N = 477 (subset of the total sample with younger siblings).

look at how frequently they did it: boys were much more likely to baby-sit less than once a week and much less likely to baby-sit regularly. There was also an interesting variation among ethnic groups. Black children were the most likely not to baby-sit at all, but at the same time those who did baby-sit were far more likely than white children to do it on a regular basis. Children from the other ethnic minorities also were more likely than white children to have regular child-care responsibilities, less likely to be completely free of them.

As with chores, a variety of factors must be considered in order to understand these patterns, including parents' attitudes toward the socialization of the children requiring care and toward the prospective caretaker child. Similarly, family structure (especially number of parents), parental employment, and the availability of child care outside the nuclear family (whether by kin or public or private agencies) are important. Our data do not enable us to address all of these factors. We can explore several, however, and draw a number of inferences.

Frequent baby-sitting was more common when parents worked, both in single-parent and in two-parent families (table 6-17). But children without a full-time homemaker parent were slightly more likely never to have child-care responsibilities. This suggests that baby-sitting by kin or professionals probably played an important role in these families. Sex differences in the amount of baby-sitting also varied with parental employment (table 6-18). The differences were quite large in the traditional two-parent, male breadwinner-housewife family, but negligible in families in which both parents worked.

Diminished sex differences in baby-sitting responsibilities in families with working mothers suggest that in these instances traditional imperatives of sex-role socialization may have been overridden: boys were forced to assume responsibilities they otherwise would not have had simply because they were the only available caretakers. To the extent that this is so, some optimism with respect to long-term redefinition of sex roles among responsibilities at home may be in order—even when the changes are not deliberate and they do not spill over immediately into other areas of personal and social life. It is also

TABLE 6-17. Baby-sitting Responsibilities, Family Structure, and Parental Labor Force Status (horizontal percentages)

Family structure and parents labor force status	Child never baby-sits	Child baby-sits once in a while	Child baby-sits more than once a week	Weighted (N)
Two parents				
One parent works	28	47	26	(123)
Both parents work	36	27	37	(128)
One parent				
Parent not in labor force	35	34	31	(96)
Parent works	31	28	41	(93)

TABLE 6-18. Children who Baby-sit Siblings more than Once a Week, Child's Sex, and Parental Labor Force Status (percentages)

Family structure and parents labor force status	Boys	Girls	Weighted (N)
Two parents			
One parent works	16	35	(123)
Both parents work	35	39	(128)
One parent			
Parent not in labor force	27	35	(96)
Parent works	36	44	(93)

possible that parents in families where the mother worked outside the home had significantly different values than other parents regarding sex roles and child-care responsibilities, independent of scheduling constraints.

The pattern in single-parent families suggests that we must be cautious, for in these cases the increased levels of child care by boys was more than matched by that of girls. This reemergence of sex differences despite presumably greater pressure on parental time probably reflected the fact that child-care responsibilities in single-parent families were more serious and less casual. Under these circumstances many parents may have been more comfortable placing a girl rather than a boy this age in charge. But even if boys' child-care responsibilities became equal to girls' only in two-parent families with a working mother, the impact would still have been important, since these responsibilities exposed boys as well as girls to nurturing roles at an early age.

Ethnic differences in child-care responsibilities increased when the mother worked. Among two-parent families (there were too few white, Asian, and other ethnic minority, single-parent families for comparison) the ethnic differences were marked when both parents worked and slight in the case of traditionally structured families (table 6-19). This was probably in large part a reflection of differences in the availability of professional baby-sitting and relatives, but it also may have been evidence of differences in values and attitudes among parents toward the preadolescent as caretaker.

Our findings suggest that at a time when children's responsibilities at home seem otherwise marginal, changes in family structure and mothers' labor force participation may signal the emergence of a significant domestic role. Whether this is good or bad for young caretakers or whether this places too much pressure on them we cannot know for certain. At the very least it indicates a clear demand for child-care alternatives and, given other findings in this chapter, ironic dependence on the contributions of some preadolescents to the family.

TABLE 6-19. Children who Baby-sit Siblings more than Once a Week and Parental Labor Force Status (percentages)

Family structure and parents labor force status	Black	White	Asian	Other	Weighted (N)
Two parents					
One parent works	27	24	*	23	(128)
Both parents work	43	26	17	*	(123)
One parent					
Parent not in labor force	29	*	*	*	(96)
Parent works	39	*	*	*	(93)

* = small *n*s

CONCLUSION

For children, whose experiences of the world of work outside the home are typically few, chores at home represent the extent of their early productive responsibilities. Our data indicated, even so, that most children's contributions to their household economies were minimal. Despite this marginality, chores appeared to reinforce certain child-rearing norms and to foster acceptance of largely traditional sex roles.

Another commonly recognized function of children's responsibilities is to inculcate an understanding of and respect for the value of money. We found that allowances and other rules regarding spending money were used by most parents to teach economic lessons. Receipt of allowances and spending money, however, was usually not connected to children's actual work experiences.

Such dissociation between productive activities and actual rewards gives preadolescents some subtle insights into the meaning of work in adult life: that the satisfactions derived from working may be few, perhaps limited to economic rewards—and even these may be disappointing. If this proves true for the children in our sample, the ambivalence many of their parents exhibited toward their own productive roles shall have been perpetuated; it was already reflected in most children's attitudes toward this domain of time use.

While some kinds of early work experiences are important for children, our data suggest that these opportunities at home and away from home are very limited for preadolescents. Hence, we must wonder how these children will come to hold positive attitudes toward work and to regard themselves as competent and productive adults.

seven

ORGANIZED ACTIVITIES

Work and play blend more readily in children's than in adults' lives. Nowhere is this more evident than in the domain we call organized activities. There the most challenging experience can be great fun and play can be taken much too seriously. Lessons, groups, clubs, and other organized, adult-led activities can turn out-of-school time use into valuable investments in the future child as well as enjoyment for the present child. The same activities can equally reflect and perpetuate many undesirable cultural qualities, including social inequality, overcompetitiveness, and sex stereotyping. Viewed from either perspective, organized activities are more than just fun and games.

In this chapter we examine some of the objectives associated with the provision of children's organized activities and then explore the actual dimensions of the domain for the children in our study. While the vast majority of children were involved in a small way at least, the quality of their experiences varied substantially.

Although readers may have an intuitive definition of the domain in mind, a precise terminology is necessary. By *organized* we mean supervised by adults and administered by some agency or formal organization. *Activities* herein encompasses clubs, groups, teams, lessons, extracurricular school programs, and squads. In short, organized activities are uses of time that are purposive, ongoing, structured, and more or less voluntarily chosen (although parental and peer pressures may influence the process of making choices).*

PROVIDING ORGANIZED ACTIVITIES FOR CHILDREN

Efforts to provide organized activities for children have a venerable, if sometimes controversial, history.[1] The tradition dates at least to the late nineteenth century, when philanthropists and settlement house leaders founded a variety of programs to ameliorate what they saw as moral, social, and environmental deprivation among the burgeoning urban immigrant working class. Some of these programs evolved into municipal agencies, and over time the private sources of funding diminished relatively. Recreation programs, for instance, were clearly rooted in this earlier era and expanded throughout the first three decades of the twentieth century with increasing public-sector support. By the Depression, the Lynds[2] and others[3] reported that a wide variety of programs for young people, many involving adult supervision, had become established as part of the range of services offered by municipalities of all sizes. In the 1930s, innovative federal relief programs, including the Works Progress Administration, National Youth Administration, and Civilian Conservation Corps, filled the budgetary breach and even expanded the level of local programming through job training and public works.[4]

Children's services today are somewhat more elaborate, but fundamentally similar to those extant by the second world war. As much as $1.5 billion, or nearly 2 percent of municipal budgets, are allocated for after-school programs, services, and facilities today.[5] It is estimated that several billion dollars more are comparably expended by private and quasi-public service agencies.[6]

Organized activities serve the needs of parents and those who provide the activities as well as needs of their young clients. It is important to understand these explicit and implicit agen-

---

*By our definition a club that a group of boys forms on its own would not be included no matter how elaborately organized its rituals might be. The Boys' Clubs of America, however, would be included because of their institutionalized nature.

das, for they are the background against which one can evaluate the place of the services in the daily lives of families.

Those who provide organized activities for children articulate several social objectives. The first of these involves child development. Children have a lot of free time that could be used to sharpen their cognitive, creative, and physical skills. In this sense, it is argued, out-of-school time can be used to supplement in-school experiences. A second objective is socialization. Organized activities can be used to teach social values and foster positive self-images, cooperative spirit, and self-discipline. These programs parallel efforts of family, school, and church to inculcate socially desirable norms and behaviors and "to build character."

Although these general objectives may be universal, services have divergent intentions and effects as well. Programs for the urban poor commonly have served the ideological and practical goal of social control: curbing delinquency and reducing violent, antisocial, or self-destructive behavior. This is pursued by instilling proper values in young people, exposing them to mainstream culture, dismantling gangs and cliques, and generally keeping them occupied. Some contemporary recreation programs also include personal and group counseling of various kinds. For the upper and middle classes program emphasis has been on opportunity enhancement. This assumes that children are growing up properly and that after-school activities are for the purpose of enrichment: providing a framework within which children can explore, improve, and expand their skills and capabilities. Most programs serve both social control and opportunity enhancement objectives, the composition of the clientele determining which is dominant. Those who provide after-school services, whether in the private or public sector, recognize that they serve many constituencies, from children seeking entertainment to politicians hoping to buy social peace to parents looking for an alternative to television as a babysitter. They recognize, too, that organized activities that fail to entertain or engross children will not achieve their other developmental, social, and educational objectives. Public and non-profit recreation and cultural programs have always had to compete with flashier, commercial alternatives for children's attention. Whether compared with old-time, "sinful" pool halls and pulp magazines or to shopping centers and television in the modern era, public recreation usually has appeared relatively dowdy, sedate, and adult-approved.

Organized activities have some of the characteristics of a market and some of a social service. As a marketplace, numerous suppliers compete for the attention of consumers—children and parents—who are mostly free to take or leave activities as they please. As with many social services, there are centralized budgeting decisions and professional guidelines for "the best interests of the child" which largely determine what will be available. The domain of organized activities is an unsettled amalgam of commerce and politics, and of the private and public sectors. As our analysis of the relationships between life circumstances and participation in activities unfolds, we shall see some of the conflicting goals and tensions—between frivolity and serious learning, social control and opportunity enhancement, and consumer choices and bureaucratic imperatives.

Service providers may have the most intense, sustained interest in these fiscal and ideological issues, but parents and children also hold strong opinions that will affect the course of future programs. For our purposes here, the providers' concerns are primarily a background against which we view the attitudes and actions of our survey respondents.[7]

In chapter three we noted that parents' satisfaction with community-based children's services—schools, libraries, parks, and recreation—varied systematically with their income and educational level, with overall neighborhood satisfaction, and with the perceived responsiveness of city government to individual needs. The higher the economic status of the neighborhood and the greater the sense of political efficacy among its residents, the more favorable were the ratings of children's services. In almost all areas surveyed, however, parents expressed relatively more dissatisfaction with recreation and parks, the agencies responsible for many organized after-school activities, than with any other services. Dissatisfaction was greatest in low-income, minority neighborhoods. The poor ratings given to these services likely reflected discontent with cutbacks induced by current fiscal conditions and the perceived poor quality of remaining programs. As far as we were able to determine, Oakland's parents were still solidly behind the general goals of after-school activities and felt that the public sector should continue to provide them.

Parents in our survey were generally very favorably disposed toward organized activities. Three out of four believed that "organized activities are an important part of a child's education," and other questionnaire items regarding their usefulness and desirability generated a similarly positive consensus. This approval held across all levels of education and income, throughout all neighborhoods, and for all ethnic groups. Most parents thought organized activities were valuable, regardless of whether their children had been involved with any in the past year or whether they had facilitated their child's involvement in any way.

Even if parents' values were often instrumental in determining what programs were offered and who took part, it was ultimately the children whose judgment carried the most weight. They could, with few exceptions, vote with their feet, terminating involvement in activities that did not satisfy their needs or interests. Organized activities were generally rated favorably by participants. Most of the activities were undertaken on the child's initiative, and only about 5 percent of the activities were explicitly disliked by the respondents. Even given the tendency for survey responses to understate dissatisfaction, this seems to be a remarkably low figure.

Another way of looking at children's satisfaction is to examine their reasons for terminating participation. Almost half the activities in which respondents had enrolled during the school year had ended for one reason or another: the course had been completed, the instructor had quit, the season had ended, or there had been some other turn of events beyond the child's control. One other reason accounted for a quarter of all terminations: as time passed children got bored. Indeed, very few children withdrew for any other reason.

There was some evidence in the survey that children who participated in organized activities were less bored with their discretionary time than nonparticipants. The respondents were asked to evaluate the statement, "After school and on week-ends, I often feel bored and don't know what to do."* The summary measure of participation in organized activities and the measure of involvement in organized sports activities were both associated with lower levels of boredom among children of all ethnic and income groups.

Given the aforementioned socialization objectives of orga-nized activities, it could be expected that involvement would produce measurable psychological effects. In fact, the children who undertook organized programs did not rate themselves appreciably differently from nonparticipants on our indicators of self-esteem or desire for more friends. Nor did controlling for ethnicity or family income elicit significant association between participation and self-concept within groups. This, of course, does not necessarily mean that the activities were having no such effects. But their impact would likely be cumulative, long-term, indirect, and linked to the influences of other types of time use.

THE ORGANIZED ACTIVITIES DOMAIN

There was tremendous diversity within the domain of orga-nized activities with regard to their substance, their structures, and their management styles. Our survey identified a wide range of leisure pursuits: over sixty different types of groups, lessons, and school activities (table 7-1). But the domain as the individ-ual child saw it was more limited: children did not actually choose from the entire array of programs. Participation, rather, was partly a function of conditions that influenced both the availability of activities and the child's interests and preferences.

A vast majority of children in the study (79 percent) were involved in at least one after-school activity during the school year (average: 2.6 activities per child), their participation con-fined largely (61 percent of all cases) to just thirteen categories of activity.

How one evaluates these global statistics depends in part on some prior expectations and theories. First, when designing the survey instrument, we entertained some fears of having a pre-

---

*This is the same measure of boredom reported in chapter four.

TABLE 7-1. Organized Activities: Lessons and Groups

Activity	Lessons		Groups		Number of* children participating	Percentages of all children (N:764)
	Boys	Girls	Boys	Girls		
Sports						
Swimming	18	11	3	2	34	4
Tennis	12	21	0	0	32	4
Skating	9	21	0	1	31	4
Martial arts	47	10	1	0	58	8
Other individual or two-person sport	1	9	9	8	27	4
Baseball	25	14	93	32	162	21
Basketball	15	7	53	4	77	10
Football	8	0	56	1	65	9
Soccer	1	2	20	4	25	3
Kickball	0	0	1	18	19	3
Other team ball sports (volleyball, softball)	3	0	7	31	41	5
Fine Arts						
Music	33	34	1	2	66	9
Dancing	5	71	0	4	77	10
Dramatics/acting	4	11	0	0	15	2
Art (drawing, painting)	35	28	0	0	63	8
Crafts (pottery, jewelry, etc.)	16	30	0	0	46	6
Clubs and organizations						
Social club			5	22	27	4
Boys' club			73	0	73	10
Girl Scouts			0	64	64	8
Boy Scouts of America			62	0	62	8
Campfire Girls			0	8	8	1
YMCA			14	5	19	3
YWCA			1	6	7	1

TABLE 7-1. Organized Activities: Lessons and Groups (Continued)

Activity	Lessons		Groups		Number of* children participating	Percentages of all children (N:764)
	Boys	Girls	Boys	Girls		
Religious						
Religious instruction or church activities	51	59	21	45	158	21
Other instruction						
Nature study or science	12	9	0	0	21	3
Cooking or sewing	19	49	0	0	66	9
Charm school	0	4	0	3	7	1
Mechanics or shop	2	2	0	0	4	1
Ethnic heritage	3	4	1	1	9	1
Other						
Other activities	2	3	0	0	5	1
Total number of activities	323	398	422	259		
Percent of total activities	45	55	62	38		

*The data in the first four columns are based on the actual number of activities children in our study were involved in, whereas the data in the fifth column represent the number of children involved in each activity listed. Thus, where columns 1-4 total more than column 5, children who took more than one activity in a given category are being represented (e.g., a child who took lessons in more than one musical instrument).

ponderance of nonusers and long lists of categories with no responses. That contingency did not materialize. That a majority of respondents did at least two activities would seem to justify our continued interest. Second, much as educators have sometimes measured social progress by the quantity of time spent in schools, so someone with a generalized belief in the value of organized activities might evaluate our summary statistics favorably, assuming the more activities a child participated in the better.[8]

But just as the amount of time spent in the classroom does not tell us much about the effect of schooling so the amount of time spent in organized activities should be only the beginning of our inquiry. Out of innumerable bits of data collected, we derived four general perspectives, each helpful for understanding the domain and its relevance for our sample population:

Subject—What is being played or learned, such as sports or music? What types of organizations are being joined, such as scouting?

Format—Is the activity done as a lesson, a group, or a school program?

Sponsorship—Who is offering the activity: a public or private institution?

Enabling conditions—Are there particular participation requirements, such as time, money, information, or transportation? Must parents facilitate participation? What level of services are provided in each neighborhood?

Subject, format, sponsorship, and enabling conditions, taken together, largely determine children's experiences with organized activities.

Subject

The most fundamental attribute of any organized activity is its subject. Preconditions and arrangements notwithstanding, a child's participation in an out-of-school program is predicated on interest or anticipated reward.

The subjects of respondents' activities were a mixture of tradition and contemporary fads. In some cases, such as scouting, the label was the same as fifty years ago, but the day-to-day program had many new dimensions. A few activities were so evanescent as to have precipitously declined in popularity in the year between our first pretest and final survey: kung fu lessons were a notable example. For the most part, however, the surveyed activities fit easily into familiar and enduring clusters, such as sports, creative and performing arts, religious activities, and social groups.

Not surprisingly, the most diversified and widespread category was sports. Various team and individual athletic pursuits accounted for 41 percent of all lessons and groups, and 34 percent of the extracurricular school activities done after school hours. More than half the children (58 percent: 71 percent of the boys, 47 percent of the girls) took part in at least one sports program.

Programs in the performing and creative arts accounted for approximately 20 percent of all groups and lessons and were used by 28 percent of the children (21 percent of the boys, 35 percent of the girls). Except for dance, which was almost exclusively a girls' activity, the arts drew children of both sexes in substantial proportions.

The third most extensive category, clubs and organizations, accounted for nearly one-fifth of all activities. This included Boy Scouts and Girl Scouts, Boys' Clubs, Campfire Girls, YMCA and YWCA, and comparable, unspecified local clubs. Of course, since a variety of things take place under the auspices of these groups, they are not strictly single-purpose activities like music lessons. These groups' programs, familiar to most readers, include varying proportions of games, sports, cultural activities, field trips, and community service (more likely recycling paper and metal than helping little old ladies crossing streets), and in some cases a fair amount of fund raising.

Religious instruction and church-related activities totaled 13 percent of all activities (62 percent of these were lessons; 38 percent group activities, such as choirs and social clubs). These activities were more frequently said to be the parents' ideas than were activities of other kinds but were not disliked by a significantly higher proportion of participants. Church-related and religious activities involved 21 percent of all children, and roughly equal proportions of boys and girls (19 and 22 percent, respectively).

Lessons in other subjects combined for a total of nearly 8 percent of all activities. Courses of instruction voluntarily undertaken by our sixth-graders included nature study, science, ethnic heritage, mechanical arts, sewing, cooking, and that elusive and ineffable asset, charm. Though the numbers in most categories were too small for rigorous analysis, they showed trends nevertheless. For instance, while charm school remained an exclusively female preserve, most of the others showed substantial involvement of boys and girls, even in stereotypically single-sex pursuits, such as cooking or shop. Studies done in the 1940s and 1950s showed these to have been strictly segregated.[9]

It was very unusual for any activity to attract youngsters from a cross section of the entire sample: the life circumstances of participants correlated fairly clearly with specific sports or fine arts programs. Not only were those who took dance lessons, for example, almost exclusively girls, they were mostly nonwhite and from middle- or low-income neighborhoods. Music lessons out of school attracted equal numbers of boys and girls who were mostly white and mostly from high-income families and neighborhoods. Individual tastes did not account for these kinds of differences. Sex difference seemed rather to reflect values in the larger culture that, although changing, still tend to saddle dance, for instance, with a "sissy" image among boys. As for class or ethnic distinctions, we suspect that the answers lie, not in the aesthetic attraction of any art form for any particular group, but in clear differences in the sponsorship, format, and enabling conditions under which they were taught in Oakland. The conditions were themselves partly a function of those same class and ethnic divisions writ large.

Format

For analytical purposes every organized activity undertaken by the children was enumerated as part of one, and only one, format: a lesson, a group, or a school program.

Lessons took place in classes or individual settings where the primary purpose was specifically to impart knowledge and to increase the child's skills and/or understanding of a particular subject. The primary purpose of a group was to do activities as part of a social situation. Thus, for example, a child could have taken basketball lessons as one activity and at a separate time and place played on a recreation center team, which would have been designated a group in this analysis. Fourteen subject categories had participants in both groups and lessons (table 7-1).

School programs were a mixture of activities that included training, performing, socializing, and assisting in the operations of the school (table 7-2). In every case involvement was voluntary and not part of the regular curriculum.

TABLE 7-2. Extracurricular School Activities

Activity	Boys	Girls	All participants	Percentage before or after school hours	Percentage during school hours
School sports teams	135	119	254	74	26
Cheerleaders or drill team	23	50	73	56	44
Chorus	64	152	216	44	56
Traffic patrol	161	149	310	40	60
Band	92	92	184	27	73
Magazine or newspaper	49	52	101	14	86
Student council	43	38	81	10	90
Music lessons	128	124	252	7	93
Office helpers	89	135	224	6	94
Tutoring	79	151	230	3	97
Other activities			87		
Percent of total activities	45	55	100	29	71

During the year of our survey our sixth-graders availed themselves of roughly equal numbers of lessons and groups (721
lessons, 681 groups). The total number of school activities
undertaken was 2,011. Only 29 percent took place outside
school hours. (In this discussion, the extra-hours subset is our
main concern.)

Lessons and groups claimed a small majority of the sample as
participants, 53 percent and 51 percent respectively. (table 7-3).
School programs outside school hours involved 42 percent of
the sample, or 322 children, including some at each of the
surveyed schools.

Even though all three formats showed broad-based attendance among sixth-graders, participants in each were dissimilar
in many respects. Lesson takers were, on average, from families
of significantly higher educational attainment and economic
status than participants in school programs. Participants in

TABLE 7-3. Participants in Lessons, Groups, and School Programs (percentages)

Ethnicity	Format			Weighted (N)
	Lessons	Groups	School programs[a]	
White	60	52	33	(134)
Black	52	56	47	(530)
Asian	48	32	28	(49)
Other	49	24	29	(51)
All children	53	51	43	(764)

[a]Includes only school programs occurring outside regular school hours.

groups ranked in between and were a more heterogeneous population. There were also some noticeable ethnic differences in levels of participation. White children comprised the highest proportion of participants in lessons, black children in groups (by a 4 percent margin) and school programs (by 14 percent). Children of other ethnic groups were less likely than blacks or whites to participate in either.

These differences indicate that format has two related meanings. First, it is a functional definition referring to the kinds of time use—learning, playing, socializing—that occurred in organized settings. Second, it is a proxy for social status. An analogy to adult leisure behavior may help illuminate this distinction. Among adults it is common to acknowledge class distinctions in the subjects of leisure-time activities. Many sports, styles of music, and other forms of recreation and culture have stereotypical, if not static, class identifications. Fox hunting, dirt biking, and racquetball conjure very different images of their typical adherents, and at times the activities become synonymous with the types of people they attract (for instance, "the horsey set"). These kinds of distinctions are less clear among preadolescents, for the range of their activities is relatively less broad and the links between subject and social status are less apparent. The use of one format instead of another, however, signifies some of these status distinctions: children who took lessons, no matter what the subjects, tended to come from more materially advantaged backgrounds than those who took none or those whose exposure was limited to programs at their public school.

Beyond these differences in activity preferences that seem linked to social status, each format had a characteristic sex profile. Lessons and school programs had very similar profiles: 45 percent boys, 55 percent girls. Groups were dominated by boys (62 percent).

One-third of lessons* and one-fifth of school programs were segregated, either all boys or all girls. Fully two-thirds of group activities were also sex-segregated, according to the children's responses.** Thus there was very little contact between children of opposite sexes in the kind of activities, and groups, where social interaction was the prominent distinguishing feature.

These findings concerning socioeconomic, ethnic, and sex differences among participants in the three formats are preliminary. Some of the differences were undoubtedly due to the formats per se. Many questions, however, cannot be answered without reference to other program characteristics considered singly or in relation to one another.

Sponsorship

Understanding the importance of program sponsorship requires a brief look at the political status of municipal recreation. The contemporary fiscal crisis of local government is forcing a reexamination of the public sector's responsibilities to children for recreation and culture. As budgets become increasingly constrained, more programs have instituted fees, cut back on the number and variety of offerings, and reduced their outreach efforts. A greater reliance on volunteers to supervise children and the "privatization" of public services both have become part of the conventional theory and practice of coping with shrinking resources in central cities, suburbs, and rural areas. Not surprisingly, many observers fear that program adjustments of this sort will create disproportionately greater difficulties for children from low-income and time-poor families.[10]

While our survey predated California's Proposition 13 by two

---

*This figure excludes individualized lessons.

**This figure excludes the Boy Scouts and Girl Scouts, Boys' Clubs, and Campfire Girls, which are single-sex by definition. With these groups included, the proportion would have been 77 percent.

years, it was conducted at a time when budget cuts of similar magnitude were being contemplated in Oakland because of a local revenue crisis. Recreation and library officials protested that they had already been "cut to the bone" by continual—but incremental rather than catastrophic—funding reductions. There has been a persistent trend toward proportionately greater reductions in services to children than in other components of leisure services provision in Oakland and other cities.[11]

Private, nonprofit youth service agencies face many similar financial problems, albeit within a different administrative context. Groups such as the YMCA and YWCA, scouting, and Boy's Clubs have to meet rising costs without pricing themselves out of the youth market. And at the same time that some public services are being privatized, some private, nonprofit agencies are growing increasingly dependent on private, state, and federal government grants. Perhaps in the long run the fiscal restructuring of recreation and cultural services will diminish the distinction between the public and private sectors. For the present, however, the dichotomy remains important and relatively clear.

Many of the basic functional differences between public and private services result in complementarity rather than competition. Public agencies traditionally have offered introductory lessons and primary exposure to athletics and the arts, leaving advanced and specialized instruction to private providers. Public programs have generally (in the past) been inexpensive if not free to the users, while most private agencies have charged fees to cover all or part of their costs. Many public agencies provide services that are neighborhood based, while most private providers seek clients from a broader population. Of course, certain religious, political, and ethnic-cultural subjects that public agencies do not normally offer are supplied under private auspices.

The children in our survey were divided into four groups in order to examine these distinctions and their consequences in greater detail: those who only participated in private activities, those who only participated in public activities, those who mixed public and private, and those who did not participate in organized activities at all.

Children using only private programs were a distinct minority (only 14 percent) even when all public school programs were excluded from consideration. Not surprisingly, these children were found more frequently in families of higher income and education (table 7-4). White and Asian children were more likely to be included than those of other ethnic groups. Blacks and whites had nearly identical public/private participation rates in the low-income categories but markedly different rates in high-income categories. High-income white children were the only group more likely to have used private programs than public ones. Comparable contingency tables were run using mother's education in place of family income, with similar results: children with highly educated parents tended to do more private activities. The "private only" children constituted the closest thing to an elite to be found in this domain.

Enabling Conditions

Children are dependent on their parents to meet many of the conditions for participating in organized activities. Since parental resources are not equal and parental attitudes concerning the activities vary, certain children may be less likely to participate in activities that have many enabling conditions. We found that lessons and privately sponsored activities tended to have more enabling conditions than other programs.

Time

Participating in activities takes time from a child's day. In some instances it also takes parent time (e.g., if a parent must drive the child to the activity). Finding time did not appear to

TABLE 7-4. Participation in Publicly or Privately Sponsored Groups and Lessons (percentages)

Family income and ethnicity	Public activities only	Private activities only	Weighted (N)
$20,000 or more			
White	19	29	(53)
Black	32	15	(65)
$10,000 or less			
White	40	10	(30)
Black	41	10	(285)

have been a problem for the children in the sample. With the average child doing one or two activities at any given point in the school year,* typically only a couple of weekday afternoons were required: that kind of time was readily available to most children. Asked why they had terminated participation in particular activities or had not been able to join ones they desired, fewer than 5 percent mentioned time constraints.

Intuitively we expected that families with all resident adults employed would have less time to facilitate a child's involvement in organized activities. In fact, few differences could be found in the actual levels of facilitation by employed and nonworking mothers:

Mothers employed full time are in some respects working harder to attain the same level of facilitation as nonworking mothers. While they manage to accomplish roughly the same amount of driving, information gathering, registering, and volunteering, to do so they must allocate a larger amount of their available time. In the first place they have literally fewer hours in which to do these tasks, especially since in most homes their housework burden is not equally shared. Secondly, they face more scheduling constraints, and have fewer options than the housewife or nonemployed parent as to when and in what ways they will facilitate their children's participation in organized activities.[12]

Family size, parents' work schedules, and other structural factors can create serious scheduling problems, but few of these factors appeared to have had a serious effect on children's levels of participation in organized activities.

Parents' Knowledge, Approval, and Facilitation of Organized Activities

Organized activities had the general approval of the vast majority of parents surveyed, but when specific attitudes and concrete actions were probed—how decisions should be made within the family regarding participation in these activities, for example—parents showed more divergence along social, economic, and ethnic lines. The matrix of parents' attitudes toward organized activities, and the accompanying cluster analysis, illustrate the divergence of two groupings. Cluster A (table 7-5)

---

*The average of 2.6 activities per child was spread over the entire school year and included many that were no longer offered at the time of our survey.

TABLE 7-5. Parents' Attitudes toward Organized Activities (matrix of measures of association [Gamma] between 7 items using scale of 1 = agree, 2 = not sure, and 3 = disagree)

	1	2	3	4	5	6	7
1 Children themselves usually know best what after-school activities they will get something out of	—	+.488	+.427	+.193	-.296	-.223	-.052
2 Children should decide themselves if they want to be in organized activities after school		—	+.410	+.100	-.410	-.328	+.104
3 Children should have more say in deciding what activities the city sets up for them			—	+.037	-.279	-.178	+.266
4 Children can learn at least as much by being with parents as by spending time in organized activities				—	+.043	+.027	-.112
5 Parents should decide what after-school activities their children should be in					—	+.460	-.011
6 If parents let their children do as they please after school they usually won't do anything worthwhile						—	+.027
7 Organized after-school activities are an important part of any child's education							

Cluster analysis: Cluster A, "Permissive," items 1, 2, 3. Cluster B, "Authoritative," items 5, 6. Coefficient of Belonging = 5.02. Coefficient of Belonging = 2.83. These are the most highly associated groupings. Coefficients for both clusters would be substantially diminished by the addition of item 4. An acceptable minimum Coefficient of Belonging denoting a cluster is 1.30. Hence both clusters A and B are highly identifiable. Cluster analysis techniques are described by Herman J. Loether and Donald G. McTavish, *Descriptive Statistics for Sociologists* (Boston: Allyn and Bacon, 1974), chap. 10.

can be labeled "permissive" and Cluster B "authoritative." [13]
Permissive parents believed that children at this age could
decide for themselves many things that authoritative parents
retained as their prerogative. It has been theorized that this
permissiveness is often the result of successful internalization of
norms by children. In other words, these permissive parents are
confident that their ends will largely be met without direct
intervention. The two items concerning the importance of
organized activities (items 4 and 7) belong to neither cluster,
since support for these programs was widespread among all
groups.

The items in the permissiveness cluster were all positively
correlated with mother's education. The authoritative cluster
was correlated with lower levels of education (table 7-6). Asian
parents tended to support the authoritative values much more
strongly than whites, with some of that support still evident
after controlling for education. Black parents also accepted
certain permissive values nearly as strongly as whites, especially
children's right to participate in the planning of municipal
recreation programs (item 3). On this issue it was only the Asian
parents who disagreed in a proportion substantially above the
mean (32 percent of Asian parents disagreed compared with 16
percent of the entire sample). This finding may reflect values
rooted in cultural experience. Although Asian children participated in many activities and at average rates, their parents
showed the lowest level of involvement in political and neighborhood issues concerning children's services. It is possible,

TABLE 7-6. "Authoritative" Attitudes Toward Organized Activities (horizontal
percentages)

Mother's education	"Parents should decide what after-school activities their children should be in."			
	Agree	Not sure	Disagree	Weighted (N)
Less than high school diploma	48	14	38	(195)
High school graduate	52	10	38	(216)
Some college	39	9	52	(214)
College graduate and above	33	7	60	(88)
All parents	46	10	44	(734)

therefore, that their lack of enthusiasm for children's involvement in planning these activities stems from their own relative distance from much public decision making.

Parents' attitudes concerning who should choose their children's activities did not always match their practices. Parents who believed that they ought to choose programs for their children were only slightly more likely than others (20 to 13 percent) to have suggested ones that their sixth-graders actually did. This dissonance between attitudes and practices can be explained partly by returning to the matter of formats. While only 5 percent of the children who took school programs credited their parents with the idea for their having participated, 26 percent of the lesson takers had been so encouraged. Of the three formats, only with regard to lessons did the likelihood of parental suggestions increase with family socioeconomic status. Apparently then, even though parents' attitudes toward decision making may have been correlated systematically with socioeconomic status, their actions were more strongly influenced by the formats of the activities. In the case of lessons this meant that parents rated most permissive in terms of stated values were most authoritative in practice. Perhaps higher-status parents, as much as their children, have internalized norms about lessons being the most constructive use of discretionary time.

The extent to which a parent could find or encourage participation in organized activities was partly a function of information received. Schools and neighborhood park and recreation services reached the majority of households with at least minimal information about their after-school or weekend activities. By contrast, three out of four surveyed parents reported that they had heard nothing about offerings of the local library or museum. Two-thirds of the parents also reported that they had received some program information through the mail or a note sent home from school "once in a while." While we are not able to evaluate the effectiveness of other forms of media and publicity, it would appear that mail and notices from school reached the most households. Some of the more specialized information that families received was the result of previous contact with the agency. Highly educated parents received more information about nonschool programs, but the difference was not significant, nor is it possible to say with certainty how much of this information was the result, rather than the cause, of a child's recent involvements.

All but a handful of lessons and groups required some written registration, with lessons being slightly more likely than groups to be handled by parents (table 7-7). Significantly more lesson registrations required a special trip for that purpose on the mother's part.

We categorized five types of approval and parental facilitation. The first four, denoting active involvement (table 7-8), all indicated significantly higher levels of activity among higher-income mothers. Greater disparities between high and low income were found in driving and volunteering, actions that required relatively more time and greater financial resources. In chapter five we saw that with regard to these forms of facilitation, parents were differentiated more by their incomes than by their time availability.

Expenses

The principal expenses for organized activities were fees or dues for membership and charges for equipment, uniforms, or other paraphernalia. Seventy-three percent of the group activities undertaken by respondents required some expenditure compared with 53 percent of lessons and just 14 percent of school programs (all of the latter were equipment rentals).*

While we do not have data on amounts, it is safe to assume that most individualized lessons or small classes were more expensive than membership in scout troops or ball teams. Incidentally, there is no evidence in our survey or in the literature that any appreciable number of children of this age paid for organized activities out of their own pockets.

Children who only used free activities outnumbered those who exclusively used fee-charging activities (tables 7-9 and

---

*It was not legal in 1976 for schools to charge for extracurricular activities though other agencies using school facilities could levy fees for certain activities. Since the passage of Proposition 13, many public schools in California, mostly high schools, have begun charging for membership on teams and in clubs.

TABLE 7-7. Registration for Groups and Lessons

Who signed child up for activity? (vertical percentages)		
	Lesson	Group
No signup necessary	3	1
Child	49	54
Mother	39	36
Someone else	8	9
Don't know/no answer	1	0
(Weighted number of activities)	(719)	(680)

If mother signed, did she make a special trip for this purpose? (vertical percentages)		
	Lesson	Group
Yes	37	22
No	61	77
Don't know/no answer	2	1
(Weighted number of activities)	(280)	(247)

TABLE 7-8. Approval and Facilitation of Organized Activities (percentages)

Mother	All mothers	Family income[a]		
		Low	Middle	High
Registered child for at least one after-school activity this year	40	37	38	53
Drove child regularly to at least one organized activity this year	22	10	27	44
Has actively sought organized programs for child to join	47	41	54	58
Volunteered in at least one organized activity for children in last year	34	27	37	50
Agrees: organized after-school activities are an important part of any child's education	75	78	76	66

[a]Low = Less than $10,000/year
Middle = $10,000-$19,999/year
High = $20,000 or more

7-10). Whites and Asians were heavier users of fee-charging programs, and income had a much stronger effect on white children's activity selection than on those of black children (table 7-11).

This finding provides another reason for carefully distinguishing among variables. Whereas in the analysis of public and private sponsorship mother's education had effects similar to those of family income, no such parallelism appeared in the analysis of free and fee-charging activities. This difference was

TABLE 7-9. Use of Lessons and Groups by Fee Structure (vertical percentages)

Category of children	
Those who took only activities that cost money	19
Those who took only free activities	28
Those who took both free and fee-charging activities	27
Those who took no organized activities	26
Weighted (N)	(764)

TABLE 7-10. Participation Exclusively in Free or Fee-charging Lessons and Groups (percentages)

Ethnicity	Free activities only	Fee-charging activities only	Weighted (N)
White	16	33	(134)
Black	33	14	(530)
Asian	17	39	(49)
Other	29	16	(51)
All children	28	19	(764)

TABLE 7-11. Participation Exclusively in Free or Fee-charging Lessons and Groups and Family Income (percentages)

Ethnicity and family income	Free activities only	Fee-charging activities only	Weighted (N)
$20,000 or more			
White	8	40	(53)
Black	20	21	(65)
$10,000 or less			
White	23	20	(30)
Black	35	13	(285)

to be expected since fees for programs are a direct drain on family finances, while the link between fees and the educational dimension of social class is more indirect.

Transportation

The data on the means of transportation taken to get home from groups and lessons show great similarities (table 7-12). Walking, bicycling, and public transit—children's autonomous means of mobility—accounted for 70 percent of the cases. Thirty percent involved chauffeuring. School-based programs were within walking or biking distance of nearly all the children's homes, so only the few who did not attend their neighborhood schools were at a disadvantage.

The parents' accounts of regularly driving their children places they wanted to go were positively associated with family income—of course, so was having a car in the first place. Other variables showed insignificant effect.

Neighborhood Facilities

The fact that more than two-thirds of the organized activities were reached by children on foot or bicycle reinforces the close-to-home quality of the domain. It is reasonable to expect, therefore, that if levels of program availability and quality vary among neighborhoods, then participation rates might reflect those differences, all other things being equal. This hypothesis was tested in several ways, with the neighborhood effects generally appearing much less pronounced than expected.

TABLE 7-12. "How Did You Get Home From This Organized Activity?" (vertical percentages)

	Lessons	Groups
Walk or bicycle	58	58
Parent drives	20	16
Other adult drives	10	14
Bus	12	12
Other means	1	1
(Weighted number of activities)[a]	(691)	(674)

[a]Excluding 35 activities that were conducted at child's home.

Principals of the sampled schools were questioned concerning the provision of various activities at their sites. Responses showed that there were some differences among schools in the clubs and teams offered to sixth-graders. These differences, however, in no way compared with the magnitude of the differences in participation levels among schools. For example, two schools in the same ethnic and socioeconomic strata that were located at opposite ends of the city were found to have nominally the same extracurricular offerings but vastly different rates of participation. Clearly, the popularity of extracurricular activities depended in part on intangible aspects of the quality and vitality of the programs, which we could not measure directly. Also, our interviews with several community leaders and children's program administrators and our survey data on neighborhood socializing patterns suggest that neighborhoods with higher rates of participation had more cohesion (as measured by variables such as population stability and level of social interaction).[14]

Disparities among neighborhoods in the provision of recreational facilities were substantial in Oakland (and they remain so). The variation arose less from the distribution of school district properties than from that of recreation centers, parks, libraries, and other municipal facilities, where many organized children's activities take place. No measure, however, showed any significant correlation between participation and the number of relevant facilities in the neighborhood.*

A summary variable of service quality yielded more interesting, though less straightforward results. Children in neighborhoods with high and medium levels of services showed somewhat higher levels of participation (table 7-13). This is not evidence of causality. Rather, it speaks to the positive relationship between neighborhood service level and neighborhood mean family income.

The connections between wealth and access to public and private facilities created some use patterns that reflected the

---

*The variables analyzed were tennis lessons, basketball group activities, all sports groups, crafts lessons, all fine arts lessons, and extracurricular school programs. None of the zero order correlations was above .09.

TABLE 7-13. Neighborhood Services and Participation in Organized Activities
(vertical percentages)

Number of activities done by child	Level of services in neighborhood[a]		
	Low	Medium	High
0	26	11	20
1	22	18	20
2 or more	52	71	60
Weighted (N)	(436)	(211)	(117)

[a]Neighborhood service summary includes measures of per capita value of investment in park and recreation facilities, number of school extracurricular activities, and size and proximity of nearest two branch libraries, as well as an indicator of specialized children's services at those branches.

dual market for activities described earlier. In neighborhoods with low levels of public facilities and services, the proportion of children who participated in organized activities only at public facilities was significantly higher than the proportion of such "public only" children living in high-service areas (table 7-14). Correspondingly, the proportion of children who used only the private sector was twice as high in the neighborhoods best served by the public sector.

TABLE 7-14. Neighborhood Services and Participation In Public and Private
Activities (vertical percentages)

Category of children	Level of service in neighborhood[a]		
	Low	Medium	High
Those who took part in private activities only	6	10	12
Those who took part in public activities only	43	36	32
Those who took part in both public and private activities	25	44	36
Those who took part in no organized activities	26	11	20
Weighted (N)	(436)	(211)	(117)

[a]See table 7-13.

Among children from low-income families, those who lived in or near areas with high levels of public services logically would have been the prime beneficiaries of the existing distribution. They were few in number, however, for only 6 percent of the 165 children from families with incomes under $5,000 lived in neighborhoods with a high rating on the service summary. Another 26 percent of poor children lived in medium-level service areas. Thus the majority of children who were most dependent on the public sector for their organized recreation opportunities did not live where they could easily make use of the best facilities.

SUBDOMAINS: SPORTS AND MUSIC ACTIVITIES

Activity clusters, such as sports, fine arts, and religious programs, form subdomains, of which sports is the largest and most varied. Although each subdomain embodies a different history and set of current circumstances, there are several commonalities. First, no subdomain is monolithic. The various activities that comprise each one attract different types of children in varying proportions, depending on the forms in which the programs are provided and on the preferences of the children. While no single social profile defines the child who is "into sports," for example, one could be drawn fairly precisely by examining participants in particular sports activities.

Second, activities in separate subdomains can be approximate functional equivalents. A child who does not or cannot fill a certain need with one activity will try to do it another way. Girls' gravitating to dance as a major outlet for expending physical energy and improving coordination may be responding to their relatively limited opportunities for participation in other sports. Boys, conversely, have few chances to take dance, but they may through athletics learn to use their bodies creatively and skillfully. Take as another example religious groups and scouts: many of their actual activities are very similar.

Third, these subdomains have some small minority of heavily involved children whose lives are truly dominated by one or two activities, be they gymnastics, violin lessons, or astronomy. Such devotees are in a class by themselves. For them time budgeting may be very urgent and parental facilitation even more critical than for the average child. Much attention has been paid in past research to the consequences of heavy training and intense competition for prodigies. By contrast the circumstances of children with average appetites for organized activities are less well known. These children are the focus of the analysis that follows.

Sports Activities

Nationally as many as twenty million children between the ages of six and sixteen take part in organized athletic programs.[15] The scale, diversity, and public visibility of these programs have all been on the increase in recent years. More kinds of sports are organized for children than in the past, the age for beginning competition has been declining, and the needs of female athletes, the handicapped, and other groups of children have been more clearly identified.

Organized sports for children are an integral part of a social, political, and economic system that extends from the neighborhood playground to the Olympic Games and to the boardrooms of multinational corporations. Sport at all levels is becoming more specialized, hierarchical, and technological. A loosely defined countermovement is emerging, however, which offers new games, new forms of coaching, and new philosophies of sport. Since sports for children have always had a strong didactic element, the conflicting philosophies get played out as a battle for the hearts, minds, and bodies of America's children. Whereas in past decades only his coach and parents were looking over the shoulder of the eleven-year-old Little Leaguer, today they are joined by an army of social and medical researchers, educators, legislators, and promoters. Luckily, contemporary eleven-year-olds may be better equipped than their predecessors to handle the pressure, for already they might have seven or eight years of competition under their belts.

In the course of expanding sports opportunities for youth, a number of longstanding educational controversies have been resurrected and some new issues raised. Common to editorials in the popular press and the measured explorations of the research journals are a set of basic concerns about the value of organized sports for children. What might the moral and psychological consequences of intense competition be? How different are opportunity structures for boys and girls, for rich and poor, for whites and blacks and other minorities? Are sports still perceived as an avenue of social mobility?

The urgency with which these questions are debated arises from concern that youth sports programs have grown in ways that inhibit them from fulfilling their alleged objectives. Building character, enhancing family stability, and providing an escape route from ghetto streets may be too much to expect, yet many sports programs continue to be promoted as though these outcomes could be achieved. While the moral and social virtues of athletic competition still command a great deal of support, the excesses of the system have produced a generation of skeptical researchers, angry parents, and disillusioned children. Psychologists Thomas Tutko and William Bruns capsulized the message of many critics when they advised parents who want to build children's characters to try something else. [16] Sociologist Harry Edwards can be persuasive when he admonishes black youth to avoid the almost certain failure of pursuing professional sports careers at the expense of their educations. [17] These critiques suggest that the problem is not individual but systemic. What must be done to encourage a child or family to try something else? Why should they relinquish their belief in sports until and unless perceived alternatives are available? Unfortunately, access to alternatives is often the prerogative of class in recreation no less than in basic education. The lasting contribution of a critical perspective may not be abandonment of organized competition but the reform of youth sports around the genuine immediate interests and developmental capacities of children.

A prerequisite to any purposeful changes in youth sports programs would be a clear picture of who is involved and under what circumstances. To this our data can contribute an understanding of the time structure of sports activities and the different participation patterns exhibited by various types of children.

For most team sports, sixth-graders are still several years away from the cutoff points for serious pursuit of competitive careers, whether amateur or professional. For other sports, such as women's gymnastics or swimming, they have practically reached the age of the most intense training and competition. Although school varsity sports are not yet a highly esteemed element of their social lives, there is substantial peer pressure to excel at sports nonetheless.

All types of children in our sample took part in sports programs during sixth grade, with the likelihood of participating in a particular activity varying according to gender, ethnicity, and family background. The attributes of subject, format, sponsorship, and enabling conditions were as helpful in understanding sports activity patterns as they were for the domain as a whole.

Subject

The most basic differences were those between the sexes (see table 7-1). The sports undertaken principally by boys included baseball, football, basketball, soccer, and martial arts. Substantial proportions of boys and girls were attracted to swimming, tennis, and ice skating (each had a female majority). Girls dominated volleyball, softball, and kickball.

This distribution reflects the programs offered to boys and girls by most public and private recreation agencies. Most sports activities, especially groups, were sexually segregated. (This accounts for the results reported earlier in this chapter since groups were the most sexually segregated format and 51 percent of group activities were sports.) The recent trend toward removing the single-sex restriction in many sports, including Little League baseball, was just beginning at the time of the survey and was not reflected in the data.

Format

Though the overall level of participation in organized sports was significantly higher for boys (71 percent) than for girls (47 percent), girls showed comparable or greater levels of interest in the smaller range of programs they were offered. Boys did a higher proportion of team sports, while girls did relatively more individualized activities. White girls participated in sports lessons at a somewhat higher rate than black girls. Black and white boys were closer in their participation rates for lessons than for groups. Most of the team sports took the form of group activities, which were primarily social and competitive, while most of the individualized sports were pursued as lessons, primarily instructional in nature.

Teams represent a different type of socialization experience than individual activities, differences corresponding to some persistent sexual stereotypes. Individualized sports allow more personalized attention to the child's development. Teams, by contrast, provide more chance for learning cooperative and competitive behavior.[18] To the extent that there are benefits from each of these social situations, the systematic channeling of boys and girls into different activities may represent a loss of opportunities for both.

General participation levels masked larger differences by sex and ethnic group in more specific categories of sport (tables 7-15 and 7-16). Black boys did not compare to black girls in the same way that white boys compared to white girls, although the

TABLE 7-15. Participation in Sports Groups and Lessons Outside School (percentages)

Ethnicity and sex	Groups	Lessons	Weighted (N)
Black			
Boys	48	32	(261)
Girls	25	20	(269)
White			
Boys	39	28	(64)
Girls	14	24	(70)
Asian			
Boys	20	12	(26)
Girls	4	15	(23)
Other			
Boys	20	4	(20)
Girls	3	10	(31)
All children	31	23	(764)

TABLE 7-16. Participation in Team, Individual and School Sports (percentages)

Ethnicity and sex	Outside school		School sponsored	Weighted (N)
	Team	Individual		
Black				
Boys	55	24	44	(261)
Girls	28	17	37	(269)
White				
Boys	44	17	31	(64)
Girls	13	23	20	(70)
Asian				
Boys	23	8	4	(26)
Girls	3	5	10	(23)
Other				
Boys	22	14	25	(20)
Girls	9	2	16	(31)
All children	36	19	33	(764)

differences between sexes were noticeably smaller in the school-sponsored activities.

The differences among ethnic groups in sports participation were in most cases greater than the differences among socioeconomic groups, however defined. This was more true for boys, where blacks consistently did more than whites, than it was for girls. We suspect that several structural and historical circumstances accounted for much of this variation.

Sports in America have always had a strong ethnic dimension that roughly represented the relative social and economic status of groups. Sports have always been one of the most visible and accessible routes of social mobility and self-expression for those whose backgrounds restricted their chances of achieving in other ways. This is not to say that there was not serious ethnic discrimination and exploitation in the sports world. There was, of course, and discriminatory practices are now somewhat more subtle than in the past.[19]

This image of social progress through sports may seem more powerful than warranted by the number of people, mostly male, who have materially benefited, but that does not lessen its importance as a cultural phenomenon. Today, black athletes still provide some of the most influential role models for black children,* and athletic prowess can still mean a chance to attend college, though it may exact a heavy price.[20]

Sponsorship

It is not surprising, given the commentary above, that the sports favored by black boys in our sample were the team sports that emulate professional leagues in which blacks play a prominent role. These sports were also the ones most often provided by schools and recreation agencies in moderate- and low-income areas. This suggests another reason why ethnic differences were so significant. Minority neighborhoods were relatively heterogeneous in family income and educational background for reasons having to do with housing and job discrimination. Since support for facilities and instruction in many sports activities was based at the neighborhood or municipal level, an ecological factor influenced the availability of programs to children regardless of individual family characteristics. For example, the costs of providing facilities and instruction needed for youth programs in skating, swimming, or tennis are very high. By comparison, facilities for team sports, such as basketball and baseball, are much less costly on a per child basis. Not surprisingly, most of the highly developed programs in individualized sports are located in affluent, mostly white suburbs. The public/private sponsorship issue is of less importance in suburbia since fees are often charged in either case and even public facilities are restricted de facto by metropolitan housing patterns.[21]

Whether public or private, sports facilities are fundamentally a form of collective consumption. In fact, some suburban communities have become specialized in the production of national- and world-class athletes in one particular sport, and their success is attributable to the modern facilities and coaching that families have chosen to provide under community auspices.

There are several implications of this pattern of program provision for our sample population. First, within Oakland most community-based opportunities were in team sports, compared

---

*The large number of former Oakland prep stars who went on to illustrious sports careers is a major source of pride for the community. Though black males predominate, the Oakland sports "hall of fame" includes world-class athletes of both sexes and a variety of ethnic backgrounds.

with publicly provided individual sports facilities in the suburbs. Second, opportunities for instruction in individualized, "exclusive" sports were mostly private or relatively expensive. The data show that individual sports were more likely than team sports to be done as lessons, to be private, to be attended outside the neighborhood, and to charge fees.

Though we had no way of measuring parents' preferences, it is reasonable to assume that middle- and upper-income parents were more likely than lower-income parents to have been exposed to the more exclusive individualized sports themselves. Tennis, for example, used to be much more restricted by ethnicity as well as by class than it is today. Since more of the white families in the sample were in the middle- or upper-income strata, their general sports/class milieu might also have contributed to their children's affinity for these kinds of activities.

Contrasting Environments for Two Subdomains

In earlier sections of this chapter we mentioned that school-sponsored activities (even those done before or after school hours) might be more accessible generally to children who were materially disadvantaged. School activities tended to have fewer requirements of any kind, including fees, equipment costs, registration, and transportation. Where there were comparable subjects offered in both school and nonschool settings, we could examine the backgrounds of participants rigorously to determine whether users of the activities outside school were from higher status families. Mother's education is presented here as a family status proxy (although family income and a measure of parental facilitation each provided similar results).

The children of highly educated parents were more likely to take part in three music-related school activities, but differences were rather modest (table 7-17). Contrast this with the distribution of children who took music lessons outside school, virtually all of which were private and fee-charging (sixty-one of sixty-seven). Participation among children with college-graduate mothers was 27 percent, compared with only one percent of children whose mothers had less than a high school diploma. The ratios were nearly identical for

TABLE 7-17. Participation in School and Outside School Musical Activities
(percentages)

| Mother's education | In-school | | | Outside school | |
	Music lessons	Band	Chorus	Music lessons	Weighted (N)
Less than high school diploma	27	17	25	1	(208)
High school graduate	33	22	28	5	(222)
Some college	36	29	30	12	(228)
College graduate and above	38	31	33	27	(90)
All children	33	24	28	9	(748)

Ratio[a] of Nonschool to School Music Activities

| Mother's education | Nonschool music compared with: | | |
	School music lessons	School band	School chorus
Less than high school diploma	.05	.08	.06
High school graduate	.15	.33	.18
Some college	.32	.40	.39
College graduate and above	.71	.87	.81

[a]The higher the value, the larger the proportion of nonschool music activities done by that group.

school chorus, band, and music classes compared with outside lessons: school was likely to be the only locus of musical activity for all but very high-status families. In this instance there were few ethnic differences that were not largely explained by family status.

None of the sports formats exhibited the monotonic relationship between participation and mother's education that was found in the case of music (table 7-18). Nor did the school/outside-school ratios vary systematically. This was because family status was less influential here than in music. Also the differences in sponsorship and enabling conditions were not as specific to the formats as they were with music. In fact, while school sports were the most unequal of the three formats in ethnic terms (having the greatest disparity between participation levels of whites and blacks), they were the most equitable format in the proportions of boys' and girls' involvement. We attribute this to the school's role as the primary provider of

TABLE 7-18. Participation in School and Nonschool Sports Activities (percentages)

| Mother's education | In-school | Outside school | | Weighted (N) |
	Sports team	Group	Lessons	
Less than high school diploma	38	29	21	(208)
High school graduate	33	30	26	(222)
Some college	35	36	24	(228)
College graduate and above	24	22	24	(90)
All children	33	31	23	(748)

| Ratio[a] of Nonschool to School Sports | | |
Mother's education	Groups/School teams	Lessons/School teams
Less than high school diploma	.78	.57
High school graduate	.92	.78
Some college	1.03	.69
College graduate and above	.91	1.00

[a]The higher the value, the larger the proportion of nonschool sports activities done by that group.

team sports for girls, whereas boys had many more chances to be involved with team sports in settings outside of school. In short, school-based extracurricular programs served as an important equalizer of opportunity but in different ways for different activities. With respect to music, they provided a chance for the culturally or economically disadvantaged. With respect to sports they were an important source of team competition for girls.

CONCLUSION

Organized activities were a significant element of children's time-use patterns: 79 percent of the children in our sample were involved during the survey year. The majority of parents strongly approved the activities, and most backed their approval with some concrete acts of facilitation. The importance of organized activities rested less on the time they consumed—the smallest number of hours of any of the five domains—than on the social functions they served.

The data show emphatically that different patterns of organized activity time use were exhibited by children of different genders, ethnicities, and socioeconomic backgrounds. In most cases, gender and ethnicity were significant in affecting the type of activity chosen, while socioeconomic variables, parent involvement, and neighborhood service context tended to influence the format, sponsorship, and conditions under which children participated. The interaction of these factors produced dual markets, such as those between the public and private sectors, and between school and nonschool settings.

Organized activities are the focus of some high expectations, both as instruments of social policy and as opportunities for fun and creativity. The differences in behavior exhibited by the children in our sample could not be attributed solely to their personal choices or individual endowments. In order to ameliorate the effects of family circumstances on children's growth and development outside school, as we have seen, it is essential to know the specific conditions under which each kind of activity is provided and to understand the nature of the social system in which it is embedded.

eight
TELEVISION

Television viewing occupies more of a child's out-of-school time than any other single activity. Despite its obvious impact on daily life, American adults are ambivalent about their own television viewing and their children's access to television. Most parents feel that children watch too much television, and many parents do not like what children watch. Parents who grew up without television, however, have an embarrassed sense of awe when they see their children watch men walk on the moon or something as colorful, lively, and interesting as *Sesame Street*. For these parents, the visual aspects of world affairs were limited to *Life* magazine or a *Movietone* summary of recent events. Audiovisual entertainment for children was an occasional weekend matinee. By contrast, today's younger parents grew up with television themselves, and they are raising their children in a similar manner.

Whether they like television for their children or not, many parents feel that they need it to occupy their children when they are too pressed, too tired, or out of ideas for something better to do. This ambivalence is partly a result of competing and contradictory norms for parents and others charged with the socialization of young children. Faced with the trade-off in time, many parents are unwilling or unable to sacrifice their own personal needs, their outside interests, or their scarce nonwork time in order to provide interesting and entertaining alternatives for their children. Keeping them away from the set when no other option presents itself is not easy, and it is not surprising to find that it often does not happen. And for parents who watch a lot themselves, turning off the television can be hard to contemplate, even if it might be desirable for adults and children alike.

A more generalized cultural ambivalence is reflected in social commentary and scholarly essays. This writing and related research expresses a tension between portraying television as an important educational and social influence on children on the one hand and as an addictive force that robs them of time, displaces family life, and convinces them that there are simple solutions to life's problems on the other. Some writers also suggest, usually without much evidence, that in generations past children used to do "better things" with their time. They conjure attics filled with model trains and other treasures, tree houses built, woods explored, books read, lazy days spent daydreaming or gathered around the radio with the family trying to imagine what "the Shadow" really knew. It is easy to forget that most of us have no such evocative images of time use among past generations of the urban poor. Children in these families typically grew up without similarly interesting things to do and little intellectual stimulation: no yards in which to play, few toys, and fewer, if any, books. For them television, a near universal in American homes since the mid-1950s, was often the most compelling and safest activity to be had.

Television today is for most children fundamental to everyday life. It would be the most deeply missed of all entertainment media if unavailable, children report.[1] Thus it deserves a special place in this study. Children in our sample watched, on average, three hours a day on school days. On weekends and holidays they watched, on average, six to eight hours a day. They were neither very selective viewers nor closely supervised. They watched as much as they did partly, and simply, because they were allowed to. To understand why, we begin this chapter by exploring some of the personal, familial, and social functions of television, concentrating on those most vital to families with preadolescent children. In the second section we turn to the social correlates of viewing. Finally, given the obvious impact of television on life out of school, we explore the effects of viewing patterns on other uses of time.

FUNCTIONS OF TELEVISION FOR CHILDREN
AND PARENTS

Social-Psychological Functions

For children television can be an escape from the problems of everyday life, a source of company when lonely, a way of satisfying some need for fantasy. Small houses, large families, and crowded cities may give children little opportunity to "get away" or "blow off steam" in a socially acceptable manner. Sitting in front of the television set a child can pretend to be, or actually can be, outside the family-dominated space. Watching television, like watching a movie but unlike reading a book, has a pace set independently of individual viewers, allowing the child to plead not to be interrupted and disturbed in the middle of something.

Coping with Everyday Life

Writing for the Surgeon General's 1970 report on television and social behavior, Jack Lyle and Heidi R. Hoffman explored children's use of different media for coping with a variety of psychosocial situations. Children were asked to choose what they would most likely do if they wanted to relax or be entertained, if their feelings were hurt, or they were angry or lonely. Television was chosen most often for relaxation and entertainment: for girls it outranked all other choices, for boys it equaled playing sports.[2] Television was also chosen fairly frequently as an antidote to hurt feelings, anger, and loneliness: nearly half the children studied reported that they were very likely to watch television when lonely. Children of both blue-collar and white-collar families said that when lonely they were twice as likely to watch television as read a book.[3]

In another study, Bradley S. Greenberg and Brenda Dervin asked teenagers to respond to thirty-four questions about why they watched television: "The[se] results indicate that TV serves some general functions for all teenagers but also serves some specific functions that vary with social class and/or race."

Low-income teenagers generally and blacks in particular gave the following responses more often than teenagers of other backgrounds:

I watch TV because

it excites me

it gives me a thrill

it keeps my mind off other things

it keeps me out of trouble

it's almost like a human companion

it brings my family together.

Furthermore, black children were significantly more likely to agree that

I watch TV because

I want to be like some of the people I see on TV

I have nothing better to do

I don't have to think of work while watching TV.[4]

Fantasy and Reality Seeking

Children, especially young children, use fantasy in their play and seek it in the media. Whether this is a felt need or simply a sometimes pleasurable activity, as it is with adults, is open to question. Escape from the routine of daily life and escape into a fantasy world are two different things often confused in the literature on children's uses of television. Wilbur Schramm argues that television is used by children overwhelmingly for fantasy.

We have advanced the theory that the mass media exist because they are useful in meeting human needs. . . . We have presented some evidence to indicate that the chief needs television meets for children are those we group under the head[ing] of fantasy, as opposed to those we call reality needs. In other words, the chief part television plays in the lives of children is that of stimulating fantasy seeking and fantasy behavior.[5]

This proposition is based largely on an analysis of what children watch, that is, the ratio of reality-oriented to fantasy-oriented programs. Very young children clearly choose the programs that are most fanciful, such as cartoons. Sixth-graders, as Lyle and Hoffman show, choose the programs that offer more than fantasy fulfillment. Family-based situation comedies and comedies rife with adolescent and preadolescent peer/teacher conflicts do not invite the viewer to "take leave of his problems in the real world" so much as they use humor to put many everyday conflicts into perspective. These conflicts are often presented in a simplistic and stereotypic form, but this, in part, is what makes the situations humorous to children. Among sixth-graders, favorite shows are drawn from many different kinds of programs, and the fantastic and violent content of these shows varies considerably. When grouped by type, family situation comedies are the overall favorite.[6]

By the time children are in the sixth grade, they enjoy watching programs featuring characters close to their own age. They often choose programs with actors of their own ethnic and social class backgrounds. In this sense, an appreciation of the predicaments of those somewhat similarly situated seems to motivate a part of the television viewing behavior of children.

Many children who watch large amounts of television, as our own data show, are also avid comic book readers. This suggests that children fill their "media time" with a mix of what is at hand and what receives parental support, whether that is watching television or reading comics, magazines, or books. In other words, heavy television viewing does not appear to displace other forms of fantasy seeking. We are not arguing that television does not provide fantasy and the opportunity for escape, but among preadolescents the evidence does not support the theory in the strong form presented by Schramm and his colleagues.

Peer Functions

Children would be hard pressed to choose not to watch any television even if they wanted to. Television is a source of play material with friends, provides topics of conversation, and is an activity that children can do together. For sixth-graders it is second only to school events as a source of conversation and as such retains special importance through high school.[7]

Although only a small proportion of children in our study reported spending a lot of time watching with friends (13 percent), Lyle and Hoffman show that about 50 percent do watch some television with friends.[8] For children among peers television bridges awkward social situations, fills play time, and provides something to talk about.

Family Social Functions

If children want to be with their parents or parents with their children on weekdays, it is likely they will meet around the television, since that is where the family tends to be. Children participating in our survey were asked if they watched television with their parents. Forty-eight percent said yes, everyday. Whether this served any function other than simply bringing the family together at the same time in the same place is an open question. For parents at the stage of life where child-rearing and work demands are greatest television may be one of the only shared activities that they have the time and energy for.

Children in 61 percent of the households in our study reported that the set was on most of the afternoon and in 84 percent of the households most of the evening. Equally important, the set was on during dinner in 59 percent of the households.

Several investigators have shown that much family television time is spent in close physical proximity but with little meaningful family interaction taking place.[9] John Robinson and his colleagues discovered that women spent four times as many hours in this way with their children as they did on primary care. For men the ratio was ten to one.

Two decades ago Hilde Himmelweit argued that "it seems likely that television, although centered on the home, does not greatly strengthen family ties, even though it may offer a spurious sense of unity. As children grow older, silent viewing increases. . . ."[10] While television may not strengthen family ties, it is a place to touch base with parents and it provides a sense of shared experience.

Child-Care Functions

Few researchers have systematically examined the child-care functions of television. While they appear to be especially important for younger children,[11] they are not insignificant for preadolescents. The fact that parents say that children's television use is a "problem" yet allow children to watch as much as they do suggests both that they have trouble controlling television use and that they may not want to. In an informal interview, one mother reported:

After a time television took on a different aspect in our household. The change was subtle, but looking back now, it's clear that a real change did take place. I suppose it was because I discovered how dependable an amusement television was, more dependable than any other . . . suddenly I realized that I was no longer using television as an experience to offer the children, but as something with value to me.[12]

The Himmelweit study, too, demonstrates anecdotally that television kept children at home, out of trouble, and distracted.[13]

Preadolescent children are considered old enough to be home alone, and some, as we have seen, baby-sit as well. The television set enables parents to plan children's time without necessarily having to be at home with them and allows older children to occupy the time of children in their care without difficulty.

Time-Filling Functions

As our data show, children do not seem to have a deliberate viewing plan: they watch whatever is on whenever they feel like it. They like what they see whatever it happens to be.

Data from the Lyle and Hoffman study confirm this lack of selectivity. The majority of sixth-grade children do not usually use a log to make program choices. In part, this may be because they know when their favorite programs are on. But for a substantial proportion of children (45 percent), first the set goes on, then a program is selected. One-third of the children indicated that there was almost always something on that they wanted to watch.[14] Apparently the availability of television as much as its content accounts for its use: television is a holding pattern between more purposive activities.

Children vary, however, in their needs and in their parents' willingness to allow them to fill time with television: many children do not and are not allowed to fill time this way. In these cases, as we shall see, the substitution of other interesting, compelling activities is both possible and likely.

These many functions of television—plus those not so clearly perceived—taken together help us understand the complexity of "overuse." In our view, each function contributes to viewing time incrementally. For example, poor parents living in unsafe neighborhoods may be more likely to tolerate a high level of television use. At the same time, poor parents generally may be more accepting of a high level of television use because they have fewer resources with which to support other time-use alternatives. Similarly, well-educated parents, who, as we shall see, are less likely to have permissive attitudes toward children's television viewing, may relent if they work or if they are otherwise pressed for time.

These examples suggest that we cannot expect to find that individual variation in television use is explained simply by the interrelations of independent variables and dependent measures. Multiple factors are relevant in different degrees in individual cases. While the most important differences were associated with ethnicity, income, and education, few variables on their own even partially explained levels of television use. Further, as we have argued in chapter three, these variables are typically not well specified in social research—serving as they do as proxies for different aspects of life-style and subculture. Failure to disaggregate the separate dimensions of these variables often leads to unwarranted assumptions. Thus, Greenberg and Dervin in their work on media patterns among the urban poor argue that "both variables—poverty and race—operate together. Because of their poverty, low-income whites and blacks are more similar to each other than either is to the general population."[15] The implication is that poverty per se is an important determinant of television use. As we shall see, however, middle-income blacks are also heavy television viewers and share much of the same television behavior and many of the attitudes toward television as lower-income blacks. On a similar note, the

National Commission on the Causes and Prevention of Violence, commenting on the effects of television a decade ago, argued that "television is a particularly potent force in . . . low-income areas or where violent life styles are common. In these instances, television does not displace parental influence: it fills a gap."[16] Here again, characteristics of family life that are disproportionately, but not universally, shared in poor or minority families are linked causally to television use without evidence.

In response to these kinds of analyses and building on the functional considerations raised here, we begin the analysis of our survey data by examining the complex correlates of television time use. We then look in some detail at the effects of three particular factors on viewing behavior: parents' time constraints, family rules concerning access to television, and the nature of the neighborhood environment.

CHILDREN'S TELEVISION TIME

No one watches more television, studies have shown, than eleven- and twelve-year-olds[17] —slightly more than 30 hours a week on average.[18] Children have about 105 available waking hours each week, of which 30 or so are spent in school. Television takes up a little less than one-half of the remaining time. Virtually all of the children in our sample reported watching every day or almost every day. Of their families, 99 percent had at least one set.

Lyle and Hoffman showed that on the four weekdays they measured, at four o'clock (prime time for most out-of-school activities) over 40 percent of sixth-graders were watching television, though they did not necessarily watch all afternoon. Lyle and Hoffman labeled one-quarter of sixth-grade children "habitual TV viewers." They watched one and one-half hours or more every measured weekday. Viewing, furthermore, has increased. Comparison with Schramm's earlier data shows viewing up on average one hour on weekdays, two hours on Sundays.[19]

We did not collect data on day-to-day viewing patterns, since for our purposes it was necessary only to be able to describe the sample relatively: light, medium, and heavy viewers. We asked parents, "On school days, about how much time does your child watch TV?" (It was anticipated that these estimates would be low, and they proved so when compared with other studies.[20] Nevertheless, we are confident of the relative validity of our measure—children in the heavy group watched considerably more television than those in the light group—although we are aware that real time variations were likely because these estimates are based on parents', not children's, reports.) In the sample as a whole slightly more than 40 percent of the children were heavy viewers (table 8-1). Gender differences were not significant in this time-use domain: boys and girls watched similar amounts of television. Therefore, in the analysis that follows we only occasionally present separate tables for boys and girls.

Although family income had some effect on television viewing, the effects of ethnicity were more notable (table 8-2). Half the black children and nearly half the other non-Asian minority children, compared with one-quarter of the white and one-quarter of the Asian children, were placed by their parents in the heavy-viewing group (three or more hours per school day). Half of this group spent more than four hours each day watching television. This significant ethnic difference remained throughout our analysis, although it was partly explained by other factors.

When we looked at each ethnic group separately, the relationships between family income and children's television-viewing

TABLE 8-1. Parents' Estimates of Children's Television-viewing Time (vertical percentages)

Child's viewing time	Black		White		All children	
	Boys	Girls	Boys	Girls	Boys	Girls
Light (less than 1-1/2 hours per day)	23	23	45	44	28	28
Medium (2 to 2-1/2 hours per day)	27	30	34	28	30	30
Heavy (3 or more hours per day)	50	47	21	27	42	42
Weighted (N)	(240)	(244)	(64)	(69)	(346)	(366)

TABLE 8-2. Parents' Estimates of Children's Television-viewing Time (percentages by family income)

Ethnicity	Less than $5,000		$5,000-$19,999		$20,000 or more		All income levels	
	Child's viewing time		Child's viewing time		Child's viewing time		Child's viewing time	
	Light	Heavy	Light	Heavy	Light	Heavy	Light	Heavy
Black	32	46	20	51	24	38	23	49
White	28	51	44	28	47	16	44	24
Total	30	47	25	44	38	25	28	42

time and between mothers' education and children's television-viewing time showed that among whites the latter relationship was stronger, that among blacks neither was significant (table 8-3).

Among white children the proportion of light viewers increased monotonically with their mothers' educational attainment. Only 10 percent of the white children from families with well-educated mothers were in the heavy-viewing group, compared with almost half the children from homes with less well-educated mothers. The same relationship held for blacks and for the sample as a whole, but it was weaker. Among blacks, mothers' educational attainment appeared to have a threshold effect on children's television viewing: only in homes with a very well-educated mother was children's television viewing dramatically affected, although here the result was a decrease in the proportion of heavy viewers rather than an increase in the proportion of light viewers.

The separate effects of income and education can be seen in the statistical regression of both on children's television time. The regression was run separately for blacks and for whites. Among blacks neither education nor income was correlated with children's viewing time, while for whites both were. Of the two variables, mother's education was the better predictor for whites, income (minimally) for blacks. The multiple correlation coefficient changes only marginally with the addition of the second variable (table 8-4). Although there were children whose television viewing was limited in all status and ethnic groups,

TABLE 8-3. Children's Television-viewing Time (horizontal percentages by ethnic group)

| Mother's education | Black | | | | White | | | | All children | | | |
| | Child's viewing time | | | Weighted (N) | Child's viewing time | | | Weighted (N) | Child's viewing time | | | Weighted (N) |
	Light	Medium	Heavy		Light	Medium	Heavy		Light	Medium	Heavy	
Less than high school diploma	27	22	51	(128)	17	42	41	(16)	23	29	48	(186)
High school graduate	21	33	46	(158)	37	21	42	(29)	25	32	43	(210)
Some college	22	26	51	(155)	45	34	21	(45)	27	29	44	(217)
College graduate and above	23	38	38	(34)	59	31	10	(42)	45	33	22	(88)

TABLE 8-4. Regression of Mother's Educational Attainment and Family Income on Children's Television-viewing Time

Ethnicity	Zero order correlation	Multiple correlation coefficient[a]
White		
Education	−.314	.314
Income	−.225	
Education and income		.331
Black		
Income	−.040	.040
Education	−.006	
Income and education		.042
All children		
Education	−.136	.136
Income	−.113	
Education and income		.148

[a]Stepwise regression

only rather well-educated white and Asian parents systematically limited viewing (or had children who systematically chose to do other activities instead).

We can pursue this exploration of the relationships between children's television viewing and mother's education, family income, and ethnicity by looking at other data available in our survey: data on when a family's television set was turned on, with whom children watched television, and family norms and values concerning television use.

With regard to when the set was turned on, we created an index of household television time: those families that had the set on most of the afternoon, at dinner, and in the evening we called "total-television households." On this measure black families outnumbered whites two to one and Asians four to one (table 8-5). Nearly three-quarters of black families, but only one-third of all other families, were joined by the television at dinner (table 8-6).

Table 8-7 presents our data on whom children watched television with. Asian children were more likely than any others to watch television alone.

Finally, with regard to family norms and values concerning television time, most children, independent of their ethnic back-

TABLE 8-5. "Total-television Households" (percentages)

Ethnicity		Weighted (N)
Black	43	(530)
White	21	(134)
Asian	10	(49)
Other	22	(51)
All children	35	(764)

TABLE 8-6. Times When Television is On (percentages)

Ethnicity	Most of afternoon	During dinner	Most of evening
Black	65	70	84
White	46	36	86
Asian	42	34	86
Other	73	34	83
All children	61	59	84

TABLE 8-7. With Whom Children Watch Television: Friends ("A lot"), Parents ("Everyday") (percentages)

	Black	White	Asian	Other	All children
Friends	18	12	6	11	16
Parents	48	46	28	39	46

grounds, could watch as much television as they wanted (table 8-8). Most of them watched, they reported, because they had nothing else to do. Black and non-Asian minority children were twice as likely as white and Asian children to be nonselective in their viewing: "If I feel like watching TV, I'll watch whatever happens to be on."

We can now begin to combine our independent variables—mothers' education, family income, and ethnicity—with our data about family viewing patterns—when, with whom, and the various norms and values—in order to sharpen our understanding of the social factors that account for variations in television use. We see, for instance, that although there were different viewing patterns among blacks of different socioeconomic status

TABLE 8-8. Television Norms and Values (percentages)

Affirmative responses to item:	Black	White	Asian	Other	All children
Can watch as much TV as want	83	74	70	71	80
Some TV programs not allowed to watch	34	40	28	41	35
Some TV programs parents like me to watch	82	67	52	81	77
Watch TV because nothing else to do	85	75	71	84	82
Watch whatever is on	61	33	33	66	54

and among whites of different socioeconomic status, the differences among whites were more pronounced. We see, furthermore, that with some items, such as "I'll watch whatever happens to be on," taking everything else into account, ethnicity itself was still the best predictor of children's behavior (table 8-9).

This was true for other items as well. Black families, for example, with highly educated mothers were twice as likely as comparable white families to have the television on during dinner, to watch television with their children, and to allow their children to watch as much television as they wanted.

The effects of family income and mother's education on viewing patterns and their differential effects among ethnic groups were not straightforward. One problem might have been that survey analyses, such as ours, demand that variables have the same shared meanings and definitions in all social groups (see chapter three). Perhaps there was less variation in children's viewing patterns by family income and mother's education in our black sample because these variables did not really tap the most crucial differences in family life, child-rearing practices,

TABLE 8-9. Television Norms, Values, and Social Patterns (percentages)

Mother's education	Television on during dinner			Television on in afternoons			Total television household		
	Black	White	All children	Black	White	All children	Black	White	All children
Less than high school diploma	78	54	68	71	68	71	55	43	48
High school graduate	68	43	61	62	50	59	38	19	33
Some college	68	34	59	61	42	56	39	20	32
College graduate and above	51	26	36	75	38	54	31	14	19

Mother's education	Watch a lot with friends			Watch with parents every day			Watch whatever is on		
	Black	White	All children	Black	White	All children	Black	White	All children
Less than high school diploma	25	33	22	53	77	53	71	54	67
High school graduate	17	16	16	48	70	49	60	45	57
Some college	14	7	12	47	42	46	52	26	47
College graduate and above	12	6	8	37	21	27	51	24	35

Mother's education	Watch as much television as want			Watch television when nothing else to do		
	Black	White	All children	Black	White	All children
Less than high school diploma	87	92	85	90	78	87
High school graduate	80	90	79	86	87	85
Some college	82	75	80	82	72	80
College graduate and above	91	54	70	80	71	76

and values among these families, as we assumed they did among white families.

The purposes served by television viewing in family life, as discussed earlier, is a compelling reason for examining the relationships of life circumstances to these broad functional contexts. The reasons for viewing change from hour to hour for each person and from person to person as well. Parents may tolerate different levels of viewing for different reasons, the product of complex factors at work in the family environment. By this logic, mothers' employment outside the home is one such factor that could be expected to influence children's viewing patterns.

A mother working full time, for instance, may want to be permissive about television viewing in order to afford herself some time free from her children, but then she may feel guilty about doing so and as a result be more restrictive. Children with working mothers in our sample were actually no more likely than others to be heavy viewers (table 8-10). This may be explained in part by the fact that a fair proportion of such children were cared for after school away from home. Hence, it is reasonable to suspect that these children have had less access to afternoon television than those children who came home directly from school.

We found that in black families the likelihood that the television would be turned on in the afternoon was affected both by mothers' labor force status and by their concerns for their children's safety. The latter also affected whether the children were heavy television viewers (table 8-11).

Analyses like these assume some form of value-added theory. In effect, they establish a mean value for the primary independent variable—say, mother's labor force status—and certain explanatory power is added by including secondary independent variables—neighborhood safety, for example.[21]

Similarly, we have already seen that mothers' educational attainment explained some of the variation in television use. So did family structure (table 8-12): the children of single parents were among the heaviest viewers. By holding mothers' educational attainment constant, we were able to examine the

TABLE 8-10. Child's Level of Television Viewing and Mother's Labor Force Status (horizontal percentages by ethnic group)

Mother's labor force status	Black				White				All children			
	Child's viewing time			Weighted (N)	Child's viewing time			Weighted (N)	Child's viewing time			Weighted (N)
	Light	Medium	Heavy		Light	Medium	Heavy		Light	Medium	Heavy	
Works full time	26	30	44	(203)	45	31	24	(40)	28	30	42	(274)
Works part time	26	20	53	(62)	49	31	20	(32)	32	29	39	(113)
Not in labor force, one-parent family	20	26	55	(112)	*	*	*	*	20	25	54	(126)
Not in labor force, two-parent family	22	29	49	(85)	47	31	22	(47)	32	32	36	(169)

* = small ns

TABLE 8-11. Television Turned on Most of Afternoon (blacks only)* (percentages)

Mother's labor force status	
Works full time	60
Works part time	53
Not in labor force	
one-parent family	74
two-parent family	74

Television turned on most of afternoon and
children's safety (blacks only)
(percentages)

Mother works full time and worries about child's safety	Television on in afternoon
A lot	74
Some	60
Not very much	54

Children's safety and heavy television viewing (blacks only)
(percentages)

Mother works full time and worries about child's safety	Child a heavy viewer
A lot	46
Some	51
Not very much	28

*ns in other ethnic groups were too small for analysis.

added value associated with their employment status and family structure (table 8-13). Apparently both might have led to greater tolerance of heavy viewing, though not in identical ways. At every level of mothers' education, single parents were significantly more likely to have children who were heavy viewers; but only the most well-educated working mothers were significantly more likely than nonworking mothers to have such children.

TABLE 8-12. Child's Level of Television Viewing, Ethnicity, and Family Structure (horizontal percentages)

Ethnicity and family structure	Child's viewing time			Weighted (N)
	Light	Medium	Heavy	
Black				
One parent	23	24	53	(237)
Two parents	24	32	44	(226)
White				
One parent	44	18	38	(29)
Two parents	46	33	21	(100)
Other				
One parent	9	44	47	(16)
Two parents	30	36	33	(77)

TABLE 8-13. Heavy Viewing Children, Mother's Education, and Other Background Characteristics (percentages of heavy viewers)

Mother's education	Mother's labor force status		Family structure	
	Works full time	Not in labor force	One parent	Two parents
Less than high school diploma	55	50	56	41
High school graduate	43	42	47	40
Some college	38	47	50	39
College graduate and above	29	14	35	19

We hypothesized that among well-educated working mothers a conflict among several factors existed: values that might lead these mothers to control children's television viewing versus relatively limited time to encourage children to do other things; and the need to use television to occupy children's time when nothing else was at hand. Mothers with less education were less likely to feel the same conflict, given their own greater use of television and more permissive attitudes toward television viewing. A similar sort of explanation held for families with single mothers. Children in these families were heavier television viewers, independent of other background factors, because single parents were likely to have less energy to control television use given the demands on their time. (Our data show that single parents themselves were likely to watch more television and less likely to perceive other time-use options.)

These more complex formulations suggested to us that the effects of life circumstances were not only direct, but were also mediated by parents' television viewing behavior and their own attitudes toward television. If parents tried to control children's television use, but they themselves watched substantial amounts, their efforts were likely to be ineffective. Indeed, the relationship between parents' and child's viewing time was strong for the sample as a whole (table 8-14). The educational attainment of a black mother had a stronger effect on her own viewing habits than on her children's. For whites the effect of mother's educational attainment was nearly equal on parents' and children's viewing habits. (The correlation of mother's educational attainment with mother's and child's viewing time was −.279 and .005 for blacks; and −.487 and −.381 for whites.)

These patterns of viewing and their linkages to parents' educational attainment are grounds for suspecting that there exists a family time-use ideology in many households, which, among other things, governs the television viewing environ-

TABLE 8-14. Mother and Child Television Viewing Compared (horizontal percentages)

Ethnicity and mother's viewing time[a]	Child's viewing time			Weighted (N)
	Light	Medium	Heavy	
Black				
Light	37	38	25	(100)
Medium	27	26	46	(221)
Heavy	8	25	66	(158)
White				
Light	63	20	16	(55)
Medium	38	44	19	(59)
Heavy	10	22	68	(19)
All mothers				
Light	44	33	22	(191)
Medium	28	31	40	(328)
Heavy	10	25	66	(189)

[a]Mother's level of viewing defined as follows: Light = one hour or less per day, Medium = one to three hours per day, Heavy = three hours or more per day.

ment. We saw evidence supporting this proposition when we looked simultaneously at children's viewing behavior and family television norms. White children in the low-viewing group were about half as likely as their peers in the high-viewing group to indicate that they could watch as much television as they wanted or that they watched whatever was on. They were also substantially different from other children in that they reported that they were not allowed to watch every program they wished (table 8-15).

We combined four variables to define "permissive television environments." These were households in which (1) the television was on during dinner; (2) children said they could watch as much as they wanted; (3) children reported watching often with friends; and (4) the mother watched a lot of television herself. We found, as might be expected, that the level of permissiveness was highly correlated with the overall amount of television children watch (table 8-16). Regardless of ethnicity, in families where norms were stricter there was less viewing. Differences remained however: 13 percent of black families,

TABLE 8-15. Television Norms and Child's Viewing Time (percentages responding "yes" to item).

Affirmative response to item	Child's viewing time	Black	White	All children
Can watch as much	Light	78	56	80
television as I want	Medium	82	83	80
	Heavy	86	94	86
Watch television	Light	87	66	80
because nothing else	Medium	80	81	80
to do	Heavy	86	84	85
Watch whatever is	Light	60	28	48
on television	Medium	50	31	48
	Heavy	65	48	61
Some programs not	Light	38	53	42
allowed to watch	Medium	27	32	30
	Heavy	36	23	34
Watch television with	Light	40	25	34
parent every day	Medium	49	63	51
	Heavy	53	61	51

TABLE 8-16. Child's Viewing Time and Television Environment (horizontal percentages)

Ethnicity and television environment	Child's viewing time			Weighted (N)
	Light	Medium	Heavy	
Black				
Permissive	21	23	57	(275)
Moderate	21	36	43	(146)
Strict	40	34	27	(63)
White				
Permissive	26	35	39	(39)
Moderate	32	39	29	(43)
Strict	69	21	10	(51)
All children				
Permissive	21	25	54	(331)
Moderate	24	37	40	(232)
Strict	49	31	20	(150)

compared with 38 percent of white families, maintained such strict rules.

While mother's education did not, in and of itself, define the television environment, it did produce differences that were somewhat stronger for whites than for blacks. A black family with a college-educated mother was more likely to be permissive (40 percent) than a comparable white family (less than 15 percent) (table 8-17). In all homes, except those of mothers with the least education, it was still a fact that the stricter the television environment, the less the amount of viewing that took place (table 8-18).

Control over children's viewing is a complex matter, because television also serves to entertain parents. If parents watch a lot of television themselves, they may be loathe to constrain their children. Hence there can be a conflict between parents' attitude toward children's viewing and their behavior with regard to controlling it. This was reflected in the data on television as a perceived family problem. Eighty percent of parents reported that the child's level of viewing was sometimes or often a problem. (A larger proportion of parents who did not feel that their children's level of television viewing was a problem had children who were light viewers.) The relationship between perceiving

TABLE 8-17. Television Environment (percentages)

Ethnicity and mother's education	Television environment	
	Permissive	Strict
Black		
Less than high school diploma	76	7
High school graduate	53	15
Some college	47	13
College graduate and above	38	29
White		
Less than high school diploma	75	8
High school graduate	38	19
Some college	28	39
College graduate and above	13	62
All children		
Less than high school diploma	64	11
High school graduate	47	19
Some college	41	20
College graduate and above	22	50

television to be a problem and controlling its use, however, was fairly weak. Only 15 percent of the black and 26 percent of the white families in which television was often a problem had a strict television control environment (table 8-19).

We have looked at television viewing and described variations among social groups and families with different orientations to time use. Ultimately we concluded that it was not so much the variations in time spent watching television that mattered as it was the factors accounting for those variations among different social groups.

TELEVISION VIEWING AND OTHER OUT-OF-SCHOOL ACTIVITIES

Given the amount of time most children spend watching television we must consider its impact on their other activities. In social science literature this has been called the problem of "displacement": simply stated television viewing takes up a lot of time, hence it must push out, or displace, other activities. [22] More complex displacement theories add that interest in television diminishes interest in other activities as well: it reduces

TABLE 8-18. Child's Viewing Time, Mother's Education, and the Television Environment (horizontal percentages)

Mother's education and television environment	Child's viewing time			Weighted (N)
	Light	Medium	Heavy	
Less than high school diploma				
Television environment				
Permissive	22	23	55	(121)
Moderate	26	39	35	(46)
Strict	26	44	29	(19)
High school graduate				
Television environment				
Permissive	21	28	51	(100)
Moderate	23	36	41	(72)
Strict	42	33	25	(39)
Some college				
Television environment				
Permissive	21	21	58	(86)
Moderate	21	40	40	(87)
Strict	52	24	23	(44)
College graduate and above				
Television environment				
Permissive	21	44	35	(18)
Moderate	34	30	36	(25)
Strict	61	31	9	(45)

TABLE 8-19. Television Perceived by Parents as a Problem (horizontal percentages by ethnic group)

"Television a problem"	Black			White		
	Television environment			Television environment		
	Permissive	Moderate	Strict	Permissive	Moderate	Strict
Often	58	27	15	46	28	26
Sometimes	63	25	12	25	32	43
Never	48	37	14	27	32	41

motivation to do other things, let alone excel at them. In part, the television-and-school-achievement debate stems from this sort of concern. Heavy television viewers are thought to be less likely to read in their spare time, less likely to be interested in reading, less able to concentrate for long periods of time, and less likely to value the written word.[23] While we do not have data with which to examine the more complex displacement theories, we are able to look at the simple relationship between levels of television viewing and participation in activities representative of our time-use domains.

In this section we will focus on two kinds of time-use, reading and participation in organized activities. The displacement effects of television viewing on these activities has been a matter for considerable debate. Researching the early diffusion and impact of television, Himmelweit and her associates noted changes in children's media behavior: a decline in reading books and comic books, listening to the radio, and going to movies. They also found a substantial decline in children's interest in the kinds of unorganized activities we described in chapter four.

Lyle and Hoffman, by contrast, found that fairly heavy television viewing is compatible with a high level of participation in organized activities and use of other media.[24] They explored the relationships separately and in the aggregate: many children were heavy television viewers and most children also did large numbers of other activities. The direct effect of viewing on each activity or type of activity, however, was not examined.

Organized Activities and Reading

A fair amount of television viewing and participation in organized activities need not be incompatible. We know that most children in our survey were involved in some organized activities and that these typically did not take up a large amount of time. The children also watched, on average, two to four hours of television a day. Nevertheless, it is surprising that the effect of different levels of viewing on participation in organized activities was as small as it was (table 8-20). Even children who were heavy television viewers managed about the

TABLE 8-20. Television Viewing and Proportion of Children Participating in Selected Organized Activities (percentages)

Ethnicity and child's viewing time	Music	Dancing	Football	Baseball	Basketball	Boy Scouts	Girl Scouts	Boys Club
Black								
Light	9	10	11	15	10	13	11	16
Medium	4	12	5	20	8	10	9	12
Heavy	2	10	10	19	9	9	6	9
Total	4	10	9	19	9	10	8	11
Weighted (N)	(21)	(53)	(44)	(98)	(48)	(49)	(39)	(58)
White								
Light	25	11	6	6	*	17	18	—
Medium	15	6	13	18	*	16	6	—
Heavy	9	8	8	6	*	6	15	—
Total	18	9	8	10	*	14	13	—
Weighted (N)	(24)	(12)	(11)	(13)	(6)	(19)	(18)	(0)
All children								
Light	18	9	8	11	6	13	12	9
Medium	7	10	6	17	6	10	8	8
Heavy	3	9	8	16	8	8	6	7
Total	8	10	8	16	7	10	8	8
Weighted (N)	(62)	(73)	(57)	(122)	(54)	(73)	(64)	(62)

* = small *n*s

same pattern of organized activities as children who watched less television. But when activities were aggregated by type, some differences emerged (table 8-21). Although among black children there were few differences in participation rates by level of viewing, among white children there were several. Almost twice as many light compared with heavy viewers took fine arts lessons or belonged to sports or any other groups. If differences could be explained by a simple displacement theory, we would have expected heavy viewers (independent of other factors) to have participated in fewer activities (independent of type). The data showed no such clear relationship.

In reading, too, we might have expected displacement to occur. Reading can occupy substantial amounts of time in a child's day and, as other studies suggest, it may well compete with television viewing. Barbara Heyns' study of out-of-school summer activities revealed that

TABLE 8-21. Television Viewing and Proportion of Children Participating in Organized Groups and Taking Lessons (percentages)

| Ethnicity and child's viewing time | Activity type | | | | |
	Lessons	Fine arts lessons	Sports lessons	All groups	Sports groups
Black					
Light	24	21	20	22	22
Medium	30	21	18	34	28
Heavy	32	21	23	30	24
Total	29	21	20	29	24
Weighted (N)	(150)	(112)	(103)	(150)	(125)
White					
Light	30	33	14	47	26
Medium	33	22	24	30	13
Heavy	26	16	16	26	14
Total	30	25	17	36	18
Weighted (N)	(41)	(34)	(24)	(50)	(25)
All children					
Light	28	27	16	30	20
Medium	30	21	18	31	21
Heavy	32	20	20	28	20
Total	30	23	18	29	20
Weighted (N)	(228)	(174)	(137)	(223)	(156)

The two activities which have the largest inverse relationship in terms of time allocation are reading and watching television. Children tend to spend equivalent amounts of time playing or pursuing hobbies irrespective of how much time is spent watching television; but reading behavior is strongly inversely related to the time spent watching television. Reading and watching television are both relatively quiescent and solitary activities, not involving much social interaction or physical activity. The total time allocated to both tends to be a fairly consistent proportion of the typical summer day. Boys are less likely to do either than are girls, yet if any two activities involve trade-offs, it would seem to be reading and watching television. The data suggest that in terms of time allocation, children choose between active and passive activities, or between playing and any other reported activities. The data suggest that these two activities are more directly interchanged than any others.[25]

Our findings show that most children sometimes read for fun when not in school. Although the proportion of all readers did not vary substantially by level of viewing, the proportion who read almost every day did (tables 8-22 and 8-23). Compared with heavy television viewers almost twice as many of the children who were light television viewers read at least five days a week. There were almost no differences, however, in terms of what children read. Books that may have demanded a greater

TABLE 8-22. Children Reading for Fun and Television-viewing Time (percentages)

Child's viewing time	Children who read for fun		
	Black	White	All children
Light	86	90	88
Medium	89	97	88
Heavy	81	78	82

TABLE 8-23. Children Reading Five or More Days a Week for Fun and Television-viewing Time (percentages)

Child's viewing time	Children who read more than five days a week		
	Black	White	All children
Light	31	46	36
Medium	24	36	26
Heavy	19	21	19

time investment than other printed media were no more likely to be read by light than by heavy viewers (table 8-24).

Family Activities and Time-Use Orientation

We also explored the effects of light and heavy television viewing on hobbies, playing outside after dinner, playing frequently in the schoolyard, number of friends, and having a library card. No consistent relationships emerged. This is not to say that television use did not affect the overall patterns of activities chosen or even particular types of activities. Rather, it suggests that children, whether light or heavy television viewers, had enough time to do many other things as well. Furthermore, it indicates that a simple displacement model may be misleading: it did not appear to be the case that level of television viewing necessarily affected participation in other activities singly.

Once again we must consider parents' and children's attitudes towards time use rather than focusing on real time constraints.

TABLE 8-24. What Children Read and Television-viewing Time (percentages)

| | Child's viewing time | | |
Child reads	Light	Medium	Heavy
Magazines			
Black	63	69	63
White	65	58	66
All children	63	64	64
Comics			
Black	84	72	81
White	55	66	64
All children	74	72	79
Books			
Black	92	97	92
White	94	88	88
All children	93	97	91
Newspapers			
Black	60	58	56
White	66	52	72
All children	63	60	60

As we have noted at several points, there exists in many families an orientation that, though often unspoken, does underlie many time-use decisions. To the extent that this is the case, we would expect to find a relationship between television viewing and other activities. For instance, children might have read more in a strictly controlled television environment, not necessarily to fill the available time, but because a positive value (either the child's or parent's) was placed on reading and other activity alternatives. Our data bore this expectation out (table 8-25): there was a fairly strong relationship between the television environment and frequent reading, visiting places of cultural interest with parents, and taking fine arts lessons.

Families that spent more time together were also more likely to control their children's television use (table 8-26). Controlling television use, given its value as entertainment and the many functions it served for children and adults, required a clear sense of the potential benefits of spending time in other

TABLE 8-25. Child's Participation in Selected Activities and the Television Environment (percentages)

Activity and ethnicity	Television environment		
	Permissive	Moderate	Strict
Takes fine arts lessons			
Black	27	27	32
White	19	34	43
All children	26	27	35
Reads every day			
Black	11	10	18
White	11	27	37
All children	12	15	22
Visits cultural places with parent			
Black	10	8	10
White	31	31	43
All children	13	11	21

TABLE 8-26. Family Activities in Homes with Strict Television Control
(percentages)

	Black	White	All children
Child goes places with parent(s) (e.g., movies, church, restaurant)			
Goes no place	7	24	11
Goes three or more places	33	44	36
Child attends cultural and recreational activities with parent(s)[a]			
Attends no activities or only one	10	23	14
Attends nine or more	20	43	30
Summary of three indexes of parent/child activities[b]			
Zero score on every index	10	12	10
Score one or more on every index	18	41	30

[a]See Appendix A, Child's Interview Schedule, Question 58.
[b]Index created from the activity sets presented in chapter five (see p. 127).

ways. In our sample it appeared to be the case that parents who limited their children's use of television actively encouraged involvement in other activities and also did many things together as a family.

CONCLUSION

While television served a multiplicity of functions for children, parents, and the larger society, its most important characteristic for many children was that it filled time. Indeed it filled more time than any other out-of-school activity—and thus became the backdrop against which the remainder of life outside school must be viewed. There was considerable social variation in the amount of television viewed and in the home television environment. In only a small proportion of homes was television viewing actively monitored and other activities encouraged. Generally, there was little support in our data for a theory that suggests that television viewing simply displaces other activities.

Given the limited and inconclusive evidence on the negative effects of television, how can we evaluate its use by children? As with other kinds of time use, this is not just an empirical problem. Even if television viewing had no measurable negative effects on children (assuming that it were possible to construct a clear cause-effect model), it could still be argued that it is an inadequate agent of socialization and a poor use of time relative to other alternatives. Furthermore, while television may have few measurable negative consequences, it has few measurable benefits for children either. Bronfenbrenner argues: "The primary danger of the TV screen lies not so much in the behavior it produces as in the behavior it prevents—the talk, the games, the family activities and the arguments through which much of the child's learning takes place and his or her character is formed."[26] Most children watch too much television given the time-use options. Their time might be better spent, in the sense that doing other things might teach them more about their world and foster development of talents, intellect, and physical abilities.

The limited amount of parental control over television, coupled with its availability, makes its use much too easy for children. Compared with most other activities, the choice process is attenuated.

It is our view that this attenuation constitutes television's primary negative effect on children. If television were a scarce resource, as it is in some homes, the value of an hour spent watching would have to be measured against the value of an hour spent doing something else. Easy access to television means that most children do not even recognize that choices and trade-offs are involved in their viewing decisions.

In addition, television is overused by children who have the poorest life chances, those who might benefit especially by exercising other alternatives. Relatively advantaged children also watch substantial amounts of television, but in the context of a more diverse out-of-school life, substantial parental intervention in and facilitation of their interests, and on average, higher scholastic achievement. Children from the least advantaged homes in our sample were almost three times as likely to be heavy television viewers as were children in the most advantaged homes, and we would argue that this further adds to their advantage deficit.

nine

CHILDREN'S TIME USE OUTSIDE SCHOOL:

PERSPECTIVES AND POSSIBILITIES

[There] was a merchant who sold pills that had been invented to quench thirst. You need only swallow one pill a week, and you would feel no need of anything to drink.

"Why are you selling those?" asked the Little Prince.

"Because they save a tremendous amount of time," said the merchant.

"Computations have been made by experts. With these pills you save fifty-three minutes in every week."

"And what do I do with those fifty-three minutes?"

"Anything you like. . . ."

"As for me," said the Little Prince to himself, "if I had fifty-three minutes to spend as I liked, I should walk at my leisure toward a spring of fresh water."

Antoine de Saint-Exupery,
The Little Prince[1]

By the time children finish high school, they have spent 11,000 hours in the classroom and roughly 65,000 hours outside. During that time they have watched about 15,000 hours of television—the dominant out-of-school activity.[2] Even so, a great deal more time has been spent on other things.

We live in a culture obsessed with achievement. We profess that children's time out of school ought to contribute to their well-being and development. But this rather straightforward ethic is by no means easily translated into behavior. We found parents positively disposed toward an enriched set of out-of-school time-use alternatives for their children, but we also found that few of the children in our study were products of interventionist homes, families that significantly and systematically directed their children's time use. Many parents told us, for instance, they would like their children to watch less television, to participate more in organized after-school activities, or to take more responsibility at home. What happened in most families? Children spent a great deal of time watching television, participating in a few organized activities, and doing very little around the house.

Most adults feel that time use out of school is important, but this does not translate readily into strategies that affect what children actually do. It is easy to lay the blame for this on one set of actors, parents, but hard to recognize that time use itself is not the singular responsibility of anyone. It is the product of relationships among parents, children, child-serving institutions, and the broader society. It is also convenient to focus on a single goal for children's out-of-school time use, say, enhancing their academic achievement. But we should accept the fact that there are actually a great number of conflicting goals to be served.

In this chapter we summarize our findings, searching the five time-use domains for commonalities and differences in children's out-of-school behavior. We then conclude by exploring a set of policy questions that the data may illuminate. These issues exemplify the problems linked to out-of-school time and the larger landscape of contemporary child rearing.

SUMMARY OF FINDINGS

Advantaged and Disadvantaged Out-of-School Lives

When we began this research we thought we would find distinct patterns of out-of-school time use among children of different backgrounds. We thought family income, parents' education, and ethnicity would differentiate children's behavior consistently. In fact, we found considerable divergence from one domain to another and little evidence of an overall pattern. Each domain appears to have a logic of its own.

What then makes one child's out-of-school life advantaged

relative to another's? This question can only be answered in terms specific to each domain. To understand why this is so, consider organized activities as an example.

Some observers believe that organized activities are important to the cognitive and social development of the young. By this standard the advantaged child would be the active participant. In fact, most children in our sample were involved in some small number of organized activities. But when we examined specific kinds of activities, we found substantial differences between the sexes. When we looked at the form of those activities, we found substantial differences among income groups with regard to enrollment in public and private programs, free and fee. But we could not necessarily say who was advantaged. We could conclude tentatively that under any circumstances these activities had the potential to be valuable social and intellectual experiences. We could conclude with less certainty that the advantaged child was the one with many options free of sex-linked and financial barriers.

Just how advantaged are these children? From the data it is hard to say. We might think, for instance, that a child enrolled in a private program is advantaged because more individual attention and presumably more expert instruction are available. But can we be certain that this child takes more away from the experience than another who is enrolled in a public-sector program of the same sort? Given the emphasis of our research, we are hard pressed to know, except with regard to access to opportunities, which children are advantaged. But the parent or service provider who advocates better programs for children cannot in practice separate questions of quality from questions of access.

Television represents an equally difficult problem. How do we define advantaged in relation to this domain? Those who genuinely believe that television is bad for children would argue that advantaged children are those who watch less and very selectively. By this standard, very few children in our sample are advantaged. Although these low-viewing children tend to share a common profile—they come from families with higher incomes and higher levels of education—even among their demographic peers they are a small minority. Of course, regarding the low television viewer as advantaged might not mean very much unless it can also be shown that this behavior is correlated with other uses of time that also represent advantaged status. But there is only limited evidence that such viewers substitute other kinds of activities that make them otherwise different from their peers. At best, we might agree that the heaviest television viewers are disadvantaged relative to others, that a significant overdose of television is simply bad for children, regardless of what they might do instead.

Useful distinctions between advantaged and disadvantaged are specific to each time-use domain, and even at this level there is ambiguity. Is the child who baby-sits for siblings each afternoon advantaged because of "adult" responsibilities or disadvantaged because baby-sitting takes time away from being a child? Are children whose parents overdetermine their out-of-school activities advantaged compared with children who are left on their own? Families must make scores of time-use trade-offs and value judgments about activities in the face of conflicting advice about what is best for children. The controversies and lack of consensus are testimony to the importance and complexity of these kinds of questions.

The Five Out-Of-School Time-Use Domains

Each out-of-school time-use domain was characterized by a pattern of its own. No single background variable or single set of variables explained them all.

Children on Their Own

Although the children in our sample mentioned an extraordinary range of activities, in their everyday lives away from parents and adults most engaged individually in a rather narrow set shaped in fairly predictable ways by sex and ethnicity. Variation across socioeconomic groups was rather minimal, probably because, in contrast with other domains, material resources are not as significant in this area of time use. With friends they participated in physically active pursuits almost exclusively. Alone they engaged in more intellectual and passive uses of time.

Boys and girls tended to play different sports, boys favoring team sports and girls individual or two-person sports. This distinction also reflected ethnic differences. Black children more often played team games; white children on their own were predominantly involved in individual sports.

Size and composition of children's peer groups did influence activities. For example, girls reporting cross-sex friendships were more likely to participate in team sports activities on their own. Reading, contrary to our expectations, was positively associated with size of peer group. Virtually all children named friends with whom they played regularly, although a surprising number of minority children other than blacks named none. Blacks reported the most friends, and this was only partly explained by the density of the neighborhoods in which they lived.

When on their own, most preadolescent children played close to home or in nearby public spaces. The nearer to home and the greater the availability of after-school programs in the school-yard, the more likely children were to play there. Even children whose parents feared for their personal safety played at a schoolyard if it was nearby, particularly in low-income areas with fewer play-space alternatives. Boys and black children generally were more mobile within and outside the neighborhood, and this, in turn, had an impact on participation rates for some activities and on the number of friends they reported.

The children did not lack free time, yet they experienced a good deal of boredom and said that they would like to have had more contact with parents and peers. Children with heavy obligations, such as jobs or baby-sitting responsibilities constraining their freedom, were even more likely to complain of boredom outside school. Contact with peers, more so than with parents, ameliorated that boredom.

Children and Parents: Time Together

We examined the question of time together by exploring the availability of parents to children, the activities they did together at home and away, and the things parents did on behalf of their children—we called this facilitation—which might have influenced the nature of out-of-school time use.

We looked at parent availability by examining the obverse: the amount of time parents spent away from home. We looked, too, at parents' whereabouts at key periods of the children's day: breakfast, afternoon, dinner time, and bedtime. Work patterns were the most powerful determinants of availability. In most families there was a parent home at key periods of the day. Parents in the poorest and the wealthiest families were most available. In white families the parent at home was often a nonworking mother in a two-parent, upper-middle-income family. In black families it was often a lower-income, nonworking, single mother. The traditional two-parent family—father working, mother at home—characterized less than one-quarter of our sample. Half the children had working mothers, and nearly half lived with single parents. Significant variations in the organization of the household were indicated by whether families ate together and by rules concerning outdoor play at dinner time and bedtimes.

Most children and parents said that they did things and went places together. White, two-parent families, and higher-income families reported higher levels of interaction both at home and away. At home, among all groups, watching television was the most frequently mentioned family activity. Children of all backgrounds were about equally likely to spend time with their parents on schoolwork.

With regard to activities away from home, we asked respondents about a range of places—some free, some that charged admission, some cultural or educational, some indoors, some outdoors. Patterns varied. Generally children from single-parent families went fewer places with parents. Parents' education and family income were less likely to affect the total number of places parents and children went together and more likely to affect the types of places they went.

On the matter of parental facilitation—driving children places, seeking out activities for them to participate in, volunteering to help with activities—we found significant social variation. Over 40 percent of the parents reported driving their children places frequently, and of these, whites drove most often and were most inclined to say that they did too much. Whites and Asians were most likely to have signed their children up for activities, lessons, or programs. Not surprisingly, single parents and working mothers were less likely to do any volunteering.

On an overall measure of child-parent interaction, there were significant differences. At comparable levels of economic status, minorities were likely to score somewhat lower. While we only examined a particular set of activities, there is clear evidence that the things families did together reflected cultural, educational, and material differences among them, and that the impact of circumstances was more apparent in this domain than in the other four.

Jobs, Chores, and Spending Patterns

Almost all of the children in our sample had some chores to do around the house each week. These chores were easy to do, took up very little time, and did not mean much subjectively to the children. Differences in the demands made upon children were associated with birth order, sex, ethnicity, and mothers' labor force status. Older brothers and sisters had more responsibilities than younger siblings; girls did more chores than boys. Some chores were considered "boys' work," some "girls' work." When the mother was employed a girl's chore responsibilities were likely to increase while a boy's were not, and generally parents said that they had to remind boys to do their chores more often than they had to remind girls.

Neither ethnicity nor socioeconomic status accounted for much variation in the level of responsibility. With respect to the assignment of specific chores, however, there were important differences. Black parents and parents with lower levels of education tended to assign children simpler chores, such as cleaning, rather than more complicated activities, such as cooking, and they were less likely to say that their children decided what chores to do. In all ethnic groups parents were divided on consensual and authoritarian models of chore assignment. There is some evidence of an incentive structure associated with chore performance: children who did more received higher allowances. Across ethnic groups there were large differences in the amounts of allowance that children received and the form that it took.

Among children in this age group opportunities to work outside the home were limited. Only 15 percent of the children held regular jobs, and these were mostly paper routes. Then, of course, there was baby-sitting, though this was confined mostly to children without younger siblings. Those who worked had higher incomes than those who did not. They tended to save more, but they also spent more on nonessentials, especially candy.

Baby-sitting at home generally represented the most demanding chore or job that children in our sample were likely to have. Forty-two percent of all children and 66 percent of those with younger siblings reported that they did some baby-sitting on a regular basis. Girls and boys were equally likely to have some such responsibility, but girls spent more time at it. In two-parent families, if the mother was employed, children of both sexes were equally likely to spend some time baby-sitting. Under any circumstances, children in single-parent families tended to do more baby-sitting than children in two-parent families.

It is in this domain that preadolescent children begin to experience the world of work. Children's resulting attitudes, at this time, suggest that many feel that work will be not creative or a positive force in their lives but merely a means to a paycheck.

Organized Activities

The vast majority of the children in our sample, 80 percent, were involved in at least one organized activity: a group or lesson outside school hours provided in a public or private setting. There were many types of organized activities available to eleven- and twelve-year-olds, hence this finding is not surprising. Only a very small minority, however, participated in three or more activities, so large time commitments were not required. Significant differences in levels of participation and types of activity choices were found between sexes and among income and ethnic groups.

Children's activities had distinct appeals. Seventy-one percent of boys, for instance, participated in a sports program, compared with 47 percent of girls. In the arts, 35 percent of girls participated compared with 21 percent of boys. In activities organized as groups, fully 62 percent of the participants were boys.

Three mutually exclusive activity formats—lessons, groups, and school programs—attracted distinct constituencies. While about half the children said that the extracurricular, organized school activities they participated in were attended half by boys and half by girls, only a fifth of the children participating in groups outside school said that these were mixed to the same degree. Public-sector facilities and programs involved children of all backgrounds. Private-sector programs were principally utilized by children from higher-status families. The same finding generally held for activities that charged fees (white children and children from higher-status families attended) and those that did not (minority children and poorer children participated in larger numbers).

Behind these aggregate patterns rested differences that can best be understood with reference to particular kinds of activities. Certain sports activities, for instance, attracted children of different sexes and from different income and ethnic groups. Ethnicity and sex combined showed especially powerful relationships. Black boys were by far the most frequent participants in team activities parallel to professional sports and provided by schools and by public recreation agencies. White boys, by contrast, were more frequent participants in individualized sports, such as swimming and tennis. Few girls were involved in team sports except at school, and it appears that competitive opportunities for girls were minimal otherwise. While boys, especially black boys, were the more numerous participants in sports activities overall, this relationship was attenuated when the type of sport in question, its format, cost, and accessibility were considered. Findings for other activities such as music also suggest a complex pattern of participation associated with similar background factors.

Organized activities did not take up large amounts of time, but they were clearly important to children. Not only did they provide opportunities to learn new things and build skills, but they were also linked to unorganized out-of-school uses of time.

Television

Perhaps more than any other time-use domain television is fully integrated into daily life. Preadolescent children are its most loyal patrons. Virtually all of the sampled children had a set at home and watched every day or almost every day. Differences in viewing patterns were tied principally to ethnicity, mothers' education, and family structure.

Just over 40 percent of the sample watched an average of three hours or more each day. Twenty-eight percent watched one and one-half hours or less. For white families, mother's educational attainment and family income were negatively correlated with children's viewing time. This was not true for blacks, although among all groups children whose mothers were college graduates watched less television on average.

"Total-television households" were defined as those in which the set was turned on (whether or not it was being watched by the sampled children) all afternoon, at dinner time, and all evening. Thirty-five percent of all households (21 percent white, 43 percent black) were total-television homes.

That a mother was employed did not make it more likely that her child would be a heavy television viewer. But if in addition she was worried about neighborhood safety, her child was very likely to be a heavy viewer. Children of single parents were only slightly more likely than children in two-parent families to watch a lot of television.

When parents were heavy television viewers, their children were far more likely to be heavy viewers, too. Mothers who watched little television had children who watched little television. In no other time-use domain was this modeling effect so apparent.

Families varied in the degree to which they controlled children's access to television. Thirteen percent of black parents and 38 percent of white parents seemed to maintain strict control, and in these homes children watched less. More educated mothers also controlled access to television, though more often in the case of whites than blacks. Control over viewing seemed to be part of a more general attitude toward time use that placed a high value on doing other things that might contribute to personal and social development.

Little evidence of simple displacement was found. Television viewing, for instance, did not influence a child's propensity to participate in organized activities, and only the most avid readers watched substantially less television.

PROBLEMS, POLICIES, AND TIME USE

Access: The Public Sector's Commitment to the Young

Out-of-school life has an important public dimension. Many of the things children do and many of the places they go bring them into contact with public institutions as providers or regulators of services. In some very basic ways government and public policy already have a powerful impact on children's lives out of school. This must be considered in light of an ongoing debate over the proper extent of government involvement in family life. Some people believe that public programs directed at out-of-school time encroach on parents' prerogatives or diminish children's autonomy. We acknowledge that there may be problems of this type, but we also hope that such concerns do not produce an overreaction endangering valuable and essential services.

As we hypothesized in chapter five, when public authorities step in, many parents bow out, assuming some activities are better left to the direction of "experts." For example, children attending schools receiving Title I ESEA Compensatory Education funds are exposed to many of the same cultural resources as children attending non-Title I schools. Availability of these activities through the schools may lead some parents to conclude that there is no reason for them to do these kinds of things with their children, this even though exposure itself may be less crucial than the parent-child interaction that takes place during the course of an excursion by the family. Parental involvement in other aspects of life out of school might be affected in a similar fashion if the public sector were to take a larger responsibility for children's time use outside school. Presumably we do not wish to encourage any diminution of the already limited levels of child-parent interaction.

Cognizant of this problem, we proceed with caution. Nonetheless, there are undeniably some interventions that could significantly affect children's time use outside school in positive ways. The public sector provides a variety of programs and facilities that have wide appeal for young people. Most children are involved in organized activities, and most children play regularly at parks, playgrounds, and other facilities managed by municipal government agencies. Children ages ten through thirteen are known to be among the principal users of these services and facilities.

There is mounting evidence that fiscal pressures on municipalities are resulting in declining commitments to child-oriented out-of-school services and facilities.[3] The implications of this trend demand attention for these services are important to children: they provide places to play, opportunities to learn new skills or sharpen existing ones, opportunities to socialize with peers, and structured and unstructured activities in managed and unmanaged settings.

California's Proposition 13 seems destined to serve as a model for similar legislation or initiatives that will affect municipal services throughout the country in the years to come. To the extent that after-school services become casualties of fiscal retrenchment (as they have in California), children's opportunities outside school will be altered in some fundamental ways. It is not just the decline of organized activities that matters but the effect on other time-use choices as well. Children utilize skills they learn in public-sector programs when they are on their own. If skill-building activities are no longer available, the range of things they are able to do will be affected, and their overall time-use opportunity set diminished. While we do not believe that the existing set of services represents any kind of ideal (there are no doubt many kinds of changes in the content of programs that ought to take place), its salience to children is beyond question. Ironically, among the earliest municipal budget reductions in communities throughout California have been many of the most effective outreach efforts and innovative programs.

The public sector provides opportunities that would not otherwise be available to some children. Children from low-income families participate in a range of cost-free programs and activities that few of them could afford if fees were charged. In those cases the public sector is clearly performing an appropriate and important compensatory role. But there is every indication that user fees are one of the most prominent mechanisms being instituted by local government agencies in response to shrinking general-fund budgets.[4] If this trend continues, the out-of-school time-use opportunities of those least able to pay will be unavoidably reduced.

Having documented the strong presence of the public sector in the daily lives of children, we believe that cutbacks in services directed at them will mean that young people are bearing an unusually large share of the adverse consequences of the taxpayers' revolt. These basic services and facilities represent an important contribution to the quality of children's out-of-school lives. We view current developments with dismay, for we see little evidence that public authorities or adults generally are willing to confront this deteriorating situation.

Out-Of-School Services and Public Responsibilities for Child Care

At various points in this volume we have discussed the problems of time-pressed parents, particularly working mothers. We have noted that time after school presents a difficult organizing problem for employed mothers, especially if they work full time. Difficult as the problem is for working parents with young children, it changes but does not necessarily diminish as those children near adolescence. It is hard for parents of preadolescents to find after-school care if they feel that their children are in need of supervision. As a result, many children are simply left alone. Under these circumstances, one would expect many parents to be interested in activities for children that provide a measure of supervision, but providers of after-school services have as yet failed to recognize and respond to this sizable and growing constituency. At present there is minimal assistance available for the time-pressed parents of preadolescents.[5] Little effort has been made on the part of public-sector officials to understand how child-care needs may be different in families with children of different ages. We believe that until children reach adolescence, parents require easily available care services oriented to children's age-specific and developmental needs.

Cutbacks in services for school-age children have followed fast on the heels of Proposition 13 at a time when increasing numbers of mothers are entering or returning to the labor force and as the number of single-parent families continues to grow. Many employed mothers have little control over their work schedules. But parents should be able to work without being preoccupied with an after-school supervision problem. More flexible working hours alone are not an adequate solution. For some parents private-sector care alternatives are adequate, but for many others private services are inaccessible: they cannot afford them even if they can find them. Hence, it is not surprising that our data indicate that often working, lower-income parents are forced to retain older children in caretaking roles.

The public sector ought to take significant responsibility for unburdening this aspect of family life, as it does in many other countries. Both parents and children suffer under the strain of after-school care: mothers are led to feel guilty because they cannot be home with their children (the societal message that they should be continues to have considerable power), and children's activities and responsibilities are unreasonably influenced by their mother's labor force status.

Adequate child care requires more than just governmental resources. In two-parent families, fathers need to assume greater household responsibilities. Employers need to be more sensitive to child-care issues and more flexible in job restructuring and shift scheduling. Regulation of private care settings should encourage, rather than inhibit the expansion of facilities at affordable rates. Yet even substantial action on all these fronts would not soon lessen the public's role in after-school services as part of the child-care system. We would expect that as we enter an era of increasing complexity in the management of family life and increasing pressures associated with rearing children, the issues of access to publicly sponsored after-school services are likely to be thrust into the spotlight of public debate.

Harnessing Out-Of-School Time to Support the Scholastic Experience

A great deal of formal and informal learning takes place away from school. Most aspects of children's lives out of school contribute to some degree to their physical, social, and intellectual development. From the perspective of many educators this is probably the single most important function of out-of-school time use.

For some time an important debate within the educational establishment has concerned the roles that parents and families can or should play in bolstering children's school achievement. Historically, many educational programs essentially excluded parents from the schooling process. The very definition of the disadvantaged child embodied in Title I of the Compensatory Education Act of 1965, for instance, seems to assume that the parent cannot or will not provide certain significant educational experiences outside school. Even so, after several generations during which educators disregarded the contribution parents could make to their children's intellectual development, the schools are now telling parents that their actions matter a great deal.[6] Educators have begun promoting parent-teacher contracts—actual, if unenforceable agreements that both sign—specifically designed to increase parents' roles (at home) in the educational process. These new directions are principally attempts to instill among the poor (who comprise the largest proportion of low achievers) an appreciation of certain interactions that occur "naturally," many believe, in the homes of higher-status families, effectively promoting better school performance.

These strategies are not without their problems. To begin addressing the possible ways in which out-of-school time could be harnessed more explicitly for educational purposes, we must first understand how the activities children do outside school affect traditional classroom learning. Similarly we must know more about what children actually do with their parents so that we can realistically assess what kinds of assistance might be forthcoming. It is not wise to take a narrow view of these parental inputs, for a particular activity in and of itself will probably not, in the long run, make a difference for an individual child. From our perspective, the idea of harnessing out-of-school time for educational support means creating a time-use environment and not just having parents adhere to a checklist of activities that children should do or that parents should do with or for them.

More specifically, we need to assess systematically which activities should be promoted for their potential educational benefit. Educators must recognize that it will not be possible to devise strong strategies designed to improve children's scholastic achievement without understanding the function and substance of out-of-school time use. Our exploratory study takes an initial look at some of the areas of out-of-school life that must be considered, for each in its way contributes to the perspectives that children bring to the classroom throughout their schooling careers.

The Parents' Dilemma

Parents not only set the tone for many time-use decisions, they also affect the child's values concerning time use. Their impact is even more direct when they establish rules and controls, facilitate some kinds of behavior and forbid others, make demands on children's time and permit certain choices.

Parents very clearly care about their children's use of time outside school. In our own data we have noted that it was a source of worry and concern, raising problems and tensions at home. Parents worry about the things children do (are they watching too much television?) and the things they do not do (are their chores and homework getting done?). They worry about the freedom their children have and ought to have. They worry about what they as parents do with their children and what they ought to do. They worry about what their children do on their own. These matters do not concern all parents to the same degree or for the same reasons. Some, for instance, may be extremely committed to having their children do a great many intellectually stimulating activities away from home; others may be concerned principally with making certain that their children "stay out of trouble," without really worrying about what they actually do. Some parents may value children's out-of-school time use for its developmental possibilities and act on those values; others may share the values but for any number of reasons not act on them. Still others feel that the real value of out-of-school time is that it teaches children to be independent, to make their own decisions and choices within the constraints of available personal, family, and community resources. These are not mutually exclusive perspectives, and, in fact, few parents appear to employ a single approach to all aspects of their children's time use. Each of the time-use domains we have examined seems to elicit its own particular response on the part of parents, and their responses may or may not be consistent in any larger sense. Since out-of-school life embraces so many different kinds of activities, one should not expect to find that parents have a rigid notion of how time ought to be spent.

Regardless of each parent's perspective on the normative questions of out-of-school life, more practical constraints intervene and mediate their behavior. Increasingly parent time is at a premium. In many families even the most basic tasks of organization and upkeep of the household are performed under pressure. While not precluding concern over the child's out-of-school life, this certainly influences the parents' opportunity to act vigorously upon their time-use aspirations for the child. Priorities being what they are, it may be that children's time use will be increasingly shaped with minimal direct parental involvement.

This is not to say that parents have withdrawn from children's out-of-school lives. In our sample, virtually all the parents and children spent some time together, even if it was mostly at home—and mostly in front of the television set. In the future parents may have a greater impact on their children's attitudes toward out-of-school time use than on their actual time-use decisions. Certainly in an era of diminishing parent time the values about the use of time that adults convey to children will matter a great deal.

All parents should regard out-of-school time as an important dimension of a child's development, and they should recognize the importance of their role in shaping children's attitudes and behaviors. But only if parents believe that out-of-school time use represents an urgent issue in terms of their children's present and future well-being can we expect any serious dialogue within families on the subject.

Responsible Work Roles

Not only do preadolescent children hold few regular jobs that expose them to the adult world of work but most contribute only minimally to the household economy. At a time when the relationship of children to school and work is undergoing careful reappraisal and critical scrutiny,[7] our data suggest some factors that affect children's work-related values and attitudes.

By the age of twelve children should begin to have some contact with the world of work. At least, they should be doing things that foster a sense of responsibility and a feeling of achievement and ability to accomplish tasks. Today, however, children know little about the way adults earn their livings. They see little evidence that work is or can be enjoyable, creative, or challenging. Work is a paycheck. At home not very much is expected of children; they have few opportunities to take on tasks that really make a difference. Their negative, or at best ambivalent, attitudes toward work should come then as no surprise.

Things could be different. With mothers at work, children could make more significant contributions to the household. Our data showed that children with important roles to play at home, though they did not necessarily like their jobs, did have higher self-esteem. We do not believe that children of this age need to be thoroughly isolated and protected from the tasks associated with being an adult. Nor do we think that children cannot learn to accept responsibility for what they actually do. Jobs around the house, however trivial, provide a valuable and valued contribution to the household economy. But if adults do not take the things children do seriously, children will not.

On the question of work outside the home, prescriptions are

necessarily cautious. The children in our sample are at a critical age with regard to their future attitudes toward jobs and careers. While we do not wish to take a step backward—children do need to be protected from abuses in the labor market—we view with concern the rather complete separation of children from work. With virtually no responsibilities outside their own homes, children have no way of learning about the kinds of things adults do for a living or of testing in the simplest ways interests they might have.

Neither are we speaking as proponents of the moral value of hard work. Rather, we are concerned that children be able to use some of their time out of school to play meaningful social roles. Similarly, remuneration should not be the only thing at issue, although there is power in earning money, for it strengthens independence. We believe that children this age ought to be able to look, not just to their parents, but to the outside world as well to satisfy some of their apparently insatiable appetites to spend and consume.

Qut-of-school time offers an opportunity to introduce children to the world of work without linking the experience exclusively to schooling. For example, public recreational and cultural agencies that already attract large numbers of children could certainly provide activities that would offer a taste of what different kinds of jobs are like, what kinds of preparation are required, and so forth. Television could also do more to incorporate these issues into programming for preadolescents. If such experiences became available, chances are children's informal games and activities would begin to reflect expanded perceptions of work.

From a practical perspective it is certainly plausible for children to devote some portion of their out-of-school time to tasks at home or away from home which include clear adultlike responsibilities. This would affect all time-use domains, probably increase children's self-esteem, and make a positive economic contribution. Failure to explore these possibilities represents lost opportunities, for our data make clear that children respond positively to the challenge of work, even in its most elementary forms.

Diminishing Sex-Linked Activity Patterns

In three time-use domains—children on their own, chores and jobs, and organized activities—activity patterns are systematically sex-linked. It is interesting to note that these domains represent a cross section of children's interactions with others: their peers and friends (on their own), their families (chores and jobs), and the public sector (organized activities). Traditions and values rooted in an earlier time are partly responsible for these persisting differences.

Today a great deal of discussion is devoted to reappraising the circumstances that led to sex stereotyping. In the context of this debate, one might have thought that public agencies providing out-of-school services to children would be at the forefront of change.

The data show a mixed record of innovation and continuing resistance to change. There was overall equality in the number of organized activities undertaken by boys and girls and evidence of more nontraditional choices by children of both sexes than in the past. Nevertheless, many programs remained available only to children of one sex or the other, particularly programs at nonschool, public and private recreation centers. Schools were the site of most of the team-sport opportunities for girls. Schools also sponsored most of the activities in which boys and girls participated together.

Support for nontraditional activity choices and settings that encourage boys and girls to participate together are essential dimensions of an environment that reduces sex-linked inequities. Under these conditions children might begin to feel that not only can they try different things in an organized setting but that they then can also do some of the same things on their own.

Families contribute to the definition of sex roles through time-use patterns in equally—if not more—powerful ways. Our data suggest that many parents reinforce traditional norms rather than encourage a break with conventional sex-linked activity patterns. Hence at home we found boys' and girls' chores distinguished fairly clearly. If this represents a microcosm of parents' attitudes toward most children's activities, we have reason to be concerned, for it appears that the next generation will have grown up with essentially the same sort of sex-role socialization as preceding ones.

CONCLUSION

In this volume we have explored children's out-of-school time use. We have described how life circumstances are associated with particular activity patterns. We have indirectly raised the issue of children's futures, linking out-of-school time use by implication to children's prospects in life.

The time-use domains we selected for study represent distinct "cuts" at a child's life. We are impressed by the commonality of experience among children in some areas of out-of-school life. At the same time, we have seen some extraordinary differences. To an extent, children seem to be growing up with different time-use opportunities and predispositions and, therefore, different values about time use, which they will carry to adulthood.

A realistic appraisal of the intellectual and social development of the young requires that a child's day not be viewed as a series of distinct, unrelated experiences but as a cohesive whole with attitudes, values, and behaviors related to and affecting one another. While we have not attempted an exhaustive documentation of children's lives, we have taken an ecological view.

The data presented here are indicators of a sort, ways of perceiving how children experience childhood. Over time, the evolution of children's activity patterns can tell us a great deal about changing conditions of childhood and how we as a culture are rearing our young and preparing them for adulthood.

We want children to have a variety of experiences outside school for we want them to be able to test themselves, pursue and develop new interests and capabilities, improve and sharpen skills, and have fun. Life outside school provides some of the most significant experiences of childhood. Jonathan Kozol has written: "I remember those times. . . . All of the hours that mattered most to us, in terms of passion, high stakes, day dreams and ideals . . . all of those hours were 'sneaked in,' 'unlicensed.' . . . We got no credit hours for them."[8] Here we have examined aspects of these hours away from school for one age group. We need to probe their meaning and impact in much greater detail as a way of understanding dimensions of children's lives that are as fundamental as any others to the experience of growing up.

APPENDIXES

Appendix A
Instruments

The Children's Time Study Survey consisted of two protocols: a child's interview and a parent's questionnaire. Interviews were administered at each respondent's home and took approximately one hour's time. Parents filled out questionnaires while the child's interview was in progress. In several instances a comparable foreign language protocol was used, and on occasion parents needed help filling out the questionnaire. The protocols reproduced here are identical to the field instruments except that parents were given gender-specific questionnaires depending on the sex of the child respondent. The questions themselves, however, were the same for parents of all respondents, regardless of the child's sex.

Three items are included in this appendix: first, the initial letter that was sent to parents prior to contact by the field staff; second, the child's interview schedule; and third, the parent's questionnaire.

UNIVERSITY OF CALIFORNIA, BERKELEY

BERKELEY · DAVIS · IRVINE · LOS ANGELES · RIVERSIDE · SAN DIEGO · SAN FRANCISCO   SANTA BARBARA · SANTA CRUZ

SURVEY RESEARCH CENTER   BERKELEY, CALIFORNIA 94720

Spring, 1976

Dear Parent:

We are writing to ask you and your child (Name of Child)
to take part in a study of sixth grade children being conducted by
the University of California.

The study is trying to learn more about children's activities
after school and the kinds of things they like to do in their free
time. This information will be used to help recreation departments,
libraries, schools and other public agencies develop programs better
fitted to children's needs and interests.

As part of this study, we would like to interview your child for
about one hour in your home. The interviewer will be asking about such
topics as indoor and outdoor play, TV watching and other types of recreation. While your child is being interviewed we would like you to fill
out a form about children's activities, your family and your neighborhood. This form will take about 45 minutes to complete.

Within the next few days an interviewer will call to ask for an
appointment at a time that will be best for you and (Name of Child).
If you have any questions, the interviewer will be happy to answer them
when she calls, or you may telephone (Name of Survey Research Center
Representative).

The sixth graders we are interviewing were chosen at random from all
areas of the city with the help of the Oakland Schools Superintendent's
Office. The information you and your child provide is most important to
us and will be kept in strictest confidence. Findings will be in a form
in which no person or family can be identified.

With your permission, we would like to give you and your child each
$2.50 for helping us to carry out this study.

Thank you for your cooperation.

Serial # _____

Confidential Form

CHILDREN'S TIME STUDY

1976

Interviewer _____ Date Assigned _____

Interviewer _____ Date Reassigned _____

	Appointment
Respondent's Name _____	Date _____
Parent's Name _____	Time _____
Address _____	
Phone # _____ ☐ None	

RECORD OF CALLS

Call #	Date	Hour	Result of Call	INDICATE TELE-PHONE CALL (T) OR HOME VISIT (H)	Int. #
1				H T	
2				H T	
3				H T	
4				H T	
5				H T	
6				H T	

By Observation: 1.W 2.B 3.MA 4. Or 5. Other _____
Comments: _____
_____
_____

Introduction

Hello—I'm _____ from the Survey Research Center at the University of California. I have an appointment with you and (CHILD'S NAME). May I come in?

Before talking with (CHILD'S NAME), I would like to ask you to answer some questions about the members of your family. I need this information because some of the questions in the interview ask about activities with brothers, sisters and others in the household.

I. First, I'd like to get an idea of who lives in this household. (RECORD IN TABLE 1.)

    1a. Are there children other than (CHILD) living here?

        Yes 1

        No (SKIP TO 2) 2

    b. Would you give me their names in order of age, beginning with the oldest? (Any others?) IF NECESSARY: How old is (CHILD)?

    2. What are the names of all the adults who live here?

    3. Is there anyone else who usually lives here, like a roomer or boarder?

    4. Have I missed anyone who is away temporarily? Any babies?

II. FOR EACH PERSON LISTED, ASK AS NECESSARY AND RECORD IN TABLE 1.

    E1. How is PERSON related to CHILD?

    E2. Is that a (boy/girl)?

    E3. How old was PERSON on (his/her) last birthday?

    IF AGE 16 OR OVER:

    E4. Is PERSON now married, widowed, divorced, separated, or has (he/she) never been married?

    E5. Does PERSON drive?

III. IF NECESSARY: Who is the head of the house? (CIRCLE PERSON NUMBER OF HOUSEHOLD HEAD.)

Include in Enumeration

a.   Everyone who usually lives here whether related or not.

b.   All persons staying or visiting here who have no other home.

c.   Persons who have a home elsewhere but are staying here most of the week while working or attending college.

Do Not Include in Enumeration

a.   College students away at school or here only on vacation and weekends.

b.   Persons away in the Armed Forces.

c.   Persons away in an institution such as a nursing home, mental hospital, or sanitarium.

d.   Persons visiting here with usual home elsewhere.

Enumeration

Name	Pers. Num. 5-6	E1 How related to respondent 9	E2 Sex 10	E3 Age 11-12	E4 Marital status 14	E5 Does PERS Drive 15
	01	Head	1. M 2. F		1. Mar 2. Sep 3. W/Dv 4. Nv M	1. Yes 2. No
	02		1. M 2. F		1. Mar 2. Sep 3. W/Dv 4. Nv M	1. Yes 2. No
	03		1. M 2. F		1. Mar 2. Sep 3. W/Dv 4. Nv M	1. Yes 2. No
	04		1. M 2. F		1. Mar 2. Sep 3. W/Dv 4. Nv M	1. Yes 2. No

Enumeration (Continued)

Name	Pers. Num. 5-6	E1 How related to respondent 9	E2 Sex 10	E3 Age 11-12	E4 Marital status 14	E5 Does PERS Drive 15
	05		1. M 2. F		1. Mar 2. Sep 3. W/Dv 4. Nv M	1. Yes 2. No
	06		1. M 2. F		1. Mar 2. Sep 3. W/Dv 4. Nv M	1. Yes 2. No
	07		1. M 2. F		1. Mar 2. Sep 3. W/Dv 4. Nv M	1. Yes 2. No
	08		1. M 2. F		1. Mar 2. Sep 3. W/Dv 4. Nv M	1. Yes 2. No
	09		1. M 2. F		1. Mar 2. Sep 3. W/Dv 4. Nv M	1. Yes 2. No
	10		1. M 2. F		1. Mar 2. Sep 3. W/Dv 4. Nv M	1. Yes 2. No
	11		1. M 2. F		1. Mar 2. Sep 3. W/Dv 4. Nv M	1. Yes 2. No
	12		1. M 2. F		1. Mar 2. Sep 3. W/Dv 4. Nv M	1. Yes 2. No

HAND PARENT QUESTIONNAIRE-BLUE FOR BOYS, YELLOW FOR GIRLS

This is the form we are asking the parents to fill out. It will take you about 45 minutes to fill complete.

OPEN TO FIRST PAGE AND REVIEW INSTRUCTIONS

If you have any questions or any problems filling it out, I'll be happy to help you as soon as I am finished talking with CHILD. You can make check marks by any questions you want to ask about after the interview is over.

NON-INTERVIEW INFORMATION

CIRCLE ONE AND COMPLETE BOX BELOW:

1. Phone—appointment made
2. Phone—refusal
3. Phone—never reached—result of visit
4. No phone—result of visit

Reason for non-interview:

☐ Indirect refusal. Two or more broken appointments, always "too busy", etc. EXPLAIN:

_____

☐ Direct refusal. (Parent or other household member said they would not cooperate) INDICATE REASON IF GIVEN:

_____

☐ No one ever at home in four calls.

☐ Parent never home in four calls, other household member seen.

☐ Respondent never at home in four calls.

☐ Inaccessible respondent. EXPLAIN (e.g.: out of town for extended stay, hospitalized, too ill for interview.)

_____

☐ Inaccessible parent. EXPLAIN AS ABOVE.

_____

☐ Respondent moved and is unlocatable.

☐ Respondent moved out of sample area.

☐ House vacant or demolished. (LIST NAME AND ADDRESS OF NEIGHBOR CONFIRMING VACANCY.)

_____

☐ Other. EXPLAIN:

_____

Result of attempted conversion by second interviewer: Int. #_____

☐ Refusal. INDICATE REASON GIVEN: _____

_____

☐ Could not find respondent/parent home in two calls.

☐ Other. _____

_____

Serial # _ _ _ _ 5/1
(1-4)
6-7/11
Time _____ A.M.
P.M.

1A. Do you ever listen to the radio?

Yes 1   8/

No 2

B. What kinds of things do you usually listen to? (CIRCLE ALL THAT APPLY)

Music 1   9/

Sports 2   10/

Talk shows 3   11/

News 4   12/

Other (SPECIFY:_____

_____) 5   13/

2A. About how many days a week do you watch TV?

    Everyday 1   *14/*

    5 or 6 days a week 2

    3 or 4 days a week 3

    1 or 2 days a week 4

    Less than that 5

    Never . . . . *(SKIP TO 3)* 6

B. What TV programs do you like best?

_____   _____ *15-16/*

3A. Do you have any hobbies, like collecting or making things?

    Yes 1   *17/*

    No . . . . *(SKIP TO 4)* 2

B. What hobbies do you have? *PROBE:* Any other hobbies?

_____ *18-19/*

_____ *20-21/*

_____ *21-23/*

4A. When you're here at home, do you spend any time reading—not for school but just reading for fun?

    Yes 1   *24/*

    No 2

B. About how many days a week do you read for fun?

    Everyday 1   *25/*

    5 or 6 days a week 2

    3 or 4 days a week 3

1 or 2 days a week 4

Less than that 5

C. I'd like to know what you read:

C1. Do you read magazines?

Yes 1   *26/*

No 2

C2. How about comics?

Yes 1   *27/*

No 2

C3. What about books?

Yes 1   *28/*

No 2

C4. Do you read newspapers, other than the funnies?

Yes 1   *29/*

No 2

IF ONLY ONE "YES" ANSWER TO C, SKIP TO 5

D. Which do you read most often—magazines, comics, books, or newspapers?

Magazines 1   *30/*

Comics 2

Books 3

Newspapers 4

5. Do you have a library card?

Yes 1   *31/*

No 2

**IF RESPONDENT HAS NO SIBS BETWEEN 6 AND 18 YEARS OLD
SKIP TO 7**

---

6. How much do you play with your (brother(s)) (or)
    (sister(s))—a lot, some, or not very much?

    A lot 1   *32/*

    Some 2

    Not very much 3

7. In the afternoon and on weekends [when you're not
    playing with your (brother(s)) (or) (sister(s))] do you
    usually play with other kids or by yourself?

    With other kids 1   *33/*

    By self . . . . *(SKIP TO 9)* 2

8A. [Not counting your (brother(s)) (or) (sister(s))], who do
    you play with most often after school and on weekends?
    What are their first names?

    *ENTER NAMES IN TABLE BELOW. WHEN ALL NAMES
    ENTERED, ASK REMAINING QUESTIONS FOR EACH
    KID NAMED.*

A. Name	B. IF NECESSARY: Is ___ a girl or a boy?		C. Does ___ go to your school?		D. Does ___ live close enough so you can walk or bike to his/her home?		E. IF YES: Does ___ live here on your block?		
	Girl	Boy	Yes	No	Yes	No	Yes	No	
	1	2	1	2	1	2	1	2	*34-37/*
	1	2	1	2	1	2	1	2	*38-41/*
	1	2	1	2	1	2	1	2	*42-45/*
	1	2	1	2	1	2	1	2	*46-49/*
	1	2	1	2	1	2	1	2	*50-53/*

9. Do you ever visit (other) friends of yours who live too
far away for you to walk there or go by bike?

   Yes 1   *54/*

   No 2

> IF NO FRIENDS OR PLAYMATES MENTIONED THUS FAR,
> SKIP TO 11

10. What kinds of things do you like to do with your friends?

    PROBE: What else do you like to do with your friends?
    PROBE FOR OTHER THAN TV WATCHING.

    _____   *55-56/*
    _____   *57-58/*
    _____   *59-60/*
    _____   *61-62/*
    _____

11. How about when you're by yourself, what do you like to do?

    PROBE: What else do you like to do when you're alone?
    PROBE FOR OTHER THAN TV WATCHING.

    _____   *63-64/*
    _____   *65-66/*
    _____   *67-68/*
    _____   *69-70/*
    _____

12. How much time do you have to do the things *you* want to
    do—a lot of time, some time, not very much, or hardly
    any time at all?

    A lot of time 1   *71/*

    Some time 2

    Not very much 3

    Hardly any at all 4

Serial # _ _ _ _ 5/1
(1-4)
6-7/12

Now let me ask you some questions about your neighborhood.

13.   How long have you lived in this neighborhood?

IF NECESSARY: What grade were you in when you
moved here? How old were you?

Grade when moved here _____	Less than 6 months . . .	1	*8/*
Age when moved here _____	6 to 11 months	2
	12 to 17 months	3
	18 to 23 months	4
	2 to 3 years	5
	4 to 5 years	6
	More than 5 years	7

14.   What do you especially like about the neighborhood?
PROBE: Anything else?

_____   *9-10/*
_____   *11-12/*
_____   *13-14/*
_____   *15-16/*
_____   *17-18/*
_____

15.   Where do you (and your friends) usually play?
CODE ALL THAT APPLY.

PROBE: Where else?

In own house or yard?   1   *19/*

In friends' houses or yards   2   *20/*

In a park   3   *21/*

School grounds or yard . . . *(SKIP TO 16B)* 4   *22/*

Other *(SPECIFY:* _____ 5   *23/*

_____

_____ *)*   *24/*

25/

16A. After school or on weekends, do you ever play in the school yard?

Yes 1   *26/*

No . . . . *(SKIP TO 17)* 2

B. About how often do you play in the school yard <u>after school or on weekends?</u>

IF NECESSARY, PROBE WITH ANSWER CATEGORIES.

Everyday 1   *27/*

5 or 6 days a week 2

3 or 4 days a week 3

1 or 2 days a week 4

Less than that 5

17. What things don't you like about this neighborhood?

PROBE: Is there anything (else/at all) that you don't like about it?

PROBE: Anything else?

☐ Nothing   *28-29/*

30-31/

32-33/

34-35/

36-37/

18A. Are there any (other) parts of the neighborhood that
     you don't like to go?

> *IF NECESSARY:* How about certain streets, playgrounds,
> parks, or vacant lots—places like that?

> Yes 1   *38/*

> No . . . . *(SKIP TO 19)* 2

B. What places? *PROBE:* Anywhere else you don't like to go?
   RECORD BELOW AND ASK C FOR EACH.

B. PLACES	C. Why don't you like to go there?	
		39-40/
		41-42/
		43-44/
		45-46/
		47-48/
		49-50/
		51-52/
		53-54/

19. How safe do you think it is going around the neighbor-
    hood by yourself—very safe, fairly safe, or not very safe?

> Very safe 1   *55/*

> Fairly safe 2

> Not very safe 3

>   *56-80/*

Now I'm going to ask you some questions about something else.

	21. A coffee shop or restaurant	22. The movies	23. A park	24. A church, synagogue, or mosque	25. A public library
A. How often do you usually go to:	Once a week or more . . . . . 1 8/ A few times a month . . . . . 2 A few times a year *(SKIP TO D)* . . . . . 3 Hardly ever/never *(SKIP TO 22)* 4	Once a week or more . . . . . 1 17/ A few times a month . . . . . 2 A few times a year *(SKIP TO D)* . . . . . 3 Hardly ever/never *(SKIP TO 23)* 4	Once a week or more . . . . . 1 26/ A few times a month . . . . . 2 A few times a year *(SKIP TO D)* . . . . . 3 Hardly ever/never *(SKIP TO 24)* 4	Once a week or more . . . . . 1 35/ A few times a month . . . . . 2 A few times a year *(SKIP TO D)* . . . . . 3 Hardly ever/never *(SKIP TO 25)* 4	Once a week or more . . . . . 1 44/ A few times a month . . . . . 2 A few times a year *(SKIP TO D)* . . . . . 3 Hardly ever/never *(SKIP TO 26)* 4
B. Do you usually go there by yourself or with someone else?	By self *(SKIP TO D)* . . . . . 1 9/ With someone else . . . . . 2 Varies *(SKIP TO D)* 3	By self *(SKIP TO D)* . . . . . 1 18/ With someone else . . . . . 2 Varies *(SKIP TO D)* 3	By self *(SKIP TO D)* . . . . . 1 27/ With someone else . . . . . 2 Varies *(SKIP TO D)* 3	By self *(SKIP TO D)* . . . . . 1 36/ With someone else . . . . . 2 Varies *(SKIP TO D)* 3	By self *(SKIP TO D)* . . . . . 1 45/ With someone else . . . . . 2 Varies *(SKIP TO D)* 3
C. Who do you usually go with? PROBE: Anyone else? CIRCLE ALL THAT APPLY. IF "FAMILY," PROBE FOR WHO GOES.	Mother . . . . . 1 10/ Father . . . . . 2 11/ Siblings . . . . . 3 12/ Other adults . . . . . 4 13/ Friends . . . . . 5 14/ Varies too much to say 6 15/	Mother . . . . . 1 19/ Father . . . . . 2 20/ Siblings . . . . . 3 21/ Other adults . . . . . 4 22/ Friends . . . . . 5 23/ Varies too much to say 6 24/	Mother . . . . . 1 28/ Father . . . . . 2 29/ Siblings . . . . . 3 30/ Other adults . . . . . 4 31/ Friends . . . . . 5 32/ Varies too much to say 6 33/	Mother . . . . . 1 37/ Father . . . . . 2 38/ Siblings . . . . . 3 39/ Other adults . . . . . 4 40/ Friends . . . . . 5 41/ Varies too much to say 6 42/	Mother . . . . . 1 46/ Father . . . . . 2 47/ Siblings . . . . . 3 48/ Other adults . . . . . 4 49/ Friends . . . . . 5 50/ Varies too much to say 6 51/
D. How do you get there most of the time? IF NECESSARY: How about the last time?	Walk or bike . . . . . 1 16/ Parent drives . . . . . 2 Other adult drives . . . . . 3 Bus . . . . . 4 BART . . . . . 5 Hitchhike . . . . . 6 Bus/BART and someone drives . . . . . 7 Other *(SPECIFY:* _____ *)* 8 Varies too much to say 0	Walk or bike . . . . . 1 25/ Parent drives . . . . . 2 Other adult drives . . . . . 3 Bus . . . . . 4 BART . . . . . 5 Hitchhike . . . . . 6 Bus/BART and someone drives . . . . . 7 Other *(SPECIFY:* _____ *)* 8 Varies too much to say 0	Walk or bike . . . . . 1 34/ Parent drives . . . . . 2 Other adult drives . . . . . 3 Bus . . . . . 4 BART . . . . . 5 Hitchhike . . . . . 6 Bus/BART and someone drives . . . . . 7 Other *(SPECIFY:* _____ *)* 8 Varies too much to say 0	Walk or bike . . . . . 1 43/ Parent drives . . . . . 2 Other adult drives . . . . . 3 Bus . . . . . 4 BART . . . . . 5 Hitchhike . . . . . 6 Bus/BART and someone drives . . . . . 7 Other *(SPECIFY:* _____ *)* 8 Varies too much to say 0	Walk or bike . . . . . 1 52/ Parent drives . . . . . 2 Other adult drives . . . . . 3 Bus . . . . . 4 BART . . . . . 5 Hitchhike . . . . . 6 Bus/BART and someone drives . . . . . 7 Other *(SPECIFY:* _____ *)* 8 Varies too much to say 0

Now let's talk about school.

26. What school do you go to?

      Name of School _____   *53-54/*

27. How long have you been going to *(NAME OF SCHOOL)*?

      Less than 1 year 0   *55/*

      1 year to 23 months 1

      2 years to 35 months 2

      3 years to 47 months 3

      4 years to 59 months 4

      5 years or more 5

28. What grade are you in?

      Sixth grade 6   *56/*

      Other *(RECONFIRM THAT YOU HAVE THE CORRECT RESPONDENT AND RECORD DETAILS BELOW)* 7

29A. How do you usually get to school—do you walk, ride a bike, take the bus, or what?

      Walk or bike . . . . *(SKIP TO 30)* 1   *57/*

      Someone drives 2

      Bus . . . . *(SKIP TO 30)* 3

      BART . . . . *(SKIP TO 30)* 4

      Bus/BART and someone drives 5

      Other *(SPECIFY:* _____

      _____ *) (SKIP TO 30)* 6

  B. Who usually drives you to (school/the bus/BART)?

      Mother or father 1   *58/*

      Other household member 2

      Someone else 3

30. On this page are some questions about school. *(HAND INSERT 1 AND PENCIL.)* I will read the questions

along with you, but I would like you to mark the answers yourself. For each question, circle the answer that is <u>most</u> true for you. Circle only one answer for each question.

(1) I like my teacher this year.

Yes 1   *59/*

No 2

No answer 3

(2) I am happy with the grades I get on my report cards.

Yes 1   *60/*

No 2

No answer 3

(3) My classroom is too noisy.

Yes 1   *61/*

No 2

No answer 3

(4) I like doing arithmetic at school.

Yes 1   *62/*

No 2

No answer 3

(5) My teacher often gives me work that is too hard.

Yes 1   *63/*

No 2

No answer 3

(6) I have many good friends at school.

Yes 1   *64/*

No 2

No answer 3

(7) Most school work is boring.

    Yes 1   *65/*

    No 2

    No answer 3

(8) I try hard at school.

    Yes 1   *66/*

    No 2

    No answer 3

(9) Some kids at school tease me a lot.

    Yes 1   *67/*

    No 2

    No answer 3

(10) I am a good reader.

    Yes 1   *68/*

    No 2

    No answer 3

(11) There are lots of tough kids at school who pick on other kids.

    Yes 1   *69/*

    No 2

    No answer 3

(12) This year, I think my teacher likes me.

    Yes 1   *70/*

    No 2

    No answer 3

(13) I wish I had gone to a different school this year.

    Yes 1   *71/*

    No 2

    No answer 3

(14) Doing school work is easy for me.

Yes 1   72/

No 2

No answer 3

Now for two questions that are a bit different.

(15) This year, my grades in reading have been:

Excellent 1   73/

Good 2

Fair 3

Poor.............................. 4

No answer 5

(16) This year, my grades in arithmetic have been:

Excellent 1   74/

Good 2

Fair 3

Poor.............................. 4

No answer 5

RETRIEVE INSERT, QUICKLY SCAN FOR DOUBLE OR MISSING ANSWERS, AND INSERT IN SCHEDULE. CODE TO THESE PAGES AFTER YOU LEAVE THE HOME.

SCHOOL ACTIVITIES

S1.   On these cards are the names of activities <u>some schools</u> have for kids *(HAND CARDS)*. I'll go through them with you, and you can hand me those that your school has. *(RECORD IN ROW S1 OF TABLE S RETRIEVE UNSELECTED CARDS.)*

S2A.   Now let's go through these cards again *(HAND SELECTED CARDS)*, and this time you hand me those for activities you have been in at any time since you started 6th grade in September. *(CIRCLE 1 "YES" IN Q2 ON TABLE S FOR EACH ACTIVITY R HAS BEEN IN AND 2 "NO" FOR ALL OTHERS.)*

   B. Are there any (other) <u>school</u> activities that aren't on the cards that you have been in at any time since you started 6th grade in September?

       Yes   1   75/

       No . . . . . .   *(SKIP TO INSTRUCTION)*   2

   C. What are they? *(RECORD NAME OF ACTIVITY UNDER "OTHER SCHOOL ACTIVITY" IN TABLE S1.)*

   > *IF NO SCHOOL ACTIVITIES: SKIP TO LESSON TABLE*
   > *IF ACTIVITIES: COMPLETE SCHOOL TABLE*

TABLE S Activity → Questions	01 Student Council or Government (8-16)	02 Student Helpers in School Office (17-25)	03 Student Traffic Patrol (26-34)
S1. ACTIVITIES SCHOOL HAS	1. School has 2. Not have (X) 3. DK (X)	1. School has 2. Not have (X) 3. DK (X)	1. School has 2. Not have (X) 3. DK (X)
S2. BEEN IN SINCE SEPTEMBER	1. Yes 2. No (X)	1. Yes 2. No (X)	1. Yes 2. No (X)
S3a. Are you still in _____?	1. Yes (SKIP TO S4) 2. No	1. Yes (SKIP TO S4) 2. No	1. Yes (SKIP TO S4) 2. No
S3b. (IF NO:) When you were in _____ did you go more than two times?	1. Yes 2. No (X) (RECORD IN TABLE ST)	1. Yes 2. No (X) (RECORD IN TABLE ST)	1. Yes 2. No (X) (RECORD IN TABLE ST)
S4. When do (did) you usually do that—during regular school hours, before school, or after school?	1. School hours 2. Before/after school 3. Varies or both 4. Can't say	1. School hours 2. Before/after school 3. Varies or both 4. Can't say	1. School hours 2. Before/after school 3. Varies or both 4. Can't say
S5. Whose idea was it for you to be in _____? Was it your own idea, your parents', a friend's, a teacher's, or was it someone else's idea?	1. Own idea 2. Parents 3. Own & parents 4. Friends/siblings 5. Teacher 6. Someone else (SPEC:_____) 7. Can't say	1. Own idea 2. Parents 3. Own & parents 4. Friends/siblings 5. Teacher 6. Someone else (SPEC:_____) 7. Can't say	1. Own idea 2. Parents 3. Own & parents 4. Friends/siblings 5. Teacher 6. Someone else (SPEC:_____) 7. Can't say
S6. Did you or your family have to buy or rent anything for you to be in _____?	1. Yes 2. No 3. Can't say	1. Yes 2. No 3. Can't say	1. Yes 2. No 3. Can't say
S7. Are (Were) the other kids in _____ mostly boys, mostly girls, or about half and half? (IF MOSTLY BOYS/GIRLS:) Were they all (boys/girls)?	1. All boys 2. Mostly boys 3. Half and half 4. Mostly girls 5. All girls	1. All boys 2. Mostly boys 3. Half and half 4. Mostly girls 5. All girls	1. All boys 2. Mostly boys 3. Half and half 4. Mostly girls 5. All girls
S8. How do (did) you feel about being in _____? Do (did) you like it a lot, like it some, or don't (didn't) you like it very much?	1. Like alot 2. Like some 3. Don't like it much	1. Like alot 2. Like some 3. Don't like it much	1. Like alot 2. Like some 3. Don't like it much
	IF NOT IN NOW, RECORD IN TABLE ST.	IF NOT IN NOW, RECORD IN TABLE ST.	IF NOT IN NOW, RECORD IN TABLE ST.

Serial # _ _ _ _ 5/1
(1-4)
6-7/14

04 School Band or Orchestra (35-43)	05 School Chorus or Glee Club (44-52)	06 School Newspaper or Magazine (53-61)	07 School Teams That Play Other Schools (62-70)	08 School Drill Team or Cheerleaders (71-79)
1. School has 2. Not have (X) 3. DK (X)	1. School has 2. Not have (X) 3. DK (X)	1. School has 2. Not have (X) 3. DK (X)	1. School has 2. Not have (X) 3. DK (X)	1. School has 2. Not have (X) 3. DK (X)
1. Yes 2. No (X)	1. Yes 2. No (X)	1. Yes 2. No (X)	1. Yes 2. No (X)	1. Yes 2. No (X)
1. Yes *(SKIP TO S4)* 2. No	1. Yes *(SKIP TO S4)* 2. No	1. Yes *(SKIP TO S4)* 2. No	1. Yes *(SKIP TO S4)* 2. No	1. Yes *(SKIP TO S4)* 2. No
1. Yes 2. No (X) *(RECORD IN TABLE ST)*	1. Yes 2. No (X) *(RECORD IN TABLE ST)*	1. Yes 2. No (X) *(RECORD IN TABLE ST)*	1. Yes 2. No (X) *(RECORD IN TABLE ST)*	1. Yes 2. No (X) *(RECORD IN TABLE ST)*
1. School hours 2. Before/after school 3. Varies or both 4. Can't say	1. School hours 2. Before/after school 3. Varies or both 4. Can't say	1. School hours 2. Before/after school 3. Varies or both 4. Can't say	1. School hours 2. Before/after school 3. Varies or both 4. Can't say	1. School hours 2. Before/after school 3. Varies or both 4. Can t say
1. Own idea 2. Parents 3. Own & parents 4. Friends/siblings 5. Teacher 6. Someone else (SPEC:_____) 7. Can't say	1. Own idea 2. Parents 3. Own & parents 4. Friends/siblings 5. Teacher 6. Someone else (SPEC:_____) 7. Can't say	1. Own idea 2. Parents 3. Own & parents 4. Friends/siblings 5. Teacher 6. Someone else (SPEC:_____) 7. Can't say	1. Own idea 2. Parents 3. Own & parents 4. Friends/siblings 5. Teacher 6. Someone else (SPEC:_____) 7. Can't say	1. Own idea 2. Parents 3. Own & parents 4. Friends/siblings 5. Teacher 6. Someone else (SPEC._____) 7. Can t say
1. Yes 2. No 3. Can't say	1. Yes 2. No 3. Can't say	1. Yes 2. No 3. Can't say	1. Yes 2. No 3. Can't say	1. Yes 2. No 3. Can t say
1. All boys 2. Mostly boys 3. Half and half 4. Mostly girls 5. All girls	1. All boys 2. Mostly boys 3. Half and half 4. Mostly girls 5. All girls	1. All boys 2. Mostly boys 3. Half and half 4. Mostly girls 5. All girls	1. All boys 2. Mostly boys 3. Half and half 4. Mostly girls 5. All girls	1. All boys 2. Mostly boys 3. Half and half 4. Mostly girls 5. All girls
1. Like alot 2. Like some 3. Don't like it much	1. Like alot 2. Like some 3. Don't like it much	1. Like alot 2. Like some 3. Don't like it much	1. Like alot 2. Like some 3. Don t like it much	1. Like alot 2. Like some 3. Don t like it much
IF NOT IN NOW, RE-CORD IN TABLE ST.	IF NOT IN NOW, RE-CORD IN TABLE ST.	IF NOT IN NOW, RE-CORD IN TABLE ST.	IF NOT IN NOW, RE-CORD IN TABLE ST.	IF NOT IN NOW, RE-CORD IN TABLE ST.

Questions	Activity →	09 Lessons in Musical Instruments (8-16)	10 Student Tutors for Other Kids (17-25)	11 Other School Club Activities (26-34)
S1. ACTIVITIES SCHOOL HAS		1. School has 2. Not have (X) 3. DK (X)	1. School has 2. Not have (X) 3. DK (X)	1. School has 2. Not have (X) 3. DK (X)
S2. BEEN IN SINCE SEPTEMBER		1. Yes 2. No (X)	1. Yes 2. No (X)	1. Yes 2. No (X)
S3a. Are you still in_____?		1. Yes *(SKIP TO S4)* 2. No	1. Yes *(SKIP TO S4)* 2. No	1. Yes *(SKIP TO S4)* 2. No
S3b. *(IF NO:)* When you were in_____ did you go more than two times?		1. Yes 2. No (X) *(RECORD IN TABLE ST)*	1. Yes 2. No (X) *(RECORD IN TABLE ST)*	1. Yes 2. No (X) *(RECORD IN TABLE ST)*
S4. When do (did) you usually do that—during regular school hours, before school, or after school?		1. School hours 2. Before/after school 3. Varies or both 4. Can't say	1. School hours 2. Before/after school 3. Varies or both 4. Can't say	1. School hours 2. Before/after school 3. Varies or both 4. Can't say
S5. Whose idea was it for you to be in ____? Was it your own idea, your parents', a friend's, a teacher's, or was it someone else's idea?		1. Own idea 2. Parents 3. Own & parents 4. Friends/siblings 5. Teacher 6. Someone else (SPEC:_____) 7. Can't say	1. Own idea 2. Parents 3. Own & parents 4. Friends/siblings 5. Teacher 6. Someone else (SPEC:_____) 7. Can't say	1. Own idea 2. Parents 3. Own & parents 4. Friends/siblings 5. Teacher 6. Someone else (SPEC:_____) 7. Can't say
S6. Did you or your family have to buy or rent anything for you to be in ____?		1. Yes 2. No 3. Can't say	1. Yes 2. No 3. Can't say	1. Yes 2. No 3. Can't say
S7. Are (Were) the other kids in ____ mostly boys, mostly girls, or about half and half? *(IF MOSTLY BOYS/GIRLS:)* Were they all (boys/girls)?		1. All boys 2. Mostly boys 3. Half and half 4. Mostly girls 5. All girls	1. All boys 2. Mostly boys 3. Half and half 4. Mostly girls 5. All girls	1. All boys 2. Mostly boys 3. Half and half 4. Mostly girls 5. All girls
S8. How do (did) you feel about being in ____? Do (did) you like it a lot, like it some, or don't (didn't) you like it very much?		1. Like alot 2. Like some 3. Don't like it much	1. Like alot 2. Like some 3. Don't like it much	1. Like alot 2. Like some 3. Don't like it much
		IF NOT IN NOW, RECORD IN TABLE ST.	IF NOT IN NOW, RECORD IN TABLE ST.	IF NOT IN NOW, RECORD IN TABLE ST.

Serial # _ _ _ _ 5/1
(1-4)
6-7/15

12	13	14	15	
35-36/ (37-45)	*46-47/ (48-56)*	*57-58/ (59-67)*	*68-69/ (70-78)*	
1. School has	1. School has	1. School has	1. School has	1. School has
2. Not have (X)	2. Not have (X)	2. Not have (X)	2. Not have (X)	2. Not have (X)
3. DK (X)	3. DK (X)	3. DK (X)	3. DK (X)	3. DK (X)
1. Yes	1. Yes	1. Yes	1. Yes	1. Yes
2. No (X)	2. No (X)	2. No (X)	2. No (X)	2. No (X)
1. Yes *(SKIP TO S4)*	1. Yes *(SKIP TO S4)*	1. Yes *(SKIP TO S4)*	1. Yes *(SKIP TO S4)*	1. Yes *(SKIP TO S4)*
2. No	2. No	2. No	2. No	2. No
1. Yes	1. Yes	1. Yes	1. Yes	1. Yes
2. No (X) *(RECORD IN TABLE ST)*	2. No (X) *(RECORD IN TABLE ST)*	2. No (X) *(RECORD IN TABLE ST)*	2. No (X) *(RECORD IN TABLE ST)*	2. No (X) *(RECORD IN TABLE ST)*
1. School hours	1. School hours	1. School hours	1. School hours	1. School hours
2. Before/after school	2. Before/after school	2. Before/after school	2. Before/after school	2. Before/after school
3. Varies or both	3. Varies or both	3. Varies or both	3. Varies or both	3. Varies or both
4. Can't say	4. Can't say	4. Can't say	4. Can't say	4. Can't say
1. Own idea	1. Own idea	1. Own idea	1. Own idea	1. Own idea
2. Parents	2. Parents	2. Parents	2. Parents	2. Parents
3. Own & parents	3. Own & parents	3. Own & parents	3. Own & parents	3. Own & parents
4. Friends/siblings	4. Friends/siblings	4. Friends/siblings	4. Friends/siblings	4. Friends/siblings
5. Teacher	5. Teacher	5. Teacher	5. Teacher	5. Teacher
6. Someone else (SPEC: ___)	6. Someone else (SPEC: ___)	6. Someone else (SPEC: ___)	6. Someone else (SPEC: ___)	6. Someone else (SPEC: ___)
7. Can't say	7. Can't say	7. Can't say	7. Can t say	7. Can t say
1. Yes	1. Yes	1. Yes	1. Yes	1. Yes
2. No	2. No	2. No	2. No	2. No
3. Can't say	3. Can't say	3. Can't say	3. Can t say	3. Can t say
1. All boys	1. All boys	1. All boys	1. All boys	1. All boys
2. Mostly boys	2. Mostly boys	2. Mostly boys	2. Mostly boys	2. Mostly boys
3. Half and half	3. Half and half	3. Half and half	3. Half and half	3. Half and half
4. Mostly girls	4. Mostly girls	4. Mostly girls	4. Mostly girls	4. Mostly girls
5. All girls	5. All girls	5. All girls	5. All girls	5. All girls
1. Like alot	1. Like alot	1. Like alot	1. Like alot	1. Like alot
2. Like some	2. Like some	2. Like some	2. Like some	2. Like some
3. Don't like it much	3. Don't like it much	3. Don't like it much	3. Don t like it much	3. Don't like it much
IF NOT IN NOW, RE-CORD IN TABLE ST.	IF NOT IN NOW, RE-CORD IN TABLE ST.	IF NOT IN NOW, RE-CORD IN TABLE ST.	IF NOT IN NOW, RE-CORD IN TABLE ST.	IF NOT IN NOW, RE-CORD IN TABLE ST.

Serial # _ _ _ _ 5/1
(1-4)
6-7/16

TABLE ST

SCHOOL ACTIVITIES TERMINATED OR DROPPED SINCE SCHOOL STARTED IN SEPTEMBER

| Activity _____ | Code ⬚⬚ | 8-9/ |

S12. Why aren't you in _____ anymore?   10-11/

PROBE: Any other reasons?   12-13/

                                                         14-15/

                                                         16-17/

| Activity _____ | Code ⬚⬚ | 18-19/ |

S12. Why aren't you in _____ anymore?   20-21/

PROBE: Any other reasons?   22-23/

                                                         24-25/

                                                         26-27/

| Activity _____ | Code ⬚⬚ | 28-29/ |

S12. Why aren't you in _____ anymore?   30-31/

PROBE: Any other reasons?   32-33/

                                                         34-35/

                                                         36-37/

GO TO TABLE L

TABLE L: LESSONS

Lessons and Classes After School

L1a. On these cards are the names of some lessons and classes that kids may take <u>after school or on weekends</u>. They may be given to one kid alone or to a group of kids all together. *(HAND CHILD CARDS.)* Please look through these cards and see if there are any that you have taken <u>since September</u>. I'll go through them with you, and if there are any that you have taken, hand them to me.

Remember, I'm asking about lessons that are given on weekends or after 3 o'clock when regular school classes end.

(RETRIEVE UNSELECTED CARDS.)

b. Have you taken any (other) lessons <u>since September</u> that are not on these cards?

Yes 3

No *(SEE INSTRUCTIONS AT BOTTOM OF PAGE)* 2

c. What are they? *RECORD RESPONSES IN SPACES 13, 14, and 15 ON TABLE L.*

IF R. HAS NOT TAKEN ANY LESSONS SINCE SEPTEMBER, RETURN TO GENERAL RETURN FROM LESSONS TABLE.

IF R. HAS TAKEN ONE OR MORE LESSONS SINCE SEPTEMBER, GO TO Q. 2 ON TABLE L.

TABLE L	01	02	03
Questions	Music lessons	Dancing lessons	Dramatics or acting lessons
L1. SINCE SEPTEMBER?	1. Yes 2. No (X)	1. Yes 2. No (X)	1. Yes 2. No (X)
L2. What kind(s) of _____ lessons are (were) you taking? *IF MORE THAN ONE KIND OF LESSON IN ANY GENERAL CATEGORY RECORD OTHER(S) IN BLANK COLUMNS AT END OF CHART*	*TYPE OF LESSON*	*TYPE OF LESSON*	*TYPE OF LESSON*
L3. When are those lessons given? During regular school hours, before school or after school?	1. School hours (X) 2. Before/after school 3. Varies or both 4. Can't say	1. School hours (X) 2. Before/after school 3. Varies or both 4. Can't say	1. School hours (X) 2. Before/after school 3. Varies or both 4. Can't say
L4a. Are you still taking _____ lessons?	1. Yes *(GO TO L5)* 2. No	1. Yes *(GO TO L5)* 2. No	1. Yes *(GO TO L5)* 2. No
L4b. *IF NO:* When you did take _____ lessons did you go more than two times?	1. Yes 2. No (X)*(RECORD IN TABLE LT.)*	1. Yes 2. No (X)*(RECORD IN TABLE LT.)*	1. Yes 2. No (X)*(RECORD IN TABLE LT.)*
L5a. Who gives (gave) those lessons? Are (were) they given by some group or organization, a private teacher, or someone else?	1. Group or Org. 2. Pvt. teacher *(GO TO L6)* 3. Other 4. DK *(GO TO L6)*	1. Group or Org. 2. Pvt. teacher *(GO TO L6)* 3. Other 4. DK *(GO TO L6)*	1. Group or Org. 2. Pvt. teacher *(GO TO L6)* 3. Other 4. DK *(GO TO L6)*
L5b. What group or organization gives (gave) them? *(RECORD NAME AS FULL AS POSSIBLE. PROBE AS NECESSARY TO LEARN IF PUBLIC OR PRIVATE.)*			
L6. Where do (did) you usually have that lesson? 1. Own home 2. Teacher or leaders' home 3. Own school 4. Other school or college 5. Public rec. area 6. Library or museum 7. YWCA or YMCA 8. Church 9. Private recreation 10. Commercial place 11. Other	01. Own home 02. Teach/Leads home 03. Own school 04. Other sch./col. 05. Public rec. area 06. Library/museum 07. YWCA/YMCA 08. Church 09. Private rec. area 10. Commercial place 11. Other	01. Own home 02. Teach/Leads home 03. Own school 04. Other sch./col. 05. Public rec. area 06. Library/museum 07. YWCA/YMCA 08. Church 09. Private rec. area 10. Commercial place 11. Other	01. Own home 02. Teach/Leads home 03. Own school 04. Other sch./col. 05. Public rec. area 06. Library/museum 07. YWCA/YMCA 08. Church 09. Private rec. area 10. Commercial place 11. Other
L7a. How did you get there the last time you went? b. How did you get home?	There / Home 1. Walk/bike 1. 2. Parent Drives 2. 3. Other HH Drives 3. 4. Other Drives 4. 5. Bus 5. 6. BART 6. 7. Bus/BART/Drive 7. 8. Other 8.	There / Home 1. Walk/bike 1. 2. Parent Drives 2. 3. Other HH Drives 3. 4. Other Drives 4. 5. Bus 5. 6. BART 6. 7. Bus/BART/Drive 7. 8. Other 8.	There / Home 1. Walk/bike 1. 2. Parent Drives 2. 3. Other HH Drives 3. 4. Other Drives 4. 5. Bus 5. 6. BART 6. 7. Bus/BART/Drive 7. 8. Other 8.

04	05	06	07	08
Art lessons, like drawing or painting	Crafts, like pottery or making jewelry	Nature study or science	Cooking or sewing	Religious instruction, like Catechism, Bible Study, or Hebrew
1. Yes 2. No (X)	1. Yes 2. No (X)	1. Yes 2. No (X)	1. Yes 2. No (X)	1. Yes 2. No (X)
TYPE OF LESSON	*TYPE OF LESSON*	*TYPE OF LESSON*	*TYPE OF LESSON*	*TYPE OF LESSON*
1. School hours (X) 2. Before/after school 3. Varies or both 4. Can't say	1. School hours (X) 2. Before/after school 3. Varies or both 4. Can't say	1. School hours (X) 2. Before/after school 3. Varies or both 4. Can't say	1. School hours (X) 2. Before/after school 3. Varies or both 4. Can't say	1. School hours (X) 2. Before/after school 3. Varies or both 4. Can't say
1. Yes *(GO TO L5)* 2. No	1. Yes *(GO TO L5)* 2. No	1. Yes *(GO TO L5)* 2. No	1. Yes *(GO TO L5)* 2. No	1. Yes *(GO TO L5)* 2. No
1. Yes 2. No (X) *(RECORD IN TABLE LT.)*	1. Yes 2. No (X) *(RECORD IN TABLE LT.)*	1. Yes 2. No (X) *(RECORD IN TABLE LT.)*	1. Yes 2. No (X) *(RECORD IN TABLE LT.)*	1. Yes 2. No (X) *(RECORD IN TABLE LT.)*
1. Group or Org. 2. Pvt. teacher *(GO TO L6)* 3. Other 4. DK *(GO TO L6)*	1. Group or Org. 2. Pvt. teacher *(GO TO L6)* 3. Other 4. DK *(GO TO L6)*	1. Group or Org. 2. Pvt. teacher *(GO TO L6)* 3. Other 4. DK *(GO TO L6)*	1. Group or Org. 2. Pvt. teacher *(GO TO L6)* 3. Other 4. DK *(GO TO L6)*	1. Group or Org. 2. Pvt. teacher *(GO TO L6)* 3. Other 4. DK *(GO TO L6)*
01.Own home 02.Teach/Leads home 03.Own school 04.Other sch./col. 05.Public rec. area 06.Library/museum 07.YWCA/YMCA 08.Church 09.Private rec. area 10.Commercial place 11.Other	01.Own home 02.Teach/Leads home 03.Own school 04.Other sch./col. 05.Public rec. area 06.Library/museum 07.YWCA/YMCA 08.Church 09.Private rec. area 10.Commercial place 11.Other	01.Own home 02.Teach/Leads home 03.Own school 04.Other sch./col. 05.Public rec. area 06.Library/museum 07.YWCA/YMCA 08.Church 09.Private rec. area 10.Commercial place 11.Other	01.Own home 02.Teach/Leads home 03.Own school 04.Other sch./col. 05.Public rec. area 06.Library/museum 07.YWCA/YMCA 08.Church 09.Private rec. area 10.Commercial place 11.Other	01.Own home 02.Teach/Leads home 03.Own school 04.Other sch./col. 05.Public rec. area 06.Library/museum 07.YWCA/YMCA 08.Church 09.Private rec. area 10.Commercial place 11.Other
There / Home 1. Walk/bike 1. 2. Parent Drives 2. 3.Other HH Drives 3. 4. Other Drives 4. 5. Bus 5. 6. BART 6. 7.Bus/BART/Drive 7. 8. Other 8.	There / Home 1. Walk/bike 1. 2. Parent Drives 2. 3.Other H I Drives 3. 4. Other Drives 4. 5. Bus 5. 6. BART 6. 7.Bus/BART/Drive 7. 8. Other 8.	There / Home 1. Walk/bike 1. 2. Parent Drives 2. 3.Other HH Drives 3. 4. Other Drives 4. 5. Bus 5. 6. BART 6. 7. Bus/BART/Drive 7. 8. Other 8.	There / Home 1. Walk/bike 1. 2. Parent Drives 2. 3.Other HH Drives 3. 4. Other Drives 4. 5. Bus 5. 6. BART 6. 7. Bus/BART/Drive 7. 8. Other 8.	There / Home 1. Walk/bike 1. 2. Parent Drives 2. 3.Other HH Drives 3. 4. Other Drives 4. 5. Bus 5. 6. BART 6. 7. Bus/BART/Drive 7. 8. Other 8.

Questions	09 Swimming lessons	10 Tennis lessons	11 Ice skating or roller skating lessons
L1. SINCE SEPTEMBER?	1. Yes 2. No (X)	1. Yes 2. No (X)	1. Yes 2. No (X)
L2. What kind(s) of _____ lessons are (were) you taking? *IF MORE THAN ONE KIND OF LESSON IN ANY GENERAL CATEGORY RECORD OTHER(S) IN BLANK COLUMNS AT END OF CHART*	*TYPE OF LESSON*	*TYPE OF LESSON*	*TYPE OF LESSON*
L3. When are those lessons given? During regular school hours, before school or after school?	1. School hours (X) 2. Before/after school 3. Varies or both 4. Can't say	1. School hours (X) 2. Before/after school 3. Varies or both 4. Can't say	1. School hours (X) 2. Before/after school 3. Varies or both 4. Can't say
L4a. Are you still taking _____ lessons?	1. Yes *(GO TO L5)* 2. No	1. Yes *(GO TO L5)* 2. No	1. Yes *(GO TO L5)* 2. No
L4b. *IF NO:* When you did take _____ lessons did you go more than two times?	1. Yes 2. No (X)*(RECORD IN TABLE LT.)*	1. Yes 2. No (X)*(RECORD IN TABLE LT.)*	1. Yes 2. No (X)*(RECORD IN TABLE LT.)*

L5a. Who gives (gave) those lessons? Are (were) they given by some group or organization, a private teacher, or someone else?	1. Group or Org.
	2. Pvt. teacher
	  (GO TO L6)
	3. Other
	4. DK *(GO TO L6)*
		1. Group or Org.
		2. Pvt. teacher
		  (GO TO L6)
		3. Other
		4. DK *(GO TO L6)*
			1. Group or Org.
			2. Pvt. teacher
			  (GO TO L6)
			3. Other
			4. DK *(GO TO L6)*

L5b. What group or organization gives (gave) them? *(RECORD NAME AS FULL AS POSSIBLE. PROBE AS NECESSARY TO LEARN IF PUBLIC OR PRIVATE.)*			
L6. Where do (did) you usually have that lesson? 1. Own home 2. Teacher or leaders' home 3. Own school 4. Other school or college 5. Public rec. area 6. Library or museum 7. YWCA or YMCA 8. Church 9. Private recreation 10. Commercial place 11. Other	01. Own home 02. Teach/Leads home 03. Own school 04. Other sch./col. 05. Public rec. area 06. Library/museum 07. YWCA/YMCA 08. Church 09. Private rec. area 10. Commercial place 11. Other	01. Own home 02. Teach/Leads home 03. Own school 04. Other sch./col. 05. Public rec. area 06. Library/museum 07. YWCA/YMCA 08. Church 09. Private rec. area 10. Commercial place 11. Other	01. Own home 02. Teach/Leads home 03. Own school 04. Other sch./col. 05. Public rec. area 06. Library/museum 07. YWCA/YMCA 08. Church 09. Private rec. area 10. Commercial place 11. Other
L7a. How did you get there the last time you went? b. How did you get home?	There Home 1. Walk/bike 1. 2. Parent Drives 2. 3. Other HH Drives 3. 4. Other Drives 4. 5. Bus 5. 6. BART 6. 7. Bus/BART/Drive 7. 8. Other 8.	There Home 1. Walk/bike 1. 2. Parent Drives 2. 3. Other HH Drives 3. 4. Other Drives 4. 5. Bus 5. 6. BART 6. 7. Bus/BART/Drive 7. 8. Other 8.	There Home 1. Walk/bike 1. 2. Parent Drives 2. 3. Other HH Drives 3. 4. Other Drives 4. 5. Bus 5. 6. BART 6. 7. Bus/BART/Drive 7. 8. Other 8.

12 Judo, Karate, Kung Fu or Aidido lessons	13 Football, basketball, or baseball clinics or lessons	14	15	16
1. Yes 2. No (X)	1. Yes 2. No (X)	1. Yes 2. No (X)	1. Yes 2. No (X)	1. Yes 2. No (X)
TYPE OF LESSON	*TYPE OF LESSON*	*TYPE OF LESSON*	*TYPE OF LESSON*	*TYPE OF LESSON*
1. School hours (X) 2. Before/after school 3. Varies or both 4. Can't say	1. School hours (X) 2. Before/after school 3. Varies or both 4. Can't say	1. School hours (X) 2. Before/after school 3. Varies or both 4. Can't say	1. School hours (X) 2. Before/after school 3. Varies or both 4. Can't say	1. School hours (X) 2. Before/after school 3. Varies or both 4. Can't say
1. Yes *(GO TO L5)* 2. No	1. Yes *(GO TO L5)* 2. No	1. Yes *(GO TO L5)* 2. No	1. Yes *(GO TO L5)* 2. No	1. Yes *(GO TO L5)* 2. No
1. Yes 2. No (X) *(RECORD IN TABLE LT.)*	1. Yes 2. No (X) *(RECORD IN TABLE LT.)*	1. Yes 2. No (X) *(RECORD IN TABLE LT.)*	1. Yes 2. No (X) *(RECORD IN TABLE LT.)*	1. Yes 2. No (X) *(RECORD IN TABLE LT.)*

1. Group or Org.
2. Pvt. teacher
   (GO TO L6)
3. Other
4. DK *(GO TO L6)*
	1. Group or Org.
	2. Pvt. teacher
	   (GO TO L6)
	3. Other
	4. DK *(GO TO L6)*
		1. Group or Org.
		2. Pvt. teacher
		   (GO TO L6)
		3. Other
		4. DK *(GO TO L6)*
			1. Group or Org.
			2. Pvt. teacher
			   (GO TO L6)
			3. Other
			4. DK *(GO TO L6)*
				1. Group or Org.
				2. Pvt. teacher
				   (GO TO L6)
				3. Other
				4. DK *(GO TO L6)*

01. Own home 02. Teach/Leads home 03. Own school 04. Other sch./col. 05. Public rec. area 06. Library/museum 07. YWCA/YMCA 08. Church 09. Private rec. area 10. Commercial place 11. Other	01. Own home 02. Teach/Leads home 03. Own school 04. Other sch./col. 05. Public rec. area 06. Library/museum 07. YWCA/YMCA 08. Church 09. Private rec. area 10. Commercial place 11. Other	01. Own home 02. Teach/Leads home 03. Own school 04. Other sch./col. 05. Public rec. area 06. Library/museum 07. YWCA/YMCA 08. Church 09. Private rec. area 10. Commercial place 11. Other	01. Own home 02. Teach/Leads home 03. Own school 04. Other sch./col. 05. Public rec. area 06. Library/museum 07. YWCA/YMCA 08. Church 09. Private rec. area 10. Commercial place 11. Other	01. Own home 02. Teach/Leads home 03. Own school 04. Other sch./col. 05. Public rec. area 06. Library/museum 07. YWCA/YMCA 08. Church 09. Private rec. area 10. Commercial place 11. Other
There Home 1. Walk/bike 1. 2. Parent Drives 2. 3. Other HH Drives 3. 4. Other Drives 4. 5. Bus 5. 6. BART 6. 7. Bus/BART/Drive 7. 8. Other 8.	There Home 1. Walk/bike 1. 2. Parent Drives 2. 3. Other HH Drives 3. 4. Other Drives 4. 5. Bus 5. 6. BART 6. 7. Bus/BART/Drive 7. 8. Other 8.	There Home 1. Walk/bike 1. 2. Parent Drives 2. 3. Other HH Drives 3. 4. Other Drives 4. 5. Bus 5. 6. BART 6. 7. Bus/BART/Drive 7. 8. Other 8.	There Home 1. Walk/bike 1. 2. Parent Drives 2. 3. Other HH Drives 3. 4. Other Drives 4. 5. Bus 5. 6. BART 6. 7. Bus/BART/Drive 7. 8. Other 8.	There Home 1. Walk/bike 1. 2. Parent Drives 2. 3. Other HH Drives 3. 4. Other Drives 4. 5. Bus 5. 6. BART 6. 7. Bus/BART/Drive 7. 8. Other 8.

TABLE L	01	02	03
Questions	**Music lessons**	**Dancing lessons**	**Dramatics or acting lessons**
L8. How often do (did) you go to ___(meetings/practice)— more than once a week, about once a week, every other week, or less often?	1. More than 1/week 2. About 1/week 3. Every other week 4. Less often 5. Can't say	1. More than 1/week 2. About 1/week 3. Every other week 4. Less often 5. Can't say	1. More than 1/week 2. About 1/week 3. Every other week 4. Less often 5. Can't say
L9. Whose idea was it for you to take ___? Was it your own idea, your parents, a friend's, or was it someone elses?	1. Own idea 2. Parents 3. Own & parents 4. Friends/siblings 5. Teachers 6. Someone else (SPEC:_____) 7. Can't say	1. Own idea 2. Parents 3. Own & parents 4. Friends/siblings 5. Teachers 6. Someone else (SPEC:_____) 7. Can't say	1. Own idea 2. Parents 3. Own & parents 4. Friends/siblings 5. Teachers 6. Someone else (SPEC:_____) 7. Can't say
L10a. How did you get signed up for the ___? Did you do it yourself, did your mother do it, or did someone else do it for you?	1. Self (GO TO L11) 2. Mother 3. Someone else (GO TO L11) 4. DK	1. Self (GO TO L11) 2. Mother 3. Someone else (GO TO L11) 4. DK	1. Self (GO TO L11) 2. Mother 3. Someone else (GO TO L11) 4. DK
L10b. IF MOTHER: Did she have to go someplace to sign you up?	1. Yes 2. No 3. DK	1. Yes 2. No 3. DK	1. Yes 2. No 3. DK
L11. Do (did) the lessons cost money or are (were) they free?	1. Cost money 2. Free 3. DK	1. Cost money 2. Free 3. DK	1. Cost money 2. Free 3. DK
L12. Did you or your family have to buy or rent anything for you to take lessons?	1. Yes 2. No 3. DK	1. Yes 2. No 3. DK	1. Yes 2. No 3. DK
L13. Do (did) you take lessons with a group of kids in a class ^ (were) they private lessons.	1. With a group 2. Pvt. (GO TO L16) 3. Both 4. Other	1. With a group 2. Pvt. (GO TO L16) 3. Both 4. Other	1. With a group 2. Pvt. (GO TO L16) 3. Both 4. Other
L14. Are (were) the other kids in the group mostly boys, mostly girls, or about half and half? (IF MOSTLY BOYS/GIRLS:) Were they all (boys/girls)?	1. All boys 2. Mostly boys 3. Half and half 4. Mostly girls 5. All girls	1. All boys 2. Mostly boys 3. Half and half 4. Mostly girls 5. All girls	1. All boys 2. Mostly boys 3. Half and half 4. Mostly girls 5. All girls
L15. IF NO FRIENDS, SKIP TO L16 Are (were) any of the kids you told me about before (REVIEW NAMES) in ___ with you?	1. Yes 2. No 3. No friends mentioned	1. Yes 2. No 3. No friends mentioned	1. Yes 2. No 3. No friends mentioned
L16. How do (did) you feel about taking ___ lessons? Do (did) you like them a lot, like them some, or don't (didn't) you like them very much?	1. Like them a lot 2. Like them some 3. Don't like them much	1. Like them a lot 2. Like them some 3. Don't like them much	1. Like them a lot 2. Like them some 3. Don't like them much
	IF NOT IN NOW, RE-CORD IN TABLE LT.	IF NOT IN NOW, RE-CORD IN TABLE LT.	IF NOT IN NOW, RE-CORD IN TABLE LT.

04	05	06	07	08
Art lessons, like drawing or painting	Crafts, like pottery or making jewelry	Nature study or science	Cooking or sewing	Religious instruction, like Catechism, Bible Study, or Hebrew
1. More than 1/week 2. About 1/week 3. Every other week 4. Less often 5. Can't say	1. More than 1/week 2. About 1/week 3. Every other week 4. Less often 5. Can't say	1. More than 1/week 2. About 1/week 3. Every other week 4. Less often 5. Can't say	1. More than 1/week 2. About 1/week 3. Every other week 4. Less often 5. Can't say	1. More than 1/week 2. About 1/week 3. Every other week 4. Less often 5. Can't say

1. Own idea
2. Parents
3. Own & parents
4. Friends/siblings
5. Teachers
6. Someone else
   (SPEC:_____)
7. Can't say
	1. Own idea
	2. Parents
	3. Own & parents
	4. Friends/siblings
	5. Teachers
	6. Someone else
	   (SPEC:_____)
	7. Can't say
		1. Own idea
		2. Parents
		3. Own & parents
		4. Friends/siblings
		5. Teachers
		6. Someone else
		   (SPEC:_____)
		7. Can't say
			1. Own idea
			2. Parents
			3. Own & parents
			4. Friends/siblings
			5. Teachers
			6. Someone else
			   (SPEC:_____)
			7. Can't say
				1. Own idea
				2. Parents
				3. Own & parents
				4. Friends/siblings
				5. Teachers
				6. Someone else
				   (SPEC:_____)
				7. Can't say

1. Self (GO TO L11)
2. Mother
3. Someone else
   (GO TO L11)
4. DK
	1. Self (GO TO L11)
	2. Mother
	3. Someone else
	   (GO TO L11)
	4. DK
		1. Self (GO TO L11)
		2. Mother
		3. Someone else
		   (GO TO L11)
		4. DK
			1. Self (GO TO L11)
			2. Mother
			3. Someone else
			   (GO TO L11)
			4. DK
				1. Self (GO TO L11)
				2. Mother
				3. Someone else
				   (GO TO L11)
				4. DK

1. Yes 2. No 3. DK	1. Yes 2. No 3. DK	1. Yes 2. No 3. DK	1. Yes 2. No 3. DK	1. Yes 2. No 3. DK
1. Cost money 2. Free 3. DK	1. Cost money 2. Free 3. DK	1. Cost money 2. Free 3. DK	1. Cost money 2. Free 3. DK	1. Cost money 2. Free 3. DK
1. Yes 2. No 3. DK	1. Yes 2. No 3. DK	1. Yes 2. No 3. DK	1. Yes 2. No 3. DK	1. Yes 2. No 3. DK
1. With a group 2. Pvt. (GO TO L16) 3. Both 4. Other	1. With a group 2. Pvt. (GO TO L16) 3. Both 4. Other	1. With a group 2. Pvt. (GO TO L16) 3. Both 4. Other	1. With a group 2. Pvt. (GO TO L16) 3. Both 4. Other	1. With a group 2. Pvt. (GO TO L16) 3. Both 4. Other
1. All boys 2. Mostly boys 3. Half and half 4. Mostly girls 5. All girls	1. All boys 2. Mostly boys 3. Half and half 4. Mostly girls 5. All girls	1. All boys 2. Mostly boys 3. Half and half 4. Mostly girls 5. All girls	1. All boys 2. Mostly boys 3. Half and half 4. Mostly girls 5. All girls	1. All boys 2. Mostly boys 3. Half and half 4. Mostly girls 5. All girls

1. Yes
2. No
3. No friends
   mentioned
	1. Yes
	2. No
	3. No friends
	   mentioned
		1. Yes
		2. No
		3. No friends
		   mentioned
			1. Yes
			2. No
			3. No friends
			   mentioned
				1. Yes
				2. No
				3. No friends
				   mentioned

1. Like them a lot
2. Like them some
3. Don't like them
   much
	1. Like them a lot
	2. Like them some
	3. Don't like them
	   much
		1. Like them a lot
		2. Like them some
		3. Don't like them
		   much
			1. Like them a lot
			2. Like them some
			3. Don't like them
			   much
				1. Like them a lot
				2. Like them some
				3. Don't like them
				   much

	IF NOT IN NOW, RE-CORD IN TABLE LT.	IF NOT IN NOW, RE-CORD IN TABLE LT.	IF NOT IN NOW, RE-CORD IN TABLE LT.	IF NOT IN NOW, RE-CORD IN TABLE LT.

	Questions	09 Swimming lessons	10 Tennis lessons	11 Ice skating or roller skating lessons
L8.	How often do (did) you go to _____ (meetings/practice)— more than once a week, about once a week, every other week, or less often?	1. More than 1/week 2. About 1/week 3. Every other week 4 Less often 5 Can't say	1. More than 1/week 2. About 1/week 3. Every other week 4. Less often 5. Can't say	1. More than 1/week 2. About 1/week 3. Every other week 4. Less often 5. Can't say

L9	Whose idea was it for you to take _____? Was it your own idea, your parents', a friend's, or was it someone elses?	1. Own idea
		2 Parents
		3. Own & parents
		4. Friends/siblings
		5. Teachers
		6. Someone else
		   (SPEC· _____)
		7. Can t say
			1. Own idea
			2. Parents
			3. Own & parents
			4. Friends/siblings
			5. Teachers
			6. Someone else
			   (SPEC· _____)
			7. Can't say
				1. Own idea
				2. Parents
				3. Own & parents
				4. Friends/siblings
				5. Teachers
				6. Someone else
				   (SPEC· _____)
				7. Can't say

L10a.	How did you get signed up for the _____? Did you do it yourself, did your mother do it, or did someone else do it for you?	1. Self (GO TO L11)
		2. Mother
		3. Someone else
		   (GO TO L11)
		4. DK
			1. Self (GO TO L11)
			2. Mother
			3. Someone else
			   (GO TO L11)
			4. DK
				1. Self (GO TO L11)
				2. Mother
				3. Someone else
				   (GO TO L11)
				4. DK

L10b.	IF MOTHER: Did she have to go someplace to sign you up?	1. Yes 2. No 3. DK	1. Yes 2. No 3. DK	1. Yes 2. No 3. DK
L11.	Do (did) the lessons cost money or are (were) they free?	1. Cost money 2. Free 3. DK	1. Cost money 2. Free 3. DK	1. Cost money 2. Free 3. DK
L12.	Did you or your family have to buy or rent anything for you to take lessons?	1. Yes 2. No 3. DK	1. Yes 2. No 3. DK	1. Yes 2. No 3. DK
L13.	Do (did) you take lessons with a group of kids in a class or are (were) they private lessons?	1. With a group 2. Pvt. (GO TO L16) 3. Both 4. Other	1. With a group 2. Pvt. (GO TO L16) 3. Both 4. Other	1. With a group 2. Pvt. (GO TO L16) 3. Both 4. Other
L14.	Are (were) the other kids in the group mostly boys, mostly girls, or about half and half? (IF MOSTLY BOYS/GIRLS:) Were they all (boys/girls)?	1. All boys 2. Mostly boys 3. Half and half 4. Mostly girls 5. All girls	1. All boys 2. Mostly boys 3. Half and half 4. Mostly girls 5. All girls	1. All boys 2. Mostly boys 3. Half and half 4. Mostly girls 5. All girls

L15.	IF NO FRIENDS, SKIP TO L16
	Are (were) any of the kids you told me about before (REVIEW NAMES) in _____ with you?
		1. Yes
		2. No
		3. No friends
		   mentioned
			1. Yes
			2. No
			3. No friends
			   mentioned
				1. Yes
				2. No
				3. No friends
				   mentioned

L16.	How do (did) you feel about taking _____ lessons? Do (did) you like them a lot, like them some, or don't (didn't) you like them very much?	1. Like them a lot
		2. Like them some
		3. Don't like them
		   much
			1. Like them a lot
			2. Like them some
			3. Don't like them
			   much
				1. Like them a lot
				2. Like them some
				3. Don't like them
				   much

		IF NOT IN NOW, RE-CORD IN TABLE LT.	IF NOT IN NOW, RE-CORD IN TABLE LT.	IF NOT IN NOW, RE-CORD IN TABLE LT.

12 Judo, Karate, Kung Fu or Aidido lessons	13 Football, basketball, or baseball clinics or lessons	14	15	16
1. More than 1/week 2. About 1/week 3. Every other week 4. Less often 5. Can't say	1. More than 1/week 2. About 1/week 3. Every other week 4. Less often 5. Can't say	1. More than 1/week 2. About 1/week 3. Every other week 4. Less often 5. Can't say	1. More than 1/week 2. About 1/week 3. Every other week 4. Less often 5. Can't say	1. More than 1/week 2. About 1/week 3. Every other week 4. Less often 5. Can't say

1. Own idea
2. Parents
3. Own & parents
4. Friends/siblings
5. Teachers
6. Someone else
   (SPEC: _____)
7. Can't say
	1. Own idea
	2. Parents
	3. Own & parents
	4. Friends/siblings
	5. Teachers
	6. Someone else
	   (SPEC: _____)
	7. Can't say
		1. Own idea
		2. Parents
		3. Own & parents
		4. Friends/siblings
		5. Teachers
		6. Someone else
		   (SPEC: _____)
		7. Can't say
			1. Own idea
			2. Parents
			3. Own & parents
			4. Friends/siblings
			5. Teachers
			6. Someone else
			   (SPEC: _____)
			7. Can't say
				1. Own idea
				2. Parents
				3. Own & parents
				4. Friends/siblings
				5. Teachers
				6. Someone else
				   (SPEC: _____)
				7. Can't say

1. Self (GO TO L11)
2. Mother
3. Someone else
   (GO TO L11)
4. DK
	1. Self (GO TO L11)
	2. Mother
	3. Someone else
	   (GO TO L11)
	4. DK
		1. Self (GO TO L11)
		2. Mother
		3. Someone else
		   (GO TO L11)
		4. DK
			1. Self (GO TO L11)
			2. Mother
			3. Someone else
			   (GO TO L11)
			4. DK
				1. Self (GO TO L11)
				2. Mother
				3. Someone else
				   (GO TO L11)
				4. DK

1. Yes 2. No 3. DK	1. Yes 2. No 3. DK	1. Yes 2. No 3. DK	1. Yes 2. No 3. DK	1. Yes 2. No 3. DK
1. Cost money 2. Free 3. DK	1. Cost money 2. Free 3. DK	1. Cost money 2. Free 3. DK	1. Cost money 2. Free 3. DK	1. Cost money 2. Free 3. DK
1. Yes 2. No 3. DK	1. Yes 2. No 3. DK	1. Yes 2. No 3. DK	1. Yes 2. No 3. DK	1. Yes 2. No 3. DK
1. With a group 2. Pvt. (GO TO L16) 3. Both 4. Other	1. With a group 2. Pvt. (GO TO L16) 3. Both 4. Other	1. With a group 2. Pvt. (GO TO L16) 3. Both 4. Other	1. With a group 2. Pvt. (GO TO L16) 3. Both 4. Other	1. With a group 2. Pvt. (GO TO L16) 3. Both 4. Other
1. All boys 2. Mostly boys 3. Half and half 4. Mostly girls 5. All girls	1. All boys 2. Mostly boys 3. Half and half 4. Mostly girls 5. All girls	1. All boys 2. Mostly boys 3. Half and half 4. Mostly girls 5. All girls	1. All boys 2. Mostly boys 3. Half and half 4. Mostly girls 5. All girls	1. All boys 2. Mostly boys 3. Half and half 4. Mostly girls 5. All girls

1. Yes
2. No
3. No friends
   mentioned
	1. Yes
	2. No
	3. No friends
	   mentioned
		1. Yes
		2. No
		3. No friends
		   mentioned
			1. Yes
			2. No
			3. No friends
			   mentioned
				1. Yes
				2. No
				3. No friends
				   mentioned

1. Like them a lot
2. Like them some
3. Don't like them
   much
	1. Like them a lot
	2. Like them some
	3. Don't like them
	   much
		1. Like them a lot
		2. Like them some
		3. Don't like them
		   much
			1. Like them a lot
			2. Like them some
			3. Don't like them
			   much
				1. Like them a lot
				2. Like them some
				3. Don't like them
				   much

	IF NOT IN NOW, RE-CORD IN TABLE LT.	IF NOT IN NOW, RE-CORD IN TABLE LT.	IF NOT IN NOW, RE-CORD IN TABLE LT.	IF NOT IN NOW, RE-CORD IN TABLE LT.

TABLE LT

ACTIVITIES TERMINATED OR DROPPED SINCE SEPTEMBER

Activity _____   Code ☐☐

L18. Why aren't you in _____ anymore?

PROBE: Any other reasons?

Activity _____   Code ☐☐

L18. Why aren't you in _____ anymore?

PROBE: Any other reasons?

Activity _____   Code ☐☐

L18. Why aren't you in _____ anymore?

PROBE: Any other reasons?

| GENERAL RETURN FROM LESSONS TABLE |

31A. Are there any (other) after school lessons or classes that you have been wanting to take?

PROBE: Any like the things we've been talking about?

Yes 1   38/

No . . . . (SKIP TO 32) 2

B. What kind of lessons or classes would you like to take?
PROBE: Any others? RECORD IN TABLE BELOW.

C. *ASK FOR EACH:* Had you thought of taking _____
before today, or did you just think of it now?

	C. Thought of:		
B. Lessons or classes would like to take	Before today	Just now	
	1	2	*39-40/*
			41/
	1	2	*42-43/*
			44/
	1	2	*45-46/*
			47/

32. Most kids we've talked with say they don't take after
     school lessons or classes. Why do you suppose that is?

     PROBE: Can you think of any (other) reasons kids don't
     take after school lessons or classes?

     Any other reasons?   ☐ Have no idea

                                                              48-49/

                                                              50-51/

                                                              52-53/

33A. Most days, do you come home right after school, do
     you stay at school for a while, or do you do something
     else?

     Come right home ...... *(SKIP TO 34)* 1   *54/*

     Stay at school ...... *(SKIP TO 34)* 2

     Something else 3

  B. Where do you <u>usually</u> go after school?

     IF MORE THAN ONE PLACE MENTIONED: Where
     do you go most often?

IF NOT MOST OFTEN: Where did you go (yesterday, the last time)?

Relative's home	1	*55/*
Other adult's home	2	
Friend's home	3	
Organization .... *(SKIP TO 34)*	4	
"Just around" .... *(SKIP TO 34)*	5	
Other *(SPECIFY:*_____		
_____ *) (SKIP TO 34)*	6	

C. Is that in this neighborhood?

Yes	1	*56/*
No	2	

D. When you're at _____ in the afternoon after school, is an adult or older kid usually there?

Adult or both ...... *(SKIP TO 34)*	1	*57/*
Older kid only	2	
Neither .... *(SKIP TO 34)*	3	

E. Is that kid at least 18 years old or older?

At least 18 years old	1	*58/*
Age 17 or younger	2	

34A. Is there usually someone here at your house in the afternoon after school?

Yes	1	*59/*
No .... *(SKIP TO 35)*	2	

B. Who is usually here? *(CIRCLE ALL THAT ARE USUALLY HERE.)*

Mother .... *(SKIP TO 35)*	1	*60/*
Father .... *(SKIP TO 35)*	2	*61/*
Babysitter	3	*62/*

Brothers/sisters   4   *63/*

Other relative *(SPECIFY:* _____

_____ *)*   5   *64/*

Other *(SPECIFY:* _____

_____ *)*   6   *65/*

C. *IF PARENT NOT PRESENT, CONSULT ENUMERA-*
   TION AND CODE OR ASK AS NECESSARY:

Is (he/she/either of them/any of them) an adult?

IF NECESSARY: Is he/she at least 18 years old?

At least one adult present   1   *66/*

No adult present   2

35A. How do you usually get (home/*PLACE R. GOES MOST*
   OFTEN) from school—do you walk, ride a bike, take the
   bus, or what?

Walk or bike . . . . *(SKIP TO 36)*   1   *67/*

Someone drives   2

Bus . . . . *(SKIP TO 36)*   3

BART . . . . *(SKIP TO 36)*   4

Bus/BART and someone drives   5

Other *(SPECIFY:* _____

_____ *(SKIP TO 36)*   6

B. Who usually drives you (here/there)?

Mother or father   1   *68/*

Other household member drives   2

Someone else   3
                                                          69-80/

Serial # _ _ _ _ 5/1
(1-4)
6-7/17

36. Do you have a bicycle?

      Yes 1   *8/*

      No 2

37. After school does (your mother/*OTHER RELEVANT
ADULT*) want to know where you are most of the time,
or are you allowed to be pretty much on your own?

      Adult wants to know 1   *9/*

      Allowed to be on own 2

38A. What usually happens at your house at dinnertime—does
everyone eat dinner together, do some of you eat
together, or does each person eat dinner when he wants?

      All eat together . . . . . . *(SKIP TO 39)* 1   *10/*

      Some eat together 2

      Each eats when wants 3

  B. Do you usually eat dinner with someone else or do you
usually eat by yourself?

      With someone else 1   *11/*

      By self . . . . *(SKIP TO D)* 2

  C. Who do you usually eat with? *(CIRCLE ALL THAT R.
USUALLY EATS WITH)*

      Mother 1   *12/*

      Father 2   *13/*

      Brothers or sisters 3   *14/*

      Other *(SPECIFY:* _____

      _____*)* 4   *15/*

  D. Does someone else usually make dinner or do you
usually make your own?

Someone else makes dinner 1   *16/*

Usually make own 2

39A. Is there a definite time when you have to come in the house before dinner, does someone call you in, or can you come in when you want?

Definite time or before dark 1   *17/*

Called to come in . . . . . . *(SKIP TO 40)* 2

Comes in when wants . . . . *(SKIP TO 40)* 3

Other *(SPECIFY:* _____

_____ *(SKIP TO 40)* 4

B. <u>*CODE OR ASK AS NECESSARY:*</u> What time do you have to come in before dinner?

Before 5:00 1   *18/*

5:00 — 5:59 2

6:00 — 6:59 3

7:00 — 7:59 4

8:00 — 8:59 5

9:00 — 9:59 6

10:00 or later 7

Before dark 8

40A. At this time of the year, what do you <u>usually</u> do after dinner on school nights? *(CIRCLE ALL THAT ARE <u>USUALLY</u> DONE.)*

PROBE: Is there anything else you usually do after supper?

In home
{
Watch TV 01 *19-20/*

Listen to radio 02 *21-22/*

Do chores 03 *23-24/*

Do schoolwork 04 *25-26/*

Read 05 *27-28/*

Play inside 06 *29-30/*

Rest, sleep, do nothing 07 *31-32/*

Go out
{
Play or go outside . . *(CODE YES IN B)* . . 08 *33-34/*
Visit friends . . . . *(CODE YES IN B)* 09 *35-36/*
}

Other *(SPECIFY:* _____

_____) 10 *37-38/*

B. *CODE OR ASK AS NECESSARY:* At this time of year, do you usually go out after dinner to play or to visit friends?

Yes 1   *39/*

No . . . . *(SKIP TO 42)* 2

41. When you go out after dinner, is there a definite time when you have to come in, does someone call you in, or can you come in when you want?

Definite time or before dark 1   *40/*

Called to come in 2

Comes in when wants 3

Other *(SPECIFY:* _____

_____) 4

Varies too much to say 5

42A. On school nights, what time are you supposed to go to bed, or don't you have a regular bed time?

Before 8:00 . . . . 01 *41-42/*

8:00 — 8:29 02

8:30 — 8:59 03

9:00 — 9:29 04

9:30 — 9:59 05

10:00 — 10:29 06

10:30 — 10:59 07

11:00 or after 08

No regular bed time . . . . . *(SKIP TO C)* 09

B. Do you usually get to bed by that time on school nights?

> Yes . . . . *(SKIP TO 43)* 1   *43/*
>
> No 2

C. *IF NO:* What time do you usually get to bed?

> Before 8:00 . . . . 01 *44-45/*
>
> 8:00 — 8:29 02
>
> 8:30 — 8:59 03
>
> 9:00 — 9:29 04
>
> 9:30 — 9:59 05
>
> 10:00 — 10:29 06
>
> 10:30 — 10:59 07
>
> 11:00 or later 08
>
> Varies too much to say 09

43A. Do you have a room of your own or do you share a room?

> Room of own . . . . *(GO TO TABLE G)* 1   *46/*
>
> Share a room 2
>
> Other *(SPECIFY:* _____
>
> _____ *) (GO TO TABLE G)* 3

B. Who do you share your room with? (CIRCLE ALL THAT APPLY)

> Brothers/sisters/other kids 1   *47/*
>
> Mother 2   *48/*
>
> Father 3   *49/*
>
> Other *(SPECIFY:* _____
>
> _____ *)* 4   *50/*

$$\boxed{GO\ TO\ TABLE\ G}$$

| TABLE G: GROUPS | ID # ☐☐☐☐☐

Let's talk now about clubs, teams, or other organizations that kids sometimes belong to. We can start with the ones that I've heard of and then there may be others you belong to that I don't know about.

G1. Have you belonged to the *(NAME OF ORGANIZATION FROM BELOW)* at any time since you started 6th grade in September? *(RECORD IN APPROPRIATE COLUMN BELOW.)*

   ASK FOR EACH ORGANIZATION

G2a. Have you belonged to any (other) sports team or League at any time since you began 6th grade in September?

   Yes 1

   No . . . . *(SKIP TO G3)* 2

  b. *IF YES:* What is the name of that (League/team); *IF NECESSARY:* What sport is that?

  c. Does an adult coach that team? *(IF YES: X SPORT BOX, RECORD NAME, AND ASK FOR ANY OTHER SPORTS OR SKIP TO G4, AS APPROPRIATE.)*

G3a. Have you belonged to any (other) social clubs or church groups since you began 6th grade in September?

   Yes 1

   No (GO TO APPROPRIATE PLACE) 2

  b. *IF YES:* What is the name of that club/group?

  c. Does an adult lead it? *(IF YES: X GROUP, RECORD NAME, AND ASK FOR ANY OTHER CLUBS/ GROUPS OR SKIP TO G14, AS APPROPRIATE.)*

	01. Boy Scouts 02. Girl Scouts	03. Boys Club of America 04. Campfire Girls	05. YMCA	06. YWCA
Boys → Girls →				
G1. IN _____ SINCE SEPTEMBER	1. Yes 2. No (X)	1. Yes 2. No (X)	1. Yes 2. No (X)	1. Yes 2. No (X)
G4. When does _____ usually meet—during regular school hours, before school or after school?	1. School hours (X) 2. Before/after school 3. Varies or both 4. Can't say	1. School hours (X) 2. Before/after school 3. Varies or both 4. Can't say	1. School hours (X) 2. Before/after school 3. Varies or both 4. Can't say	1. School hours (X) 2. Before/after school 3. Varies or both 4. Can't say
G5. Do you still belong to the _____?	1. Yes (SKIP TO G8) 2. No	1. Yes (SKIP TO G8) 2. No	1. Yes (SKIP TO G8) 2. No	1. Yes (SKIP TO G8) 2. No
G6 IF NO: When you did belong to _____, did you go more than two times?	1. Yes 2. No (X) (RECORD IN GT)	1. Yes 2. No (X) (RECORD IN GT)	1. Yes 2. No (X) (RECORD IN GT)	1. Yes 2. No (X) (RECORD IN GT)
G7. Who (sponsors/runs) that (team, club, organization)?	(X)	(X)	(X)	(X)
G8. Where do (did) you usually meet? 1. Own home (GO TO G10) 2. Teacher's or Leader's home 3. Own school 4. Other school or college 5. Public rec. area 6. Library or museum 7. YWCA or YMCA 8. Church 9. Private recreation area 10. Commercial place 11. Other	01. Own home (GO TO G10) 02. Teacher/leaders home 03. Own school 04. Other school/college 05. Public rec. area 06. Library or museum 07. YWCA or YMCA 08. Church 09. Private rec. area 10. Commercial place 11. Other	01. Own home (GO TO G10) 02. Teacher/leaders home 03. Own school 04. Other school/college 05. Public rec. area 06. Library or museum 07. YWCA or YMCA 08. Church 09. Private rec. area 10. Commercial place 11. Other	01. Own home (GO TO G10) 02. Teacher/leaders home 03. Own school 04. Other school/college 05. Public rec. area 06. Library or museum 07. YWCA or YMCA 08. Church 09. Private rec. area 10. Commercial place 11. Other	01. Own home (GO TO G10) 02. Teacher/leaders home 03. Own school 04. Other school/college 05. Public rec. area 06. Library or museum 07. YWCA or YMCA 08. Church 09. Private rec. area 10. Commercial place 11. Other
G9a. How did you get there the last time you went? b. How did you get home?	There / Home 1. Walk/Bike 2. Parent Drives 3. Other HH Drives 4. Other Drives 5. Bus 6. BART 7. Bus/BART/Drive 8. Other	There / Home 1. Walk/Bike 2. Parent Drives 3. Other HH Drives 4. Other Drives 5. Bus 6. BART 7. Bus/BART/Drive 8. Other	There / Home 1. Walk/Bike 2. Parent Drives 3. Other HH Drives 4. Other Drives 5. Bus 6. BART 7. Bus/BART/Drive 8. Other	There / Home 1. Walk/Bike 2. Parent Drives 3. Other HH Drives 4. Other Drives 5. Bus 6. BART 7. Bus/BART/Drive 8. Other

Boys →	01. Boy Scouts	03. Boys Club of America	05. YMCA	06. YWCA
Girls →	02. Girl Scouts	04. Campfire Girls		
G10. How often do (did) you go to _____ (meetings/practice)—more than once a week, about once a week, every other week, or less often?	1. More than 1/week 2. About 1/week 3. Every other week 4. Less often 5. Can't say	1. More than 1/week 2. About 1/week 3. Every other week 4. Less often 5. Can't say	1. More than 1/week 2. About 1/week 3. Every other week 4. Less often 5. Can't say	1. More than 1/week 2. About 1/week 3. Every other week 4. Less often 5. Can't say
G11. Whose idea was it for you to be in _____? Was it your own idea, your parents, a friend's, or was it someone else's idea?	1. Own idea 2. Parents 3. Own & parents 4. Friends/siblings 5. Leader/coach 6. Someone else (SPEC: _____) 7. Can't say	1. Own idea 2. Parents 3. Own & parents 4. Friends/siblings 5. Leader/coach 6. Someone else (SPEC: _____) 7. Can't say	1. Own idea 2. Parents 3. Own & parents 4. Friends/siblings 5. Leader/coach 6. Someone else (SPEC: _____) 7. Can't say	1. Own idea 2. Parents 3. Own & parents 4. Friends/siblings 5. Leader/coach 6. Someone else (SPEC: _____) 7. Can't say
G12a. How did you get signed up for the _____? Did you do it yourself, did your mother do it, or did someone else do it for you?	1. Self (SKIP TO 13) 2. Mother 3. Someone else (SKIP TO 13)	1. Self (SKIP TO 13) 2. Mother 3. Someone else (SKIP TO 13)	1. Self (SKIP TO 13) 2. Mother 3. Someone else (SKIP TO 13)	1. Self (SKIP TO 13) 2. Mother 3. Someone else (SKIP TO 13)
G12b. IF MOTHER. Did she have to go someplace to sign you up?	1. Yes 2. No 3. DK	1. Yes 2. No 3. DK	1. Yes 2. No 3. DK	1. Yes 2. No 3. DK
G13. Do (did) you have to pay dues or insurance to belong to _____?	1. Yes 2. No 3. DK	1. Yes 2. No 3. DK	1. Yes 2. No 3. DK	1. Yes 2. No 3. DK
G14. Did you or your family have to buy or rent anything for you to belong to _____?	1. Yes 2. No 3. DK (SKIP TO G16)	1. Yes 2. No 3. DK (SKIP TO G16)	1. Yes 2. No 3. DK	1. Yes 2. No 3. DK
G15. Are (were) the other kids (in/on) the _____ mostly boys, mostly girls, or about half and half? IF MOSTLY BOYS/GIRLS: Were they all (boys/girls)?	1. All boys 2. Mostly boys 3. Half and half 4. Mostly girls 5. All girls *(crossed out)*	1. All boys 2. Mostly boys 3. Half and half 4. Mostly girls 5. All girls *(crossed out)*	1. All boys 2. Mostly boys 3. Half and half 4. Mostly girls 5. All girls	1. All boys 2. Mostly boys 3. Half and half 4. Mostly girls 5. All girls
G16. IF NO FRIENDS, SKIP TO G17. Are (were) any of the kids you told me about before (REVIEW NAMES) in _____ with you?	1. Yes 2. No 3. No friends mentioned	1. Yes 2. No 3. No friends mentioned	1. Yes 2. No 3. No friends mentioned	1. Yes 2. No 3. No friends mentioned
G17. How do (did) you feel about being in the _____? Do (did) you like it a lot, like it some, or don't (didn't) you like it very much?	1. Like it a lot 2. Like it some 3. Don't like it much	1. Like it a lot 2. Like it some 3. Don't like it much	1. Like it a lot 2. Like it some 3. Don't like it much	1. Like it a lot 2. Like it some 3. Don't like it much
	IF NOT IN NOW, RECORD IN	IF NOT IN NOW, RECORD IN	IF NOT IN NOW, RECORD IN	IF NOT IN NOW, RECORD IN

	07 1 ☐ Sport 2 ☐ Group	08 1 ☐ Sport 2 ☐ Group	09 1 ☐ Sport 2 ☐ Group	10 1 ☐ Sport 2 ☐ Group
G2a.-3a. SPORT OR GROUP?				
G2b.-3b. NAME OF SPORT/GROUP *(WRITE IN)*				
G2c.-3c. ADULT COACH/LEADER				
G4. When does _____ usually meet—during regular school hours, before school or after school?	1. School hours (X) 2. Before/after school 3. Varies or both 4. Can't say	1. School hours (X) 2. Before/after school 3. Varies or both 4. Can't say	1. School hours (X) 2. Before/after school 3. Varies or both 4. Can't say	1. School hours (X) 2. Before/after school 3. Varies or both 4. Can't say
G5. Do you still belong to the _____?	1. Yes *(SKIP TO G7)* 2. No	1. Yes *(SKIP TO G7)* 2. No	1. Yes *(SKIP TO G7)* 2. No	1. Yes *(SKIP TO G7)* 2. No
G6. *IF NO.* When you did belong to _____, did you go more than two times?	1. Yes 2. No (X) *(RECORD IN GT)*	1. Yes 2. No (X) *(RECORD IN GT)*	1. Yes 2. No (X) *(RECORD IN GT)*	1. Yes 2. No (X) *(RECORD IN GT)*
G7. Who (sponsors/runs) that (team, club, organization)?				
G8. Where do (did) you usually meet? 1. Own home *(GO TO G10)* 2. Teacher's or Leader's home 3. Own school 4. Other school or college 5. Public rec. area 6. Library or museum 7. YWCA or YMCA 8. Church 9. Private recreation area 10. Commercial place 11. Other	01. Own home *(GO TO G10)* 02. Teacher/leaders home 03. Own school 04. Other school/college 05. Public rec. area 06. Library or museum 07. YWCA or YMCA 08. Church 09. Private rec. area 10. Commercial place 11. Other	01. Own home *(GO TO G10)* 02. Teacher/leaders home 03. Own school 04. Other school/college 05. Public rec. area 06. Library or museum 07. YWCA or YMCA 08. Church 09. Private rec. area 10. Commercial place 11. Other	01. Own home *(GO TO G10)* 02. Teacher/leaders home 03. Own school 04. Other school/college 05. Public rec. area 06. Library or museum 07. YWCA or YMCA 08. Church 09. Private rec. area 10. Commercial place 11. Other	01. Own home *(GO TO G10)* 02. Teacher/leaders home 03. Own school 04. Other school/college 05. Public rec. area 06. Library or museum 07. YWCA or YMCA 08. Church 09. Private rec. area 10. Commercial place 11. Other
G9a. How did you get there the last time you went? **b.** How did you get home?	*There / Home* 1. Walk/Bike 2. Parent Drives 3. Other HH Drives 4. Other Drives 5. Bus 6. BART 7. Bus/BART/Drive 8. Other	*There / Home* 1. Walk/Bike 2. Parent Drives 3. Other HH Drives 4. Other Drives 5. Bus 6. BART 7. Bus/BART/Drive 8. Other	*There / Home* 1. Walk/Bike 2. Parent Drives 3. Other HH Drives 4. Other Drives 5. Bus 6. BART 7. Bus/BART/Drive 8. Other	*There / Home* 1. Walk/Bike 2. Parent Drives 3. Other HH Drives 4. Other Drives 5. Bus 6. BART 7. Bus/BART/Drive 8. Other

G2a.–3a. SPORT OR GROUP?	07 1 ☐ Sport 2 ☐ Group	08 1 ☐ Sport 2 ☐ Group	09 1 ☐ Sport 2 ☐ Group	10 1 ☐ Sport 2 ☐ Group
G10 How often do (did) you go to _____ (meetings/practice)—more than once a week, about once a week, every other week, or less often?	1. More than 1/week 2. About 1/week 3. Every other week 4. Less often 5. Can't say	1. More than 1/week 2. About 1/week 3. Every other week 4. Less often 5. Can't say	1. More than 1/week 2. About 1/week 3. Every other week 4. Less often 5. Can't say	1. More than 1/week 2. About 1/week 3. Every other week 4. Less often 5. Can't say
G11. Whose idea was it for you to be in _____? Was it your own idea, your parents, a friend's, or was it someone else's idea?	1. Own idea 2. Parents 3. Own & parents 4. Friends/siblings 5. Leader/coach 6. Someone else (SPEC._____) 7. Can't say	1. Own idea 2. Parents 3. Own & parents 4. Friends/siblings 5. Leader/coach 6. Someone else (SPEC._____) 7. Can't say	1. Own idea 2. Parents 3. Own & parents 4. Friends/siblings 5. Leader/coach 6. Someone else (SPEC._____) 7. Can't say	1. Own idea 2. Parents 3. Own & parents 4. Friends/siblings 5. Leader/coach 6. Someone else (SPEC._____) 7. Can't say
G12a. How did you get signed up for the _____? Did you do it yourself, did your mother do it, or did someone else do it for you?	1. Self (SKIP TO 13) 2. Mother 3. Someone else (SKIP TO 13)	1. Self (SKIP TO 13) 2. Mother 3. Someone else (SKIP TO 13)	1. Self (SKIP TO 13) 2. Mother 3. Someone else (SKIP TO 13)	1. Self (SKIP TO 13) 2. Mother 3. Someone else (SKIP TO 13)
G12b. IF MOTHER. Did she have to go someplace to sign you up?	1. Yes 2. No 3. DK	1. Yes 2. No 3. DK	1. Yes 2. No 3. DK	1. Yes 2. No 3. DK
G13. Do (did) you have to pay dues or insurance to belong to _____?	1. Yes 2. No 3. DK	1. Yes 2. No 3. DK	1. Yes 2. No 3. DK	1. Yes 2. No 3. DK
G14. Did you or your family have to buy or rent anything for you to belong to _____?	1. Yes 2. No 3. DK	1. Yes 2. No 3. DK	1. Yes 2. No 3. DK	1. Yes 2. No 3. DK
G15. Are (were) the other kids (in/on) the _____ mostly boys, mostly girls, or about half and half IF MOSTLY BOYS/GIRLS. Were they all (boys/girls)?	1. All boys 2. Mostly boys 3. Half and half 4. Mostly girls 5. All girls	1. All boys 2. Mostly boys 3. Half and half 4. Mostly girls 5. All girls	1. All boys 2. Mostly boys 3. Half and half 4. Mostly girls 5. All girls	1. All boys 2. Mostly boys 3. Half and half 4. Mostly girls 5. All girls
G16. IF NO FRIENDS, SKIP TO G17 Are (were) any of the kids you told me about before (REVIEW NAMES) in _____ with you?	1. Yes 2. No 3. No friends mentioned	1. Yes 2. No 3. No friends mentioned	1. Yes 2. No 3. No friends mentioned	1. Yes 2. No 3. No friends mentioned
G17. How do (did) you feel about being in the _____? Do (did) you like it a lot, like it some, or don't (didn't) you like it very much?	1. Like it a lot 2. Like it some 3. Don't like it much	1. Like it a lot 2. Like it some 3. Don't like it much	1. Like it a lot 2. Like it some 3. Don't like it much	1. Like it a lot 2. Like it some 3. Don't like it much

TABLE GT

GENERAL RETURN FROM GROUPS TABLE

44. On this page are some questions about the way you feel. *(HAND INSERT 2 AND PENCIL.)* I will read the questions along with you, but I would like you to mark the answers yourself. For each question, circle the answer that best describes the way you feel. Circle only one answer for each question.

(1) I wish I had more close friends.

Yes 1   *51/*

No 2

No answer 3

(2) I have to do lots of things I don't like to do.

Yes 1   *52/*

No 2

No answer 3

(3) I would like to spend more time doing things with my parents.

Yes 1   *53/*

No 2

No answer 3

(4) I can do many things well.

Yes 1   *54/*

No 2

No answer 3

(5) If I could change, I would be somewhat different from myself.

Yes 1   *55/*

No 2

No answer 3

(6) Making friends is hard for me.

Yes 1   *56/*

No 2

No answer 3

(7) After school and on weekends, I often feel bored
and don't know what to do.

Yes 1   *57/*

No 2

No answer 3

*RETRIEVE INSERT, QUICKLY SCAN FOR DOUBLE OR MISSING
ANSWERS, AND INSERT IN SCHEDULE. CODE TO THIS PAGE
AFTER YOU LEAVE THE HOME.*

58-80/

Serial # _ _ _ _ 5/1
(1-4)
6-7/18

45A. Are you supposed to do any work or chores around the
house at least once a week?

Yes 1   *8/*

No . . . . *(SKIP TO 46)* 2

B. Here is a list of chores. *(HAND BLUE CARD)* As I read
along with you, tell me which ones you really do at least
once a week.

*ENTER IN TABLE BELOW. INCLUDE CHORES DONE
ON ALTERNATE WEEKS OR ROTATING SCHEDULE.*

C. Are there any other chores you do at least once a week?
What are they? *ENTER IN TABLE BELOW.*

D. *FOR EACH CHORE R. DOES:* How many days a week
do you _____ ?

*IF CHORES DONE ON ALTERNATE WEEKS OR
ROTATING SCHEDULE, ASK ABOUT LAST WEEK
AND CODE "0" FOR THOSE NOT DONE LAST WEEK.*

Chores	Does at least once a week. Yes	No	IF YES: How many days a week do you do _____?								
Make your bed— Do you do that at least once a week?	1	2	0	1	2	3	4	5	6	7	*9-10/*
Clean your room	1	2	0	1	2	3	4	5	6	7	*11-12/*
Help clean the rest of the house	1	2	0	1	2	3	4	5	6	7	*13-14/*
Set the table . . .	1	2	0	1	2	3	4	5	6	7	*15-16/*
Clear the table . .	1	2	0	1	2	3	4	5	6	7	*17-18/*
Do the dishes . . .	1	2	0	1	2	3	4	5	6	7	*19-20/*
Work in the yard	1	2	0	1	2	3	4	5	6	7	*21-22/*
Empty waste baskets or take out the garbage . .	1	2	0	1	2	3	4	5	6	7	*23-24/*
Feed the pets . . .	1	2	0	1	2	3	4	5	6	7	*25-26/*
Help cook	1	2	0	1	2	3	4	5	6	7	*27-28/*
Other *(SPECIFY BELOW:)*											
_____	1	2	0	1	2	3	4	5	6	7	*29-30/*
_____	1	2	0	1	2	3	4	5	6	7	*31-32/*

46.   *(IF NO YOUNGER KIDS IN HOUSEHOLD, SKIP TO 47.)*

A. Do you ever take care of (the younger kids/your younger
_____) when your (parents/mother/father)
(aren't/isn't) here? I mean, do you ever babysit (them/
him/her)?

Yes   1   *33/*

No . . . . *(SKIP TO 47)*   2

B. About how often do you do that—almost every day, four or five times a week, two or three times a week, once a week, or less than that?

Almost every day	1	*34/*
4 or 5 times a week	2	
2 or 3 times a week	3	
Once a week	4	
Less often	5	

47A. Do you have a regular paid job outside your home that you do at least once a week?

PROBE: For example, do you deliver newspapers or do paid babysitting for some other family at least once a week?

Yes	1	*35/*
No .... *(SKIP TO 48)*	2	

B. What kind of paid job do you have? *PROBE:* Any others? *RECORD ALL JOBS IN TABLE BELOW AND THEN ASK C AND D FOR EACH.*

PAID JOBS DONE EACH WEEK *PROBE:* Any others?	C. How many days a week do you do that? *IF VARIES:* How about last week.	D. About how much money do you earn each week for that? *IF VARIES,* How about last week?	
1. Paper rt. 2. Babysit 3. Other *(SPEC:_____ _____)*	1 2 3 4 5 6 7	$ __ __.__ __	*36-41/*
1. Paper rt. 2. Babysit 3. Other *(SPEC:_____ _____)*	1 2 3 4 5 6 7	$ __ __.__ __	*42-47/*
1. Paper rt. 2. Babysit 3. Other *(SPEC:_____ _____)*	1 2 3 4 5 6 7	$ __ __.__ __	*48-53/*

48A. Do you get spending money from your (parents/mother/
   father)?

      Yes   1   *54/*

      No . . . *(SKIP TO BOXED INSTRUCTIONS)* . . .   2

B. Do they give it to you just when you ask for it or do you
   get a regular allowance?

      When ask for it . . . . *(SKIP TO 49)*   1   *55/*

      Regular allowance   2

      Both   3

C. How often do you get your allowance?

      Once a week   1   *56/*

      Every other week   2

      Once a month   3

      Other *(SPECIFY:* _____ *)*   4

D. How much do you usually get?

    IF VARIES OR UNCERTAIN: How about the last time?

      Allowance . . . . $ __ __ . __ __   *57-60/*

> **IF R. HAS NO SPENDING MONEY OR JOB EARNINGS**
> **GO TO 50**

49A. What do you usually do with the money you get from
   (your (parents/mother/father)) (and) (your job)?

    IF VARIES OR UNCERTAIN: How about the last
   time?   *61-62/*

                                                    63-64/

                                                    65-66/

                                                    67-68/

B. Is there anything you have to spend at least part of your
   money on—like bus fare, lunch, things like that?

      Yes   1   *69/*

      No . . . . *(SKIP TO 50)*   2

C. What kinds of things do you have to spend it on?

   PROBE: Anything else?

   70-71/

   72-73/

   74-75/

   76-77/

                                            Serial # _ _ _ _ 5/1
                                                  (1-4)
                                                6-7/19

Now I'd like to ask about things you do with your (parents/mother/
father).

50A. First let's talk about weekends. How often do you do
     things with your (parents/mother/father) on weekends—
     every weekend, most weekends, some weekends, or
     hardly ever?

     Every weekend   1   *8/*

     Most weekends   2

     Some weekends   3

     Hardly ever . . . . *(SKIP TO 51)*   4

   B. What kind of things do you and your (parents/mother/
      father) do together on weekends?

      PROBE: Is there anything else you do together with
      your (parents/mother/father) on weekends?

*ENTER ALL IN TABLE BELOW AND CODE OR ASK
C AND D AS NECESSARY.*

Activity	Office Code	CODE OR ASK AS NECESSARY					
		−C− Do you usually do that with your mother, your father, or both of them together			−D− Where do you usually do that?		
		Both	Mother	Father	At home	Not at home	
	− −	1	2	3	1	2	*9-12/*
	− −	1	2	3	1	2	*13-16/*
	− −	1	2	3	1	2	*17-20/*
	− −	1	2	3	1	2	*21-24/*
	− −	1	2	3	1	2	*25-28/*
	− −	1	2	3	1	2	*29-32/*
	− −	1	2	3	1	2	*33-36/*

Here are some things you might have done with your (parents/mother/
father) on weekends or during the week. (You may have mentioned some
of them already.)

51A. Did you go grocery shopping with your (parents/mother/
father) during the last week or two?

Yes 1   *37/*

No 2

B. Did you watch TV together in the last week or two?

Yes 1   *38/*

No 2

C. Did you and your (parents/mother/father) run errands
together in the last week or two, say to the cleaners, the
bank, the hardware store or anyplace like that?

Yes 1   *39/*

No 2

D. What about working together around the house or yard? Did you do that with your (parents/mother/father) in the last week or two?

Yes	1	*40/*
No	2	

E. Did your (parents/mother/father) help you with your school work in the last week or two?

Yes	1	*41/*
No	2	

52A. Do you and your (parents/mother/father) ever work together on hobbies or special projects?

Yes	1	*42/*
No . . . . *(SKIP TO 53)*	2	

B. About how often do you do that?

PROBE WITH ANSWER CATEGORIES AS NECESSARY.

At least once a week	1	*43/*
2 or 3 times a month	2	
About once a month	3	
Less often	4	

53A. How about games? Do you ever play games together with your (parents/mother/father)?

Yes	1	*44/*
No . . . . *(SKIP TO 54)*	2	

B. About how often do you play games together?

At least once a week	1	*45/*
2 or 3 times a month	2	
About once a month	3	
Less often	4	

54. We've talked a lot about the things you usually do.
Now I'd like to find out what you did just
yesterday.

> *IF YESTERDAY WAS NOT A SCHOOL DAY, SKIP TO C.*

A. Did you go to school yesterday or were you out sick or
something like that?

      Went to school 1   *46/*

      Out sick or other . . . . . *(SKIP TO 56)* 2

B. Think about yesterday afternoon—what did you do
right after school let out?

> *RECORD ANSWER ON FIRST LINE OF FOLLOWING TABLE*
> *AND CONTINUE WITH TABLE*

C. Think about yesterday morning—what did you do
right after you got up?

> *RECORD ANSWER ON FIRST LINE OF FOLLOWING TABLE*
> *AND CONTINUE WITH TABLE*

YESTERDAY TABLE

What did you do right after (school let out/you got up)? What did you do next?	Who was with you? *PROBE: Anyone else?* *CODE ALL THAT APPLY*	Where was that?	*IF DIFFER-ENT PLACE* How did you get there?
	0. Alone 1. Parent 2. Other adult 3. Siblings 4. Friends 5. Other_____	[ ] Own home	[ ] Walk/bike
	0. Alone 1. Parent 2. Other adult 3. Siblings 4. Friends 5. Other_____	[ ] Same as above [ ] Own home	[ ] Walk/bike
	0. Alone 1. Parent 2. Other adult 3. Siblings 4. Friends 5. Other_____	[ ] Same as above [ ] Own home	[ ] Walk/bike
	0. Alone 1. Parent 2. Other adult 3. Siblings 4. Friends 5. Other_____	[ ] Same as above [ ] Own home	[ ] Walk/bike
	0. Alone 1. Parent 2. Other adult 3. Siblings 4. Friends 5. Other_____	[ ] Same as above [ ] Own home	[ ] Walk/bike
	0. Alone 1. Parent 2. Other adult 3. Siblings 4. Friends 5. Other_____	[ ] Same as above [ ] Own home	[ ] Walk/bike

CONTINUE ON NEXT PAGE IF NECESSARY

What did you do right after (school let out/you got up)? What did you do next?	Who was with you? *PROBE:* Anyone else? *CODE ALL THAT APPLY*	Where was that?	*IF DIFFER-ENT PLACE* How did you get there?
	0. Alone 1. Parent 2. Other adult 3. Siblings 4. Friends 5. Other_____	[ ] Own home	[ ] Walk/bike
	0. Alone 1. Parent 2. Other adult 3. Siblings 4. Friends 5. Other_____	[ ] Same as above [ ] Own home	[ ] Walk/bike
	0. Alone 1. Parent 2. Other adult 3. Siblings 4. Friends 5. Other_____	[ ] Same as above [ ] Own home	[ ] Walk/bike
	0. Alone 1. Parent 2. Other adult 3. Siblings 4. Friends 5. Other_____	[ ] Same as above [ ] Own home	[ ] Walk/bike
	0. Alone 1. Parent 2. Other adult 3. Siblings 4. Friends 5. Other_____	[ ] Same as above [ ] Own home	[ ] Walk/bike
	0. Alone 1. Parent 2. Other adult 3. Siblings 4. Friends 5. Other_____	[ ] Same as above [ ] Own home	[ ] Walk/bike
	0. Alone 1. Parent 2. Other adult 3. Siblings 4. Friends 5. Other	[ ] Same as above [ ] Own home	[ ] Walk/bike

> IF YESTERDAY WAS NOT A SCHOOL DAY, SKIP TO 56

55A. Was yesterday an ordinary day or was it different in some way?

　　　　　Ordinary day . . . . *(SKIP TO 57)* . . . . 1　　47/

　　　　　Different in some way 2

B. What was different about yesterday?

PROBE: Anything else that was different about it?

　　　　　　　　　　　　　　　　　　　　　　　　　　　48-49/

　　　　　　　　　　　　　　　　　　　　　　　　　　　50-51/

　　　　　　　　　　　　　　　　　　　　　　　　　　　52-53/

　　　　　　　　　　　　　　　　　　　　　　　　　　　54-55/

> GO TO 57

56. Even though yesterday wasn't a school day (for you), I'd still like to find out what you do in the afternoon after you've been to school. What kinds of things do you usually do in the afternoon after school lets out?

PROBE: Anything else?

　　　　　　　　　　　　　　　　　　　　　　　　　　　56-57/

　　　　　　　　　　　　　　　　　　　　　　　　　　　58-59/

　　　　　　　　　　　　　　　　　　　　　　　　　　　60-61/

　　　　　　　　　　　　　　　　　　　　　　　　　　　62-63/

　　　　　　　　　　　　　　　　　　　　　　　　　　　64-65/

　　　　　　　　　　　　　　　　　　　　　　　　　　　66-67/

　　　　　　　　　　　　　　　　　　　　　　　　　　　68-69/

　　　　　　　　　　　　　　　　　　　　　　　　　　　70-80/

Serial # _ _ _ _ 5/1
(1-4)
6-7/20
8/

57. On this page are some questions about watching TV. *(HAND INSERT 3 AND PENCIL.)* I will read the questions along with you, and I would like you to mark your answers yourself. For each question circle the answer that is most true for you. Circle only one answer for each question.

    (1)   Most days I am allowed to watch as much TV as I want. *CIRCLE YES OR NO.*

            Yes 1   *9/*

            No 2

            No answer 3

    (2)   My friends and I spend a lot of time watching TV together.

            Yes 1   *10/*

            No 2

            No answer 3

    (3)   There are some TV programs I am not allowed to watch.

            Yes 1   *11/*

            No 2

            No answer 3

    (4)   There are some TV programs my parents like me to watch.

            Yes 1   *12/*

            No 2

            No answer 3

(5)   A lot of times I watch TV because I can't think of anything else to do.

Yes   1   *13/*

No   2

No answer   3

(6)   If I feel like watching TV, I'll watch whatever happens to be on.

Yes   1   *14/*

No   2

No answer   3

(7)   Usually I only watch TV programs I like a lot.

Yes   1   *15/*

No   2

No answer   3

(8)   My parents and I watch TV together almost every day.

Yes   1   *16/*

No   2

No answer   3

(9)   At my house the TV is on most of the <u>afternoon</u>.

Yes   1   *17/*

No   2

No answer   3

(10) At my house the TV is usually on during <u>dinner</u>.

Yes   1   *18/*

No   2

No answer   3

(11) At my house the TV is on most of the <u>evening</u>.

Yes   1   *19/*

No 2

No answer 3

RETRIEVE INSERT, QUICKLY SCAN FOR DOUBLE OR MISSING ANSWERS, AND INSERT IN SCHEDULE. CODE TO THESE PAGES AFTER YOU LEAVE THE HOME.

58A. On these cards are the names of places kids sometimes go. *(HAND R. CARDS ARRANGED IN NUMBERED ORDER.)* I'll read through the cards with you, and you pick out the cards with the names of places you have been to. Just hand them to me.

ENTER ALL IN TABLE AND ASK B AND C AS INDICATED

PLACE	—A— EVER GONE	—B— *IF EVER GONE:* Have you been to ___ since you've been in the sixth grade?	—C— *IF GONE IN 6TH GRADE:* Who did you go with the last time you went to ___? *PROBE:* Who else? *CODE TO THE LOWEST NUMBER*	
(1) The Oakland Museum	1. Yes → 2. No/DK (X)	1. Yes → 2. No/DK (X)	0. Alone 1. School class 2. Parents 3. Other adult 4. Siblings 5. Friends 6. Other 7. Not sure	*20-22/*
(2) Knowland Park and Zoo	1. Yes → 2. No/DK (X)	1. Yes → 2. No/DK (X)	0. Alone 1. School class 2. Parents 3. Other adult 4. Siblings 5. Friends 6. Other 7. Not sure	*23-25/*

PLACE	—A— EVER GONE	—B— IF EVER GONE: Have you been to _____ since you've been in the sixth grade?	—C— IF GONE IN 6TH GRADE: Who did you go with the last time you went to _____? PROBE: Who else? CODE TO THE LOWEST NUMBER	
(3) Lake Merritt	1. Yes → 2. No/DK (X)	1. Yes → 2. No/DK (X)	0. Alone 1. School class 2. Parents 3. Other adult 4. Siblings 5. Friends 6. Other 7. Not sure	26-28/
(4) The San Francisco Aquarium	1. Yes → 2. No/DK (X)	1. Yes → 2. No/DK (X)	0. Alone 1. School class 2. Parents 3. Other adult 4. Siblings 5. Friends 6. Other 7. Not sure	29-31/
(5) The San Francisco Planetarium	1. Yes → 2. No/DK (X)	1. Yes → 2. No/DK (X)	0. Alone 1. School class 2. Parents 3. Other adult 4. Siblings 5. Friends 6. Other 7. Not sure	32-34/
(6) The Lawrence Hall of Science	1. Yes → 2. No/DK (X)	1. Yes → 2. No/DK (X)	0. Alone 1. School class 2. Parents 3. Other adult 4. Siblings 5. Friends 6. Other 7. Not sure	35-37/

PLACE	—A— EVER GONE	—B— *IF EVER GONE:* Have you been to _____ since you've been in the sixth grade?	—C— *IF GONE IN 6TH GRADE:* Who did you go with the last time you went to _____? *PROBE:* Who else? *CODE TO THE LOWEST NUMBER*	
(7) The Oakland Coliseum	1. Yes → 2. No/DK (X)	1. Yes → 2. No/DK (X)	0. Alone 1. School class 2. Parents 3. Other adult 4. Siblings 5. Friends 6. Other 7. Not sure	38-40/
(8) The San Francisco Exploratorium	1. Yes → 2. No/DK (X)	1. Yes → 2. No/DK (X)	0. Alone 1. School class 2. Parents 3. Other adult 4. Siblings 5. Friends 6. Other 7. Not sure	41-43/
(9) An ice skating or roller skating rink	1. Yes → 2. No/DK (X)	1. Yes → 2. No/DK (X)	0. Alone 1. School class 2. Parents 3. Other adult 4. Siblings 5. Friends 6. Other 7. Not sure	44-46/
(10) Redwood Park	1. Yes → 2. No/DK (X)	1. Yes → 2. No/DK (X)	0. Alone 1. School class 2. Parents 3. Other adult 4. Siblings 5. Friends 6. Other 7. Not sure	47-49/

PLACE	—A— EVER GONE	—B— *IF EVER GONE:* Have you been to _____ since you've been in the sixth grade?	—C— *IF GONE IN 6TH GRADE:* Who did you go with the last time you went to _____ ? *PROBE:* Who else? *CODE TO THE LOWEST NUMBER*	
(11) Marine World	1. Yes → 2. No/DK (X)	1. Yes → 2. No/DK (X)	0. Alone 1. School class 2. Parents 3. Other adult 4. Siblings 5. Friends 6. Other 7. Not sure	*50-52/*
(12) Tilden Park	1. Yes → 2. No/DK (X)	1. Yes → 2. No/DK (X)	0. Alone 1. School class 2. Parents 3. Other adult 4. Siblings 5. Friends 6. Other 7. Not sure	*53-55/*
(13) Alameda Beach	1. Yes → 2. No/DK (X)	1. Yes → 2. No/DK (X)	0. Alone 1. School class 2. Parents 3. Other adult 4. Siblings 5. Friends 6. Other 7. Not sure	*56-58/*
(14) Lake Temescal	1. Yes → 2. No/DK (X)	1. Yes → 2. No/DK (X)	0. Alone 1. School class 2. Parents 3. Other adult 4. Siblings 5. Friends 6. Other 7. Not sure	*59-61/*

PLACE	−A− EVER GONE	−B− *IF EVER GONE:* Have you been to _____ since you've been in the sixth grade?	−C− *IF GONE IN 6TH GRADE:* Who did you go with the last time you went to _____? *PROBE:* Who else? *CODE TO THE LOWEST NUMBER*	
(15) Lake Chabot	1. Yes → 2. No/DK (X)	1. Yes → 2. No/DK (X)	0. Alone 1. School class 2. Parents 3. Other adult 4. Siblings 5. Friends 6. Other 7. Not sure	62-64/

59   Now just think about your own neighborhood and what there is to do here. What kinds of things should there be to make it more fun for kids living here?

PROBE: Tell me anything at all that you think would make this a better place for kids.

Anything else?

65-66/

67-68/

69-70/

71-72/

73-74/

That completes the interview. Thank you very much for your help.

Time _____   A.M.
            P.M.

Month of Interview	Day of the Month:	Day of the Week:
April 1 75/	___ ___ 76-77/	Sunday 1 78/
May 2		Monday 2
June 3		Tuesday 2
		Wednesday 4
		Thursday 5
		Friday 6
		Saturday 7

Serial # _ _ _ _ 5/1
(1-4)
6-7/21

INTERVIEWER OBSERVATIONS

1.. Sex of respondent.

    Boy 1   8/

    Girl 2

2. Respondent's ethnicity:

    White 1   9/

    Mexican-American 2

    Other Spanish-American 3

    Black 4

    Asian-American 5

    Other (SPECIFY: _____

    _____) 6

3. Mother's ethnicity:

    White 1   10/

    Mexican-American 2

    Other Spanish-American 3

    Black 4

    Asian-American 5

Other *(SPECIFY:* _____

_____) 6

Not present 7

4. Father's ethnicity:

White 1   *11/*

Mexican-American 2

Other Spanish-American 3

Black 4

Asian-American 5

Other *(SPECIFY:* _____

_____) 6

Not present 7

5. What language was the interview conducted in?

English 1   *12/*

Spanish 2

Other *(SPECIFY:* _____

_____) 3

6. Did the respondent have any difficulty understanding the questions?

Yes 1   *13/*

No 2

7. Did the respondent have any difficulty reading the answer cards?

Yes 1   *14/*

No 2

8. What was the respondent's initial attitude about being interviewed?

Very interested or enthusiastic 1   *15/*

Somewhat interested 2

Indifferent 3

Somewhat reluctant 4

Very reluctant 5

9. What was the respondent's attitude during the interview?

Friendly and eager, volunteered information 1   *16/*

Cooperative but not particularly eager 2

Indifferent 3

Often irritated or hostile—seemed anxious to
get the interview over with 4

10. How truthful did the repondent appear to be?

Truthful 1   *17/*

Somewhat evasive 2

Untruthful 3

11. Was the respondent very shy, fairly shy, not at all shy?

Very shy 1   *18/*

Fairly shy 2

Not at all shy 3

12a. Did the respondent have any obvious physical dis-
abilities or impairments?

Yes 1   *19/*

No . . . . *(SKIP TO 13)* 2

b. What type of disability?

Crippled 1   *20/*

Facial disfigurement 2

Serious speech impediment 3

Deaf 4

Very overweight 5

Very underweight 6

Other *(SPECIFY:* _____

_____ *)*   7

13a. Where was the respondent's mother during most of the interview?

>   In the same room ...... *(SKIP TO 14)* 1   *21/*
>
>   In another room .... *(SKIP TO c)* 2
>
>   Sometimes in same room, sometimes
>   elsewhere 3

b. For how much of the interview was the respondent's mother present?

>   During most of the interview 1   *22/*
>
>   During about half of the interview 2
>
>   During about one-quarter of the interview 3
>
>   During less than one-quarter of the interview 4

c. When the mother was out of the room, do you think she could overhear what you and the respondent were saying?

>   Definitely yes 1   *23/*
>
>   Probably yes 2
>
>   Probably not 3
>
>   Definitely not 4

14a. Was anyone else (besides the mother) present or within hearing distance during the interview?

>   Yes 1   *24/*
>
>   No .... *(SKIP TO 15)* 2
>
>   Not sure .... *(SKIP TO 15)* 3

b. About how long was someone else present or within hearing distance?

>   During most of the interview 1   *25/*
>
>   During about half of the interview 2
>
>   During about one-quarter of the interview 3
>
>   During less than one-quarter of the interview 4

c. Who was present? *(CODE ALL THAT APPLY)*

Father	1	*26/*
Other adult	2	*27/*
Sibling <u>over</u> age of five	3	*28/*
Sibling under 5 years of age	4	*29/*
Friend of respondent	5	*30/*

15. What was the general atmosphere of the household?

Noisy, chaotic, many distractions	1	*31/*
Some noise and distractions	2	
Quiet, calm, practically no distractions	3	

16. Other comments about the respondent:

32/

33/

THE PARENT'S QUESTIONNAIRE

17. Who filled out the parent questionnaire? *(WRITE IN ENUMERATION #   )*   *34-35/*

18. How cooperative was the parent who filled out the self-administered questionnaire?

Very cooperative	1	*36/*
Fairly cooperative	2	
Fairly uncooperative	3	
Very uncooperative	4	

19a. Was s/he able to fill out the questionnaire by herself or himself or did s/he require help from you?

By self .... *(SKIP TO 20)*	1	*37/*
Required help	2	

b. How much help did s/he require in filling out the questionnaire?

A little	1	*38/*

	Some	2	
	A lot	3	
	R. had to be interviewed. Could not do questionnaire at all	4	

20. Did the parent speak English with you?

	Yes	1	*39/*
	No	2	

21. Did the parent speak English with the child?

	Yes	1	*40/*
	No	2	

22. Other comments about the parents:

41/

42/

23. Comments about the parent-child relationship:

43/

44/

FOR ALL HOUSEHOLDS — WHETHER INTERVIEW COMPLETED OR NOT

---

24. Description of building containing the housing unit.

1. One-family house   *45/*
2. Two-family house
3. Three-family house or apt.
4. Four-family house or apt.
5. Building with 5 to 9 apartments
6. Building with 10 to 19 apartments
7. Building with 20 to 49 apartments
8. Building with 50 or more apartments
9. Other (*SPECIFY:* _____)

25. Does the building containing this housing unit also contain space for non-residential purposes, such as a store, office, warehouse, etc?

    1. Yes   *46/*

    2. No

26. Which of the following best describes the building containing this housing unit?

    Building is separated from adjacent buildings by open space on all sides 1   *47/*

    Building has common or abutting wall with adjacent building on one side only 2

    Building has common or abutting wall with at least two adjacent buildings 3

27. Description of the street (one block, both sides) on which unit is found.

    1. Residential only   *48/*

    2. Residential with one or two stores only

    3. Three or more commercial properties, mostly retail

    4. Three or more commercial properties, mostly wholesale or industrial

    5. Other (*SPECIFY:* _____)

28. Description of racial composition of street (one block, both sides) on which housing unit is found.

    1. All White   *49/*

    2. Mostly White

    3. About half White, half Black

    4. Mostly Black

    5. All Black

    6. Other (*SPECIFY:* _____)
       (*e.g., mostly Latino, Asian etc.*)

    7. Could not determine

PARENT'S QUESTIONNAIRE

This questionnaire was administered to parents of male respondents. An identical form in the female gender was administered to parents of female respondents.

UNIVERSITY OF CALIFORNIA, BERKELEY

BERKELEY · DAVIS · IRVINE · LOS ANGELES · RIVERSIDE · SAN DIEGO · SAN FRANCISCO   SANTA BARBARA · SANTA CRUZ

CHILDHOOD AND GOVERNMENT PROJECT

SCHOOL OF LAW (BOALT HALL)
BERKELEY, CALIFORNIA 94720
TELEPHONE (415) 642-0912

Dear Parent:

This study is trying to learn about the ways children spend their time when they are not in school. We are talking with sixth grade students throughout the Bay Area to find out what they do after school, what they especially like to do, and why.

We are asking parents to help by filling out this question-naire which will give us important information about their children, their families, and their neighborhoods. When the study is done, we hope to know more about the kinds of programs that can best serve children when they are not in school.

The questions should take about 45 minutes to answer. Your answers are confidential. Neither your name nor your child's name will ever appear in any report.

Thank you for your cooperation.

INSTRUCTIONS FOR COMPLETING THIS QUESTIONNAIRE

All questions about your son refer to _____
who is now being interviewed. For each question, put an "x" in the box
next to the answer that is most true for you.

FOR EXAMPLE: How long have you lived in Oakland?

- ☐ Less than 6 months

- ☐ 6 to 11 months

- ☒ 1 to 3 years

- ☐ 3 to 5 years

- ☐ 5 to 10 years

- ☐ More than 10 years

Please check only one answer for each question unless the question
itself asks you to do something else.

If you have any questions or any problem filling this out, the interviewer will be happy to help you as soon as she is done talking with
your son.

1-4/

5/2

6-7/01

PART I

THIS SECTION IS ABOUT YOUR NEIGHBORHOOD

1. How long have you lived in Oakland?

1 ☐ Less than 6 months	4 ☐ 3 to 5 years	*8/*
2 ☐ 6 to 11 months	5 ☐ 5 to 10 years	
3 ☐ 1 to 3 years	6 ☐ More than 10 years	

2. How long have you lived at this address?

1 ☐ Less than 6 months	4 ☐ 3 to 5 years	*9/*
2 ☐ 6 to 11 months	5 ☐ 5 to 10 years	
3 ☐ 1 to 3 years	6 ☐ More than 10 years	

3. Do you rent or own your home?

    1 ☐ Rent   *10/*

    2 ☐ Own

    3 ☐ Other : (Please explain) _____

4. Are there enough places in your neighborhood for your son to play safely?

    1 ☐ Yes   *11/*

    2 ☐ No

    3 ☐ Not sure

5. Has there ever been a problem of traffic safety for children in your neighborhood?

    1 ☐ Yes   *12/*

    2 ☐ No

    3 ☐ Not sure

6. How often do you talk with your neighbors?

    1 ☐ Often   3 ☐ Hardly ever   *13/*

    2 ☐ Sometimes   4 ☐ Never

7. How often do you exchange things (like tools or recipes) with your neighbors?

    1 ☐ Often   3 ☐ Hardly ever   *14/*

    2 ☐ Sometimes   4 ☐ Never

8. How often do you and your neighbors visit each other's homes?

    1 ☐ Often   3 ☐ Hardly ever   *15/*

    2 ☐ Sometimes   4 ☐ Never

9. How many of your son's friends live within walking or bicycling distance of your home?

    1 ☐ Almost all of them   *16/*

    2 ☐ About half

    3 ☐ Only a few

4 ☐ None

5 ☐ Not sure

10. How many of his friends live within a block of your home?

1 ☐ Almost all of them   *17/*

2 ☐ About half

3 ☐ Only a few

4 ☐ None

5 ☐ Not sure

11. <u>How satisfied are you with</u>:

a. Recreation programs for children in your neighborhood?

1 ☐ Very satisfied   3 ☐ Somewhat dissatisfied   *18/*

2 ☐ Somewhat satisfied   4 ☐ Very dissatisfied

b. Parks in your neighborhood?

1 ☐ Very satisfied   3 ☐ Somewhat dissatisfied   *19/*

2 ☐ Somewhat satisfied   4 ☐ Very dissatisfied

c. Safety from crime in your neighborhood?

1 ☐ Very satisfied   3 ☐ Somewhat dissatisfied   *20/*

2 ☐ Somewhat satisfied   4 ☐ Very dissatisfied

d. The way your neighborhood looks?

1 ☐ Very satisfied   3 ☐ Somewhat dissatisfied   *21/*

2 ☐ Somewhat satisfied   4 ☐ Very dissatisfied

e. Your son's school?

1 ☐ Very satisfied   3 ☐ Somewhat dissatisfied   *22/*

2 ☐ Somewhat satisfied   4 ☐ Very dissatisfied

12. <u>Compared to other areas in this city</u>, how well do you think your neighborhood is served by:

a. Schools

   1 ☐ Better than average   3 ☐ Below average   *23/*

   2 ☐ Average   4 ☐ Not sure

b. Police

   1 ☐ Better than average   3 ☐ Below average   *24/*

   2 ☐ Average   4 ☐ Not sure

c. Recreation programs for children

   1 ☐ Better than average   3 ☐ Below average   *25/*

   2 ☐ Average   4 ☐ Not sure

d. Parks

   1 ☐ Better than average   3 ☐ Below average   *26/*

   2 ☐ Average   4 ☐ Not sure

e. Libraries

   1 ☐ Better than average   3 ☐ Below average   *27/*

   2 ☐ Average   4 ☐ Not sure

f. Buses

   1 ☐ Better than average   3 ☐ Below average   *28/*

   2 ☐ Average   4 ☐ Not sure

13. Is it easy for children in this neighborhood to use A.C. buses?

   1 ☐ Yes   *29/*

   2 ☐ No

   3 ☐ Don't know

14. Is it easy for children in this neighborhood to get to libraries?

   1 ☐ Yes   *30/*

   2 ☐ No

   3 ☐ Don't know

15. Is it easy for children in this neighborhood to get to parks and playgrounds?

    1 ☐ Yes   *31/*

    2 ☐ No

    3 ☐ Don't know

16. Are children afraid to walk around your neighborhood during the day?

    1 ☐ Yes   *32/*

    2 ☐ No

    3 ☐ Not sure

17. How much do you have to worry about children's safety in this neighborhood?

    1 ☐ A lot   *33/*

    2 ☐ Some

    3 ☐ Not very much

18. What do you think your chances would be of getting something done in each of the following situations?

    a. How good are your chances of getting the city to give better police and fire protection to your neighborhood?

        1 ☐ Good chance   3 ☐ Poor chance   *34/*

        2 ☐ Fair chance   4 ☐ Not sure

    b. How good are your chances to get the principal of your child's school to act on a complaint or suggestion?

        1 ☐ Good chance   3 ☐ Poor chance   *35/*

        2 ☐ Fair chance   4 ☐ Not sure

    c. How good are your chances of getting the city to stop someone from putting up a building that would be bad for your neighborhood?

        1 ☐ Good chance   3 ☐ Poor chance   *36/*

        2 ☐ Fair chance   4 ☐ Not sure

d. How good are your chances of finding a way to
talk to someone on the city council about a
neighborhood problem?

1 ☐ Good chance   3 ☐ Poor chance   *37/*

2 ☐ Fair chance   4 ☐ Not sure

e. How good are your chances of getting a traffic
light or a stop sign put on a street in your
neighborhood?

1 ☐ Good chance   3 ☐ Poor chance   *38/*

2 ☐ Fair chance   4 ☐ Not sure

19a. If you were going to move somewhere else, would
you want to live in a neighborhood pretty much
like the one you live in now?

1 ☐ Yes   3 ☐ Not sure   *39/*

2 ☐ No
↓
IF NO:

> 19b. Why would you want to live in a   *40-41/*
> different neighborhood?

20. If you were going to move somewhere else, how
hard do you think it would be to find housing that
would meet your needs?

1 ☐ It would be very easy to find housing   *42/*

2 ☐ It would be fairly easy

3 ☐ It would be fairly hard

4 ☐ It would be very hard

PART II

THIS SECTION IS ABOUT YOUR SON AT SCHOOL AND AT HOME

21. How many different schools has your son gone to since beginning kindergarten?

    1 ☐ One—only the school he goes to now   *43/*

    2 ☐ 2 schools

    3 ☐ 3 schools

    4 ☐ 4 schools

    5 ☐ 5 or more

22. How long has he been going to the school he goes to now?

    1 ☐ Less than 6 months   3 ☐ 1 to 3 years   *44/*

    2 ☐ 6 months to 1 year   4 ☐ More than 3 years

23. How does your son feel about school?

    1 ☐ He likes school a lot   *45/*

    2 ☐ He likes school some

    3 ☐ He doesn't like school very much

    4 ☐ He doesn't like school at all

    5 ☐ Not sure

24. How is your son doing in reading this school year?

    1 ☐ Excellent   3 ☐ Fair   *46/*

    2 ☐ Good   4 ☐ Poor

                        5 ☐ Not sure

25. How is he doing in arithmetic this school year?

    1 ☐ Excellent   3 ☐ Fair   *47/*

    2 ☐ Good   4 ☐ Poor

                        5 ☐ Not sure

26. After school lets out at 3 o'clock, what does your son usually do?

    1 ☐ He usually comes straight home   *48/*

    2 ☐ He usually stays at school for awhile

    3 ☐ He usually goes somewhere else before coming home

27. After school and on weekends, does your son usually play by himself, with brothers or sisters, or with other children?

    1 ☐ Usually plays by himself   *49/*

    2 ☐ Usually plays with brothers or sisters

    3 ☐ Usually plays with other children

    4 ☐ Other: (Please explain) _____

28. How many TV sets do you have in your house?

    1 ☐ None   3 ☐ 2 TV's   *50/*

    2 ☐ 1 TV   4 ☐ 3 TV's or more

29. How many days a week does your son usually watch TV?

    1 ☐ Everyday   *51/*

    2 ☐ 5 or 6 days a week

    3 ☐ 3 or 4 days a week

    4 ☐ 1 or 2 days a week

    5 ☐ Hardly ever or never

    6 ☐ Not sure

30. On school days about how much time does he usually spend watching TV?

    1 ☐ No time   5 ☐ About 3 to 3½ hours   *52/*

    2 ☐ Less than 1 hour   6 ☐ About 4 to 4½ hours

    3 ☐ About 1 to 1½ hours   7 ☐ About 5 to 5½ hours

    4 ☐ About 2 to 2½ hours   8 ☐ Not sure

31a. Does your son have chores or jobs that he is supposed to do around the house <u>at least once a week</u>?

    1 ☐ Yes   2 ☐ No (Go to Question 32) *53/*

    ↓

    IF YES:

31b. Which chores does he do <u>at least once a week</u>? <u>CHECK ALL THE CHORES HE DOES</u>.

    1 ☐ Makes own bed   *54/*

      ☐ Cleans own room

      ☐ Helps clean rest of house

      ☐ Sets table

      ☐ Clears table

      ☐ Does the dishes

      ☐ Works in yard

      ☐ Empties waste baskets or garbage

      ☐ Feeds pets

      ☐ Helps cook

      ☐ Other: (Please list)_____ *64/*

31c. How often do you have to remind your son to do his chores or jobs at home?

    1 ☐ Almost everytime he does them   *65/*

    2 ☐ A few times a week

    3 ☐ A few times a month

    4 ☐ Hardly ever

31d. How is it decided what chores your son will do?

    1 ☐ I or some other adult in the family decides what chores he will do   *66/*

    2 ☐ He decides for himself what chores to do

    3 ☐ We decide together what chores he will do

32. Are there certain things you ask or encourage your son to do in his free time after school or on weekends or is he mostly left to do things he wants to do?

    1 ☐ Mostly left to do things he wants to do   *67/*

    2 ☐ Asked or encouraged some of the time

    3 ☐ Asked or encouraged a lot of the time

33. Would you like to see your child do more of any of the things listed below in his free time?

CHECK ALL THAT ARE TRUE FOR YOU

    1

   ☐ Play more with friends   *68/*

   ☐ Play more with brothers or sisters

   ☐ Read

   ☐ Watch TV

   ☐ Be in organized groups, like the Scouts

   ☐ Take lessons or classes in things like music or crafts

   ☐ Other: (Please write in) _____

   ☐ None of these things   *75/*

34. How often does your son work with you or other adults in the family around the house or yard?

    1 ☐ Hardly ever or never   3 ☐ A few times a month   *76/*

    2 ☐ About once a month   4 ☐ Once a week or more

35. About how often does he work on hobbies or special projects with you or other adults in the family?

    1 ☐ Hardly ever or never   3 ☐ A few times a month   *77/*

    2 ☐ About once a month   4 ☐ Once a week or more

1-4

5/2

36. On school days, is there a definite time your son is supposed *6-7/02*

to be in the house around dinnertime or can he come in
when he wants?

1 ☐ Come in when wants   8/

2 ☐ In before dark

3 ☐ Definite time

4 ☐ When called

5 ☐ Other: (Please explain) _____

37. At this time of year, do you usually let your son play
outside on school nights after dinner?

1 ☐ Yes   2 ☐ No (Go to Question 38)   9/
       ↓
     IF YES:

> 37b. How often does he usually play outside
>   after dinner on school nights?
>
>   1 ☐ Everyday or almost everyday   10/
>
>   2 ☐ A few times a week
>
>   3 ☐ A few times a month
>
>   4 ☐ Hardly ever or never

38. Does your son have a regular bedtime on school nights?

1 ☐ Yes   2 ☐ No   11/

39. About what time is he usually in bed on school nights?

1 ☐ No special time   5 ☐ 9:30 to 9:59 p.m.   12/

2 ☐ 8:00 to 8:29 p.m.   6 ☐ 10:00 to 10:29 p.m.

3 ☐ 8:30 to 8:59 p.m.   7 ☐ 10:30 to 10:59 p.m.

4 ☐ 9:00 to 9:29 p.m.   8 ☐ 11:00 p.m. or later

40. How independent is your son in doing things for himself
around the house?

1 ☐ Very independent   13/

2 ☐ Fairly independent

3 ☐ Not very independent

41. How independent is he in doing things on his own <u>away from home</u>?

    1 ☐ Very independent   *14/*

    2 ☐ Fairly independent

    3 ☐ Not very independent

42. How shy is your son?

    1 ☐ Very shy   3 ☐ Not very shy   *15/*

    2 ☐ Fairly shy   4 ☐ Not shy at all

43. Does your son have any health problems that keep him from doing things other children his age do?

    1 ☐ Yes   2 ☐ No (Go to Question 44) *16/*

    ↓

    IF YES:

> 43b. What kind of things does he have trouble doing?   *17-18/*

44. How often do the following things come up as problems with your son? CHECK ONE BOX FOR EACH.

	Often	Sometimes	Almost never or never	
	1	2	3	
a. Watching too much TV	☐	☐	☐	*19/*
b. Watching certain programs you don't like him to watch	☐	☐	☐	
c. Going too far away from home	☐	☐	☐	
d. Playing with children that you don't like	☐	☐	☐	

		Often	Sometimes	Almost never or never	
		1	2	3	
e.	Wanting to do things that cost too much money.	☐	☐	☐	
f.	Being late for meals . . .	☐	☐	☐	
g.	Forgetting to do house-hold chores	☐	☐	☐	
h.	Playing in parts of the neighborhood you don't like him to go. . .	☐	☐	☐	26/

45. How far would you like to see your son go in school?

    1 ☐ Some high school   27/

    2 ☐ Finish high school

    3 ☐ Technical school after high school

    4 ☐ Some college

    5 ☐ Finish college

    6 ☐ Graduate or professional school

46. How far do you suppose he <u>will</u> go in school?

    1 ☐ Some high school   28/

    2 ☐ Finish high school

    3 ☐ Technical school after high school

    4 ☐ Some college

    5 ☐ Finish college

    6 ☐ Graduate or professional school

PART III

THIS SECTION IS ABOUT PLACES YOUR SON GOES WITH THE FAMILY OR WITH HIS FRIENDS

47. About how often does your son go places with you or other adults in the family—including things like shopping, doing errands, eating out, visiting?

1 ☐ A few times a week   3 ☐ About once a month   *29/*

2 ☐ A few times a month   4 ☐ Less often

48. Has he gone with you or another adult in the family to any of the following places in the last month?

PLEASE CHECK YES OR NO FOR EACH.

Gone with an adult member of your family to:	In the last month		
	YES	NO	
	1	2	
a. A restaurant or coffee shop	☐	☐	*30/*
b. Shop for groceries	☐	☐	
c. Visit friends or relatives	☐	☐	
d. A movie	☐	☐	
e. A sports event	☐	☐	
f. A library	☐	☐	
g. An event at his school	☐	☐	
h. A park	☐	☐	
i. A museum	☐	☐	
j. A play or concert	☐	☐	*39/*

49a. Do you have any relatives living in the Bay Area?

1 ☐ Yes   2 ☐ No (Go to Question 50) *40/*
   ↓
IF YES:

> 49b. About how often does your son go with you or other adults in the family to visit relatives?
>
>   1 ☐ Hardly ever or never   *41/*
>   2 ☐ A few times a year
>   3 ☐ About once a month
>   4 ☐ A few times a month
>   5 ☐ Once a week or more

50. Do you or anyone else in the household have a car?

    1 ☐ Yes   2 ☐ No (Go to Question 53) *42/*

51. Do you have a driver's license?

    1 ☐ Yes   2 ☐ No (Go to Question 53) *43/*

52a. Do you ever drive your son places he wants to go after school or on weekends?

    1 ☐ Yes   2 ☐ No (Go to Question 53) *44/*

    ↓

    IF YES:

> 52b. About how often do you drive your son places he wants to go?
>
>   1 ☐ Almost everyday   *45/*
>
>   2 ☐ A few times a week
>
>   3 ☐ A few times a month
>
>   4 ☐ About once a month
>
>   5 ☐ Less often
>
> 52c. Do you feel that you have to spend too much time driving him places?
>
>   1 ☐ Yes   2 ☐ No   *46/*

53. When your son wants to go someplace after school or on weekends, does he mostly depend on you or another adult to take him or does he usually go on his own?

    1 ☐ Mostly depends on me or another adult to take him   *47/*

    2 ☐ He goes some places on his own

    3 ☐ He goes most places on his own

54. After school and on weekends, how often does your son go places <u>outside the neighborhood</u> by himself or just with friends?

    1 ☐ Everyday or almost everyday   *48/*

    2 ☐ A few times a week

    3 ☐ A few times a month

4 ☐ Less often

5 ☐ Never

55. After school and on weekends, how often does he take A.C. buses by himself to go places he wants to go?

    1 ☐ Everyday or almost everyday   *49/*

    2 ☐ A few times a week

    3 ☐ A few times a month

    4 ☐ Less often

    5 ☐ Never

56a. Did your son go with the family on a vacation during the past year?

    1 ☐ Yes   2 ☐ No (Go to Question 57) *50/*

    ↓

    IF YES:

> 56b. How long was the vacation?
>
>   1 ☐ 1 or more weekends   *51/*
>
>   2 ☐ 3 to 7 days
>
>   3 ☐ 8 to 14 days
>
>   4 ☐ 15 to 30 days
>
>   5 ☐ More than 1 month

PART IV

THIS SECTION IS ABOUT ORGANIZED AFTER SCHOOL ACTIVITIES

These questions are about organized activities for children that meet after school or on weekends. We call them organized activities because they meet regularly and are run by adults. They include:

After school lessons or classes like music, crafts, dancing, and swimming lessons.

Recreation programs like those at the YMCA, at parks and recreation centers, and in school yards after school lets out.

Adult led groups and clubs, like Scouts, church youth groups, and organized sports teams.

57. Has your son done any organized activities like those mentioned above since school started in September?

    1 ☐ Yes   2 ☐ No   *52/*

58. In general, how do you feel about your son doing these kinds of activities? <u>CHECK ONLY ONE</u>.

    1 ☐ I would rather not have my son in these activities.   *53/*

    2 ☐ It's up to him, it doesn't matter to me one way or the other.

    3 ☐ I like my son to spend at least some time in these activities.

    4 ☐ I like my son to spend a lot of time in these activities.

59. About how often do you get notices through the mail or sent home from school about organized activities your son could join?

    1 ☐ Often   *54/*

    2 ☐ Once in a while

    3 ☐ Hardly ever or never

60. Have you ever tried to find organized activities for your son to join or after school lessons for him to take?

    1 ☐ Yes   2 ☐ No   *55/*

61. How much do you hear about after school or weekend activities for children at the following places?

<u>CHECK ONE BOX FOR EACH.</u>

	A lot	A little	Nothing	
	1	2	3	
a. Your son's school	☐	☐	☐	*56/*

	A lot	A little	Nothing
	1	2	3

b. The nearest park or recreation center . . . . ☐ ☐ ☐

c. Your local library . . . . ☐ ☐ ☐

d. The Oakland Museum . . . . . . ☐ ☐ ☐ *59/*

62. Please check whether you mostly agree or mostly disagree with each of the following statements.

	Mostly agree	Mostly disagree	Not sure
	1	2	3

a. Children should decide themselves if they want to be in organized activities after school . . . . ☐ ☐ ☐ *60/*

b. Organized after school activities are an important part of any child's education . . . . ☐ ☐ ☐

c. Parents should decide what after school activities their children should be in . . . . ☐ ☐ ☐

d. If parents let their children do as they please after school they usually won't do anything worthwhile . . . . ☐ ☐ ☐

e. Children should have more say in deciding what activities the City sets up for them . . . . ☐ ☐ ☐

f. Children can learn at least as much by being with parents as by spending time in organized activities . . . . ☐ ☐ ☐

	Mostly agree	Mostly disagree	Not sure
	1	2	3

g. Children themselves usually know best what after school activities they will get something out of . . . . ☐   ☐   ☐   *66/*

63. Most decisions about after school activities and programs for children are made by people in the city government. What do you think would be the best way to make decisions about children's programs? CHECK ONLY ONE.

     1 ☐ These decisions should be made by people in city government.   *67/*

     2 ☐ These decisions should be made by the city, but they should find out what people in each neighborhood want.

     3 ☐ These decisions should be made by the people living in each neighborhood.

     4 ☐ It doesn't matter to me how these decisions are made.

     5 ☐ Have no opinion on this.

64. If more decisions about after school activities and programs were made by the people in your neighborhood, would you want to go to meetings to help make these decisions?

     1 ☐ Yes   2 ☐ No   *68/*

65. Suppose decisions were being made by residents of each neighborhood.

    a. Do you think these programs would interest more children, about the same, or fewer children?

       1 ☐ More children   *69/*

       2 ☐ About the same

       3 ☐ Fewer children

       4 ☐ Not sure

b. Do you think programs in your neighborhood would change a lot or would they stay about the same as they are now?

1 ☐ Programs would change a lot   70/

2 ☐ Programs would stay about the same

3 ☐ Not sure

66a.   Do you think your neighborhood needs more activities, programs or facilities for children?

　　　1 ☐ Yes   2 ☐ No (Go to Question 67) 71/
　　　　↓
　　　IF YES:

> 66b. Are there any activities or facilities that you
>   would especially like to see? <u>PLEASE
>   WRITE IN.</u>   72-73/

67a.   Are there any organized activities that you would especially like your son to do?

　　　1 ☐ Yes   2 ☐ No (Go to Question 68) 74/
　　　　↓
　　　IF YES:

> 67b. What activities are these? <u>PLEASE WRITE IN.</u>   75-76/
>
>
>
> 67c. Is there a reason why he isn't doing them now?   77-78/
>   <u>PLEASE WRITE IN.</u>

1-4/

5/2

6-7/03

PART V

THIS SECTION IS ABOUT RAISING CHILDREN

68. As children grow up, they start to do more things on their own without help from parents. Please check what grade you think your son will be in when he becomes ready to do each of the following by himself.

	Activity	When he will be ready to do this by himself without your help?			
		Does this already	7th or 8th grade	9th or 10th grade	11th grade or after that
		1	2	3	4
a.	Pick out his own clothes at the store	☐	☐	☐	☐ *8/*
b.	Decide for himself <u>what</u> TV programs to watch	☐	☐	☐	☐
c.	Decide for himself <u>how much</u> TV to watch . . .	☐	☐	☐	☐
d.	Decide when to go to bed on Friday and Saturday nights	☐	☐	☐	☐
e.	Set his own bedtime on school nights	☐	☐	☐	☐
f.	Decide whether to join any organized after school activities	☐	☐	☐	☐
g.	Visit a friend outside the neighborhood without telling you before he goes	☐	☐	☐	☐
h.	Go to San Francisco by bus or BART with				

		When he will be ready to do this by himself without your help?			
	Activity	Does this already	7th or 8th grade	9th or 10th grade	11th grade or after that
		1	2	3	4
	other kids his own age	☐	☐	☐	☐
i.	Decide for himself what chores to do	☐	☐	☐	☐
j.	Go out alone in the neighborhood after dark	☐	☐	☐	☐ *17/*

69. How important do you think the following things are for your son? For each, check whether you think it is very important, somewhat important, not too important, or not important at all.

	How important is it for your son to:	Very important	Somewhat important	Not too important	Not important at all
		1	2	3	4
a.	Become well-educated	☐	☐	☐	☐ *18/*
b.	Obey even those family rules he feels are unfair	☐	☐	☐	☐
c.	Have an interesting job or career someday	☐	☐	☐	☐
d.	Bring his friends home	☐	☐	☐	☐
e.	Get very good grades in school . .	☐	☐	☐	☐

How important is it for your son to:	Very important	Somewhat important	Not too important	Not important at all
	1	2	3	4
f. Make a lot of money someday . .	☐	☐	☐	☐
g. Take part in organized after school activities	☐	☐	☐	☐
h. Become ambitious	☐	☐	☐	☐
i. Obey even those laws which most people ignore	☐	☐	☐	☐ 26/

70. Do you agree or disagree with these two statements about raising children?

    a. Children around age 11 or 12 usually know what's best for them.

        1 ☐ Agree   27/

        2 ☐ Disagree

        3 ☐ Not sure

    b. Girls should be raised more strictly than boys.

        1 ☐ Agree   28/

        2 ☐ Disagree

        3 ☐ Not sure

71. How important are each of the following in affecting what happens to children as they grow up? For each, check whether you think it is very important, somewhat important, not too important, or not important at all.

		Very important	Somewhat important	Not too important	Not important at all	
		1	2	3	4	
a.	Good schooling . .	☐	☐	☐	☐	*29/*
b.	The neighborhood they are raised in	☐	☐	☐	☐	
c.	Having good luck	☐	☐	☐	☐	
d.	Having a "close" family	☐	☐	☐	☐	
e.	The child's IQ . . .	☐	☐	☐	☐	
f.	How hard he or she tries	☐	☐	☐	☐	
g.	God's will	☐	☐	☐	☐	
h.	Having a lot of money in the family	☐	☐	☐	☐	
i.	Going to church . .	☐	☐	☐	☐	
j.	The kinds of friends they have	☐	☐	☐	☐	*38/*

Now please go back over this list and choose the <u>two things</u> that you think are the most important in affecting what happens to children and circle the letters of your choices below.

a	b	c	d	e	f	g	h	i	j

39-40/
41-42/

PART VI

THIS SECTION IS ABOUT YOUR OWN ACTIVITIES

72. Here is a list of clubs and organizations that some people belong to. Please put an "x" next to any that you yourself belong to.

    1 ☐ Church or synagogue   *43/*

        ☐ Church-connected groups

        ☐ Labor union

        ☐ Business or civic groups

        ☐ Professional groups

        ☐ Neighborhood or community group

        ☐ Social or card-playing group

        ☐ Sports teams

        ☐ Country club

        ☐ Parent-teacher groups, like the PTA

        ☐ Political club or organization

        ☐ Other club or group: (Please list)

        _____

        _____

        _____

        ☐ None   *55/*

73. Some people spend a lot of time doing volunteer work or going to meetings. Others do not have the time or have too many other things to do. Have you done any of the following in the past few years?

    PLEASE CHECK YES OR NO FOR EACH.

Have you:	In the past few years	
	Yes	No
	1	2
a. Been a room mother or done regular volunteer work for any of your children's classes at school	☐	☐ *56/*

	In the past few years	
Have you:	Yes	No
	1	2

b. Worked as a leader or volunteer with any organized activities for children— like the Scouts, a church group, or Little League . . . . ☐ ☐

c. Gone to a meeting of the City Council or School Board . . . . ☐ ☐

d. Gone to a meeting of some other City government agency, like the planning commission . . . . ☐ ☐

e. Done regular volunteer work for a church, charitable, or community organization . . . . ☐ ☐

f. Worked to correct a traffic safety problem or other problem in your neighborhood . . . . ☐ ☐ *61/*

74a. Are you going to school now?

    1 ☐ Yes   2 ☐ No (Go to Question 75) *62/*
    ↓
    IF YES:

> 74b. Are you a part time or full time student?
>
>   1 ☐ Part time   *63/*
>
>   2 ☐ Full time
>
>   3 ☐ Other: (Please explain)

75. How many days a week do you usually watch TV?

    1 ☐ Everyday   *64/*

    2 ☐ 5 or 6 days

    3 ☐ 3 or 4 days

    4 ☐ 1 or 2 days

    5 ☐ Hardly ever or never

76. About how much time do you usually spend watching TV each day?

    1 ☐ No time   *65/*

    2 ☐ About 1 hour or less

    3 ☐ About 1 to 2 hours

    4 ☐ About 2 to 3 hours

    5 ☐ About 3 to 4 hours

    6 ☐ About 4 to 5 hours

    7 ☐ More than 5 hours

77a. Do you ever use the public library?

    1 ☐ Yes   2 ☐ No (Go to Question 78) *66/*
    ↓
    IF YES:

> 77b. How often do you use the public library?
>
>   1 ☐ Hardly ever   *67/*
>
>   2 ☐ Every few months
>
>   3 ☐ About once a month
>
>   4 ☐ A few times a month or more

PART VII

FAMILY INCOME, PARENT'S EDUCATION AND OCCUPATION

78. Please check the amount that comes closest to your total family income <u>before taxes</u> last year in 1975. (Include all forms of income.)

    1 ☐ Less than $3,000   *68/*

    2 ☐ $3,000 to $4,999

    3 ☐ $5,000 to $7,999

    4 ☐ $8,000 to $9,999

    5 ☐ $10,000 to $14,999

    6 ☐ $15,000 to $19,999

    7 ☐ $20,000 to $24,999

8 ☐ $25,000 to $29,999

9 ☐ More than $30,000

79. What is the highest level of school you have completed?

    1 ☐ 8th grade or less *69/*

    2 ☐ Some high school

    3 ☐ High school graduate

    4 ☐ Some college

    5 ☐ College graduate

    6 ☐ Graduate or professional school

80. What is the highest level of school your son's father (or stepfather) has completed?

    1 ☐ 8th grade or less *70/*

    2 ☐ Some high school

    3 ☐ High school graduate

    4 ☐ Some college

    5 ☐ College graduate

    6 ☐ Graduate or professional school

1-4/
5/2
6-7/04

81a. Which best describes you?

    1 ☐ Self employed *8/*

    2 ☐ Employed by someone else

    3 ☐ Full time housewife—no job outside home (Go to Question 82)

    4 ☐ Unemployed (Go to Question 82)

    5 ☐ Retired (Go to Question 82)

  b. Do you work full time or part time?

    1 ☐ Full time *9/*

    2 ☐ Part time

c. What is your occupation? (DESCRIBE WHAT YOUR
    JOB IS)

_____ *10-11/*

_____ *12-13/*

d. Which days do you work?

    CHECK ALL THE DAYS THAT YOU WORK.

        1

    ☐ Monday   *14/*

    ☐ Tuesday

    ☐ Wednesday

    ☐ Thursday

    ☐ Friday

    ☐ Saturday

    ☐ Sunday   *20/*

e. Do you have regular working hours?

    1 ☐ Yes   2 ☐ No (Go to Question 82) *21/*
    ↓
    IF YES:

f.	What time do you usually leave for work?	
	_____ A.M./P.M.	*22-25/*
	What time do you usually get home from work?	
	_____ A.M./P.M.	*26-29/*

IF YOU ARE MARRIED, PLEASE ANSWER QUESTION 82.
IF NOT MARRIED, GO TO QUESTION 83.

82a. Which best describes your husband or wife?

    1 ☐ Self employed   *30/*

    2 ☐ Employed by someone else

    3 ☐ Full time housewife—no job outside home (Go to
        Question 83)

4 ☐ Unemployed (Go to Question 83)

5 ☐ Retired (Go to Question 83)

b. Does he or she work full time or part time?

1 ☐ Full time   *31/*

2 ☐ Part time

c. What is his or her occupation? (DESCRIBE HIS OR HER JOB)

_____ *32-33/*

_____ *34-35/*

d. Which days does he or she work?

CHECK ALL THE DAYS HE OR SHE WORKS.

1

☐ Monday   *36/*

☐ Tuesday

☐ Wednesday

☐ Thursday

☐ Friday

☐ Saturday

☐ Sunday   *42/*

e. Does he or she have regular working hours?

1 ☐ Yes   2 ☐ No (Go to Question 83) *43/*
↓
IF YES:

f. What times does he or she usually leave for work?
_____ A.M./P.M. *44-47/*
What time does he or she usually get home from work?
_____ A.M./P.M. *48-51/*

83. Would you like to receive a summary of this study when it is finished?

    1 ☐ Yes   2 ☐ No   *52/*

84. We may want to talk with you again about this study. May we get in touch with you again at some future time?

    1 ☐ Yes   2 ☐ No   *53/*

Appendix B
Sample Design and Field Results*

This appendix describes the sample design and reports field procedures, field outcomes, and the calculation of weights for the Oakland survey of the Children's Time Study.

THE STUDY POPULATION

The study sample was drawn in the spring of 1976 from the 4,100 sixth-grade students attending public elementary schools in Oakland, California. The children were distributed among fifty-eight neighborhood elementary schools ranging in enrollment from about a dozen to almost 200 sixth-grade students.

Oakland's elementary schools are neighborhood schools. They draw the overwhelming proportion of their students from officially designated school attendance areas. Hence the composition of each school's student body rather closely reflects the characteristics of the neighborhood in which it is located.

Racial and ethnic minorities predominate among the overall school district population. In 1974-75, 65.1 percent of Oakland's elementary school students were black, 7.5 percent had Spanish surnames, 5.2 percent were Asian, 2.7 percent were members of other minorities, and 19.6 percent were white. The

*By William L. Nicholls, II, Center for Human Factors Research, U.S. Bureau of the Census (formerly assistant director, Survey Research Center, University of California, Berkeley).

schools varied greatly in ethnic composition. Some schools were predominantly white, some predominantly black, and some predominantly Asian. A number of schools were heterogeneous with no single ethnic group comprising a majority of the student population.

Many of the city's sixth-grade students come from low-income families. In 1974-75, almost two-fifths (38.3 percent) lived in homes supported by Aid to Families with Dependent Children (AFDC). Approximately one-fifth of the sixth-grade students attend schools where less than 10 percent of the students are from AFDC families, while one-third attend schools where the majority of the students are from AFDC homes. While the schools with predominantly black enrollments tend to have large proportions of AFDC children, there are important exceptions. Oakland has a large and growing middle-class black population. This is reflected in the fact that several elementary schools have high proportions of black children from families of middle-class status.

Not all of the sixth-grade children attending Oakland's public schools reside in the city of Oakland. Approximately 2 percent have officially recorded home addresses outside the city. Some are the children of teachers in the Oakland public schools, while others live in adjacent cities but attend Oakland schools under exchange agreements with other school districts. These agreements permit children living near the city boundaries to attend schools in other communities if they are closer to their homes. It is suspected that an even larger proportion actually lived outside the city but filed fictitious or unverifiable addresses with the school authorities. Under similar exchange arrangements an unknown number of children residing in Oakland attend public schools in Berkeley, Emeryville, and other nearby cities.

For the purposes of this study, the survey population was defined as children who (1) were enrolled in the sixth grade of the Oakland public schools in January 1976; (2) resided in the city of Oakland; and (3) had not moved from the city or to another elementary school attendance area between the time of sample selection and completion of the field work. By these criteria, approximately 3,950 of the 4,169 enrolled sixth-grade students were eligible to participate in the study.

SAMPLING METHODS

Overview

As a first step in the sampling process, Oakland's public elementary schools were divided into high, medium, and low socioeconomic groupings (or master strata) according to the percentage of children at the school from AFDC homes.* By the method used, about 20 percent of the sixth-graders attended high socioeconomic status (SES) schools, about 20 percent attended medium SES schools, while 60 percent attended low SES schools.

To ensure that enough students would be interviewed at each SES level to make reliable statistical comparisons, sixth-graders from high and medium SES schools were sampled at a higher rate than those from low SES schools. Specifically, 30 percent of the sample was drawn from students in high SES schools, 30 percent from those in medium SES schools, and 40 percent from low SES schools. This meant that students from high and medium SES schools had a chance of about three in ten of being interviewed while those in low SES schools had a chance of approximately one in nine.

Within each SES stratum sixth-graders were selected by a two-stage process. First, a sample of schools was drawn by probability methods. Then, school records were consulted to obtain the names, addresses, and telephone numbers of randomly selected sixth-grade students. The sampling procedures were designed to provide from thirty-five to forty-one completed interviews per sampled school.

A total of twenty schools was chosen, about one-third of the elementary schools in the city. These included six schools each of high and medium SES and eight of low SES. Interviews were completed with approximately 19.4 percent of the sixth-grade students eligible for the study.

Stratification

To allow each elementary school principal to decide whether to permit his or her school to be included in the study, the

---

*The reasons for choosing AFDC as a principal stratifying criteria are explained in the following section.

initial selection of sites took place at the start of the 1975-76 school year. In designing the sample, therefore, it was necessary to rely on stratification criteria from both the current and the previous school year and on projected sixth-grade enrollments.

Four stratification criteria were considered in developing homogeneous strata of schools: (1) ethnic composition; (2) percentage of children from AFDC families as of January 1976; (3) average income of all families living in the school attendance area estimated from 1970 U.S. Census figures; and (4) CTBS* standardized reading test scores. The percentage of children from AFDC families was selected as a better measure of socioeconomic status than census-based family income, both because it was more current and because it referred exclusively to the families in the area with children. Average reading scores were eliminated as a stratification criterion when they were found to be closely correlated in each school with the percentage of children from AFDC homes. Analysis indicated, however, that average reading scores reached a fairly stable low plateau when the percentage of children from AFDC homes reached about 35 to 40 percent. This suggested an approximate, but meaningful cutting point to delineate low socioeconomic neighborhoods.

Three socioeconomic master strata were defined by the proportions of children from AFDC homes. High SES school attendance areas were defined as those with less than 10 percent of their grade-school children from AFDC homes; low SES neighborhoods were defined as those with 37.6 percent or more AFDC students. The 37.6 percent cutoff point was somewhat arbitrary and selected in part to control stratum sizes.

To avoid selection of schools with too few sixth-grade students, for the next stage of sampling schools with a projected sixth-grade enrollment of less than forty students were combined with adjacent schools of similar character. These combined schools were then treated as single schools in further stratification and sampling. This reduced the total number of possible primary sampling units from fifty-eight to fifty-two.

The schools within each SES master stratum were then divided into three or four individual strata by a combination of

---

*Comprehensive Tests of Basic Skills.

ethnic and socioeconomic criteria. These criteria, which are summarized in table B-1, were varied from one master stratum to the next to accommodate their predominant characteristics and to provide individual strata of approximately equal numbers of projected sixth-grade students for better control of sample size.

To illustrate the process, the high SES master stratum was divided into three substrata of approximately 250 to 300 students each. Stratum 1 consisted of schools with less than 2 percent of the student body from AFDC homes. These schools also happened to have student bodies that were 80 percent or more white and Asian. Stratum 2 consisted of schools with 2.0 to 9.9 percent AFDC children and 75 percent or more white and Asian student bodies. Stratum 3 included schools within the same AFDC range but with less than 75 percent white and Asian students.

The medium and low SES master strata also employed finer breakdowns of the percentage of AFDC children for further stratification but varied in their ethnic composition. For the medium SES master stratum, school compositions of approximately 50 percent whites and Asians were used, while for the low SES master stratum the criterion was about 80 percent black. It should be emphasized that the three master strata were intended to form a strict hierarchy along a single continuum. The individual strata within them were meant only to form groupings of schools that were relatively homogeneous in ethnicity and socioeconomic status.

Selection of Schools and Interview Targets

From each of the ten final strata, two schools were selected without replacement and with probability proportionate to their projected numbers of sixth-grade students in 1975-76. When a two-schools combination was chosen, it was treated as a single sampling unit with approximately forty sixth-graders selected between them. This occurred twice, making a total of twenty-two schools representing twenty selections.

A target number of completed interviews was calculated for each school to keep the sample self-weighting within master

TABLE B-1. Sampling Strata

Master stratum	Stratum	Stratification criteria			Population		Target sample	
		AFDC children (percentage)	White and Asian (percentage)	Black (percentage)	Schools[a]	Sixth-grade students[b]	Schools	Sixth-grade students
I (High SES)	1	0.0- 1.9	(>80)[c]	d	4 (4)	274	2 (2)	77
	2	2.0- 9.9	≥75	d	5 (4)	255	3 (2)	72
	3	2.0- 9.9	<75	d	5 (4)	265	2 (2)	74
	Total	0.0- 9.9	d	d	14 (12)	794	7 (6)	223
II (Middle SES)	4	(17.2-28.4)[c]	≥50	d	4 (4)	266	2 (2)	75
	5	19.9-30.9	<50	d	5 (4)	276	3 (2)	77
	6	31.0-37.6	<50	d	5 (5)[e]	266	2 (2)	75
	Total	10.0-37.6	d	d	14 (13)	808	7 (6)	227
III (Low SES)	7	(37.6-52.4)	d	<80	8 (8)[e]	633	2 (2)	74
	8	43.6-48.4	d	≥80	7 (6)	610	2 (2)	71
	9	48.5-54.4	d	≥80	7 (7)	697	2 (2)	82
	10	54.5-99.9	d	≥80	9 (7)	627	2 (2)	73
	Total	37.6-99.9	d	d	31 (28)	2,567	8 (8)	300
Grand Total					58 (52)	4,169	22 (20)	750

[a]The first figure is the total number of schools with sixth-grade students. The second figure in parentheses is the reduced number of schools after those with less than 40 sixth-grade students have been combined with adjacent schools.

[b]The numbers of sixth-grade students reported here are projections for 1975-76 prepared in the summer of 1975.

[c]Figures in parentheses were not used to define strata but provide supplementary information about the strata.

[d]Not a criterion for this master stratum.

[e]One large school was split between strata 6 and 7 and was reported in the count of schools for both of these strata. This school was not selected in the sample for either stratum.

strata. For combined schools, the target was allocated between them by their relative projected enrollments. Stratum (rather than school) targets are shown in the last column of table (B-1). The target for each school was one-half its stratum target, rounded to the nearest whole number when necessary.

The principal of each selected school was contacted to secure his or her approval of the study before the next stage of sampling was undertaken. Approval was obtained for twenty-one of the twenty-two schools approached. The principal of one school asked that it be dropped from the sample in the belief that the survey might exacerbate existing conflicts between staff and parents. This one school was replaced by another from the same stratum.

Selection of Students

Students were selected from each sampled school by simple random sampling from the roster of sixth-grade students enrolled in February 1976. Several groups of students were excluded from the survey at this point.

The first were students with officially recorded home addresses outside the city of Oakland, who, therefore, fell outside the definition of the study population. In total, this amounted to about 2 percent of the sixth-grade enrollments.

The second were students who presented special interviewing problems. It was decided, for example, that no more than one child would be interviewed in each household. Consequently, when twins living in the same household were randomly selected, only one was considered eligible for an interview. A few additional students were omitted because they did not speak English or Spanish, because they had previously been interviewed in pretests, or because their parents had helped review the interview forms. In total, these exclusions represented about 1 percent of the sixth-grade enrollments, of which two-thirds were exclusions of half of a set of twins.

The third group, comprising about 5 percent of the sixth-grade enrollments, were students with no current home addresses or telephone numbers in their school records. In some cases, the school records contained an entry that this missing information was not to be pursued further. No attempts were made to obtain home addresses or telephone numbers if they were absent from the school records. It is suspected that at least some of these students resided outside of Oakland or in attendance areas for schools other than the ones they were attending. These losses were spread rather evenly over all three SES master strata.

To allow for refusals and other field losses, each school was oversampled by about 25 percent. The resulting lists of sampled students were then maintained in random order and the excess cases assigned for interviews only to replace refused interviews and other field losses as they occurred. Halfway through the fieldwork, the sampling targets were revised for each school to take account of discrepancies between the projected and the actual 1975-76 enrollments and to make adjustments for ineligible respondents identified through school records and field contacts. In virtually all schools, the revised targets of completed interviews were closely approximated or exceeded.

FIELDWORK METHODS

Since the respondents were young children, it was thought advisable to have an interviewing staff consisting of young women. It was felt that they would appear less threatening to respondents than either male interviewers or older women. Since the majority of child respondents were black, special efforts were made to employ black interviewers.

A total of twenty-two interviewers participated in the study. Each attended a two- to four-day training session and completed at least two practice interviews before receiving a first assignment. The length of training varied with the interviewer's prior experience.

All interviews were completed in the respondents' homes. An advance letter was mailed to the mother or guardian of each child describing the purpose of the survey and explaining that mother and child would each receive $2.50 for their participation. The interviewer then telephoned the home to arrange an appointment for the interview. If the home did not have a telephone, a personal visit was made for this purpose.

In most cases, agreement to participate was readily obtained.

The honorarium for the child, which was paid in cash at the completion of the interview, appears to have been quite important in the favorable reception.

When the interviewer arrived at the home, a household enumeration was completed with the parent. The parent, in almost every case the child's mother, was then asked to complete a lengthy questionnaire while the child was being interviewed. This had the double advantage of securing parent and child data concurrently and of making possible a more confidential interview with the child while the parent was occupied with the questionnaire. If a parent had difficulty reading the questionnaire, and some did, the interviewer offered to help after finishing the child's interview.

The first interviews were completed on April 8, 1976, and the last on June 23, 1976, approximately two weeks after the close of school.*

FIELD OUTCOMES

Response Rates

During the course of the fieldwork a few additional children were identified as ineligible for an interview by the definition of the study population. These included children whose actual place of residence was outside Oakland or who had moved away from Oakland or to another school attendance area prior to the date of interview.

Interviews were completed with 87.2 percent of the remaining children who were sampled for the survey and not known to be ineligible. The parents of 10.6 percent of sampled children declined to permit an interview, 1.5 percent could not be found at home in repeated calls, and 0.7 percent were lost for other reasons, such as serious illness of the parent or child or the inability to complete a reinterview (table B-2).

Response rates varied only slightly from school to school and from stratum to stratum (table B-3). At least 80 percent of the

---

*Verification of the fieldwork indicated that it was necessary to conduct partial or total reinterviews with approximately 9 percent of the sample. This was done during the summer months.

TABLE B-2. Field Outcomes by Master Stratum

| | Master stratum | | | | | | | | |
| | I (High SES) | | II (Middle SES) | | III (Low SES) | | City total | |
Interview outcome	number	percentage	number	percentage	number	percentage	number	percentage
Ineligible for study[a]	2	0.8	8	2.9	7	1.9	17	1.7
Eligible for study	249	99.2	268	97.1	359	98.1	876	98.3
Total sample	251	100.0	276	100.0	366	100.0	893	100.0
Completed interview	233	89.6	236	88.1	305	85.0	764	87.2
Refused interview	22	8.8	29	10.8	42	11.7	93	10.6
Never at home	4	1.6	3	1.1	6	1.7	13	1.5
Inaccessible and other[b]	—	—	—	—	6	1.6	6	0.7
Total eligible	249	100.0	268	100.0	359	100.0	876	100.0

[a]Includes children living outside of Oakland or moving from Oakland or to another school prior to the intended date of interview. Also includes two families who moved to unlocatable, new addresses.

[b]Includes one family where the child respondent was too ill to be interviewed, one family where the parent was too ill to participate, and four families scheduled for reinterviews but who moved from Oakland before they could be reached.

TABLE B-3. Completed Interviews by School and Stratum and Analysis Weight

Master stratum	Stratum	School	Eligible sample	Completed interviews		Stratum response rate	Analysis weight
				Number	Percentage of those eligible		
I (High SES)	1	1	41	37	90.2%	89.3%	0.652
		2	43	38	88.4%		0.735
	2	1	39	35	89.7%	92.6%	0.705
		2	42	40	95.2%		0.619
	3	1	48	42	87.5%	86.9%	0.604
		2	36	31	86.1%		0.708
		Total	249	223	89.6%	89.6%	—
II (Middle SES)	4	1	41	36	87.8%	88.0%	0.642
		2	42	37	88.1%		0.878
	5	1	46	43	93.5%	87.0%	0.648
		2	46	37	80.4%		0.600
	6	1	48	44	91.7%	89.2%	0.630
		2	45	39	86.7%		0.688
		Total	268	236	88.1%	88.1%	—
III (Low SES)	7	1	42	37	88.1%	86.5%	1.317
		2	54	46	85.2%		1.371
	8	1	48	41	85.4%	83.1%	1.413
		2	35	28	80.0%		1.655
	9	1	47	40	85.1%	86.5%	1.661
		2	42	37	88.1%		1.544
	10	1	42	36	85.7%	83.5%	1.477
		2	49	40	81.6%		1.554
		Total	359	305	85.0%	85.0%	—
Grand Total			876	764	87.2%	87.2%	—

sampled eligible students at each sampled school were interviewed, while the stratum response rates varied only from 83.1 to 92.6 percent. The response rates of boys and girls were virtually identical, 87.4 and 87.0 percent, respectively.

There is some evidence that black families were somewhat less likely to participate in the study than others. Since race and ethnicity were not indicated in the school records and could not be determined with certainty if the home was not visited, the ethnicity of families never reached is not known. Among those visited, however, only 3.1 percent of the white families and 2.8 percent of the Hispanic-American families declined to be interviewed contrasted with 7.9 percent of the black families. Nevertheless, the response rate even in predominantly black areas was sufficiently high so that this minor bias should be negligible.

Matching Interviewer Backgrounds

For several reasons, the goal of having children interviewed by interviewers of their own background could not be met in all cases. Although the interviewing staff included black, white, and Chinese interviewers, it was not large enough to include the full range of ethnic groups sampled. In addition, since the family's race or ethnicity was not known with certainty in advance, race matching could only be approximated by assigning white interviewers to predominantly white areas and black interviewers to predominantly black areas. When they encountered children of a different background in their assignments, they were instructed to complete those interviews. The alternative of terminating such interviews early and sending another interviewer at a later time often proves embarrassing for all parties and generally does not seem advisable.

Eighty-nine percent of the white children were interviewed by white interviewers, while 72 percent of the black children were interviewed by black interviewers (table B-4). The residual

TABLE B-4. Race of Interviewer by Ethnicity of Child Respondent
(horizontal percentages)

Ethnicity of child respondent	Race of interviewer		Total (N)
	White	Black	
White	88.6	11.4	(185)
Black	27.8	72.2	(457)
Asian-American	97.1	2.8	(70)
Hispanic-American	51.3	48.7	(39)
Other	23.1	76.9	(13)
Total	50.0	50.0	(764)

percentages of cross-race interviewing generally represent white children residing in predominantly black areas and vice versa.

Virtually all the Asian children were interviewed by white interviewers, often accompanied by the Chinese staff member who interpreted for the parent when necessary. About half the Mexican-American and other Hispanic respondents were interviewed by white interviewers and half by black. Again, the race of the interviewer depended primarily on whether the neighborhood to which she was assigned was predominantly white or black.

WEIGHTING

Since children were sampled from the low SES master stratum at a lower rate than from the high and medium master strata, sample estimates are based on weighted results. The weights employed throughout the analysis compensate for the varying probability of selection by master stratum and also for (1) deviations of actual school enrollments from September projections; (2) estimated losses from ineligibility; and (3) the small variations in response rates from school to school.

The weights were prepared at the school level so that all sampled children in the same school received the same weight. A preliminary set of weights was first calculated to provide estimated population numbers for each individual stratum of children who (1) were enrolled in the sixth grade of the Oakland public schools in January 1976; (2) resided in the city of Oakland; and (3) had not moved from the city or to another elementary school attendance area between January 1976 and the date of interview. The final noninteger, case-attached weights were obtained by multiplying the preliminary weights by a constant to reduce the weighted total of sample cases to the actual sample size. The final weights are shown in the last column of table B-3.

SUMMARY

In summary, 764 children attending sixth grade in the Oakland public schools were interviewed with the unusually high completion rate of 87.2 percent of the sampled eligible cases. When weighted, the sample data provide accurate estimates of the study population with calculable confidence intervals. Moreover, since response rates of 80 percent or better were obtained from both sexes, all socioeconomic groups, and all twenty sampled schools, sampling biases are negligible.

NOTES

Notes

Preface

1. John Dewey, "My Pedagogic Creed," *The School Journal* 54, no. 3 (January 16, 1897): 78.

2. John Dewey, *Democracy and Education* (New York: Macmillan, 1916), p. 89.

3. See, for example, Victor Rubin and Elliott A. Medrich, "More Than Fun and Games: The Predicament of Recreational and Cultural Services for Children" (Children's Time Study, Schools of Law and Education, University of California, Berkeley, 1981); and Mary Berg and Elliott A. Medrich, "Children in Four Neighborhoods: The Physical Environment and Its Effect on Play and Play Patterns," *Environment and Behavior* 12, no. 3 (September 1980): 320-348.

1. Life out of School

1. George Gallup, *The Gallup Opinion Index*, no. 135 (October 1976); no. 119 (May 1973); no. 47 (May 1969); no. 102 (December 1973), (Princeton: The American Institute of Public Opinion); Richard Bloom, Martin Whiteman, and Martin Deutsch, "Race and Social Class as Separate Factors Related to the Social Environment," *American Journal of Sociology* 70 (January 1965): 471-476; William Brink and Lewis Harris, *Negro Revolution in America* (New York: Simon and Schuster, 1964); Arlene Skolnick, "Caste and Class in the American Family," mimeographed (Institute of Human Development, University of California, Berkeley, January 1977).

2. Christopher Jencks et al., *Inequality* (New York: Harper & Row, 1972), pp. 53 and 255.

3. James S. Coleman et al., *Equality of Educational Opportunity* (Washington, D.C.: Government Printing Office), pp. 73-74.

4. James S. Coleman, "The Concept of Equality of Educational Opportunity," *Harvard Educational Review* 37 (Summer 1968): 21.

5. For a discussion of this point see Charles S. Benson, Stuart Buckley, and Elliott A. Medrich, "A New View of School Efficiency: Household Time Contributions to School Achievement," in *School Finance Policy in the 1980s: A Decade of Conflict*, ed. James Guthrie (Cambridge, Mass.: Ballinger Publishing Co., 1980), pp. 169-204.

On the related school achievement question see Judith Roizen, "School Achievement and Out-of-School Life," working paper (Children's Time Study, Schools of Law and Education, University of California, Berkeley, 1981); and Charles S. Benson, "Household Production of Human Capital: Time Uses of Parents and Children as Inputs," in *Toward Efficiency and Equity in Educational Finance*, eds. Walter W. McMahon and Terry Geske (Boston: Allyn and Bacon, 1980).

6. Sara L. Lightfoot, *Worlds Apart* (New York: Basic Books, 1978), pp. 4-5.

7. Urie Bronfenbrenner, *The Ecology of Human Development* (Cambridge, Mass.: Harvard University Press, 1979). By way of comparison see Roger Barker and Herbert Wright, *Midwest and Its Children: The Psychological Ecology of an American Town* (Evanston, Ill.: Row Peterson, 1955).

8. Bronfenbrenner, *Human Development*, p. 21.

9. These issues are examined in chap. 6 of this volume.

10. For a review of some of the major work in this area see, for example, Robert Lineberry, "Mandating Urban Equality: The Distribution of Municipal Public Services," *Texas Law Review* 53, no. 26 (1974): 25-59; The Ford Foundation, *The Next Step: Toward Equality of Public Service* (Summary of the Conference on Public Service Equalization Litigation, New York, May 16-17, 1974); Steven D. Gold, "The Distribution of Urban Government Services in Theory and Practice," *Public Finance Quarterly* 2 (January 1975): 107-116; Charles S. Benson and Peter Lund, *Neighborhood Distribution of Local Public Services* (Berkeley: Institute of Governmental Studies, 1969); Allen D. Mandel, "Changing Patterns of Local Urban Expenditure," in *Public Expenditure Decisions in the Urban Community*, ed. Howard Schaller (Washington, D.C.: Resources for the Future, Inc., 1965), pp. 19-37; Frank S. Levy, Arnold J. Meltsner, and Aaron Wildavsky, *Urban Outcomes: Schools, Libraries and Streets* (Berkeley, Los Angeles, London: University of California Press, 1974); Seymour Gold, *Urban Recreation Planning* (Philadelphia: Lea and Fabinger, 1973); Harry Hatry and Diana R. Dunn, *Measuring the Effectiveness of Local Government Services* (Washington, D.C.: The Urban Institute, 1971).

11. Ralph Smith, "Sources of Growth of the Female Labor Force, 1971-1975," *Monthly Labor Review* 100 (August 1977): 28. For a recent review, see June O'Neill, "Trends in the Labor Force Participation of Women," in *Work, Family, and Community: Summary Proceedings of an Ad Hoc Meeting*, ed. Cheryl D. Hayes (Washington, D.C.: National Academy of Sciences, 1980), pp. 28-38.

12. Kenneth Keniston et al., *All Our Children* (New York: Harcourt Brace, 1977), p. 12.

13. Ibid, p. 17. This perspective should be viewed in the context of a larger debate over the family and its future. Exemplary writings exploring aspects of this question include: Mary Jo Bane, *Here to Stay: American Families in the Twentieth Century* (New York: Basic Books, 1976); Christopher Lasch, *Haven in a Heartless World* (New York: Basic Books, 1977); Eli Zaretsky, *Capitalism, The Family and Personal Life* (New York: Harper and Row, 1976); Jessie Bernard, *The Future of Marriage* (New York: Bantam Books, 1972); idem, *The Future of Motherhood* (New York: Dial Press, 1974); Heather Ross and Isabel Sawhill, *Time of Transition: The Growth of Families Headed by Women* (Washington, D.C.: The Urban Institute, 1975); Jerome H. Skolnick and Arlene Skolnick, eds., *Families in Transition: Rethinking Marriage, Sexuality, Childrearing and Family Organization* (Boston: Little Brown, 1971); and Lois W. Hoffman and Ivan Nye, eds., *Working Mothers: An Evaluative Review of the Consequences for Wife, Husband and Child* (San Francisco: Jossey Bass, 1974).

14. Alexander Szalai, "Trends in Contemporary Time Budget Research," in *The Social Sciences: Problems and Orientations*, ed. Szalai (The Hague: Mouton, 1968); idem, "Trends in Comparative Time Budget Research," *The American Behavioral Scientist* 9, no. 9 (May 1966): 3-8, John Robinson, *How Americans Use Time* (New York: Praeger, 1977); F. Stuart Chapin, Jr., *Human Activity Patterns in the City* (New York: John Wiley, 1974); Sebastian deGrazia, *Of Time, Work and Leisure* (Garden City, N.Y.: Anchor Books, 1964), pp. 85-90; John Robinson and Philip Converse, "Social Change Reflected in the Use of Time," in *The Human Meaning of Social Change*, eds. Angus Campbell and Philip Converse (New York: Russell Sage, 1972); and Alexander Szalai, ed., *The Use of Time* (The Hague: Mouton, 1972). Related literature pertinent specifically to studies of children are cited in chap. two.

15. Time-use patterns change from season to season, particularly the specific content of activities. We conducted this survey in the spring, hoping to profile out-of-school life at a time when activity choices were not simply reflecting constraints of unfavorable weather. The spring season in Northern California tends to be warm and relatively dry. Furthermore, once daylight-saving time begins in April, many children spend a good deal of their afternoons and evenings out of doors. We would expect that a similar survey conducted in midwinter would yield somewhat different activity patterns linked to the weather: children would be less mobile, spending more time at home engaging in a greater number of passive or sedentary activities.

2. The Study of Time and Time Use

1. Staffan B. Linder, *The Harried Leisure Class* (New York: Columbia University Press, 1970), p. 2.

2. Gerald Gutenschwager, "The Time Budget–Activity Systems Perspective in Urban Research and Planning," *Journal of the American Institute of Planners* 39, no. 6 (November 1973): 378.

3. Victor Rubin, "The Time Budget Research Tradition: Lessons for Planning with Young People," working paper (Children's Time Study, Schools of Law and Education, University of California, Berkeley, September 1978), pp. 2-4.

4. F. Stuart Chapin, Jr., *Human Activity Patterns in the City* (New York: Wiley, 1974), pp. 9 and 33-34.

5. Sebastian deGrazia, *Of Time, Work and Leisure* (Garden City, N.Y.: Anchor Books, 1962), chap. 4.

6. L. Gordon and E. Klopov, *Man After Work* (Moscow: Progress Publishers, 1975), p. 59.

7. For recent reviews of efforts to categorize types of time use see United Nations, UNESCO, *Progress Report on the Development of Statistics of Time Use*, 1979; and William Michelson, ed., *Public Policy in Temporal Perspective* (The Hague: Mouton, 1978). An earlier statement appears in Alexander Szalai, "Trends in Contemporary Time Budget Research," in *The Social Sciences: Problems and Orientations*, ed. Szalai (The Hague: Mouton, 1968).

8. Alexander Szalai et al., *Use of Time*, p. 1.

9. Chapin, *Human Activity Patterns*, chap. 2. Most of the time geography literature is in Swedish, but a good summary and extensive bibliography can be found in Allan R. Pred, "Urbanisation, Domestic Planning Problems and Swedish Geographic Research," *Progress in Geography* (London: Edward Arnold Publishers, 1973) 5: 1-76.

10. George A. Lundberg et al., *Leisure: A Suburban Study* (New York: Columbia University Press, 1934).

11. Pitirim A. Sorokin and Clarence Berger, *Time Budgets of Human Behavior* (Cambridge, Mass.: Harvard University Press, 1939).

12. The Opinion Research Corporation's 1957 national sample of "yesterday" activities; the J. A. Ward study of 7,000 household time budgets kept over a two-day period (see deGrazia, *Of Time, Work and Leisure*, pp. 460-463); the University of Michigan, Institute for Social Research 1965 survey of how Americans use time, overviewed in John Robinson, *How Americans Use Time* (New York: Praeger, 1977); and the international time-use study conducted by the European Coordination Centre for Research and Documentation in Social Sciences in twelve countries, involving 30,000 adults, summarized in Szalai, *Use of Time*.

13. Szalai, *Use of Time*, chap. 1.

14. For reviews of important twentieth-century time-budget studies, see Alexander Szalai, "Contemporary Time Budget Research"; Szalai, *Use of Time*, chap. 1; Robinson, *How Americans Use Time*; Chapin, *Human Activity Patterns*; deGrazia, *Of Time, Work and Leisure*; John Robinson and Philip Converse, "Social Change Reflected in the Use of Time," in *The Human Meaning of Social Change*, ed. Angus Campbell and Philip Converse (New York: Russell Sage, 1972).

15. Kathryn E. Walker and Margaret E. Woods, *Time Use: A Measure of Household Production of Family Goods and Services* (Washington, D.C.: American Home Economics Association, Center for the Family, 1976). Home economists and agricultural economists have studied extensively the allocation of time among household and domestic chores. For a sampling of this research, much of which was conducted prior to World War II, see the following: I. F. Arnquist and E. H. Roberts, *The Present Use of Work Time of Farm Homemakers*, Washington State College Agricultural Experiment Station Bulletin, no. 234 (Pullman: Washington State College, 1929); I. Z. Crawford, *The Use of Time by Farm Women*, University of Idaho Agricultural Experiment Station Bulletin, no. 146 (Moscow: University of Idaho Press, 1927); D. Dickins, *Time Activities in Homemaking*, Mississippi Agricultural Experimental Station Bulletin, no. 424 (Jackson: University Press of Mississippi, 1945); I. H. Gross, *Home Management of Working and Non-working Homemakers with Young Children*, Michigan Agricultural Experiment Station Quarterly Bulletin, vol. 27 (East Lansing: University of Michigan, February 1955); B. M. Kuschke, *Allocation of Time by Employed Married Women in Rhode Island*, Rhode Island State College Agricultural Experiment Station Bulletin, no. 267 (Kingston: Rhode Island State College, 1938); S. L. Manning, *Time Use in Household Tasks by Indiana Families*, Purdue University Agricultural Experiment Station Research Bulletin, no. 837 (Lafayette, Ind.: Purdue University, 1968); M. Muse, *Time Expenditures on Homemaking Activities in 193 Vermont Farm Homes*, University of Vermont Agricultural Experiment Station Bulletin, no. 514 (Burlington: University of Vermont, 1945); J. O. Rankin, *The Use of Time in Farm Homes* Nebraska Agricultural Experiment Station Bulletin, no. 230 (Lincoln: University of Nebraska, 1928); R. E. Steidl, "Use of Time During Family Meal Preparation and Cleanup," *Journal of Home Economics* 50 (1958): 447-450; U.S., Department of Agriculture, Bureau of Human Nutrition and Home Economics, *Time Costs of Homemaking—A Study of 1,500 Rural and Urban Households* (Washington, D.C.: Government Printing Office, 1944); M. Whittemore and B. Neil, *Time Factors in the Business of Home Making in Rural Rhode Island*, Rhode Island State College Agricultural Experiment Station Bulletin, no. 221 (Kingston: Rhode Island State College, 1927); M. Wilson, *Time*

Used in the Operation of Representative Oregon Households: A Preliminary Report (Corvallis: School of Home Economics, Oregon State Agricultural College, 1930).

16. Examples of journey-to-work studies that have utilized time-budget data are: The Editors of *Fortune* magazine, *Exploding Metropolis* (Garden City: Doubleday, 1958); Kate K. Liepman, *The Journey to Work* (London: Paul, Trench, Trubner, 1944); Allan Voorhees and associates, *Factors and Trends in Trip Lengths* (Washington Highway Research Board, 1968); Gutenschwager, "Time Budget," p. 381; Jean Gottman, *Megalopolis* (New York: Twentieth Century Fund, 1961); Anthony Wallace, "Driving to Work," in *Context and Meaning in Cultural Anthropology*, ed. Melford Spiro (New York: Free Press, 1965), pp. 277-292.

17. See, for example, Hilda Himmelweit, A. Oppenheim, and P. Vince, *Television and the Child* (London: Oxford University Press, 1958); Rolf Meyersohn, "Television and the Rest of Leisure," *Public Opinion Quarterly* (Spring 1968): 102-112. See also chap. 8 of this volume.

18. Survey Research Center, Institute for Social Research, University of Michigan, *A Study of Adolescent Boys* (New Brunswick, N.J.: Boy Scouts of America, 1956).

19. U.S., Outdoor Recreation Resources Review Commission, *National Recreation Survey: Study Report 19* (Washington, D.C.: Government Printing Office, 1962).

20. British Travel Association and University of Keele, *The Pilot National Recreation Survey: Report No. 1* (July 1967).

21. For a sampling of this research, see Herbert Gans, "Recreation Planning for Leisure Behavior" (Ph.D. diss., University of Pennsylvania, 1957); Donald L. Foley, "The Use of Facilities in a Metropolis," *American Journal of Sociology* 56 (November 1950): 238-246; Bernard Berelson, *The Library's Public* (New York: Columbia University Press, 1949); Charles S. Benson and Peter Lund, *Neighborhood Distribution of Local Public Services* (Berkeley: University of California, Institute of Governmental Studies, 1969); Ralph Conant, *The Public Library and the City* (Cambridge, Mass.: MIT Press, 1965); Seymour Gold, "Nonuse of Neighborhood Parks," *Journal of the American Institute of Planners* 38, no. 6 (November 1972): 369-378; Frank Levy, Arnold Meltzner, and Aaron Wildavsky, *Urban Outcomes: Schools, Libraries and Streets* (Berkeley, Los Angeles, London: University of California Press, 1974); Herbert Bangs and Stuart Mahler, "Users of Local Parks," *Journal of American Institute of Planners* 36, no. 5 (September 1970): 330-334.

22. Converse and Robinson, "Social Change," p. 22.

23. See, for example, sections of Robert S. Lynd and Helen Lynd, *Middletown in Transition* (New York: Harcourt Brace, 1929); Robert J. Havighurst et al., *Growing Up in River City* (New York: John Wiley, 1962); Celia B. Stendler, *Children of Brasstown* (Urbana: University of Illinois Press, 1949).

24. See Anthea Holme and Peter Massie, *Children's Play: A Study of Needs and Opportunities* (London: Michael Joseph, 1970); Kevin McGrath, "Children in Their Own Time," *Where* 107 (August 1975): 202-212; Davis McEntire, *Leisure Activities of Youth in Berkeley, California* (Berkeley: Berkeley Council of Social Welfare, 1952); James S. Coleman, *The Adolescent Society* (New York: Free Press, 1961); Survey Research Center, *Adolescent Boys*; Ann Bellingham and Barbara Hird, "Pilot Survey of Existing Leisure Time Provisions for Children Aged 5-14 in the London Boroughs of Kensington, Chelsea, and Greenwich" (London: Inner London Education Authority, 1972); Central Advisory Council for Education, *Out of School* (London: Her Majesty's Stationery Office, 1948); Barbara Heyns, *Exposure and the Effects of Schooling* (New York: Academic Press, 1978).

25. Hans Meyerhoff, *Time in Literature* (Berkeley and Los Angeles: University of California Press, 1960), p. 27.

26. Ibid, p. 95.

27. Jean Piaget, *The Origins of Intelligence in Children* (New York: International University Press, 1952); idem, *The Child's Conception of the World* (New York: Harcourt Brace, 1929); idem, *Le Developpement de la notion de temps chez l'enfant* (Paris: Presses Universites France, 1929).

28. Paul Fraisse, *The Psychology of Time* (New York: Harper and Row, 1963).

29. Wilbur Schramm, Jack Lyle, and Edwin Parker, *Television in the Lives of Our Children* (Stanford: Stanford University Press, 1961), pp. 213-216. For additional discussion of the estimation problem, see Robinson, *How Americans Use Time*, chap. 2.

30. Philippe Aries, *Centuries of Childhood* (New York: Vintage, 1962), chap. 4.

31. Converse and Robinson, "Social Change," pp. 34-45.

32. Herbert Blumer, *The World of the Youthful Drug User* (Berkeley: School of Criminology, University of California, 1967).

33. Lillian Rubin, *Worlds of Pain* (New York: Basic Books, 1976), pp. 38-39.

34. Arlene Skolnick, "Caste and Class in the American Family," draft (Childhood and Government Project, School of Law, University of California, Berkeley, January 1977), p. 6.

35. Jules Henry, "White People's Time, Colored People's Time," *Transaction* (March/April 1965): 34.

36. Margherita McDonald, Carson McGuire, and Robert Havighurst, "Leisure Activities and the Socioeconomic Status of Children," *American Journal of Sociology* 54 (May 1949): 505-519.

37. Survey Research Center, *Adolescent Boys*, p. 111.

38. Bernard Goldstein, *Low Income Youth in Urban Areas* (New York: Holt, Reinhart, 1967), pp. 121-128.

39. M. Ward Cramer, "Leisure Time Activities of Economically Privileged Children," *Sociology and Social Research* 34 (May/June 1950): 444-450.

40. Stendler, *Brasstown*, chap. 5.

41. A. B. Hollingshead, *Elmtown's Youth* (New York: John Wiley, 1943), p. 299.

42. Lynd and Lynd, *Middletown*, chaps. 17 and 18.

43. Goldstein, *Low Income Youth*, chap. 7.

44. R. Clyde White, "Social Class Differences in the Use of Leisure," *American Journal of Sociology* 61 (September 1955): 145-150.

45. Urie Bronfenbrenner, "Socialization and Social Class Through Time and Space," in *Readings in Social Psychology*, eds. E. E. Maccoby, T. M. Newcombe, and E. L. Hartley (New York: Holt, Rinehart, 1958), pp. 400-425.

46. Elliott A. Medrich, "Measuring the Child's Use of Time: A Comment on Methodology and Survey Instruments," working paper (Children's Time Study, Schools of Law and Education, University of California, Berkeley, Fall 1977).

47. Heyns, *Effects of Schooling*, chaps. 7 and 8.

48. Coleman, *Adolescent Society*, p. 13.

49. Pauline M. Vaillancourt, "Stability of Children's Survey Responses," *Public Opinion Quarterly* (November 1977): 373-387.

50. R. G. Niemi, *How Family Members Perceive Each Other* (New Haven: Yale University Press, 1974).

51. Elliott A. Medrich, "Test-retest: Response Stability in the Children's Time

Study Survey," working paper (Children's Time Study, Schools of Law and Education, University of California, Berkeley, 1980).

52. Charles S. Benson, Stuart Buckley, and Elliott A. Medrich, "A New View of School Efficiency: Household Time Contributions to School Achievement," in *School Finance Policy in the 1980s: A Decade of Conflict*, ed. James Guthrie (Cambridge, Mass.: Ballinger, 1980) pp. 169-204; Charles S. Benson, "Household Production of Human Capital: Time Use of Parents and Children As Inputs," in *Toward Efficiency and Equity in School Finance*, ed. Walter W. McMahon and Terry Geske (Boston: Allyn and Bacon, 1980).

3. The Setting and the Sample

1. For a review of the issue of children's mobility, Roger Hart, *Children's Experience of Place* (New York: Irvington Publishers, Inc.); Donald L. Foley, "The Use of Facilities in a Metropolis," *American Journal of Sociology* 56 (November 1950): 238-246; Nelson J. Foote et al., *Housing Choices and Housing Constraints* (New York: McGraw Hill, 1960); Kevin Lynch et al., *Growing Up in Cities* (Cambridge, Mass.: MIT Press, 1977); Gerald Suttles, *The Social Construction of Communities* (Chicago: University of Chicago Press, 1972); and idem, "Community Design: The Search for Participation in a Metropolitan Society," in *Metropolitan America in Contemporary Perspective*, eds. Amos H. Hawley and Vincent P. Rock (New York: John Wiley, 1975), pp. 235-98. For additional references, see chap. 4 of this volume.

2. Mary Berg and Elliott A. Medrich, "Children in Five Neighborhoods," working paper (Children's Time Study, Schools of Law and Education, University of California, Berkeley, 1977); and idem "Children in Four Neighborhoods: The Physical Environment and Its Effect on Play and Play Patterns," *Environment and Behavior* 12, no. 3 (September 1980): 320-348.

3. The names of the five neighborhoods have been changed. They are, however, descriptions of neighborhoods actually in the Time Study Survey sample. These neighborhoods were visited in Summer 1976, after the fieldwork was completed. Informants had been child respondents in the spring survey.

4. City of Oakland, Department of City Planning, "Proposed Open Space, Conservation and Recreation Element of the Oakland Comprehensive Plan," January 1976, pp. 55-71.

5. For a summary of problems associated with the measurement of social status and class, see Richard P. Coleman and Lee Rainwater, *Social Standing in America: New Dimensions of Class* (New York: Basic Books, 1978).

4. Children on Their Own

1. The most celebrated and in some ways an extreme view of this process is that of Philippe Aries, *Centuries of Childhood* (New York: Vintage Press, 1962). He argues that the concept of childhood is virtually the invention of the last few centuries of Western European culture.

2. Urie Bronfenbrenner, *Two Worlds of Childhood* (New York: Simon and Schuster, 1970), p. 102.

3. See, for example, Leslie Fiedler's analysis in *Love and Death in the American Novel* (Cleveland: World Publishing Company, 1962), chap. 15.

4. William Golding, *Lord of the Flies* (New York: Capricorn Books, 1959).

5. Jean Piaget, *The Moral Judgment of the Child* (New York: The Free Press, 1965), chap. 1.

6. These open-ended questions were posed deliberately in colloquial terms. Children's responses to such queries are generally poised between preference and behavior, regardless of the precise formulation of the question. Preferences reflect actual experience, while reports of behavior are heavily influenced by wishes. Consequently, these responses need not be interpreted as measures purely of preference or behavior. Imprecision on this point, we felt, was inevitable in a multipurpose survey instrument, and we preferred to ask children about their activities on their own in terms as little removed as possible from their actual experience.

We feel justified in having made this choice because when we did press in the direction of behavioral reports with a more specific, closed-ended question, we evoked rather different responses. We asked, "What do you usually do after dinner?" and coded this more specific question into a small number of predetermined, nonexclusive categories. The results were much less varied, revealing a less active pattern than the open-ended questions did.

Selected Activities after Dinner
(percentages of children responding in each category)

Activity	
Television	79
Listening to music	16
Chores	28
Schoolwork	45
Reading	26
Playing inside	18
Nothing/resting	6
Playing outside	46
Visiting friends	9
Weighted (N)	(764)

This divergence between responses to the closed- and open-ended questions reflects the fact that the two open-ended questions (see text) tap not only children's actual activities but also their interests, not only what children do but also what they would most likely do given the chance. Hence, they give us some idea of the significance of various kinds of activities to particular groups of children. Another reason for the divergence between responses to closed- and open-ended questions is that questions about activities after dinner restrict answers to a time period when children are less likely to be with friends. This presumably explains the less active pattern.

7. The table on p. 383 shows the percentage of total responses falling into various summary categories. It gives a picture of how children's time is allocated. It does not tell us how many children engage in any given activity. For example, it shows that television viewing accounted for 16 percent of children's total responses; in contrast table 4-1 shows that the 34 percent of children actually mentioned television viewing as an activity they did when they were alone.

8. Given the nature of our data, this analysis draws only indirectly on material related to the psychology and anthropology of children's play. For a recent survey of

Children's Activities on Their Own

"What do you like to do when you are *alone*?"
(percentages of total responses in each activity category)

Activity	All children	Boys	Girls	Blacks	Whites	Asians	Other
Hobbies	13	15	12	12	19	12	11
Music	10	8	12	8	13	10	20
Television viewing	16	17	14	16	11	22	18
Reading or homework	24	20	27	23	22	31	29
Physical activities	20	15	16	22	20	13	15
"Playing"	7	5	9	8	6	3	1
Other responses	10	20	11	12	9	9	6
Total number of responses	(1673)	(795)	(878)	(1092)	(347)	(127)	(108)
Mean number of responses per child	2.2	2.1	2.2	2.1	2.6	2.6	2.1

"What do you like to do with your friends?"
(percentages of total responses in each activity category)

	All children	Boys	Girls	Blacks	Whites	Asians	Other
Hobbies, media, television viewing, reading	7	6	7	5	10	8	7
Team sports	35	45	26	40	22	25	32
Bicycling/ skateboarding	12	13	11	11	15	13	10
Other physical activities	14	11	17	13	17	17	15
"Going places"	7	5	9	7	5	7	9
"Playing"	16	13	19	15	19	20	16
Socializing	6	5	8	6	8	8	7
Other responses	2	1	4	2	3	2	3
Total number of responses	(2447)	(1198)	(1258)	(1694)	(465)	(143)	(151)
Mean number of responses per child	3.2	3.2	3.2	3.2	3.5	2.9	3.0

that literature, see Helen B. Schwarzman, *Transformations: The Anthropology of Children's Play* (New York: Plenum Press, 1979). Earlier collections of articles include, J. Bruner, A. Jolly, and K. Sylva, eds., *Play: Its Role in Development and Evolution* (New York: Basic Books, 1976) and R. Herron and B. Sutton-Smith, eds., *Children's Play* (New York: John Wiley, 1971). Mention should also be made of the classic *Homo Ludens* by J. Huizinga (Boston: Beacon Press, 1955) and of Erik H. Erikson, "Sex Differences in the Play Configurations of American Pre-adolescents," in *Childhood in Contemporary Cultures*, eds. Margaret Mead and Martha Wolfenstein (Chicago: University of Chicago Press, 1955).

9. Children gave fewer responses than we were prepared to code, and they tended to give "team sports" and "reading" as answers to different questions. Our findings in this regard, therefore, are not artifacts of the question design.

10. For a recent summary of related research, see *Reading Teacher* 29, no. 8 (May 1976).

11. See Zick Rubin, *Children's Friendships* (Cambridge, Mass.: Harvard University Press, 1980) and references therein.

12. Talcott Parsons, "The School Class as a Social System: Some of Its Functions in American Society," *Harvard Educational Review* 29 (Fall 1959): 297-318.

13. James S. Coleman, *The Adolescent Society* (New York: Free Press, 1961).

14. James S. Coleman, *Equality of Educational Opportunity* (Washington, D.C.: Government Printing Office, 1966).

15. Lee Rainwater, *Behind Ghetto Walls: Black Families in a Federal Slum* (Chicago: Aldine Publishing Co., 1970), chap. 11.

16. Carol Stack, *All Our Kin: Strategies for Survival in a Black Community* (New York: Harper and Row, 1974).

17. Eliot Liebow, *Tally's Corner* (Boston: Little Brown, 1967).

18. John C. Condry, Jr. and Michael L. Siman, "Characteristics of Peer and Adult Orientation of Children," *Journal of Marriage and the Family*, 36, no. 3 (August 1974): 552. This study attempts to give empirical grounding to many of the peer group issues raised by Bronfenbrenner in *Two Worlds of Childhood*.

19. For a useful discussion of the size of friendship groups, sex roles, and the types of games children play, see Janet Lever, "Sex Differences in the Complexity of Children's Play," *American Sociological Review* 43 (1978): 471-483.

20. See chap. 7, especially "Sports Activities."

21. Some hints of this dimension of reading motivation can be found in the descriptions offered by educators like Herbert Kohl, *36 Children* (New York: Signet, 1968); or James Herndon, *The Way It Spozed to Be* (New York: Simon and Schuster, 1968), especially chap. 36.

22. Victor Rubin and Elliott A. Medrich with Hedva Lewittes and Mary Berg, "Children's Out-of-School Services and the Urban Fiscal Crisis" (Berkeley: Children's Time Study, Schools of Law and Education, University of California, Berkeley, 1980).

23. Iona and Peter Opie, *Children's Games in Street and Playground* (London: Oxford University Press, 1969), p. 10.

24. Donald L. Foley, "The Use of Facilities in a Metropolis," *American Journal of Sociology* 56 (November 1950): 238-246; Nelson J. Foote et al., *Housing Choices and Housing Constraints* (New York: McGraw Hill, 1960); Gerald Suttles, "Community Design: The Search for Participation in a Metropolitan Society" in *Metropolitan America in Contemporary Perspective*, ed. Amos H. Hawley and Vincent P. Rock (New York: John Wiley, 1975), pp. 235-298; and Kevin Lynch et al., *Growing Up in Cities* (Cambridge, Mass.: MIT Press, 1977).

25. Robin Moore and Donald Young, "Childhood Outdoors: Toward a Social Ecology of the Landscape," in *Children and the Environment*, ed. Irwin Altman and Joachim F. Wohlwill (New York: Plenum Publishers, 1978), pp. 83-130.

26. See Mary Berg and Elliott A. Medrich, "Children in Four Neighborhoods: The Physical Environment and Its Effect on Play and Play Patterns," *Environment and Behavior* 12, no. 3 (September 1980): 320-348.

27. Bruno Frappat, "French Children in 1976: Seen and Not Heard," *Le Monde*, 7 November 1976, p. 3.

28. Many of the issues of children's range, independence and autonomy are reviewed in Roger Hart, *Children's Experience of Place* (New York: Irvington Publishers, 1979), chaps. 1-3 and Appendix A-1.

29. Three excellent and comprehensive overviews have recently appeared, William Michelson et al., eds., *The Child in the City*, 2 vols. (Toronto: University of Toronto Press, 1979); Colin Ward, *The Child in the City* (London: Architectural Press, 1978); and Hart, *Children's Experience of Place*.

30. One particularly useful study is that of Robert Maurer and James C. Baxter, "Images of the Neighborhood and City Among Black-, Anglo-, and Mexican-American Children," *Environment and Behavior* 4 (1972): 351-388.

31. Barry Wellman, "Crossing Social Boundaries: Cosmopolitanism Among Black and White Adolescents," *Social Science Quarterly*, 52, no. 3 (1971).

32. Berg and Medrich, "Four Neighborhoods."

33. See, for example, the analyses in Samuel Bowles and Herbert Gintis, *Schooling in Capitalist America: Education and the Contradictions of Economic Life* (New York: Basic Books, 1976) and John Ogbu, *Caste and Class: The American System in Cross Cultural Perspective* (New York: Academic Press, 1978).

34. See references in chap. 7.

35. We have discussed these issues in Charles S. Benson, Stuart Buckley and Elliott A. Medrich, "A New View of School Efficiency: Household Time Contributions to School Achievement, in *School Finance Policy in the 1980s: A Decade of Conflict*, ed. James Guthrie (Cambridge, Mass.: Ballinger Publishing Co., 1980), pp. 169-204.

36. Judith Roizen, "School Achievement and Out-of-school Life," working paper (Children's Time Study, Schools of Law and Education, University of California, Berkeley, 1981).

5. Children and Parents: Time Together

1. William H. Whyte, *The Organization Man* (New York: Doubleday, 1956), p. 162.

2. Urie Bronfenbrenner, *Two Worlds of Childhood* (New York: Russell Sage Foundation, 1970), p. 99.

3. Quoted in Allison Davis, *Social Class Influence Upon Learning* (Cambridge, Mass.: Harvard University Press, 1952), pp. 10-11.

4. John Demos, *A Little Commonwealth: Family Life in Plymouth Colony* (New York: Oxford University Press, 1976), p. 43.

5. Michael Young and Peter Willmot, *The Symmetrical Family* (New York: Pantheon Books, 1973), p. 68.

6. Rose F. Kennedy, *Times to Remember* (New York: Bantam Books, 1975), p. 80.

7. Jacob Riis, *The Battle with the Slum* (London: Macmillan Co., 1902), p. 100.

8. Daniel P. Moynihan, ed., *On Understanding Poverty: Perspectives from the Social Sciences* (New York: Basic Books, 1968), p. 6.

9. Oscar Lewis, "The Culture of Poverty," ibid., p. 191.

10. Lee Rainwater, "The Problem of Lower Class Culture and Poverty War Strategy," ibid., p. 247.

11. Kenneth Keniston et al., *All Our Children* (New York: Harcourt Brace, 1977), chap. 6. See also Benjamin Spock, *Baby and Child Care* (New York: Praeger Books, 1970). Spock writes (p. 563):

> TO WORK OR NOT TO WORK? Some mothers *have* to work to make a living. Usually their children turn out all right, because some reasonably good arrangement is made for their care. But others grow up neglected and maladjusted. It would save money in the end if the government paid a comfortable allowance to all mothers of young children who would otherwise be compelled to work. . . . A few mothers, particularly those with professional training, feel that they must work because they wouldn't be happy otherwise. I wouldn't disagree if a mother felt strongly about it, provided she had an ideal arrangement for her children's care. After all, an unhappy mother can't bring up very happy children.

12. The evidence is reviewed in Lois W. Hoffman, "The Effects of Maternal Employment," in *Work, Family and Community: Summary Proceedings of an Ad Hoc Meeting*, ed. Cheryl D. Hayes (Washington, D.C.: National Academy of Sciences, 1980), pp. 47-55.

13. In *The First Years of Life* (New York: Avon, 1975), Burton White takes a strong position on time-use related issues, and by implication he finds maternal employment problematic. But neither White's work nor the developmental agenda of programs like Home Start indicate agreement regarding the "costs" of maternal employment to the child.

14. The distinction between primary and nonprimary activities is described on pp. 101-102.

15. See, for example, Alexander Szalai et al., eds., *The Use of Time* (The Hague: Mouton, 1972); F. Stuart Chapin, Jr., *Human Activity Patterns in the City: Things People Do in Time and Space* (New York: John Wiley, 1974); John Robinson, *How Americans Use Time* (New York: Praeger 1977); and Kathryn Walker and Margaret Woods, *Time Use: A Measure of Household Production of Goods and Services* (Washington, D.C.: American Home Economics Association, 1976).

16. See chap. 1, note 15.

17. Robinson, *How Americans Use Time*, p. 69.

18. See chap. 4, "How Children View Their Time."

19. Walker and Woods, *Time Use*, p. 106.

20. Ibid., p. 106.

21. Ibid., pp. 126-127.

22. We have adapted the concept of time poverty from Clair Vickery's two-dimensional (material resources and time availability) definition of poverty. In her paper, "The Time Poor: A New Look at Poverty," *The Journal of Human Resources* 12, no. 1 (Winter 1977): 28, she writes:

> In this definition, the necessity of home production for the well-being of the household's members is emphasized. Then a measure of this generalized poverty standard is used to estimate the number of additional female-headed families who would be counted as poor because of a deficiency of nonmarket time. The policy implications of the new definition are explored by using the index to distinguish among poor, and to estimate the potential poverty population.

23. In his research, Chapin (*Human Activity Patterns*) reports that black parents spend less time on family activities than whites and that fewer blacks report engaging in "family activities." There are few other comparable data sources with which we can compare our findings.

24. This notion is explored by Robert Coles in "The Art Museum and the Pressures of Society," *Art News* (January 1975): 24-33.

25. Charles S. Benson, "Household Production of Human Capital: Time Uses of Parents and Children as Inputs," in *Toward Efficiency and Equity in Educational Finance*, ed. Walter W. McMahon and Terry Geske (Boston: Allyn and Bacon, 1980); and Charles S. Benson, Stuart Buckley, and Elliott A. Medrich, "The New Efficiency: Time Use Contributions to School Achievement," in *School Finance Policy in the 1980s: A Decade of Conflict*, ed. James Guthrie (Cambridge, Mass.: Ballinger Publishers, 1980) pp. 169-204.

26. For an extended discussion of this issue, see Judith Roizen, "School Achievement and Out-of–school Life," working paper (Children's Time Study, Schools of Law and Education, University of California, Berkeley, 1981).

6. Jobs, Chores, and Spending Patterns

1. Ruth Sidel, *Women and Childcare in China* (New York: Hill and Wang, 1972); and William Kessen, ed., *Childhood in China* (New Haven: Yale University Press, 1975).

2. For example, Seymour L. Wolfbein, ed., *Labor Market Information for Youths: Papers on the Occasion of a Working Conference on the Role of Information in Improving the Transition from School to Work* (Philadelphia: Temple University Press, 1975) and references therein.

3. Samuel Bowles and Herbert Gintis, *Schooling in Capitalist America: Education and the Contradictions of Economic Life* (New York: Basic Books, 1976).

4. W. Norton Grubb and Marvin Lazerson, "Rally 'Round the Workplace: Continuities and Fallacies in Career Education, *Harvard Educational Review* 45, no. 4 (November 1975): 451-474.

5. Philippe Aries, *Centuries of Childhood* (New York: Knopf, 1962).

6. On this subject, see Michael B. Katz, *Class, Bureaucracy and Schools* (New York: Praeger, 1975); and David Stern, Sandra Smith, Fred Doolittle, "How Children Used to Work," *Law and Contemporary Problems* 39, no. 3 (Summer 1975). This latter paper also documents the contribution of children to household economies at different times in the eighteenth, nineteenth, and early twentieth centuries.

7. In Norman Denzin, ed., *Children and Their Caretakers* (New Brunswick, N.J.: Transaction Books, Dutton, 1973).

8. Robert Dreeben, *On What Is Learned in School* (Reading, Mass.: Addison Wesley Press, 1968).

9. See, for example, Jack Lyle and Heidi R. Hoffman, "Children's Use of Television and Other Media," in Eli A. Rubinstein et al., eds., *Television and Social Behavior, Reports and Papers*, 5 vols., *Television in Day-to-Day Life: Patterns of Use* (Washington, D.C.: Government Printing Office, 1972): 4:215.

10. Mary Engel, Gerald Marsden, and Sylvia W. Pollock, "Child Work and Social Class," *Psychiatry* 34 (May 1971).

11. Our findings are consistent with those of the only comprehensive time budget assessment of children's contribution to the domestic economy, Walker and Woods's 1976 study of 1,300 white, two-parent families in Syracuse, New York. The following table reproduces that study's estimate of the time contributed by children of two

age groups to domestic production in families of varying sizes with working and nonworking mothers. We computed from Walker and Woods's data the value of children's contributions independent of the extra housework time associated with greater numbers of children. As the second part of the table shows, it appears that the net value is positive only when there are several children, all of them older than those in our sample. In general, Walker and Woods conclude that in families where mothers were employed, teenagers twelve through seventeen contributed on average 10 percent of the total time the family spent on housework (including child care) and 5 percent in families where mothers were not employed. Children six through eleven contributed about 5 percent in both cases. See Kathryn E. Walker and Margaret Woods, *Time Use: A Measure of Household Production of Family Goods and Services* (Washington, D.C.: Center for the Family of the American Home Economics Association, 1976), p. 58, Table 3.40.

Time Value in Hours of Children's Contribution to Household

| Size of family | Children aged 12-17 | | Children aged 6-11 | |
| | Mother | | Mother | |
	Not working	Working	Not working	Working
1 child	1.2	1.1	.4	.6
2 children	1.1	1.6	.6	.6
3 children	2.2	2.9	1.0	1.5
4 children	2.2	3.2	1.5	1.0
5-6 children	2.8	3.6	1.6	1.0
7-9 children	3.4	—	2.6	—
Total	2.0	2.2	1.1	1.0

Net Gain to Family in Hours of Time Resulting from Children's Contribution

(Less extra time mother spends each day at housework with additional child[ren])

| Size of family | Children aged 12-17 | | Children aged 6-11 | |
| | Mother | | Mother | |
	Not working	Working	Not working	Working
1 child	−.5	−.3	−1.3	−.8
2 children	−1.6	−.6	−2.1	−1.6
3 children	−.2	+.5	−1.4	−.8
4 children	−.8	+.7	−1.5	−1.5
5-7 children	−.5	+1.0	−1.7	−1.5
7-9 children	−.3	—	−1.1	—

12. Barbara Ehrenreich and Deirdre English, *For Her Own Good: A Hundred Years of Experts' Advice to Women* (New York: Vintage Press, 1978).

13. For some details on changes over time, see Kathryn E. Walker, "Time Use in Families, A New Study: Implications for Understanding Family Life," research paper in Consumer Economics and Public Policy, RP 78-7, (Ithaca: Cornell University, 1978), pp. 13-15.

14. Walker and Woods, *Time Use*, p. 36.

15. Melvin Kohn et al., *Class and Conformity: A Study in Values with a Reassessment* (Chicago: University of Chicago Press, 1977).

16. Basil Bernstein, ed., *Theoretical Studies Towards a Sociology of Language*, vol. 1, *Class, Codes and Control* (London: Routledge & Kegan Paul, 1974).

17. See especially David Cohen and Marvin Lazerson, "Education and the Corporate Order," *Socialist Revolution* 2, no. 2 (March/April 1972): 47-72.

18. On children as consumers, see Elliott A. Medrich, "Children as Economic Actors," working paper (Childhood and Government Project, School of Law, University of California, Berkeley, 1976).

19. Eliot Liebow, *Tally's Corner* (Boston: Little Brown, 1967).

20. Margaret Mead, *The School in American Culture* (Chicago: University of Chicago Press, 1951).

21. A good example is Robert I. Levy, *Tahitians: Mind and Experience in the Society Islands* (Chicago: University of Chicago Press, 1973). For a summary of this literature, see Thomas Weisner and Ronald Gillimore, "My Brother's Keeper: Child and Sibling Caretaking," *Current Anthropology* 18, no. 2 (June 1977).

7. Organized Activities

1. Victor Rubin and Elliott A. Medrich with Hedva Lewittes and Mary Berg, "Children's Out-of-School Services and the Urban Fiscal Crisis" (Berkeley: Children's Time Study, Schools of Law and Education, University of California, Berkeley, 1980), is a detailed account of that history which elaborates the points made here. Other valuable historical summaries are: Harold D. Meyer and Charles K. Brightbill, *Community Recreation* (Englewood Cliffs, N.J.: Prentice-Hall, Inc., 1956), pp. 1-26; Herbert J. Gans, "Recreation Planning for Leisure Behavior: A Goal Oriented Approach" (Ph.D. diss., University of Pennsylvania, 1957), pp. 20-46; Clarence E. Rainwater, *The Play Movement in the United States: A Study of Community Recreation* (Chicago: University of Chicago Press, 1922); Cary Goodman, *Choosing Sides: Playground and Street Life on the Lower East Side* (New York: Schocken Books, 1979); Virginia Frye, "Development of Parks and Recreation" in *Managing Municipal Leisure Services*, ed. Sidney Lutzin (Washington, D.C.: International City Management Association, 1973); and Jack W. Berryman, "The Rise of Highly Organized Sports for Preadolescent Boys," in *Children in Sport: A Contemporary Anthology*, eds. Richard A. Magill, Michael J. Ash, and Frank L. Smoll (Champaign, Illinois: Human Kinetics Publishers, 1978), pp. 3-18.

2. Robert S. Lynd and Helen M. Lynd, *Middletown in Transition* (New York: Harcourt Brace and Co., 1937), pp. 290-292.

3. Nettie P. McGill and E. N. Matthews, *The Youth of New York City* (New York: Macmillan Co., 1940); George A. Lundberg, M. Komarovsky, and M. McInerny, *Leisure: A Suburban Study* (New York: Columbia University Press, 1934).

4. Robert E. Myers, "Controlling the Poor: The Undeclared Goal of Public Recreation" (Ph.D. diss., University of California, Berkeley, 1974); H. Dan Corbin, *Recreation Leadership* (Englewood Cliffs, N.J.: Prentice-Hall, Inc., 1953), pp. 7-8; Harry Hopkins, *Spending To Save: The Complete Story of Relief* (New York: W. W. Norton and Co., 1936).

5. U. S., Bureau of the Census, *Statistical Abstract of the United States* (Washington, D.C.: Government Printing Office, 1977), chap. 9. This and most other descriptions of local government budgets do not specify the proportion of funds allocated to

children's programs. For useful descriptions of the components of municipal recreation and culture budgets see Lutzin, *Municipal Leisure*, chaps. 12 and 13; and Charles S. Benson and Peter B. Lund, *Neighborhood Distribution of Local Public Services* (Berkeley: Institute of Governmental Studies, University of California, 1969), chaps. 1 and 6.

6. It was not possible to estimate the sizable outlays of these kinds of organizations with precision. However, a brief survey of expenditures by the Boy Scouts and Girl Scouts, the Boys' Clubs of America, the YMCA and YWCA youth divisions and several other of the larger nongovernmental youth-serving agencies indicates that even these figures represent low estimates. To provide more accurate estimates it would be necessary to study an extraordinary number of organizations of all sizes that provide programs for young people. The six largest youth organizations reach a combined total of 36 million clients each year. (Information gathered from agency representatives at the National Workshop on Television and Youth, Washington, D. C., March 1980).

7. Rubin, Medrich, Lewittes and Berg, "Children's Out-of-School Services and the Urban Fiscal Crisis." This monograph includes extensive analysis of interviews with administrators and field personnel in libraries, recreation programs, museums, and other children's services as well as an analysis of parents' attitudes toward neighborhood services.

8. Many of the recreation studies cited in chap. 2 embody this outlook.

9. See, for example, Davis McEntire, *Leisure Activities of Youth in Berkeley, California* (Berkeley: Berkeley Council of Social Welfare, 1952), pp. 10-37.

10. Some of these trends are described in Mark David Menchik and Anthony H. Pascal, *The Equity Effects of Restraints on Taxing and Spending* (Santa Monica: Rand Corp., May, 1980); "Proposition 13 Cuts Rate of Spending Growth," *Los Angeles Times*, 1 October 1978, pp. 1, 3, and 14; and James N. Danziger, ed., symposium on "Rebellion on Fiscal Policy: Assessing the Effects of California's Proposition 13," *The Urban Interest* (Spring 1979): 59-92. For an early attempt to apply the Children's Time Study data to these trends, see Victor Rubin and Elliott A. Medrich, "Childcare, Recreation and the Fiscal Crisis," *Urban and Social Change Review* 12, no. 1 (Winter 1979): 22-28.

11. In Oakland in 1976 a school board member estimated that a 15 percent cut in the overall Parks and Recreation Department budget would have meant effectively a cutback of 54 percent in children's services, given the department's priorities. The trend was somewhat less noticeable in 1978 and 1980, when the overall magnitude of the cuts was greater.

12. Rubin and Medrich, "Childcare," p. 25.

13. These terms are adapted from research on parenting styles conducted by Diana Baumrind. In some respects the data in our analysis would fit an "authoritarian" as well as an "authoritative" style, and we did not delve deeply enough here to distinguish rigorously between them. For definitions of all three styles and a recent summary of Baumrind's work, see Herbert Yahraes, "Parents as Leaders: The Role of Control and Discipline," in *Families Today: A Research Sampler on Families and Children*, vol. 1, ed. Eunice Corfman (Washington, D.C.: National Institute of Mental Health, 1979), pp. 289-298.

14. Mary Berg and Elliott A. Medrich, "Children in Four Neighborhoods: The Physical Environment and Its Effect on Play and Play Patterns," *Environment and Behavior* 12, no. 3 (September 1980).

15. Magill, Ash, and Smoll, *Children in Sport*, p. iv.

16. Thomas Tutko and William Bruns, *Winning Is Everything and Other American*

Myths (New York: Macmillan Co., 1976). See also Terry Orlick and Cal Botterill, *Every Kid Can Win* (Chicago: Nelson-Hall Co., 1975).

17. Harry Edwards, "The Black Athletes: 20th Century Gladiators for White America," in *Sport Sociology: Contemporary Themes*, ed. Andrew Yiannakis et al. (Dubuque: Kendall-Hunt Publishing Co., 1976), p. 172.

18. Eleanor Emmons Maccoby and Carol Nagy Jacklin, *The Psychology of Sex Differences* (Stanford: Stanford University Press, 1974), pp. 247-254.

19. See, for example, Harry Edwards, *The Revolt of the Black Athlete* (New York: Free Press, 1969); and Daniel M. Landers, ed., *Social Problems in Athletics* (Urbana: University of Illinois Press, 1976).

20. For example, Mark Naison's articles for the weekly newspaper *In These Times* (1979); and Joseph Durso, *The Sports Factory* (New York: Quadrangle Books, 1975).

21. E. Gareth Hoachlander, "Privatizing the Public Domain: Metropolitan Residential Patterns and Distributions of Local Public Spending" (Ph.D. diss., University of California, Berkeley, 1978). This study shows the disparities in expenditures on children's services among Bay Area communities.

8. Television

1. Wilbur L. Schramm et al., *Television in the Lives of Our Children* (Stanford: Stanford University Press, 1961), p. 49.

2. Jack Lyle and Heidi R. Hoffman, "Children's Use of Television and Other Media," in the U. S. Surgeon General's Scientific Advisory Committee on Television and Social Behavior, *Reports and Papers*, vol. 4, *Television in Day-to-Day Life: Patterns of Use* (Washington, D.C.: Government Printing Office, 1972), p. 181.

3. Ibid., p. 186.

4. Bradley S. Greenberg and Brenda Dervin, *Use of the Mass Media by the Urban Poor* (New York: Praeger, 1970), pp. 45-46.

5. Schramm, *Television*, p. 73.

6. Lyle and Hoffman, "Children's Use of Television," pp. 146-147.

7. Ibid., p. 172.

8. Ibid., p. 166.

9. Hilde Himmelweit, et al., *Television and the Child: An Empirical Study of the Effect of Television on the Young* (London: Oxford University Press, 1958), p. 39-380. See also John Robinson, *How Americans Use Time* (New York: Praeger, 1977), pp. 69-71.

10. Himmelweit, *Television and the Child*, p. 383.

11. Marie Winn, *The Plug-In Drug* (New York: Bantam Books, 1978), chap. 13.

12. Ibid., p. 179-180.

13. Himmelweit, *Television and the Child*, p. 384.

14. Lyle and Hoffman, "Children's Use of Television", p. 145.

15. Greenberg and Dervin, *Use of the Mass Media*, p. 4.

16. National Commission on the Causes and Prevention of Violence, "Statement on Violence in Television Entertainment Programs" (Washington, D.C.: Government Printing Office, 1969), p. 7.

17. Measuring children's viewing levels has proven to be a complex but tractable task. Schramm, *Television*, has demonstrated that different methods of reporting— diary, child and parent record, aided and unaided program recall—produce distinct estimates. For example, parent estimates of children's television viewing time tend to be low, while children's unaided estimates tend to be high. Aided recall and full-

family interviews, while the most reliable forms of reporting, are time-consuming and expensive. Our own study used parent estimates of children's viewing time; other studies reported here used diaries and aided recall.

18. Lyle and Hoffman, "Children's Use of Television," pp. 130-132.

19. Schramm, *Television*, p. 31.

20. Ibid., and Appendix IV; see also Lyle and Hoffman, "Children's Use of Television," pp. 130-132.

21. Neil Smelser, *Theory of Collective Behavior* (New York: Free Press, 1963), pp. 13-14. Smelser writes that: "Every stage in the value-added process, therefore, is a necessary condition for the appropriate and effective addition of values in the next stage. The sufficient condition for the final production, moreover, is the combination of every necessary condition, according to a definite pattern."

22. Himmelweit, *Television and the Child*, pp. 35-36.

23. Ibid., p. 308; also Barbara Heyns, *Exposure and the Effects of Schooling* (Washington, D.C.: National Institute of Education, 1976), pp. 300-304.

24. Lyle and Hoffman, "Children's Use of Television," pp. 163-164.

25. Heyns, *Exposure*, p. 301. For a recent review paper exploring reading-television trade-offs, see Robert Hornick, "Out of School Television and Schooling: Hypotheses and Methods" (Philadelphia: Annenberg School of Communications, University of Pennsylvania, 1980).

26. Urie Bronfenbrenner cited in Kenneth Keniston et al., *All Our Children*, (New York: Harcourt Brace, 1977), p. 54.

9. Children's Time Use Outside School: Perspectives and Possibilities

1. Antoine de Saint-Exupery, *The Little Prince* (New York: Harcourt Brace, 1943).

2. Evelyn Kaye, *The Family Guide to Children's Television* (New York: Pantheon, 1974), p. 7.

3. A selected set of articles reviewing these developments includes Children's Rights Group, "A Preliminary Analysis of the Effects of Proposition 13 on Services for Children in California" (San Francisco, June 1978); State of California, Department of Finance, *A Study of the Local Government Impacts of Proposition 13: K-12 School Districts* (Sacramento: State Department of Finance, March 1979); Paul Terrell, *California Human Services Two Years After Proposition 13* (Millbrae: Calif. Chapter, National Association of Social Workers, April 1980); and Victor Rubin, "Living with Less: Proposition 13 and Children's Services," in *The Future of Education: Policy Issues and Challenges*, ed. Kathryn Cirincione-Coles (Beverly Hills: Sage Publications, 1981).

4. The increasing role of user fees in local government services in California is well reflected in several recent reports including: California Joint Legislative Audit Committee, "School Fees" (Sacramento: Joint Legislative Audit Committee, December 1979); Anthony H. Pascal et al., "Fiscal Containment of Local and State Government" (Santa Monica: Rand Corporation, September 1979); Albert S. Rodda, "Fiscal Implications of Jarvis II for the State of California and Agenices of California Local Government" (Sacramento: State Finance Committee, January 1980); California, Assembly, Minority Ways and Means Committee, "Analysis of the Potential Impact of Proposition 9" (Sacramento: Assembly of the California Legislature,

March 1980); and Mark D. Menchik and Anthony H. Pascal, *The Equity Effects of Restraints on Taxing and Spending* (Santa Monica: Rand Corporation, May 1980).

5. For a review of some of these issues, see Joan Lipsitz, *Growing Up Forgotten* (Lexington, Mass.: Lexington Books, 1977); idem, *Barriers: A New Look at the Needs of Young Adolescents* (New York: The Ford Foundation, 1979).

6. Charles S. Benson, Stuart Buckley, and Elliott A. Medrich, "A New View of School Efficiency: Household Time Contributions to School Achievement," in *School Finance Policy in the 1980s: A Decade of Conflict*, ed. James Guthrie (Cambridge, Mass.: Ballinger Publishing Co., 1980), pp. 169-204.

7. Linkages between school and work, and summaries of the current debate over future directions are explored in W. Norton Grubb, "Schooling and Work: The Changing Context of Education," in *Education Finance and Organization Research Perspectives for the Future*, ed. Charles S. Benson et al. (Washington, D.C.: Government Printing Office, 1980), pp. 191-218; Samuel Bowles and Herbert Gintis, *Schooling in Capitalist America* (New York: Basic Books, 1976); W. Norton Grubb and Marvin Lazerson, "Rally 'Round the Workplace: Continuities and Fallacies in Career Education," *Harvard Educational Review* 45, no. 4 (1975): 451-475; Eleanor Farrar McGowan and David K. Cohen, "Career Education—Reforming School through Work," *The Public Interest* 46 (Winter 1977): 28-47; and David Stern, "Wages and Other Rewards: What People Want or Get from Their Jobs and How Education Makes a Difference (or Does It?)" (Paper prepared for the U. S. National Institute of Education, 1977).

8. Jonathan Kozol, *The Night Is Dark and I Am Far from Home* (Boston: Houghton Mifflin, 1974), p. xii.

Index

Achievement: and child-parent time, 113; family as factor of, 4, 8; life out of school and, 3-5, 8, 243-244; scholastic, 3-4, 89-90, 98-99, 136, 220, 243-244; and television viewing, 65, 207, 220; values of, 229-230; and work skills, 136

Adolescence, 6

Age segregation, 6, 64, 96

Aid to Families with Dependent Children, 44, 45, 360-363

Allowances, 157, 235; and chores, 235; ethnic differences in, 149; family income and, 149, 150; questions on, 305-306; and working, 139

Aries, Philippe, 22, 134

Automobile, 79, 83, 120, 122-123, 173, 178, 181, 234; in child-parent time, 122

Babysitting, 137, 152-153, 236. *See also* Sibling child care

Bedtime: as factor of child-parent time, 106, 107, 108-111; ethnic differences in, 111, 130; and family structure, 108-111; questions on, 294-295, 338

Benson, Charles S., xv, xvi

Berg, Mary, 83

Berger, Clarence, 17

Bernstein, Basil, 147

Bicycle, 79, 83, 181

Blumer, Herbert, 23

Boredom, 35, 85, 86-87, 92, 233; ethnic differences in, 87; and organized activities, 162-163; questions on, 302; and reading, 87; sex differences in, 87

Bowles, Samuel, 133, 136

Bronfenbrenner, Urie, 27, 70; on child development, 5-6; on child-parent interaction, 63-64, 86, 95; on television viewing, 227

Bruns, William, 186

Buckley, Stuart, xv

Care: nonphysical, 101-103; physical, 101, 102

Chapin, F. Stuart, Jr., 14-15, 17

Childhood: images of, 64, 89; invention of, 134

Child-parent time, 11-12, 86, 94-130, 239, 243, 245; and achievement, 113; automobile as factor of, 122; and bedtime,